THE HANDBOOK OF INTERNATIONAL LOAN DOCUMENTATION

The Handbook of International Loan Documentation

2ND EDITION

SUE WRIGHT

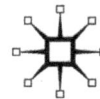

© Sue Wright 2014

All rights reserved. No reproduction, copy or transmission of this publication may be made without written permission.

No portion of this publication may be reproduced, copied or transmitted save with written permission or in accordance with the provisions of the Copyright, Designs and Patents Act 1988, or under the terms of any licence permitting limited copying issued by the Copyright Licensing Agency, Saffron House, 6–10 Kirby Street, London, EC1N 8TS.

Any person who does any unauthorized act in relation to this publication may be liable to criminal prosecution and civil claims for damages.

The author has asserted her right to be identified as the author of this work in accordance with the Copyright, Designs and Patents Act 1988.

First edition published 2006
Second edition published 2014 by
PALGRAVE MACMILLAN

Palgrave Macmillan in the UK is an imprint of Macmillan Publishers Limited, registered in England, company number 785998, of Houndmills, Basingstoke, Hampshire RG21 6XS.

Palgrave Macmillan in the US is a division of St Martin's Press LLC, 175 Fifth Avenue, New York, NY 10010.

Palgrave Macmillan is the global academic imprint of the above companies and has companies and representatives throughout the world.

Palgrave® and Macmillan® are registered trademarks in the United States, the United Kingdom, Europe and other countries.

ISBN: 978–1–137–46758–4

This book is printed on paper suitable for recycling and made from fully managed and sustained forest sources. Logging, pulping and manufacturing processes are expected to conform to the environmental regulations of the country of origin.

A catalogue record for this book is available from the British Library.

Library of Congress Cataloging-in-Publication Data

Wright, Sue (Solicitor)
   [International loan documentation]
   The handbook of international loan documentation / Sue Wright. – 2nd edition.
     pages cm
   Includes bibliographical references and index.
   ISBN 978–1–137–46758–4
   1. Loans, Foreign – Law and legislation. 2. Commercial loans – Law and legislation. 3. Loans, Foreign – Law and legislation – England. 4. Commercial loans – Law and legislation – England. I. Title.

K1094.3.W75 2014
658.15′242—dc23
                                                          2014026154

For Dave, Amy, Leo, Hilary and Claude

Contents

List of Statutes and Conventions	x
List of Cases	xii
Preface to the Paperback Edition	xv
Acknowledgements	xvi

Introduction — 1
General Introduction — 1
Section 1: Principal Types of Loans — 3
Section 2: Loan Agreement Overview — 8
Section 3: LIBOR-based Lending — 15
Section 4: Scope of the Loan Agreement — 24
Section 5: Optional Provisions Published by the LMA in 'Kit' Form — 32
Section 6: Commodification of Debt — 36
Section 7: Asset and Project Finance — 40
Section 8: Quasi Security and Financial Indebtedness — 43

PART 1   Administrative Provisions

1 Interpretation — 51
  Clause 1: Definitions and Interpretation — 51
   Section 1 – An Introduction — 51
   Section 2 – The LMA Definitions — 54

2 The Facility — 78
  Clause 2: The Facility — 78
  Clause 3: Purpose — 82
  Clause 4: Conditions of Utilization — 83

3 Utilization — 91
  Clause 5: Utilization — 91
  Clause 6: Optional Currencies — 94

4 Repayment, Prepayment and Cancellation — 98
  Clause 7: Repayment — 98
  Clause 8: Prepayment and Cancellation — 99

5	**Costs of Utilization**		**106**
	Clause 9: Calculation of Interest		106
	Clause 10: Interest Periods		109
	Clause 11: Changes to Calculation of Interest		112
	Clause 12: Fees		119
6	**Additional Payment Obligations**		**121**
	Clause 13: Tax Gross up and Indemnities		121
		Section 1 – An Introduction	121
		Section 2 – The Clause	125
		Section 3 – FATCA	131
	Clause 14: Increased Costs		133
		Section 1 – An Introduction	133
		Section 2 – The Clause	135
	Clause 15: Indemnities		137
	Clause 16: Mitigation		138
	Clause 17: Costs and expenses		138

PART II Guarantee, Representations, Undertakings and Events of Default

7	**Guarantee**		**143**
	Clause 18: Guarantee and Indemnity		143
8	**Representations, Undertakings and Events of Default**		**152**
	Clause 19: Representations		152
		Section 1 – An Introduction	152
		Section 2 – The LMA Term Loan Representations	161
	Clauses 20–22: Undertakings – Introduction		175
	Clause 20: Information Undertakings		179
	Clause 21: Financial Covenants		183
	Clause 22: General Undertakings		196
		Section 1 – The LMA Undertakings	196
		Section 2 – Other Common Undertakings	212
	Clause 23: Events of Default		220
		Section 1 – Introduction	220
		Section 2 – The LMA Events of Default	223

PART III Boilerplate and Schedules

9	**Changes to Parties**		**249**
	Clause 24: Changes to Lenders		249
		Section 1 – Methods of Transfer	249
		Section 2 – Transfers of Secured Loans	257
		Section 3 – The LMA Term Loan	262
	Clause 25: Changes to the Obligors		268

10 The Finance Parties — 271
- Clause 26: Role of Agent and Arranger — 271
- Clause 27: Conduct of Business by the Finance Parties — 277
- Clause 28: Sharing Among Finance Parties — 277

11 Administration — 280
- Clause 29: Payment Mechanics — 280
- Clause 30: Set off — 282
- Clause 31: Notices — 283
- Clause 32: Calculations and Certificates — 283
- Clause 33: Partial Invalidity — 284
- Clause 34: Remedies and Waivers — 284
- Clause 35: Amendments and Waivers — 285
- Clause 36: Confidentiality — 287
- Clause 37: Counterparts — 288

12 Governing Law and Enforcement — 289
- Clause 38: Governing Law — 289
- Clause 39: Enforcement — 290

13 Schedules — 293
- Schedule 1: Parties — 293
- Schedule 2: Conditions Precedent — 293
- Schedule 3: Requests — 297
- Schedule 4: Mandatory Costs Formula — 298
- Schedule 5: Form of Transfer Certificate — 298
- Schedule 6: Form of Assignment Agreement — 298
- Schedule 7: Accession Letter — 298
- Schedule 8: Form of Resignation Letter — 299
- Schedule 9: Form of Compliance Certificate — 299
- Schedule 10: Existing Security — 299
- Schedule 11: Form of Confidentiality Undertaking — 299
- Schedule 12: Timetables — 300
- Schedule 13: Legal Opinions — 300
    - Section 1 – Introduction — 300
    - Section 2 – Form of Opinion — 303

Appendix 1 Some English Law Concepts — 315
- Section 1: Some Basic Concepts — 315
- Section 2: Security — 327
- Section 3: Guarantees — 339

Appendix 2 Glossary of Terms Used in International Lending — 346

Bibliography — 374

Index — 377

List of Statutes and Conventions

STATUTES AND REGULATIONS

1878
The Bills of Sale Acts 1878 and 1882	333

1890
s2 Partnership Act 1890	67, 68
s3 Partnership Act 1890	68, 312

1925
Law of Property Act s94 (2)	338
Law of Property Act 1925 s136	332

1967
s3 Misrepresentation Act 1967	323, 324

1971
s1 Powers of Attorney Act 1971	323

1977
s2(2) Unfair Contract Terms Act 1977	323
s3 Unfair Contract Terms Act 1977	282, 323
s27 Unfair Contract Terms Act 1977	324

1986
s123 Insolvency Act 1986	234, 235, 343, 359
s214 Insolvency Act 1986	246, 373
s238 Insolvency Act 1986	343
s239 Insolvency Act 1986	365
Rule 12.3(2A) Insolvency Rules 1986	68

1989
Rule 4.90 Insolvency Rules 1986	264
s1(2) Law of Property (Miscellaneous Provisions) Act 1989	322

1999
Contracts (Rights of Third Parties) Act 1999	77

2000
Financial Services and Markets Act 2000	39

2002
Enterprise Act 2002 — 330

2003
Financial Collateral Arrangements (No 2) Regulations 2003 — 335

2004
Pensions Act 2004 — 219

2006
s40(1) Companies Act 2006 — 293, 305
s170(4) Companies Act 2006 — 344
s172 Companies Act 2006 — 343
s251 Companies Act 2006 — 175, 369

2007
Money Laundering Regulations 2007 — 183

2009
Banking Act 2009 — 60

2011
Overseas Companies (Execution of Documents and Registration of Charges) (Amendments) Regulations 2011 (SI 2011/2194) — 334

EU REGULATIONS AND DIRECTIVES

Regulation 1346/2000 Insolvency Regulation — 216
Regulation 44/2001 (Brussels Regulation) as recast by regulation 2012/2015 — 292
Regulation 864/2007 (Rome II) — 289
Regulation 593/2008 (updating the Rome Convention) — 366
Regulation 575/2013 (the Capital Requirements Regulation), known together with the fourth capital requirements directive 36/2013, as CRD IV) — 133, 136, 348, 353
Regulation 462/2013 — 67

INTERNATIONAL CONVENTIONS

Brussels Convention of 1926 Relating to Maritime Liens and Mortgages — 336
Geneva Convention of 1948 on the International Recognition of Rights in Aircraft — 336
Cape Town Convention on International Interests in Mobile Equipment 2001 — 336
United Nations Convention on the Recognition and Enforcement of Foreign Arbitral Awards — 290

List of Cases

Abu Dhabi National Tanker Co v Product Star Shipping (No 2) (1993) 1 Lloyds Rep 397	314
Argo Fund Ltd v Essar Steel Ltd [2006] 2 All E.R. (Comm) 104	37
ARM Asset Backed Securities SA (2013) EWHC 3351 Ch	216, 234
Ashborder BV v Green Gas Power Ltd (2004) EWHC 1517	205, 210, 331
Associated British Ports v Ferryways NV & anor (2009) EWCA Civ 189	147
Aviva Insurance Ltd v Hackney Empire Ltd [2013] 1 W.L.R. 3400	147
Badeley v Consolidated Bank (1888) LR 38 Ch D	68
Bank of Scotland Plc v Constantine Makris and Ben O'Sullivan (2009) EWHC 3869	147
Barclays Bank v Quistclose [1968] UKHL4	82
BNP Paribas SA v Yukos Oil Co (2005) EWH C 1321 (Ch)	239
BNY Corporate Trustee Services Ltd v Eurosail – UK- 2007- 3BL Plc [2013] UKSC 28	235
British Waggon Co v Lea & Co (1879–80) LR 5 QBD 149	253
Carlill v Carbolic Smoke Ball Company (1892) 2QB 484	251
Cattles plc v Welcome Financial Services and others [2010] EWCA Civ 599	149
Central London Property Trust Ltd v High Trees House Ltd (1947) KB 130	356
Re Charge Card Services (1987) Ch 150	336
Chemco Leasing SpA v Rediffusion plc (1987) 1 FTLR 201	343
Cherry v Boultbee (1839) 4 My & Cr 442	149
China & South Seas Bank Ltd v Tan (1990) 1 AC 536	147
Clayton's case (Devagnes v Noble 1816 1 Mer 572)	144
Concord Trust v The Law Debenture Corp plc (2005) 1 WLR 1591	239, 240, 314
Re Cosslett (Contractors) Ltd (1998) Ch 495	329
Close Bros v Ridsdale (2012) EWHC 3090	147
Criterion Properties v Stratford UK Properties LLC [2004] 1 W.L.R. 1846	102

Cukurova Finance International Ltd v Alfa Telecom Turkey Ltd 2009 WL 908215	335
Customs & Excise Commissioners v Broomco Ltd (1984) formerly Anchor Foods Ltd 2000 WL 1084449	234
Dearle v Hall (1828) 3 Russ 1	333
Deutsche Bank v Khan (2013) EWHC 482 (Comm)	282
Director General of Fair Trading v First National Bank Plc 2002 1 AC 481	108
Dunlop Pneumatic Tyre Co Ltd v New Garage & Motor Co Ltd (1915) AC 79	364
Enviroco Ltd v Farstad Supply [2011] 1 W.L.R. 921	73
Re Eurofood IFSC Ltd [2006] EUECJ C-341/04	216
Fons HF (in liquidation) v Corporal Limited and Pillar Securitisation [2014]EWCA Civ 304	40
Gabriel v Little and others [2013] EWCA Civ 1513	82
General Produce Co v United Bank Ltd (1979) 2 Lloyds Reps 255	340
Goldsoll v Goldman (1915) 1 Ch 292	284, 304
Goodridge v Macquarie Bank Limited [2010] FCA 67 (Australian case)	251
Griffith v Tower Publishing (1897) 1 Ch 21	253
Grupo Hotelero Urvasco SA v Carey Value Added SL [2013] EWHC 1039	233, 244
Habibsons Bank Ltd v Standard Chartered Bank (Hong Kong) Limited [2010] EWCA Civ 1335	251
Heald v O'Connor (1971) 2 AER 1105	340
Hedley Byrne & Co Ltd v Heller (1964) AC 465	324
Holme v Brunskill (1877) 3 QBD 495	147
Hooper v Western Counties and South Wales Telephone Co Ltd (1892)68 LT 78	103
Hughes v Metropolitan Ry (1877) 2 App Cas 439	284
Jet2.Com Limited v Blackpool Airport Limited [2012] EWCA Civ 417	177
Kleinwort Benson Ltd v Malaysian Mining Corp (1989) 1 AER 785	343
Lancashire County Council v Municipal Mutual Insurance Limited (1997) QB 897	314
Lester v Garland (1808) 15 Ves 248	56
Re Lonergan, ex p Sheil (1876–77) LR 4 Ch D 789	68
Lordsvale Finance plc v Bank of Zambia (1996) QB 752	108
Luckins v Highway Motel (Caernarvon) Pty Ltd (1975) 133 CLR 164	336

Ludgate Insurance Co Ltd v Citibank (1998) Lloyds Rep 221	314
Marplace (Number 512) Limited v Chaffe Street (a firm) [2006] EWHC 1919 Ch	209
Mauritius Commercial Bank Ltd v Hestia Holdings [2013] EWHC 1328 (Comm)	291
McGuinness v Norwich and Peterborough Building Society [2010] EWHC 2989 (Ch)	144
Meritz Fire & Marine v Jan de Nul [2011] 2 Lloyds Rep 379	341
Mills and others v HSBC Trustee (C.I.) Ltd and others [2009] EWHC 3377 (Ch)	149
Morris v Agrichemicals Ltd (1998) AC 214	336
Re Mytravel Group [2004] EWCA Civ 1734	211
National Westminster Bank Plc v Spectrum Plus Limited (2005) 3 W.L.R. 58	331
North Shore Ventures Ltd v Anstead Holdings (2011) EWCA Civ 230	147
NML Capital v Argentina (2013 US case)	171
Polak v Everett (1875–76) LR 1 QB 669	147
Re PFTZM Ltd [1995] BCC 280	175
Red Sea Tankers v Papachristidis [1997] 2 Lloyd's Rep. 547	275
Rolled Steel Products (Holdings) Ltd v British Steel Corp and others (1986) Ch 246	344
Rothschild case (french)	291
Re SSSL Realisations (2002) Ltd [2006] EWCA Civ 7	149
Strategic Value Master Fund Ltd v Ideal Standard International Acquisition S.A.R.L. & Ors [2011] EWHC 171 (Ch)	245
Sumitomo Bank v Banque Bruxelles Lambert (1997) 1 Lloyds Law Reports 487	271
Tele2 International Card Co SA v Post Office (2009) EWCA Civ 9	285
Thomas v Thomas (1842) 2 QB 851	322
Tolhurst v Associated Portland Cement Manufacturers (1900) Ltd (1903) AC 414	253
Torre Asset Funding Ltd v The Royal Bank of Scotland (2013) EWHC 2670 Ch	221, 272, 273
Triodos Bank v Dobbs (2005) EWCA Civ 630	147
Twinsectra Ltd v Yardley [2002] UKHL 12	82
Vossloh v Alpha Trains [2010] EWHC 2443 (Ch)	341
White v Davenham Trust Ltd (2011) EWCA Civ 747	148
Wulff v Jay (1871–72) LR 7 QB 756	147

Preface to the Paperback Edition

This second edition of *The Handbook of International Loan Documentation* was prompted by the major changes in the documentation and practice of loan documentation that have occurred since the first edition was published in 2005.

The financial crisis of 2007–2008, and the increased regulation and litigation which followed it, gave rise to a host of new issues as well as some useful judicial decisions on the wording of the documents. Interest rates, in particular, became the subject of much discussion both as a result of concerns over the accuracy of LIBOR as a benchmark rate and as a result of changes in bank funding arrangements following the crisis. This has led to the substantial revision of the sections in the book dealing with interest.

There are also new sections on defaulting lenders; commodification of debt; the Euro crisis; FATCA; sanctions and anti-corruption legislation; and on the impact of recent court decisions on the loan agreement wording. I have also taken the opportunity to expand the sections of the book dealing with financial covenants and with other undertakings other than those contained in the investment grade LMA loan agreement.

As ever my thanks go to the many delegates who have attended my loan documentation courses over the years. Their questions and comments have been invaluable in inspiring this book in the first place as well as in highlighting contentious issues. Thanks also are due to the partners, staff and clients at Norton Rose, where I gained my practical experience in international finance.

Sue Wright

Acknowledgements

This book was inspired by the questions and comments of the many delegates who have attended my loan documentation courses over the years. Their questions, often difficult and insightful, and based on their widely differing backgrounds and areas of expertise, have been indispensable in helping to widen my own perspective on the documentation, and in highlighting issues of concern. My thanks to those many delegates who have inspired me to investigate those issues which are discussed in this book. My thanks also go to the partners, staff and clients at Norton Rose, where I obtained my practical experience of international finance, without which this book would have been impossible. Thanks are also due to those who have been kind enough to spare their valuable time to review parts of the manuscript of this book at its various stages of development, and to provide comments and suggestions. In particular I would like to thank Staffan Avenius (Nordea Bank), Anne-Marie Godfrey (Deacons), Kenneth Gray (Norton Rose), Alexey Ievlev (ING Bank), Jonathan Porteous (Stevens and Bolton LLP), Richard Powell (Mundays) and Paul Rogerson (ABN Amro) for their kind assistance. The comments, information and support provided have been enormously helpful in getting this book from conception to completion. Finally, of course, I would like to thank the Loan Market Association for their permission to use their primary form documents in this text, and the Dutch Bankers Association, for consenting to the use of their 'parallel debt' wording.

PS To Leo, thanks too for your comments, which will be included if a humorous version of this book is ever commissioned.

Introduction

GENERAL INTRODUCTION

How to use this book

A word of caution is necessary at the outset. This book seeks to give readers the tools to enable them to negotiate loan agreements efficiently (i.e. with minimum expense in terms of time and money) and effectively (i.e. to result in a document which closely suits their corporate needs, whether they are borrower or lender). For this book to succeed in its aim it must be used appropriately – that is, as an aid to, and not as a substitute for, proper understanding of the commercial position of the parties. Readers need to keep in mind that loan agreements are used in widely differing commercial situations.

0.001

Some examples (among the numerous possibilities) are:

0.002

- secured loans made to start-up companies owned by entrepreneurs;
- structured loans to special purpose companies, designed to achieve a particular tax effect or for the purpose of a particular project;
- loans to **investment grade** corporates designed to provide them with **liquidity**.

The basic precedent for all these situations will be remarkably similar, but the changes to that precedent which are appropriate in each case will vary enormously. Comments which are made in this book will only be appropriate in some (usually a minority) of the circumstances in which a loan agreement will be used. One size does not fit all. Moreover, there will be many comments which ought to be made in specific transactions which are not made in this book. The comments included are not intended to be (nor can they be) exhaustive. The comments in the book are intended to give the reader a better understanding of what the loan agreement does and does not say, and to provide readers with a full set of tools with which to ensure that the final agreement meets their commercial objectives.

0.003

0.004 However, the most important commercial objective of the parties to a loan transaction is to reach an agreement on the documents quickly (time is money) and in a way which gives all involved confidence in their ongoing relationship (and does not result in disproportionate legal fees). If this is to be achieved, parties must identify the points they wish to make with care, and only make comments which are commercially significant in the context of the particular transaction. Failure to do this will backfire as the **counterparty** will quickly lose patience, probably resulting in a negotiation which fails to achieve the parties' real commercial objectives.

0.005 Readers are therefore urged to ensure that they do not lose sight of the ultimate commercial objectives, and that they use this book only as an aid to better understanding of the agreements, not as a 'checklist' of comments – a purpose for which this book was not designed and is not appropriate.

What should I be looking for in this loan agreement? Why does it have to be so long?

0.006 This Introduction sets the scene for the discussion of the loan agreement by

- describing the main categories of loans (in Section 1 at 0.008);
- providing an overview of the loan agreement (in Section 2 at 0.035);
- looking at **LIBOR**-based lending (in Section 3 at 0.081);
- discussing the scope of the agreement, including who can be affected by it, and whose activities can have an effect under it (in Section 4 at 0.121);
- describing certain optional provisions, including provisions for dealing with defaulting lenders, which the Loan Market Association[1] ('LMA') publishes in 'kit' form (in Section 5 at 0.152);
- looking at the commodification of debt (in Section 6 at 0.183), including the influence of non-bank lenders and **credit derivatives;**
- providing a brief overview of asset and project finance (in Section 7 at 0.207); and
- describing (in Section 8 at 0.234) various commercial arrangements which, while not amounting to borrowing or giving **security** in a legal sense, amount to the commercial equivalent and therefore have to be treated in a similar manner for the purposes of the loan agreement.

0.007 This book uses the loan agreements that are published by the LMA as the starting point for its discussions. In general, the LMA recommended form for an unsecured term loan to an investment grade borrower is used as the basis for discussion, and is referred to in this book as the 'LMA Term Loan'.

---

[1] The Loan Market Association was established in 1996 as a forum for dealing with issues relating to the syndicated loan market. It was established to promote the trading of interests in loans. See 0.036–0.046.

The book follows the structure and numbering of the LMA Term Loan, and references to clauses, unless stated otherwise, are to clauses of the LMA Term Loan. The text also comments on situations and documents which differ from the LMA Term Loan. Such comments are indicated by shaded text.

SECTION 1: PRINCIPAL TYPES OF LOANS

Loans can be classified with reference to a number of characteristics. The principal categories are discussed here.   0.008

1 Classification on the basis of availability

Perhaps the main characteristic for categorizing loans is the issue of availability.   0.009

Term loan

A term loan is a loan which is made available to the borrower on the basis that it will be repaid by specified instalments over a set period of time. Once repaid it cannot be redrawn. It is generally used for a specific financing requirement such as an **asset** purchase. It is a long-term debt on the borrower's balance sheet.   0.010

Demand loan

A **facility** which the lenders make available but which the lenders are able to cancel or require repayment of at any time (or 'on demand') may be called an 'uncommitted facility' (because the lenders are not committed to maintain its availability) or a 'demand facility'. Facilities of this type do not require lengthy documentation as there is no need for **undertakings** or **Events of Default**, the lenders being free to terminate the facility at will. The lack of a commitment by the lenders is clearly a significant disadvantage to a borrower.   0.011

Overdraft facility

An overdraft facility is a facility that the borrower may draw on, repay and then draw on again. This is as distinct from a term loan which, once the borrower has repaid, cannot be reborrowed. An overdraft facility is used for situations where the borrower has fluctuating financing requirements (e.g. for **working capital**). By having the ability to repay and reborrow, the borrower is able to ensure that levels of borrowing at any time do not exceed the financial requirements of the borrower at that time. An overdraft facility may be committed or uncommitted. In a **committed facility**, the lenders would commit to lend up to a specified sum for a given period, for example, 12 months. The borrower could draw up to the limit at any time, repay as it wished and have the comfort of being able to draw again, up to the limit,   0.012

at any time within the committed period.[2] If the facility is uncommitted or if the period of the commitment is short then the facility will be a **current liability** on the borrower's balance sheet, with the implications which that carries for the borrower's liquidity. Given its short-term (and in some cases, uncommitted) nature, lengthy documentation will not be required.

Revolving credit

0.013 A **revolving credit** is a committed facility which operates in a similar way to an overdraft (in that it may be repaid and reborrowed) but is of longer term. It is a long-term debt on the borrower's balance sheet. The documentation will be very similar to that for a term loan. The maximum amount available may remain the same throughout the facility period or it may reduce over time.

2 Classification on the basis of the lenders' credit decision

0.014 The second key characteristic of a loan is the question of the type of credit risk which the loan represents for the lenders. That is, what are they relying on in their assessment of the borrower's ability to repay the loan? Borrowers repay loans either by selling assets; by using income generated from a particular asset or project; or out of their general corporate resources. While this is a very broad generalization, these are the distinctions which underlie the classification of loans as 'corporate finance', '**asset finance**' and '**project finance**'.

Corporate finance

0.015 A corporate finance transaction (when the expression is used in this context, not in its wider meaning which encompasses corporate financings based on the **capital markets**) is one in which there is neither a specific asset nor a specific stream of income on which the lenders' credit decision is based, but rather they are relying on the general financial position of the borrower. This is also known as '**balance sheet lending**'.

Asset finance

0.016 An asset finance transaction is one in which the future value of the asset concerned is a key factor in the lenders' credit risk. This, of course, has major implications for the security and the documentation, as discussed in Section 7 of this Introduction at 0.207–0.218.

Project finance

0.017 A project finance transaction is one in which the income generated by the project which is being financed is a key factor in the lenders' credit decision. It is described in more detail in Section 7 of this Introduction at 0.219.

---

[2] However, the borrower will need to pay a commitment fee to the lenders for any part of the facility which the borrower is not using at any time, and which the lenders remain committed to lend.

In the context of asset and project financing, it should be noted that the lenders are often taking a mixture of asset risk, project risk and corporate risk. For example, lenders providing ship finance (which is regarded as asset finance) will not only assess the future value of the ship, they will often also look at the operator's balance sheet and financial ratios and at the likely income which the ship will generate. In other words, the lenders will take asset, project, and corporate risk within a facility which is traditionally regarded as an asset finance transaction.

0.018

Limited recourse financing

Some transactions (most commonly project finance) are put together on a '**limited recourse**' basis. This involves the lenders accepting that they will only be repaid out of specified assets. This may be done by having a contractual limitation on recourse (see Box 0.1).

0.019

Alternatively, and more commonly, it may be done structurally, by establishing a special purpose entity which will only own the assets (e.g. project assets and income) to which the lenders are intended to have recourse, with the lenders lending to that entity.

0.020

> **Box 0.1**
> Under a contractual limitation on recourse, the lenders agree with the borrower only to pursue certain assets, such as income from the project in question, and that if the income in question is insufficient, the lenders will suffer a loss and will not be able to claim further repayment from the borrower.

3 Classification on the basis of the purpose of the loan

The third major attribute of a loan for classification purposes is the question of its purpose. While there are as many purposes as there are borrowers those purposes fall into categories which are commonly used to describe loans.

0.021

Acquisition (or 'Leveraged') finance

Acquisition finance or **leveraged finance** is finance used to acquire a company. It has become a highly active market, particularly attractive to **hedge funds**. The financing arrangements are highly structured with a number of different tiers of lending and the relationship between the tiers regulated by an **intercreditor agreement**. The Loan Market Association produces template documents for the loan (which is referred to in this book as the 'Leveraged LMA') and for the intercreditor agreement.

0.022

Bridge finance

Bridge finance is finance made available to bridge a gap. For example, a company may require financing for a corporate acquisition. It may intend to

0.023

raise the bulk of that finance through issuing bonds on the capital markets but need interim finance to cover the period during which circulars are issued to the public, etc. A bridge finance loan (which is usually high margin, short-term debt provided by the relationship bank) could bridge the gap.

Mezzanine finance or venture capital

0.024 **Mezzanine finance** or **venture capital** is finance used where traditional finance is not available in sufficient amounts to meet the borrower's needs. Generally companies meet their financing requirements by a mixture of debt (borrowing from third parties) and **equity** (the company's own money, either as invested by shareholders or as profits which would otherwise be available to shareholders). Where the level of debt is high compared to the amount of equity, the company is described as 'highly **leveraged**' or 'highly geared'.[3] Where equity plus the amounts available from traditional lenders will be insufficient to meet the need, borrowers may approach mezzanine financiers to make up the difference. These financiers specialize in providing funds for a particular project, such as a major acquisition, which supplement moneys available from traditional lenders for that project. The finance they provide will be subordinate to the traditional loan. It will carry more risk and therefore the **margin** will be higher. Generally the mezzanine financier will also require some form of '**equity kicker**' – that is, in addition to the margin they will require a share in any profits from the transaction. The finance may be provided by way of **subordinated debt** or by way of **preference shares**.

Refinancing

0.025 Refinancing is finance made available to repay existing debt. This may be done to achieve less onerous undertakings or more favourable margins; to reflect new corporate structures; to increase leverage; as part of a restructuring following a default; or for numerous other reasons.

Mismatch facilities

0.026 These are facilities which seek to match the difference between what is available to a borrower from a given source and what the borrower needs. For example, in a **securitization** a borrower may require a mismatch facility to bridge the gap between dates of payment of **receivables** and due dates on **commercial paper** issued.

Swingline facilities

0.027 **Swingline facilities** are facilities which are available to meet short-term liquidity needs (such as to replace funds which, but for a market disruption,

---

[3] Hence the description of acquisition finance as 'leveraged' finance. Traditionally, there would be a 'senior' facility and a mezzanine facility. More recently it is more common for the leveraged acquisition finance to take the form of a mixture of loan finance and capital markets finance.

would have been available to a borrower by the issue of commercial paper). They will be available with minimum (same day) notice and only to cover short-term needs. They often have a maximum period for **advances** to be outstanding of 3–5 days.

4 Classification on the basis of the number of lenders

Syndicated loans

Syndicated loans are made available by a number of lenders who all join together to make the loan. With the exception of certain fees, which are for the benefit of individual lenders in the syndicate, the lenders have equal rights (or rather, rights proportionate to the amount each has lent – i.e. **pro rata**) against the borrower under a single loan agreement. 0.028

Club loans

These are syndicated loans where there are few syndicate members. The lenders, who are called a **club** and who will participate in the loan, are known from the outset and there will be no need to market the facility to the wider banking community as with a large syndicate. 0.029

Bilateral facilities

Bilateral facilities are made by a single lender to a single borrower. 0.030

5 Miscellaneous categories

Sovereign debt

This is debt made available to a sovereign entity. 0.031

Export credit

Export credit is debt that is supported in some way (e.g. by some form of guarantee of payment) by a government in order to encourage exports from their country. 0.032

Acceptance credit facility

Under an **acceptance credit facility**, instead of the lenders agreeing to lend money to the borrower, they agree to accept[4] bills of exchange or letter of credit on behalf of the borrower. The terms of the facility document will be similar to the term loan with changes reflecting the mechanical differences in the forms of financial support. 0.033

---

[4] In other words, to agree to make payment under.

PIK Financings

0.034 PIK financings are debts on which the borrower does not pay interest, but instead the interest is added to the **principal** amount of the debt. In other words, the interest is capitalized. The letters 'PIK' stand for payment in kind. There are many different types of PIK financings. Commonly they are done through the capital markets, when the borrower will issue '**PIK notes**', or they may be made through the loan markets. They may have a '**toggle**' which means that the holder of the note has a choice – he can elect to receive interest or alternatively, choose to capitalize the interest, in which case the rate will be higher than if he elected for payment.

SECTION 2: LOAN AGREEMENT OVERVIEW

0.035 The loan agreement is generally produced by the lenders' lawyer. Its purpose is to ensure that the lenders have all the rights and powers they require, bearing in mind that, at least in a simple, single drawdown, term loan, the lenders will have handed over a large sum of money and received in exchange, this document (plus perhaps security). Therefore, by custom, the lenders have what is a major negotiating advantage – the right to produce the first draft of the agreement.

1 The Loan Market Association recommended forms

0.036 In London, LMA has produced recommended forms for unsecured, corporate risk term loans and revolvers.[5] These are now widely accepted as a common negotiating platform, albeit often with variations reflecting a law firm's own preferences.

0.037 The first LMA documents were introduced in 1999 with a number of aims, including, in particular, the aim of promoting efficiency in the original negotiation of the loan, and, subsequently, on its transfer, to facilitate review of the agreement by proposed investors. The recommended form for use for an unsecured loan to an investment grade borrower was negotiated and agreed by representatives of borrowers, lenders, and law firms, with the aim of producing documents which were not overly favourable to any party. It is worth noting that the other forms of loans issued by LMA have not been negotiated with the Association of Corporate Treasurers (representing borrowers) and therefore those documents do not have the

---

[5] The forms available are for multicurrency term, revolving, or combined term and revolving, facilities, including a version with a letter of credit facility included. There is also an option, discussed in 3.006 onwards, for a swingline (Dollars or Euros). Numerous other facilities have been added to the suite of documents, including a form for use in a leveraged transaction, one for use in developing countries, a pre export finance facility and a real estate facility.

benefit of this even-handed approach.⁶ To a large extent, these documents have been successful in their aims and it has become market practice to use these documents as a basis for loan documentation in the London market and beyond.

0.038 The LMA recognized, on launch of the recommended forms, that some provisions would need to be negotiated on a case-by-case basis. They therefore divided the loan into 'hard' and 'soft' provisions, with the soft provisions (**representations**, **undertakings**, financial covenants, events of default, transferability and **conditions** precedent) being put forward simply as a starting point, which would need negotiation on a case-by-case basis. The remainder of the agreement (the 'hard' provisions) was expected, in most cases, not to require adjustment.

0.039 A number of adjustments to the recommended form will need to be made in any given transaction, mostly in relation to the 'soft' provisions, but often also including adjustment to the 'hard' provisions.

- 0.040 Some parts of the recommended form have been left blank as there is no standard market practice for these provisions. Such provisions need to be negotiated on a one-off basis. Examples are the financial covenants and the material adverse change clause.
- 0.041 If the loan is to be secured then a number of the provisions may be drawn more tightly than for the LMA Term Loan, which assumes an unsecured loan. The Leveraged LMA (designed for use in leveraged or acquisition finance) is often used as a prompt for the types of additional undertakings and Events of Default which may be needed for a secured loan, although this needs to be done with a significant degree of caution since many areas of the document are really not appropriate outside the leveraged market.⁷
- 0.042 The document will need tailoring to reflect the credit decision – that is, additional representations, undertakings, and events of default are likely to be necessary, reflecting specific concerns relating to the borrower's business. In particular, if the lenders are taking any project or asset risk in the transaction, substantial additions will be needed as discussed in Section 7 of this Introduction at 0.208–0.233.
- 0.043 The lenders may have certain policy requirements, for example, as to transferability which they wish to have incorporated.
- 0.044 The borrower may have certain policy requirements, for example, as to agreeing cross acceleration clauses only, which they have agreed with the lenders.

---

⁶ The Association of Corporate Treasurers issues guidance on the LMA Term Loan and the Leveraged LMA from time to time – giving detailed commentary of issues for borrowers to look out for. These are available from the website of the Association of Corporate Treasurers at www.treasurers.org

⁷ An obvious example is the '**clean up period**' which gives the borrower a period of time after the loan is advanced (and the target company acquired) in which to comply with certain specified undertakings.

0.045 • Certain provisions have been put forward by LMA as optional riders to the LMA Term Loan (such as the provisions on defaulting lenders); which the parties may want to have incorporated. These are discussed in Section 5 of this Introduction at 0.152 onwards.

0.046 • Other more detailed points may need to be adjusted as mentioned in the remainder of this book.

2 Loan agreement structure

Function of the clauses

0.047 Each provision of the agreement is of one of three types:

0.048 • first, there are the administrative provisions – dealing with calculation of interest, mechanics of advances, repayment, and the like;[8]

0.049 • second are the information and business restriction provisions (see Box 0.2) such as representations, undertakings and events of default;[9]

0.050 • third, there are the boilerplate clauses dealing with important issues such as **indemnities**, notices, **jurisdiction**, and the relationship between the lenders (such as the agency clause).[10]

Box 0.2
Negotiation should usually focus on two areas of the agreement. First the business restriction provisions, since this is the part of the agreement which will have a significant ongoing effect on how the borrower conducts its business, and how much power the lenders can wield. The second key area is those parts of the administrative provisions under which the borrower may find that the interest rate they are required to pay is higher than the interest rate they expected to pay. There are three clauses of concern here: the **market disruption clause**; the increased costs clause; and the grossing up clause, all of which are discussed in some detail elsewhere.

Stages of the transaction

0.051 The business restriction provisions of the agreement seek to protect the lenders at three different stages of the transaction.

0.052 *Before drawing.* First, the document protects the lenders, before any money is lent, through those provisions which operate to release the lenders from their obligations to advance funds. At this stage, the lenders

---

[8] In the LMA Term Loan, these provisions are in clauses 1–17.
[9] In the LMA Term Loan, these provisions are in clauses 18–23.
[10] In the LMA Term Loan, these provisions are in clauses 24–39.

have three types of protection operating at the same time: the due diligence (which the lender and their lawyer will conduct prior to signature of the loan agreement), the borrower's representations (in clause 19 of the LMA Term Loan), and the conditions precedent (in clause 4 of the LMA Term Loan) (see Box 0.3).

> **Box 0.3**
> In other words, the borrower is being asked to state that certain facts are true (in the representations), to prove that they are true (in the conditions precedent), and the lenders are also checking that they are true (in the due diligence).

0.053 This triple layer of protection is designed to minimize the risk of error. As a practical issue it means that the conditions precedent, representations and legal opinions duplicate each other to a large extent, so that if adjustments are made to one area in a loan agreement, it will often be necessary to make corresponding adjustments to the other areas.

0.054 *After drawing.* Second, the document protects the lenders after the money has been lent and while it is outstanding. This is the remit of the undertakings (or **covenants**). Their role is to ensure that the status quo (or something near to that) is maintained during the life of the loan and that the lenders are given the information they need (see Box 0.4).

> **Box 0.4**
> Except in limited recourse transactions such as some project finance, it makes little difference whether any particular issue is dealt with as an undertaking or as an Event of Default (in some cases, only after a **grace period** expires) since a breach of undertaking is an Event of Default. The tradition is to include as undertakings those things which the borrower can promise (e.g. not to grant security) and as Events of Default those which it cannot (e.g. material adverse change).

0.055 *Termination.* Third, the document sets out the circumstances which the lenders regard as changing the position so completely that they require the right to be repaid immediately. These are the Events of Default[11] – which give the lenders the right to accelerate the loan. In practice, often the result of an Event of Default is a renegotiation not an **acceleration**, but it is the existence of the right to accelerate which gives the lenders the necessary leverage to renegotiate.

---

[11] Or compulsory prepayment events – see clause 8.2 in 4.012.

3 Key concerns

Borrower's concerns

A borrower's key concerns in reviewing the documents are:

Control

0.056 • to what extent do they remain free to conduct their business as they see fit and to what extent do they require consent for their activities?

0.057 • if they need consent (see Box 0.5) for some acts – what level of consent is needed (e.g. Majority Lenders' consent or unanimous consent of all lenders) and might any requirement for consent impose unacceptable delays in their action (e.g. do they need freedom to act if there is no response to a request within a specified period of days)?

0.058 • How easy will it be to get consent and does the agreement give them any flexibility to deal with the situation if they have difficulties getting the required level of consent? Hence the '**Snooze you lose**' and '**Yank the Bank**' provisions discussed at Box 11.6 on page 287 and 4.026.

0.059 • what companies within their group are restricted?[12]

> **Box 0.5**
> At some point in the negotiations, the lender may make the point that the borrower should not be too concerned about giving the lenders rights to object to certain things, because the lenders will only use their rights when it is sensible to do so. Nevertheless, borrowers should treat this argument with caution and seek to negotiate an agreement which will enable them to conduct their business with minimum need to make requests for consents or waivers because
>
> • requests for consent will involve the borrowers spending time and money (and, in some cases, the lenders charge a fee for consents);
> • if consent is required, the lenders may take the opportunity to raise other issues of concern to them and link those to the issue of consent;
> • there may be a change in personnel or policies at the lenders' office which may result in a different approach to the granting of waivers and consents;
> • wherever the lenders have the right to accelerate their loan then other lenders will have the same right under their **cross default** clauses.

Certainty of funds

0.060 • in what circumstances might the loan cease to be available? This includes not only the undertakings and Events of Default but also the possibility of the lenders defaulting on their obligations;[13]

---

[12] See discussion on the scope of the agreement in 0.121.
[13] See 0.155 for 'Defaulting Lender' provisions.

- are all the Events of Default within the borrower's control (e.g. change of ownership of the borrower[14])?   0.061
- are all the Events of Default objectively tested or are some matters of opinion, and, if so, by what standards can an opinion be tested? For example, is the Event of Default limited by concepts of materiality or reasonableness?[15]   0.062
- should some of the events which are expressed to be Events of Default more properly result in a change in margin rather than a right to accelerate, for example, minor breach of a financial ratio?[16]   0.063

Pricing
- In what circumstances will the interest rate be different to the rate expected? The borrower will want to focus on the increased cost clause, the market disruption clause and the grossing up clause; and   0.064

Scope
- *The scope of the agreement* – as discussed in Section 4 of this Introduction at 0.121.   0.065

Lenders' concerns

Lenders' key concerns in reviewing the agreement are: 0.066

- equality with other creditors (this is one of the reasons for the **pari passu** clause (clause 19.12), the **negative pledge** (clause 22.3), and the cross default clause (clause 23.5) in an unsecured facility);   0.067
- ensuring they are provided with sufficient information, in good time (clause 20);   0.068
- protection of their profit (by the ability to pass on changes in costs such as changes in regulatory cost – clause 14);   0.069
- certainty as to the effect of the agreement (hence the importance of the choice of law and jurisdiction clauses at clauses 38 and 39);   0.070
- ability to withdraw (i.e. right to accelerate) if there is a change in circumstances which may affect the lenders' view of the credit risk involved (clause 23);   0.071
- maintenance of the borrower's assets and income – hence financial ratios at clause 21 and asset or project specific covenants;   0.072
- reputational, regulatory and political risks, including the risk of imposition of exchange control regulations, or redenomination of the loan in the event of a change in currency (such as in the event of a Euro break up), and risks of breaching anti-corruption, money laundering or similar regulations or expectations.[17]   0.073

---

[14] See discussion of clause 8.2 in 4.012 and see also the discussion of clause 23 in 8.215.
[15] See the discussion of clause 23 in 8.216.
[16] See discussion of clause 21 in 8.117.
[17] See 4.009.

4 Hazards in reviewing a loan agreement

0.074 Five principal difficulties arise in reviewing a loan agreement, which are worth highlighting here. These are the difficulty of spotting what is not there; the potential for conflict between different parts of the agreement; the significance of the precise wording of the definitions; appreciating the impact of repeating representations; and the difficulty of negotiating a document which is presented as being a market standard. These issues are discussed in turn in the following paragraphs.

Spotting what is not there

0.075 It is easy to see and comment on what is there, but harder to spot what is not there. In order to see the wood for the trees it is often helpful to summarize the key issues before reading the draft agreement. This will help the reader to spot what is not there and minimize the risk of being drawn into making minor comments on what is there while failing to spot the bigger picture.

Potential conflict between provisions

0.076 Potential conflicts arise because, as discussed at 0.051–0.055, the agreement protects the lenders at three different stages.[18] Any particular issue is therefore touched on in a number of different places in the agreement, some of which may conflict with others (see Box 0.6).

0.077 It is therefore sensible, as well as reading the agreement from start to finish, to check, in relation to each key issue, how it is dealt with at each point of the agreement (conditions precedent, representations, repeating representations, undertakings, and events of default) to get a complete picture and also to ensure that any conflicts between the provisions are ironed out. This is worth doing on later drafts as well as initially, because changes negotiated in one area of the document are often inadvertently missed in corresponding parts of the agreement.

> **Box 0.6**
> For example, to find out in what circumstances litigation against the borrower can impact on the loan, it will be necessary to look at the representations, conditions precedent, repeating representations, undertakings and the events of default. See also 8.074.

Definitions

0.078 Loan agreements contain detailed definitions. There are a number of reasons for this. One reason is to keep the complexities out of the body of the agreement. Another is to avoid ambiguity. The difficulty for the reader is that

---

[18] The provisions of the representations and conditions precedent, and the wording of any attached legal opinion, are also inter-related.

it is hard to comment on (or to fully appreciate the implications of) any particular definition out of context. It is sensible to start reviewing any loan agreement, not at the definitions, but, instead, at the operative clauses (those which operate to actually do something as opposed to the definitions clause which simply describes things). When a defined term (usually signified by capital letters, but see 1.004) is encountered, return to review its definition. This will make it easier to appreciate the detail of the definition.

Repeating representations

A final word of caution relates to the repeating representations. As we will see in relation to clause 19 of the LMA Term Loan (8.001 onwards), certain representations may be repeated during the life of the loan. After full **drawdown** on a term loan, the result of this is that, if a repeating representation becomes untrue, the lenders will be entitled to accelerate the loan. The same result would have been achieved by phrasing the issue as an undertaking (if it is something which the borrower can promise) or an Event of Default (if not). By using a repeating representation instead, the possibility of conflict between different parts of the document has been increased.[19]

0.079

Market practice

It can be difficult to negotiate a document which is presented as a market standard, particularly where lenders feel that suggested changes may hinder syndication, as this is not something which can readily be tested by the borrower. Similarly, borrowers will not wish to waste time, money and goodwill trying to achieve something which the lenders regard as non-negotiable. The best protection against this is to use lawyers who are active in the market and who know what can be achieved and what cannot. Nevertheless, regardless of whether any provision is market standard or not, borrowers need to ensure that they are happy with what the clause says and not accept risks simply because other borrowers have agreed to accept those risks. After all, not all borrowers have the same commercial constraints – there may be reasons why other borrowers found the risk acceptable which might not apply to this one.

0.080

SECTION 3: LIBOR-BASED LENDING

1 Interbank markets

Lenders borrow money in order to lend. In addition to the equity invested by shareholders, lenders borrow in the capital markets (e.g. by issuing bonds or commercial paper), in interbank markets and from their deposit holders. For the purpose of international lending, depending on the currencies concerned, most (not all) loans in a currency for which LIBOR exists are

0.081

---

[19] See further Section 1 of the commentary on clause 19 in 8.001.

LIBOR-based – and, despite the mix of funding sources, the documentation is written on the fiction that the lenders are funding themselves solely by raising money in an interbank market. This may be a domestic currency market (e.g. borrowing Sterling in London) or a **Eurocurrency**[20] market (e.g. borrowing Dollars in Tokyo) (see Box 0.7). Market practices (e.g. period required for notice of drawing, what constitutes a banking day, conventions for number of days in a year for calculating annualized payments, and the like) are different as between the domestic and international markets.

> **Box 0.7**
> This explains the distinction between *Euribor* (which is the domestic interbank interest rate for borrowing Euros in one of its home countries) and *Euro Libor* (which is the international interbank interest rate for borrowing Euros in London).

0.082　Whether the lenders are funding themselves in a domestic or an international market, if a payment falls due in the relevant currency, then, in order to get value for a payment made in that currency (and not continue to be charged interest on it) the lenders' correspondent banks need to be open for business in the principal financial centre for the currency concerned. So, for example, to make a payment in Yen, Tokyo must be open.[21]

2 Cost-plus lending

0.083　LIBOR-based lending is a 'cost-plus' basis of lending (as opposed to an inclusive basis).

0.084　An inclusive basis is where the lender charges a single rate, such as its **base rate**, which encompasses all its costs of funding and some profit. This rate will be set at a level which allows a fair degree of variation in the lenders' costs to be absorbed without its having to change its base rate. The base rate will be changed from time to time when there are step changes in the lender's funding costs. The lender is free to change its base rate whenever it thinks fit – the only comfort for the borrower being that competition between banks will restrict this. Any such change in base rate will take effect immediately under the loan agreement. The rate which the lender will charge to the borrower will usually be higher than the base rate, with the amount of uplift reflecting the perceived credit risk of the borrower.

0.085　The cost-plus basis of charging interest, on the other hand, historically involves the lender agreeing a fixed level of profit (the Margin) with the

---

[20] 'Eurocurrency' is used here in its historical sense of meaning a currency being traded outside its home country. It does not necessarily involve Europe.
[21] For a discussion of interbank payment systems see Goode *Commercial Law* 4th edn, chapter 17.

borrower and charging the borrower interest at the lender's actual costs plus the agreed Margin.

3 History of LIBOR-based lending

0.086   LIBOR-based lending originated in the 1960s when Middle Eastern countries deposited the Dollars they received from the sale of oil with London banks. The London banks started to use these funds to lend to customers, charging, as the interest rate, the cost at which the particular bank could borrow Dollars in the London interbank markets (LIBOR) plus a fixed profit – the Margin.

0.087   At that time, the London interbank market was totally unregulated and there were two principal concerns. Firstly there was a concern that the US would stop the trading of Dollars in London, for example by imposing exchange control restrictions. Hence the market disruption clause,[22] which was designed to ensure that if the market for lending Dollars in London was unavailable then the bank could fund the Dollars wherever they could and pass on the cost of funds to the borrower instead of charging the LIBOR component of the interest rate.

0.088   The second concern was that the market might stop being unregulated. Hence the loan agreement included an increased cost clause[23] which provided that if there were a change in law or regulation which increased the bank's costs or reduced its profits from the loan then the lender could pass those costs on to the borrower.

0.089   The structure of the loan agreement devised then was designed to ensure that the Margin – which was the bank's profit – was protected. All other costs other than changes in tax rates were passed on to the borrower.

0.090   Since then, principally as a result of (i) increased regulation; and (ii) the invention of a **Screen Rate** of LIBOR, the assumptions on which the loan agreement was originally based – that LIBOR is the lenders' funding cost, and their profit is the Margin, is increasingly a fiction. We will look at each of these issues in turn now.

4 Changing regulatory environment

0.091   In a LIBOR-based loan, the risks of all eventualities which may result in the lender incurring additional costs are passed on to the borrower through the '**yield** protection' clauses.[24] These clauses are designed to protect the lender against regulatory costs (discussed here) as well as other costs.[25]

---

[22] Discussed in 5.026 onwards.
[23] Discussed in 6.036 onwards.
[24] The increased cost clause (clause 14), the market disruption clause (clause 11.2), and the gross-up clause (clause 13.2(c)).
[25] Principally, **withholding tax** (discussed in the context of clause 13) and the cost incurred if there is a market disruption (discussed in the comments on clause 11.2).

0.092   There are two main types of regulatory costs which a lender may seek to pass on to a borrower under a loan agreement in which interest is calculated on a 'cost-plus' basis. These are

0.093   • Costs of compliance with the various Basel regulations[26] discussed in some detail in Chapter 6; and

0.094   • Costs (known as 'Mandatory Costs') of contributing to the running costs of the banking regulator, discussed at 0.101

What are the Basel Regulations there for?

0.095   Banking is an inherently risky business, fundamental to the wellbeing of economies. It is therefore highly regulated, and compliance with these regulations is costly for lenders. There are two principal types of risk which the Basel regulations seek to protect against: capital adequacy and liquidity.

Capital adequacy

0.096   One reason why banking is a risky business is that banks are highly geared. That is, most of the money they lend is borrowed from someone else. This means that a comparatively small loss can wipe out the banks' capital and result in the bank being unable to repay those from whom they have borrowed money – that is, the deposit holders. Put simply, banks are taking risks with other people's money. This is the reason for the capital adequacy regulations.

0.097   These regulations require banks to have a minimum amount of capital, with reference to the risks involved in their particular business. The riskier the business, the more of their own money (as opposed to money borrowed from depositors) must be used. In other words more shareholders' funds (or capital) are required for more risky types of business (see Box 0.8).

> **Box 0.8**
> The amount of capital required depends on the types of business conducted by the banks, with different degrees and types of risk having a different effect. Any changes in the level of capital required in relation to any given transaction will have an impact on the lender's profit for that transaction, and any additional costs resulting from such changes[27] are therefore generally passed on to the borrower for that transaction. See further clause 14 at 6.036.

---

[26] The Basel Regulations are commonly referred to as '**Basel I, Basel II and Basel III**' reflecting the three principal points of time at which these proposals were produced. They are the work of the Basel Committee of the G10 originally, (now the G20) – being a grouping of nations providing a forum for international economic cooperation.

[27] Or rather, from changes in regulation or application of regulation, which result in such changes in the level of capital required.

Liquidity

The second key risk which a bank runs is liquidity risk. The role of a bank is to transform short-term debt (customer deposits) into long-term debt (loans to customers) – which is an inherently risky activity.[28] Banks borrow money from deposit holders but allow them to withdraw funds with little or no notice – in other words, the banks borrow on a short-term basis from their deposit holders, supplementing this by short-term borrowing in the interbank markets. The bank then lends that money to their customers on a long-term basis. This of course gives rise to the risk that customers will require repayment at a time when there are insufficient new deposits from other customers, insufficient maturing loans and insufficient ability of the banks to borrow the necessary funds elsewhere – this is the liquidity risk.

0.098

This liquidity risk is something peculiar to financial institutions – outside the financial sector, firms invariably match the **tenor** of their financing to the tenor of the asset being financed. In other words, if they wanted to fund long-term assets, they would borrow money on a long-term basis to do that, rather than doing what banks do – and borrow on a short-term basis thus incurring the liquidity risk.

0.099

The regulations in Basel I, II and III are designed to try to reduce these two risks – the capital adequacy risk and the liquidity risk. It is worth noting at this stage that one effect of these regulations is to encourage banks to have a variety of sources of funds and to reduce the extent to which they raise funds in the interbank markets so as to reduce their liquidity risk. Hence the disconnect discussed between the documentation and the banks' actual funding arrangements. The Basel Regulations are discussed in more detail at 6.037 onwards.

0.100

Mandatory Costs

The second regulatory cost which the lenders may seek to pass on is 'Mandatory Costs'. Central banks in many jurisdictions require banks which are active in those jurisdictions to place deposits, often interest free, with the central bank. The income from these deposits is used to help fund the regulatory activity of the central bank. In England, there is an additional requirement for banks and other regulated institutions to pay fees to the banking regulators (the Prudential Regulation Authority and the Financial Conduct Authority) for their supervisory role. The amount of these fees and deposits are based on the amount of the lender's 'eligible liabilities' or 'modified eligible liabilities' (including any deposits obtained to fund LIBOR-based loans). An increase in borrowing by the bank to fund a new loan increases the lender's 'eligible liabilities' and so increases the amounts of fees and deposits required by the regulatory authorities. So,

0.101

---

[28] It is similar in nature to financing a long-term asset, such as a house, by borrowing on a credit card – when the credit card bill arrives, the bill can only be paid by borrowing again.

5 Personal LIBOR and the Screen Rate of LIBOR

0.102 Typically, interest under a Eurocurrency loan agreement, where the lender is treated as funding itself in London, will be charged at LIBOR plus Margin.

0.103 LIBOR means the London Interbank Offered Rate. The first letter of 'LIBOR' stands for London, and will be different if the lender is treated as funding itself in a different market. For example, if the loan is in Swedish Krona, there is no LIBOR quote for that currency, so the Lenders are likely to want to refer instead to the rate at which the funds are available in Stockholm – hence the Stockholm Interbank Offered Rate (or 'STIBOR').

0.104 Originally, LIBOR referred to the lenders' actual funding costs. However, in the early 1990s, the **Screen Rate** of LIBOR was invented, as discussed further at 1.060. This is intended to represent the rate of interest at which a prime bank could borrow from another bank in a specified currency on a specified date, for a specified period, in the London Interbank Market. It is intended to set a benchmark rate, being the rate at which prime banks *ought* to be able to fund themselves in the interbank markets at the relevant time – regardless of their actual funding costs (see also Box 0.9).

> **Box 0.9**
> Therefore, simply saying LIBOR is meaningless. The expression only has a meaning in relation to:
>
> - a specified currency;
> - a set duration; and
> - determined at a set time.
>
> For example, six month $ LIBOR on $10 million and three month Euro LIBOR on 10 million Euros are different. It is also necessary to define whether the intention is to refer to a Screen Rate or to a particular bank's actual rate of LIBOR.

0.105 The practice in the London market is that a lender wishing to fund itself in the interbank market enters into a commitment to borrow two **business days** before the money is required and the rate of LIBOR will be settled at the time the commitment is made. The moneys are borrowed for the

---

[29] The practice of charging Mandatory Costs in addition to the Margin and LIBOR is becoming less widespread, as discussed further in the commentary on clause 9.1 in 5.002.

specified period (typically one, three, or six months,) and repaid, together with interest, at the end of that period.[30]

6 Alternatives to LIBOR

As mentioned above, LIBOR is no longer an accurate reflection of most banks' overall funding costs, since they no longer fund the loan exclusively in the interbank markets.

0.106

Despite the changes in the lenders' funding arrangements, LIBOR has become a proxy for their funding costs for the purpose of the documentation. That is, they accept that their funding costs will differ from LIBOR and rely on the Margin to cover not just profit but also this cost differential. LIBOR is used as a benchmark rate (see Box 0.10).

0.107

> **Box 0.10**
> This puts pressure on the documentation. Should indemnities such as **Break Costs** and the market disruption clause be based on the Bank's actual funding costs or on the basis of its fictional costs? Similarly, given that the Margin includes some costs, the question arises as to which costs should have been included in the Margin and which justify additional claims being made on the Borrower.[31]

During the financial crisis of 2007/2008 many lenders started to question the accuracy of the Screen Rate of LIBOR – eventually resulting in a wholesale review of the benchmark and (among other things) a reduction of the currencies and durations for which LIBOR was quoted. This is discussed further in the commentary on the market disruption clause at 5.026 onwards.

0.108

This review resulted in the need for alternative benchmarks for pricing loans in those currencies for which LIBOR no longer existed. Alternatives used or suggested included:

0.109

- central bank rates;
- rates in domestic interbank markets (e.g. STIBOR); or
- LIBOR for a continued currency combined with cost of swapping into the relevant currency.

The view of the Association of Corporate Treasurers is that central bank rates are inappropriate because they would be unattractive to non-financial lenders and the documents would need extensive amendment. The

0.110

---

[30] See commentary on definition of LIBOR in 1.042 onwards for a further discussion of LIBOR.
[31] See for example, 6.044 in relation to increased costs, 5.033 onwards in relation to market disruption and 1.012 in relation to Break Costs.

disadvantages of using domestic rates are that those rates are not available internationally. The third option of using LIBOR plus **swap** costs is complex. For the time being, for those currencies for which there is no LIBOR, the most common solution is to use the equivalent in the domestic market (such as STIBOR – or Stockholm Interbank Offer Rate – for Swedish Krona). For those currencies for which LIBOR still exists, it is still used as the basis for the documentation, although there is increasing tension between the documents and the reality and increasing pressure to find alternatives.

7 Summary of interest provisions in LMA Term Loan

0.111 In the interests of simplicity, below you will find a summary of the mechanics for calculating interest and other ongoing payments contained in the LMA Term Loan. The details of each point are discussed elsewhere.

0.112
- The LMA Term Loan provides that interest will be paid at LIBOR[32] plus Margin (clause 9.1). Sometimes clause 9.1 requires Mandatory Costs to be paid in addition to LIBOR plus Margin. There are then various fall back mechanisms dealing with the possibility that there is no Screen Rate for the relevant currency and Interest Period.[33] These are described here, and, in diagrammatic form, in Figure 0.1 on page 23

0.113
- LIBOR is defined to mean the Screen Rate (unless the optional provisions referred to below at 0.119 are used).

0.114
- If there is a Screen Rate for the relevant currency but not for the relevant **Interest Period**, LIBOR is defined to mean a rate (the 'Interpolated Rate') which is calculated with reference to the nearest available LIBOR figures

0.115
- If there is no Screen Rate for the relevant currency or if it is not possible to calculate an interpolated rate then LIBOR is defined to mean the Reference Bank Rate, which is a rate quoted by certain specified banks on the basis of the same criteria used to calculate the Screen Rate

0.116
- If the Reference Bank Rate mechanism fails (see 1.058) or if the Screen Rate does not reflect the rate at which a set percentage of lenders can fund in the relevant interbank market then the market disruption clause kicks in, and the borrower will need to pay each lender's 'cost of funds' plus Margin.[34]

---

[32] If the Loan is in Euros, lenders have the option of choosing Euribor instead, but for all other currencies for which LIBOR exists, the lenders are assumed to be funding in London.
[33] See definition of LIBOR at 1.042.
[34] See discussion of the market disruption clause in 5.026 onwards.

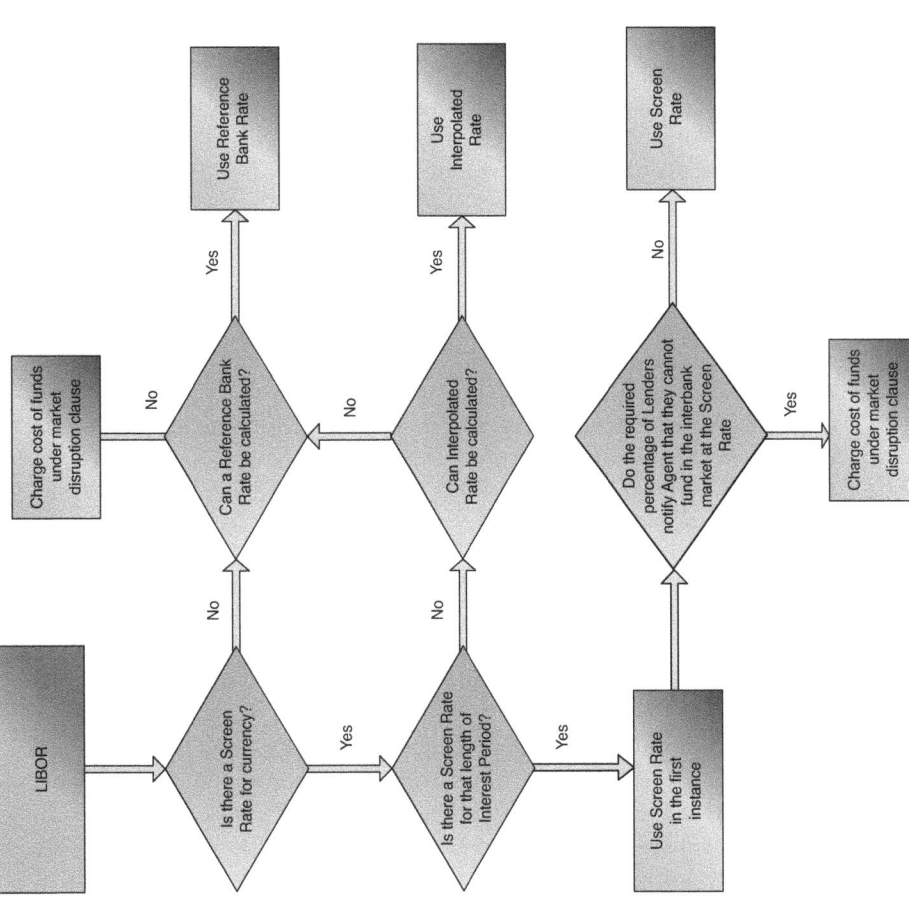

Figure 0.1 Summary of LMA interest rate provisions

- 0.117 • Additionally, the borrower may be required to make additional payments under the increased costs clause[35] if the lenders' costs change due to a change in regulation or in application of a regulation.
- 0.118 • The borrower may also be required to '**gross up**' interest payments if there is a withholding tax.[36]
- 0.119 • There are optional provisions (contained in the 'kits' described at Section 5 of this Introduction at 0.152) for using the Reference Bank Rate as the primary method of determining LIBOR, rather than the Screen Rate. This may be useful for currencies for which there is no Screen Rate as discussed at 0.108.
- 0.120 • There are also optional provisions in the 'kits' for a two-tier market disruption clause, designed to relegate the 'standard' market disruption provisions to more extreme circumstances.[37]

SECTION 4: SCOPE OF THE LOAN AGREEMENT

0.121 In every loan agreement, some fundamental issues relating to the scope of the agreement need to be addressed,

- Who can make use of the facility?
- Who are the lenders, the **Agent**, and the Security **Trustee**?
- Who can be called on to repay?
- Whose activities can cause difficulty for the borrower under the loan agreement?

0.122 See Box 0.11 on page 25 for a description of the concepts used in the LMA Term Loan to address some of these issues discussed in the paragraphs below.

1 Who can make use of the facility?

0.123 In many loan agreements only certain named persons may use the facility. In other cases (including the LMA Term Loan) additional group companies may make use of the facility subject to certain conditions. Those additional companies will become party to the loan agreement at a future date by a mechanism agreed at the start.[38] Borrowers will wish to ensure that this process is a mechanical one, as far as possible, and that the conditions precedent do not effectively make the extension of the loan to new group members discretionary on the part of the lenders.

---

[35] Discussed in 6.036.
[36] See discussion of the grossing up clause in 6.015 onwards.
[37] If this option is chosen, then a new set of banks is introduced (confusingly, the 'Alternative Reference Banks', with the banks which would normally have been Reference Banks being renamed as the 'Base Reference Banks'!) to give a quote based on the same criteria as the Screen Rate which will then apply to the whole loan unless a more extreme market disruption occurs. This is discussed further in 5.037.
[38] See clause 25 in 9.060.

> **Box 0.11**
>
> THE LMA STRUCTURE
>
> The LMA Term Loan describes the various categories of persons affected by the agreement by the following definitions:
>
> - *'Original Borrowers'* These are the companies in the group which are initially entitled to borrow as specified in a schedule to the agreement.
> - *'Original Guarantors'* These are the companies specified in a schedule to the agreement which are initially required to guarantee the loan.
> - *'Company'* This is the ultimate holding company of the group or sub-group (which may or may not also be a borrower or guarantor).
> - *'Borrowers'* These are the members of the group which, at any particular time, have borrowed or remain entitled to borrow moneys under the facility. This will be the Original Borrowers plus any other company in the group which has been accepted by the lenders as a borrower but excluding any who are no longer entitled to borrow under the agreement.
> - *'Guarantors'* These are the members of the group which, at any particular time, are liable under guarantees of the loan. This will be the Original Guarantors plus any additional group companies which have guaranteed the loan but excluding any whose guarantees have been released.
> - *'Obligors'* These are the borrowers and the guarantors.
> - *'Group'* This is the Company and all its Subsidiaries[39] at any given time.

2 Who are the lenders?

Most commonly there will be a syndicate with the identity of lenders changing from time to time and new lenders becoming party to the agreement at a future date, by a mechanism agreed at the start.[40] Borrowers will wish to be sure that any changes in lenders or in the **lending office** do not cause any adverse consequences, such as additional costs under the **gross-up** clause,[41] for the borrower. The original Agent and Security Trustee will be specified, but there may be provisions allowing these roles to be passed on to others over time.

0.124

3 Who can be called on to repay?

Often there will be specified guarantors in addition to the borrowers. The LMA Term Loan also contains a mechanism for guarantors to change[42]

0.125

---

[39] See definition of 'Subsidiary' in 1.062.
[40] See clause 24 in 9.043.
[41] See clause 13 in 6.016.
[42] See clause 25 in 9.063 onwards.

(subject to approval of the lenders) allowing flexibility, for example, if the holding company wishes to dispose of a group member which is a guarantor or to release it from those requirements of the agreement which relate to guarantors.

4 Whose activities can cause difficulties for the borrowers under the loan agreement?

0.126 What is the scope of the loan agreement in relation to the group? For example, do financial ratios relate to the consolidated position of the group as a whole? Are there negative undertakings relating to companies in the group which are not borrowers? (See Box 0.12 on page 27 for a diagram of the position under the LMA Term Loan).

0.127 This issue is of particular importance to all parties.

0.128 • Lenders need to ensure that the agreement provides them with sufficient powers in relation to all those issues which are relevant to their credit decision, which may well extend to issues involving members of the group which are neither borrowers nor guarantors.

0.129 • Borrowers will be concerned to insulate themselves as far as possible from problems which may arise in other parts of the group. They will also want to avoid the possibility that activities of other group members, particularly those over which the borrowers have no control, may result in the withdrawal of the borrowers' funding.

0.130 • The ultimate holding company will want to maintain the flexibility to restructure the group and, if appropriate, sell parts of it, without interference by the various lenders to group members under their different financing arrangements.

0.131 The parties therefore need to address the following questions, considered in turn here:

0.132 • Is consent of lenders required to the sale of a group member or acquisition of a new group member?[43]

0.133 • Should certain companies be excluded from the undertakings altogether?[44]

0.134 • Which (if any) provisions should relate to group companies which are neither borrowers nor guarantors?[45]

---

[43] See 0.136
[44] See 0.138.
[45] See 0.142.

Box 0.12

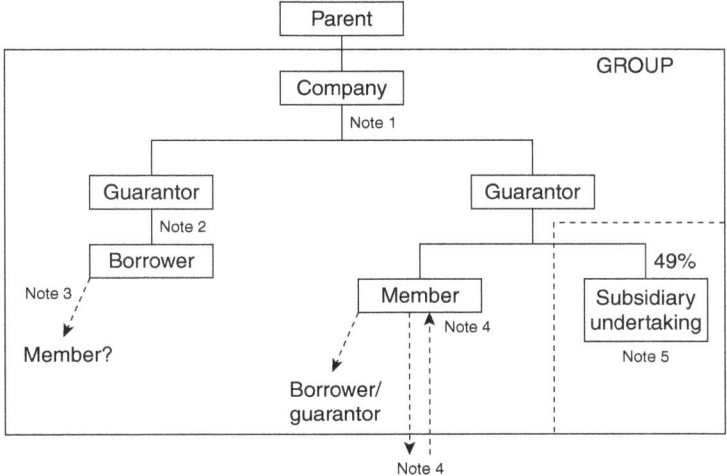

(Based on the assumption that selling of shares in Group companies is permitted under the no disposals undertaking)

Note 1 The 'Company' administers the facility. It assumes miscellaneous payment and other obligations. The loan must be prepaid if there is a change of control of the Company. Note that if the Company is not the ultimate holding company of the group it is important to ensure that a change of 'ultimate' control triggers the clause. Even if the borrower's shareholders do not change, if the shareholders of the shareholders change, the lenders will want that to trigger the clause

Note 2 Guarantors must remain in the Group, unless they resign as guarantors, which they can do with the consent of all Lenders. They are bound by the undertakings relating to 'Obligors'.

Note 3 Borrowers must remain in the Group unless they resign as borrowers. They may resign as borrowers if they repay those advances which were made to them and if there is no **Default** at the time of their resignation. They are bound by the undertakings relating to 'Obligors'.

Note 4 Members of the Group are bound only by the 'Group' undertakings (summarized in Box 0.16), which are less extensive than the 'Obligor' undertakings. They need not remain in the Group. They may become Borrowers or Guarantors subject to certain conditions, including delivery of a satisfactory legal opinion.

Note 5 If this company is effectively controlled by a Group member it may be a 'Subsidiary Undertaking', and, if such companies are included in the definition of 'Subsidiary', it will be affected by the Loan Agreement in the same way as other Group companies.

0.135
- Do the lenders have different concerns in relation to different members of the group?[46] So, for example,
  - Should some provisions be tested on a group-wide, as opposed to an individual company, basis?
  - Should some provisions allow transactions between different group members?

Is consent of the lenders required to sale or acquisition of a group member?

0.136 Some loan agreements restrict the borrowers from forming subsidiaries[47] and restrict group members from being sold out of the group. A common way to achieve this is to attach a group structure chart to the agreement and require the borrowers to undertake to make no changes to the group structure from that indicated in the chart. Of course, the no disposals undertaking also prevents the disposals of subsidiaries unless appropriate carve-outs are negotiated.

0.137 Other loan agreements prevent sale of a subsidiary less explicitly, as they include undertakings relating to specific named group companies or companies which are members of the group on the day of the loan agreement's signature. The result is that such companies cannot be sold out of the group, since, if they were, the continued compliance with the relevant provisions would be outside the control of the group. See Box 0.13 for a description of the position under the LMA Term Loan.

Should certain companies be excluded from the undertakings entirely?

0.138 Two types of companies are often excluded from the undertakings in the loan agreement, being insignificant companies and non-recourse companies.

Box 0.13
The LMA Term Loan requires Obligors to remain members of the group,[48] but, on the face of it, it allows other group members to be sold (although there needs to be an adjustment to the no disposals clause to achieve this), and allows new companies to become part of the group. Change in the control of the group gives lenders the right to require to be prepaid.[49] By virtue of the provisions allowing Obligors to cease to be Obligors,[50] even Borrowers can be sold out of the group as long as they first repay any loan they have borrowed and as long as that is not prohibited by the no disposals clause. Guarantors can only be released from their obligations (and hence become free to be sold) with consent of all lenders.

---

[46] See 0.147.
[47] Indeed, in a loan to a single borrower which has no subsidiaries it is usually sensible to either include potential future subsidiaries in the undertakings or to include an undertaking against forming subsidiaries to ensure that the purpose of the negative undertakings cannot be avoided through activities of unregulated subsidiaries.
[48] See clause 23.9 in 8.265.
[49] See clause 8.2 in 4.012.
[50] See clause 25 in 9.062.

Insignificant companies Borrowers will often ask for insignificant companies to be exempted from the undertakings. Often the test of significance for this purpose looks at the **Tangible Net Worth** of the company concerned and exempts it if that represents a minor (e.g. less than 5%) part of the Tangible Net Worth of the group. This is often calculated with reference to the latest audited accounts at the relevant time.

0.139

Comment Borrowers need to be cautious with this approach as a company which was once exempt may be caught at a later point if its relative importance in the Group changes. This may even result in an **Event of Default** by virtue of things done while the company was exempt. If this type of exception has been agreed, the group needs to keep a check on whether exempt companies might cross the threshold and cease to be exempt (see Box 0.14).

0.140

Box 0.14

An example might assist. Assume that a loan agreement includes a negative pledge clause saying '*The Company shall ensure that no ... [Material Subsidiary] shall ... permit to subsist any Security.*' Assume that

(a) the company grants security at a time when it is not a Material Subsidiary; and
(b) the value of the company increases relative to that of the Group and it becomes a Material Subsidiary.

Unless the security falls within one of the exceptions to the negative pledge clause, the company will need to discharge the security before it becomes a Material Subsidiary in order to avoid being in breach, as the covenant is not to '*permit Security to subsist*'.

Non-recourse companies The second type of company which is commonly exempted is a company which is established for the purpose of a particular non-recourse transaction. These companies are established as vehicles for particular projects. The argument for excluding them from the provisions of the loan agreement is that difficulties with the project vehicle are usually not the responsibility of the group and therefore should not impact on the group's commercial borrowing. (If excluded from the undertakings, they would also then be excluded for all purposes, including, e.g. financial ratios.) Hence a definition of 'Non-Recourse Company' is often inserted (see Box 0.15 on page 30).

0.141

> **Box 0.15**
> 'Non-Recourse Company' means, at any relevant time, a company which, at such time, has no Financial Indebtedness other than Non-Recourse Indebtedness.
> 'Non-Recourse Indebtedness' means Financial Indebtedness incurred by a company (the 'Project Company') for the purposes of financing a particular project where
>
> (i) the principal assets and business of the Project Company are constituted by that project; and
> (ii) the provider of the Financial Indebtedness has no recourse against any member of the Group or its assets except the assets of the Project Company comprised in the project.

Which provisions should be extended to relate to group companies which are not Obligors?

0.142 Borrowers, as noted earlier, want the undertakings and other provisions to apply only to Obligors and not to be extended to any other company in the group. There are three main reasons for this.

0.143 • The result of extending the provisions to a company which is not an Obligor will usually be that a downturn in that other company's financial fortunes will cause a potential problem for the borrower.

0.144 • The borrower may not be in a position to control the activities of that other company, and therefore may be unable to prevent that other company from doing things which cause an Event of Default under the borrower's loan.

0.145 • The group may wish to maintain flexibility as to company sales and purchases.[51]

0.146 Given that lenders have no claim against group companies which are not Obligors it may be questioned why, for example, the negative pledge or the no disposals covenant extend to those companies. Often the lenders will justify this on the basis that, whatever the legal situation, if a subsidiary were to have financial difficulties (such as those caused by cross default,[52] or which may be heralded by **asset stripping**[53] or a breach of the negative pledge[54]) the ultimate holding company may well find itself bound up with the financial difficulties of its subsidiary, even if not legally bound to support it. The solution needs to be agreed on a case-by-case basis and usually on a clause-by-clause basis, taking account of the credit decision. The result

---
[51] See 0.136.
[52] See clause 23.5 in 8.231.
[53] See clause 22.4 in 8.174.
[54] See clause 22.3 in 8.135.

(as in the LMA Term Loan – see Box 0.16) may well be that some clauses will apply to all group members and others to Obligors only. However, any extension of any clause to companies which are not Obligors needs very careful consideration by the borrower, as to whether it is justified, and acceptable, in the context of the particular group.[55]

Box 0.16
The LMA Term Loan provides for the following undertakings to relate to group companies (as opposed to Obligors).

- Representations (clauses 19.1, 19.3, 19.9 and 19.13) as to corporate existence: that performance is not a breach of applicable constitution, law or contract; that there is no material breach of contract; and that there is no litigation – limited in each case to Subsidiaries of Obligors.
- Representations (clause 19.10 and 19.11) as to information provided and absence of material adverse change.
- Financial information (clause 20.1 requiring consolidated financial statements for the Company).
- Information generally (clause 20.4).
- Negative pledge (clause 22.3).
- No disposals (clause 22.4).
- No merger (clause 22.5).
- No change of business (of the group, not individual members) clause 22.6.
- Cross default (clause 23.5).
- **Insolvency** (clauses 23.6 and 23.7).
- Execution of judgments (clause 23.8).

Do the lenders have different concerns about different members of the group?

0.147 In agreeing which clauses should extend to group members and which should be limited to Obligors, or perhaps to Obligors and their Subsidiaries, the parties also need to consider whether the lenders may have specific concerns in relation to individual group members or whether they are looking at the overall financial position of the group. For example, are the lenders concerned to ensure that value is maintained in those parts of the group (the Obligors) against which they have a direct claim, or are they content that the value is maintained in the group as a whole? Are they satisfied as to the efficacy of all the guarantees they have or are there some upstream guarantees in the structure which might be problematic in the jurisdiction of the guarantor or of its assets[56]?

---

[55] If the eventual agreed position is that some provisions extend beyond the Obligors, the borrower may seek to mitigate this by providing for extended grace periods for Events of Default which relate to companies that are not Obligors.
[56] See the discussion in A1.082.

0.148 The answer will impact (among other things) on the following questions:

0.149
- whether any relevant limits, such as the effect which is to be treated as material for the purpose of the definition of 'Material Adverse Effect'[57] or the threshold amount for the negative pledge,[58] or the test of change of business,[59] is set on a company-by-company basis (and then, whether it is set with reference to any Obligor or with reference to any group member) or with reference to the position of the group as a whole.

0.150
- negative undertakings – the borrowers may request that these relate to the group as a whole and that transactions between group members should be excluded from, for example, the no disposals clause. The lenders, on the other hand, may be happy to permit such transactions as between Obligors, but not between other group members (see Box 0.17).

> **Box 0.17**
> For example, in relation to the no disposals undertaking at clause 22.4,[60] the borrower may request the ability to transfer assets between group members without the restrictions of that clause. The lenders, on the other hand, may be concerned to ensure that specific assets remain within a company to which the lenders have direct access, in which case they may agree the exception, but only in relation to transactions between Obligors.

0.151
- at which levels the financial ratios are tested. The lenders may require ratios to be tested both at a consolidated level (probably excluding any companies such as non-recourse companies which have been excluded from the undertakings), and also for particular Obligors. If certain companies have been excluded from the financial covenants, the lenders may well want to restrict certain transactions which benefit those companies, such as making loans or giving security.

SECTION 5: OPTIONAL PROVISIONS PUBLISHED BY THE LMA IN 'KIT' FORM (OR BY CROSS REFERENCE TO THE LEVERAGED LMA)

0.152 There are a number of provisions which the LMA has published in the form of optional provisions which can be included in the LMA Term Loan at the option of the parties. Many of these provisions ought to be included in any loan agreement. They are discussed separately here in order to give

---

[57] See definition of 'Material Adverse Effect' in 1.052.
[58] See clause 22.3(c)(x) in 8.168.
[59] See clause 22.6 in 8.188.
[60] See 8.174.

an overview of how they operate. Where appropriate, they will also be discussed in more detail in the clauses where they appear.

1 Borrowers and affiliates purchasing in the secondary market

The first of these optional supplements relates to the possibility that a Borrower or one of its Affiliates might purchase an interest in the loan in the **secondary market**. The LMA Term Loan includes a footnote in the transfer clause which cross refers to the provisions of the Leveraged LMA dealing with this issue. Those provisions provide for two options as to how to deal with this. The first option prohibits it. The second option permits it but provides that the purchaser's offer to purchase must be capable of being accepted by all the lenders pro rata so that the borrower cannot pick and choose which lender to buy out (just as they cannot choose who to prepay). This option also provides that the purchaser will not have any voting rights in relation to its share of the loan. 0.153

Comment Where there is a senior and junior loan, senior lenders might also want to consider adding similar provisions preventing the junior lenders or their affiliates from buying into the senior loan and influencing voting there primarily to protect their own position in the junior loan. 0.154

2 Defaulting lender provisions

In June 2009, as a result of the 2008 financial crisis, the LMA published a number of clauses addressing lender default. These clauses (which the LMA refer to as the 'LMA Finance Party Default and Market Disruption Clauses' and which I will refer to as the 'Defaulting Lender Provisions') deal with: 0.155

- how to deal with the position where a lender is in financial difficulty; 0.156
- what to do if the Agent were in financial difficulty – and in particular how to ensure that this does not interfere with the flow of payments between the borrower and its lenders; 0.157
- how to deal with a lender which is in financial difficulties when the facility provides for **letters of credit** to be issued, with the issuing bank relying on indemnities from syndicate members; and 0.158
- how to ensure that the interest calculation mechanism provides an appropriate way of remunerating the lenders during periods of severe market disruption. 0.159

We will deal with each of the defaulting lender issues in turn. The interest mechanisms are dealt with in the market disruption clause. 0.160

Lender Default

0.161 The six main consequences which the LMA clauses provide for are that:

0.162
- The Borrower ought not to be obliged to pay a **commitment fee** to a lender which is unlikely to be able to comply with its obligation to advance the undrawn **commitment**;[61]

0.163
- The borrower ought to be able to bring in a different lender (referred to in the LMA Term Loan as an 'Increase Lender') to commit to advance the sums which the defaulting lender has not yet advanced;[62]

0.164
- The defaulting lender's vote in syndicate meetings should be calculated on the basis of amounts it has actually advanced and should not take into account its undrawn commitment (since it may well not be able to comply with its obligations to advance that);[63]

0.165
- The borrower ought also be able to remove the defaulting lender from the facility entirely (i.e. also in relation to sums already drawn) and replace it with a more acceptable lender;[64]

0.166
- The borrower ought not to be obliged to repay that lender's participation in a revolving credit until the end of the **availability period** for that revolving credit;[65]

0.167
- If the defaulting lender fails to respond promptly to requests for consent and the like, then its vote should be disregarded.[66]

0.168 Of course the documents also need to address the question of what is a Defaulting Lender and the Defaulting Lender Provisions define this to mean a lender which fails to advance moneys when due or which makes it clear that it will not perform its obligations under the agreement or in relation to which insolvency procedures are commenced.

Impaired Agent

0.169 Next the Defaulting Lender Provisions deal with the situation where problems arise in relation to the Agent. This would be of concern to all parties because the Lenders take a credit risk on the Agent, in relation to monies paid through the Agent; and also because the Agent may become unable to continue to perform its communication role for the syndicate.

0.170 The Defaulting Lender Provisions deal with this by providing that:[67]

0.171
- The Majority Lenders can remove the Agent and replace him with a new Agent;

---

[61] See 5.045.
[62] See 2.003.
[63] See 11.028.
[64] See Box 4.4 on page 105.
[65] See 4.004.
[66] See 11.029.
[67] See 10.018.

- Payments need not be made through Agent, but may either be made direct to the appropriate recipient or may be paid to a **trust** account with a third party bank (having a specified minimum credit **rating**) to be held on trust for the relevant recipient;
- Communications need not be made through Agent but may be given directly between the parties; and
- Of course, these provisions are only workable if the borrower knows who the lenders are, so there is also a provision that the Agent must supply the borrower with a list of lenders and their Commitments and administrative details, either on request or at monthly intervals.

The concept which is used to define a problem Agent is that of an 'Impaired Agent'. The idea is similar to that of a Defaulting Lender but recognizing the many different circumstances in which payments need to be made by Agents. So it is defined to mean an Agent which fails to make a payment when due or which makes it clear that it will not perform its obligations under the agreement (in each case, whether in its capacity as Agent, or, if applicable, as a Lender) or in relation to which insolvency procedures are commenced.

Letter of Credit Facilities

The next area of concern is the situation where a defaulting lender participates in a letter of credit facility (see Box 0.18).

The problem here is that it is common for a single lender to issue the letter of credit and to rely on indemnities from syndicate members in respect of any payments made by the issuing lender under the letter of credit. Of course, if a syndicate member gets into financial difficulties the issuing bank will be concerned about –

- existing letters of credit – will the defaulting bank make payment when required? as well as about
- future letters of credit – it will not want to be obliged to issue additional letters of credit when it knows there is a problem with a syndicate member.

Box 0.18

A letter of credit is a method of payment used, for example, in export finance. A buyer wants to be sure that he only pays for goods when they have been shipped, but the seller does not want to ship them until he knows he will be paid. So the buyer's bank issues a letter of credit, which is essentially a promise by the bank to make payment on behalf of its customer, once proof of shipment is given. Once payment is made by the bank issuer it is entitled to receive repayment from its customer.

Under a letter of credit facility, the bank agrees that it will not require immediate repayment but that the amount paid on behalf of the customer will take the form of a loan, repayable over time. If the facility is syndicated then, once the issuing bank makes payment under the letter of credit, it will require each syndicate member to reimburse it for that lender's share of the sum paid.

0.180 The general position should be, just as in a syndicated loan, that it is the borrower who is taking the credit risk on the syndicate members. To achieve this, the Defaulting Lender Provisions provide that: the Issuing Bank may require a defaulting lender to provide cash **collateral** for its participation in the facility, but that, if it fails to provide that, the borrower has the option to provide cash collateral (or can be required to do so if the letter of credit has already been issued). The document goes on to provide that if no cash collateral is provided, the Issuing Bank can reduce amounts of unissued letters of credit by the amount of that lender's **participation**.

0.181 Note also that these provisions apply not only to defaulting lenders but also to lenders of below a specified rating.

0.182 The Defaulting Lender Provisions also include optional provisions allowing the borrower to appoint more than one bank as the bank which will issue letters of credit under the loan agreement. The purpose is to allow a fallback position if one of the banks appointed to that role gets into financial difficulties.

SECTION 6: COMMODIFICATION OF DEBT

0.183 The credit crunch of 2007–2008 was widely seen as resulting from the massive commodification of debt which has happened since the invention of securitization and credit derivatives. These instruments gave rise to the growth of the so-called 'shadow banking system' – with all the challenges which that gives rise to for regulators and for borrowers.

0.184 This part of the Introduction gives a brief description of the growth and influence of non-bank lenders on the loan market and highlights some of the complications which this creates for the documents.

0.185 There are three key issues to consider.

0.186 • The first is the fact that there may be lenders in the syndicate which are not banks.

0.187 • The second issue is that the direct lenders to the borrower may not have retained the credit risk in relation to the loan, but may have sold it on, and this may influence their motivation when it comes to requests for consent and the like.

0.188 • The third issue is that the increased trading of loans has led to a convergence between market practices in the loan markets and capital markets, as investors increasingly participate in both markets

We will look at each of these issues in turn

1 Non bank lenders as direct lenders

0.189 Pension funds, insurance companies, hedge funds and 'CLOs'[68] all participate in loans. This has been the case for many years but the increased regu-

---

[68] CLO stands for Collateralised Loan Obligation. It is an investment which can be issued to purchasers, giving them a share in the **pool** of assets (loans) underlying the CLO.

lation and state of the financial markets (in Europe at least), have added impetus to this as banks retrench and companies have to look elsewhere for funds. The LMA Term Loan allows interests in the loan to be transferred to any entity which is *'regularly engaged in ... investing in ... financial assets.'*[69] So there is very broad scope for different types of entities to buy into the loan. Even if the borrower restricted that clause so that the loan could only be transferred to a bank or financial institution, a decision in 2006[70] in the UK held that this encompassed 'a legally recognised form or being which carries on its business in accordance with the laws of its place of creation and whose business involves commercial finance.'

Involvement of non-banks as direct lenders has a number of consequences: 0.190

- Some of these entities may also trade in shares so they may not want to receive non-public information from the borrower as that may restrict their ability to trade the shares. The LMA Term Loan has addressed this by allowing lenders to nominate a third party to receive information on their behalf so as to filter out any non-public information;[71] 0.191
- Some of these entities may not have the duties of confidentiality which a bank has – hence the introduction of a confidentiality clause in the LMA Term Loan imposing duties of confidentiality on lenders;[72] 0.192
- Many of these lenders do not want to be consulted on anything other than major issues – they do not have the manpower to deal with requests and are used to investing in bonds which have much less restrictive undertakings than loans. This gives rise to two issues: 0.193
  - they may not respond to requests for consent (making consent harder to achieve unless there is a snooze you lose clause[73]) and 0.194
  - They may prefer the loan to have less onerous undertakings (the so-called '**covenant lite**' transactions discussed at 8.073, which were criticized as being part of the issues behind the credit crisis and which are re emerging); 0.195
- Many of the standard provisions of the LMA Term Loan are based on the assumption that the lenders are banks funding themselves in the London interbank markets and subject to banking regulation. Examples are the market disruption clause, the definition of Break Costs and the provisions relating to Mandatory Costs. These provisions may need adjusting for non-bank lenders. 0.196

---

[69] LMA Term Loan clause 24.1 discussed in 9.043.
[70] In the case Argo Fund Ltd v Essar Steel Ltd [2006] 2 All E.R. (Comm) 104.
[71] See 10.016.
[72] See 11.031.
[73] See Box 11.6 on page 287.

2 Direct lenders transferring credit risk

0.197 Turning to the second issue – lenders may not have kept the credit risk of the loan but may have sold that on through credit derivatives. The most popular form of credit derivative is a **credit default swap** (or 'CDS'). It is effectively rather like insurance in that the lender of record, in exchange for a fee, receives compensation if there is a 'Credit Event' such as failure to pay, **bankruptcy** or restructuring. The **lender of record** is known as the 'purchaser' – buying credit protection; and the counterparty is the 'seller' – selling credit protection (see Box 0.19).

> **Box 0.19**
> A Credit Default Swap may be issued in relation to a particular debt, or in relation to a bundle of debts of a given type. For example they could relate to debts of a particular borrower or from a particular country or with some other particular characteristic (such as sub-prime mortgage debt). A buyer of protection does not need to hold the debt to enter into such an arrangement. A seller of protection may also offer protection against different tranches of risk – such as the first 5% of loss. Credit Default Swaps are discussed in more detail in relation to clause 24 at 9.021.

0.198 The result of this is that there is an active market for credit risk which can be traded without trading the underlying debt itself. A lender which has purchased credit protection may have little motivation to support the company in difficult times, and borrowers are unlikely to know whether their lenders have purchased credit protection or not.[74] The market for **distressed debt** also leads to difficulties in organizing restructurings not only because of the difficulty in identifying all the relevant stakeholders but also because of their different incentives. Some investors in distressed debt may be following a 'loan to own' policy – with the intention of taking over the company or its assets in a restructuring.[75]

0.199 The upside of all this is increased sources of funds, particularly in times when banks are retrenching. The downside is increasing difficulties in organizing restructurings, or even just in obtaining consents, and stress on the documentation which was drafted to deal with relationships in a very different financial landscape from that which exists today.

---

[74] See further 9.035 onwards.
[75] Some examples of this are discussed at 'Trading places: distressed debt trading in the US and UK restructuring markets' in Butterworths Journal of International Banking and Financial Law July/August 2013.

3 Convergence with capital markets

It is also worth noting that this commodification of debt has increased the liquidity of loan investments, leading to some convergence between practices in the loan markets and the capital markets – (see Box 0.20) particularly in the leveraged acquisition market where investors commonly invest in both types of debt – that is, they take participations in traditional loans and also invest in debt instruments in the capital markets. One well-known example is the so-called 'covenant lite' loan – a loan with less onerous undertakings than has been traditional in the loan market, but which is acceptable to investors who traditionally invest in the capital markets.

0.200

> **Box 0.20**
> For some companies needing to raise money, they have the option of raising it from the public, instead of approaching banks or other lenders. This is what is meant by the 'capital markets'. The most familiar form is for a listed company to issue shares, but the capital markets deal in many forms of investments, including debt instruments, commonly referred to as bonds or notes. From the borrowers' point of view, issuing bonds is similar to raising money through a loan from banks, in that the bond issue will raise a given amount of funds, on which the borrower must pay interest, and which must be repaid on specified dates. In the meantime the borrower will need to comply with various undertakings which they have agreed to in the documentation.

There are still significant differences between financing in the loan markets and in the capital markets, principally in:

0.201

- the amount of publicity involved – loans are confidential while bond issues involve the provision to the public of extensive amounts of information;

0.202

- the amounts of money which can be raised (and its cost) – the size and liquidity of the capital markets enables borrowers to raise more money more cheaply than by using loan finance;

0.203

- less restrictive terms of financing in the capital markets in terms of the undertakings and events of default;

0.204

- raising money in the capital markets – is not possible for all companies as they need to be large enough, and sufficiently creditworthy to be able to attract the investors;

0.205

- the degree of regulation involved – the accepted view (uncertainty around which has recently been clarified, see Box 0.21 on page 40) has been that loan agreements are not specified investments under the <u>Financial Services and Markets Act 2000</u>, whereas bonds and similar instruments issued in the capital markets are regulated.

0.206

> **Box 0.21**
> The recent case of Fons HF (in liquidation) **v** Corporal Limited and Pillar Securitisation [2014]EWCA Civ 304 however held that, contrary to the accepted view, loan agreements are **debentures** (defined as an instrument which evidences a debt). The case did not concern regulatory issues but the implications of the decision are that if a loan agreement is a debenture then it is a regulated investment. Nevertheless the Financial Services Authority has confirmed that they do not regard the case as having altered the previously accepted position.[76]

SECTION 7: ASSET AND PROJECT FINANCE

1 Asset finance

0.207 Asset finance is financing of an asset (often a moveable asset) where the lender regards the value of the asset being financed as a significant factor in its credit assessment. The expression is commonly used for ship finance, aircraft finance, financing of rolling stock, satellites, containers and other major assets.

0.208 Key issues in asset finance, which need to be addressed by the documents[77] and by due diligence, include:

0.209
- conflict of law (e.g. the law chosen for the loan agreement, the law applicable to the security, and the law in the place where the asset is at the time any security comes to be enforced);

0.210
- whether to structure the transaction as a **mortgage** financing or as a **title financing**;[78]

0.211
- liabilities of a financier (such as the issue of whether the financier will be exposed to environmental liabilities, either simply as a result of taking security over the asset, or as a result of ownership of it in a title finance arrangement, or as a result of the enforcement of security over the asset);

0.212
- detention rights of third parties relating to the asset, if it is a moveable asset. The issue here is to identify what parties may be entitled to detain the asset and prevent its profitable use. Examples are the **lien** which a repairer has on an asset until the repair bill is paid and the right of port states to detain vessels for safety reasons;

---

[76] The letter explains the implications of the case and is available from the website at www.citysolicitors.org.uk (search 'Fons').

[77] See, for example, the comments at 0.016 in relation to asset finance and Section 2 of the commentary on the undertakings in 8.200 onwards.

[78] See 0.234.

- maintenance of the asset – the lenders will want to be sure that the asset is properly maintained and, perhaps, that funds are set aside for this purpose;   **0.213**
- preservation of the value of the asset generally, including loan to value ratios;[79]   **0.214**
- insurance – the lenders will want to have security over the asset's insurance so that, if there is damage to it, the lenders have replacement security. They will also want to be satisfied as to the insurance for potential liabilities to third parties arising in respect of the use of the asset;   **0.215**
- impact of insolvency – are there risks that enforcement of security on the asset may be impeded as a result of insolvency proceedings such as **administration** in England, or that transactions such as guarantees may be vulnerable to be unwound in the event of an insolvency?   **0.216**
- registration – where does the asset and any security on it need to be registered and what are the consequences of non-registration?   **0.217**
- ability to sell the asset free of liens and other interests – and can the lender exercise self-help remedies, or will any sale have to be effected by a court?   **0.218**

2 Project finance

Project finance consists of lending against the income of a project. It usually involves: **0.219**

- the development or exploitation of a right, natural resource or other asset;
- limited recourse lending;
- income capture with the debt being repaid out of the revenue generated by the project.

In relation to the loan agreement, key characteristics will be: **0.220**

- strict undertakings in relation to the key contracts in the project, (see Box 0.22 on page 42 for an illustration of some common key contracts) for example, undertakings not to amend them, **assignments** of these contracts to the lenders, and direct agreements between lenders and the counterparties to those contracts – allowing the lenders step-in rights (i.e. the right to step in and perform the contract on behalf of the borrower);   **0.221**

---

[79] See commentary on clause 21 in 8.123.

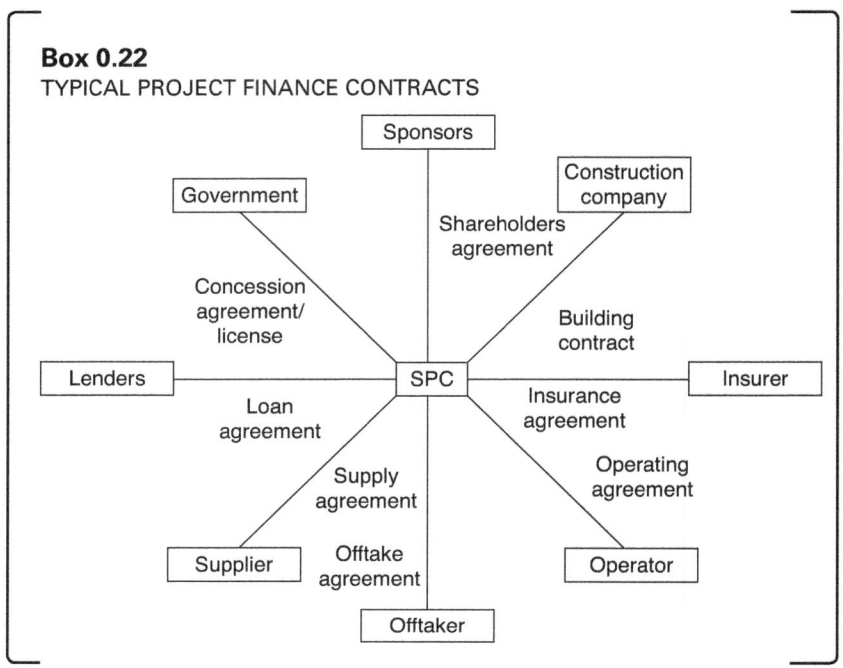

Box 0.22
TYPICAL PROJECT FINANCE CONTRACTS

0.222	• the availability of funds from the lenders will be dependent on the rateable contribution from other lenders and/or **sponsors**;
0.223	• extensive information provision for the lenders;
0.224	• detailed project forecasts and budgets agreed in a financial model before the loan agreement is signed, with variations from the base case having numerous consequences, such as restricting drawings of the loan; restricting payment of **dividends**; changing the Margin; setting the amounts of repayments; and ultimately, triggering an Event of Default;
0.225	• long drawdown period during construction, with interest possibly being capitalized, and drawings paid to a **disbursement account**;
0.226	• detailed expert evidence required as to the state of the project at various points during the drawdown period, as conditions precedent to further drawing;
0.227	• 'waterfall' for payment (see Box 0.23 on page 43) of project income;
0.228	• often, release of certain security (e.g. completion guarantee) once evidence of completion of the construction phase is provided;
0.229	• special purpose company undertakings – restricting the ability of the borrower to undertake other activities;[80]
0.230	• security over all project assets;

---

[80] See Section 2 of the commentary on clause 22 – general undertakings in 8.190 onwards.

> **Box 0.23**
> The 'waterfall' is the expression commonly used to describe the series of accounts used to hold income generated in a project finance transaction. Typically these include:
>
> - The revenue or operating account, into which income is paid and which is used to hold up to an agreed sum to pay for ordinary operating expenses;
> - The debt service reserves account, which builds up an agreed cushion to pay for future **debt service**;
> - The maintenance reserves account, which builds up an agreed cushion to pay for major maintenance costs;
> - The distribution account – available to pay dividends to sponsors, subject to certain conditions.

- limited recourse to sponsors (shareholders in the project company); **0.231**
- extensive insurance undertakings; **0.232**
- additional events of default if: **0.233**
  - remaining development cost exceeds available funding;
  - ratios are not met;
  - insurance becomes voidable;
  - any relevant consent or licence is altered;
  - any physical damage occurs to project assets;
  - the project is abandoned;
  - **force majeure** occurs under a project document in excess of a specified period;
  - the project is expropriated;
  - completion is delayed; or
  - any project document is terminated.

SECTION 8: QUASI SECURITY AND FINANCIAL INDEBTEDNESS

1 Quasi security[81]

Quasi security means arrangements which have the same commercial effect as security. It comprises both title financing and other arrangements. **0.234**

Title financing is using title (or ownership to property) instead of security, such as is done in finance leases or hire purchase agreements (as discussed here). Most title financing arrangements involve the separation of legal ownership (or title) to an asset from the economic ownership of the asset (or the commercial risks and rewards which go with ownership such as the risk or reward of a loss, or gain in value of the asset). There are many different reasons for using title finance. In some cases, a tax or accounting **0.235**

---

[81] See generally Richard Calnan 'Taking Security' 3rd edn, 2013 in 6.33 onwards.

advantage is sought. In others, the structure is used as an alternative to security because of unavailability of satisfactory security in the relevant jurisdiction. Whatever the purpose of the arrangements, their commercial effect is equivalent to the effect of security (but see also Box 0.24 on page 45). Therefore any provisions in a loan agreement which deal with security must also deal with these arrangements.

0.236 Other arrangements, such as rights of **set off**, do not amount to title financing but can also have a similar impact to security and therefore are discussed together with title financing in this Section 8.

0.237 Examples of title financing include the following:

Finance or capital leases (as opposed to operating leases)

0.238 **Finance leases** are leases in which the lessor (or owner) is simply a financier and the lessee has the commercial risks and benefits of ownership. The lessor funds the purchase of the asset and receives rent through the lease sufficient to pay off the funding cost plus interest. Once paid, the lease may continue at a nominal rent or the asset may be sold, with proceeds payable to the lessee. The effect is as though the lessor had lent the funds to the lessee and the lessee had given security over the asset. **Hire purchase** is simply an example of a finance lease in which, once rent has been paid sufficient to pay the funding cost plus interest, the lessee acquires title to the asset for no significant further payment.

0.239 It should be noted that at the time of writing the accounting treatment of a finance lease is different from the accounting treatment of an operating lease. This has been widely criticized (including, for example, by the Securities and Exchange Commission in the US in their report on off balance sheet financings in 2005). As a result, the Financial Accounting Standards Board in the UK together with the International Accounting Standards Board, are working on a project to change the accounting treatment of leases and to require an organization to recognize assets and liabilities arising from leases. The way in which this would be done is as yet unsettled at the time of writing (August 2014)

0.240 Therefore if the documentation refers to finance leases, it might be sensible to define them by reference to their effect rather than their accounting treatment. For example a finance lease could be defined as a lease under which the lessee has substantially all the risks and rewards of ownership. Alternatively the document could clarify that the reference is intended to be a reference to the accounting treatment of the lease at the date the loan agreement is signed.

0.241 This issue may also give rise to difficulties with financial ratios – if the accounts are produced on a different basis in the future that will of course have an effect on the numbers. This highlights the role of the provisions dealing with frozen or moving **GAAP** discussed in Chapter 8 at 8.083.

Title retention

If a seller gives credit to the purchaser of an asset and retains title to the asset until paid, the commercial effect is as if the purchaser had given security over the asset for the amount of the credit.[82] 0.242

Another example is an instalment sale agreement, or a conditional sale agreement under which title only passes on payment of the final purchase instalment or fulfilment of other conditions. 0.243

> **Box 0.24**
> Title financing is often used as an alternative to security but careful **due diligence** is necessary, not only as to the legal effect but also as to the tax, accounting, and regulatory effect. The person who is treated as the 'owner' of the asset for accounting purposes may be different from the 'owner' for tax purposes; the 'owner' for regulatory purposes;[83] and the owner for other legal purposes. In some countries, the structure will not be treated, for legal purposes, in accordance with its apparent effect, but will be '**recharacterized**' in accordance with its substantive effect. This may lead to a requirement that such arrangements be registered as though they were security (as in New York) or to the arrangements not being effective at all.

Selling receivables but keeping the associated risk (as in some securitizations)

A distinction needs to be drawn between situations where the receivables are sold together with the risk[84] and where they are sold but the risk is retained by the seller. 0.244

For example, compare the situation where 0.245

- debts with a face value of $10 million are sold for $8 million and 0.246
- the same debts are sold at the same price but the seller keeps the risk (e.g. by giving a **guarantee** to the buyer of the payment of the debts). 0.247

Assume the debtors pay only $6 million. In the first case, that is of no concern to the seller. In the second, the seller must compensate the buyer. The commercial effect of the second case is as though the seller had borrowed $8 million from the buyer and given security over the receivables.

---

[82] In some countries, the seller is automatically given a security interest for unpaid purchase moneys so that title retention would be unnecessary.

[83] For example, is a temporary owner of shares under a repo treated as the owner for regulatory purposes such as duty to disclose major shareholdings?

[84] Often referred to as a 'true sale', and, depending on the purpose of the securitization, the requirement of a true sale may be key to its effectiveness.

Forward sale

0.248 This may be illustrated by an example. Let us assume that a manufacturer of watches, in order to raise finance, agrees with a 'lender' in January, for a price paid by the 'lender' at that time, that the next 500 watches produced will belong to the 'lender'. In other words, the 'lender' will purchase the watches in advance of their manufacture.[85] The 'lender' may then appoint the manufacturer as his agent to sell the watches with a requirement that a certain part of the sale proceeds be paid over to the 'lender' and with the manufacturer guaranteeing to make up any shortfall between the proceeds of sale recovered by the 'lender' and the advance price originally paid by the 'lender' plus 'interest'. The commercial effect is as though the manufacturer had given security over the watches to raise a loan.

Forward purchase (as in repos)

0.249 This is an arrangement where a company owns an asset, such as shares, and, in order to raise finance, sells those shares to a financier for, say, $5 million, and agrees to repurchase them in six months' time for $6 million. The commercial effect is very similar to the situation if the company had borrowed $5 million and given the shares as security.

Set off

0.250 **Set off** is a procedural rule which allows a party which owes money to another to reduce the amount he pays to that other by an amount which that other party owes to him.

0.251 The availability of this right of set off is a matter of law in the courts in which it is asserted. It may have the same commercial effect as security in some cases. For example, if a borrower of a loan of $10 million has a bank account with its lender with $5 million deposited, and the lender, if unpaid, can set off the amount in the bank account (leaving it with no obligation to pay over the deposit and with the amount of its loan reduced to $5 million), the commercial effect is as though the lender had security over the bank account.[86]

Cash deposits

0.252 Depositing money with a party could have the same commercial effect as security either because of the set-off rights which will arise or because of formal or informal arrangements allowing that other party to forfeit the sums deposited in certain circumstances or because those sums are part of a payment mechanism.[87]

---

[85] To be effective, the relevant jurisdiction would need to recognize agreements to sell future property as being binding.

[86] But a right of set-off is not as good as security in all cases (and may even be better than security in some instances). See A1.066.

[87] See Goode '*Legal Problems of Credit and Security*' 5th edn, 2013, in 1.42.

Trust arrangements

If a company holds an asset on trust for others then that asset is, just as it would be if security had been given over it, not available to that company's creditors generally in the insolvency of the company. A **trust** can therefore have the same commercial effect as security.[88]

0.253

2 Financial indebtedness

In considering quasi security it is also useful to look at the breadth of arrangements by which finance can be raised and which can have the same commercial effect as borrowing money. Examples of such arrangements are described here.

0.254

Acceptance credit facility

This is an agreement by a lender to accept (or become liable for) bills of exchange issued by the company. Under this arrangement the lender agrees to make payment to a third party under the **bill of exchange** on behalf of the company. The effect is as if the lender lent the equivalent amount to the company.

0.255

Bonds (like notes or commercial paper)

Bonds are simply promises to pay, which are traded in the capital markets. A company will issue a bond (or note, or paper) which will be purchased in the capital markets and then traded. The purchase price will be paid to the company. The company has effectively borrowed the amount paid to it.

0.256

Note purchase facility

This is a facility under which a financier agrees to buy **promissory notes** issued by the company.

0.257

Loan stock

Money borrowed from investors and represented by certificates which can be sold by the investors in whole or in part. Loan stock may be secured, in which case it is known as debenture loan stock. It may be convertible into shares on terms specified in the stock, in which case it is known as convertible loan stock.

0.258

Seller's credit

Where a seller sells goods but agrees to delayed payment.

0.259

---

[88] In fact, it may amount to a registrable security interest – see Goode 'Legal Problems of Credit and Security' 5th edn, 2013 at 1–57 and compare 1–42.

Forward sale

0.260 Selling assets which are not owned yet may amount to borrowing money. For example, assume a furniture store sells furniture and requires payment in advance of the purchase of that furniture by the store. The store has effectively borrowed money from its customers.

Other title financing

0.261 Other methods of title financing discussed above amount to borrowing on a secured basis, being finance leasing, forward purchase (e.g. repos) and selling receivables on recourse terms.

PART 1
ADMINISTRATIVE PROVISIONS

This Part deals with those parts of a loan agreement which are mechanical in nature: the definitions, procedures for drawdown, calculation of interest, and the like. These provisions are contained in clauses 1–17 of the LMA Term Loan.

1 Interpretation

CLAUSE 1: DEFINITIONS AND INTERPRETATION – SECTION 1 – AN INTRODUCTION

1 Introduction

Loan agreements contain detailed definitions. This helps,   **1.001**

- to ensure consistency between different provisions of the document;
- to avoid ambiguity; and
- to keep the complexities out of the body of the agreement (see Box 1.1).

> **Box 1.1**
> For example, in the operative provisions, a simple statement can be made, such as *The Borrower shall not create any Encumbrances other than Permitted Encumbrances.* The general purpose of this provision is easily understood, while its application, and therefore its impact on the borrower, is only understood by reviewing the detail in the definitions.

There are traps for the unwary in using definitions. Principally these are: **1.002**

- reading (or not reading) the definitions in context;
- appreciating (or failing to appreciate) that the definitions may need different meanings in different contexts;
- avoiding circular definitions; and
- avoiding including operative provisions.[1]

We look at each of these issues here.

Definitions out of context

It is hard to comment on, or to fully appreciate the implications of, any particular definition out of context (see Box 1.2 on page 52).   **1.003**

---

[1] Provisions which 'operate' or actually do something as opposed to the provisions of the definitions in clause 1 which are merely descriptive.

> **Box 1.2**
>
> For example, appreciating whether the definition of 'Financial Indebtedness' should or should not include **derivative** transactions depends on the reader knowing where the definition will be used and with what purpose.[2]

It may therefore be sensible to skip the definitions clause and start reading from the operative clauses starting at clause 2 (or, rather, at clause 1.2, for reasons discussed here). When a defined term is encountered, its definition can then be reviewed in context. This makes it easier to appreciate the detail of the definition.

The suggestion is to commence reading at clause 1.2, so as to be aware of any words which have been defined by that clause without that fact being flagged by the use of capital letters.

1.004 Clause 1.2 is intended to deal with references to *concepts* (such as a person) as opposed to *specific words* (such as '**Encumbrance**'). In this interpretation clause, concepts are broadened without their being given capital letters (see Box 1.3).

> **Box 1.3**
>
> So you can see there is no attempt to define 'person' – instead of saying 'person **means** ABC' the statement is that 'person **includes** ABC'. The idea is to **extend** the ordinary meaning, not to provide a complete definition.

This can lead to the existence of the wider meaning which has been given to the concept being overlooked. It is therefore sensible to read the interpretation clause (clause 1.2) before reviewing the operative clauses and to make special note of the words and concepts which have been defined without being capitalized (see Box 1.4).

> **Box 1.4**
>
> For example, assume clause 23.13 is drafted to say '*On, and at any time after, the occurrence of an Event of Default which is continuing, the Agent may…[accelerate the Loan]*'.
>
> On its own, this appears clear. However, it needs to be read in the context of clause 1.2(d) which defines the word '*continuing*'.[3] When that meaning is taken into account, the reader will appreciate that clause 23.13 has a somewhat different meaning than would have been understood from reading clause 23.13 alone.

---

[2] See comments on the definition of Financial Indebtedness at 1.037 for a discussion on the inclusion of derivatives in this definition.

[3] See comments on clause 1.2(d) at 1.067.

Different meanings in different contexts

While the definitions help to ensure consistency throughout the document it may be that consistency is not required in some cases. 1.005

Borrowers frequently request that adjustments be made to a definition which, on consideration, the lenders may wish to make in some instances (e.g. the negative pledge) but not others (e.g. the conditions precedent) (see Box 1.5).

> **Box 1.5**
> For example, the borrowers may request a definition of 'Permitted Encumbrances' which allows the creation of a wide variety of security interests over the company's property. The lenders may be willing to agree to this request in the context of the negative pledge but may want to be more restrictive as to the security interests which may exist at the date of the first **advance** of the loan. In that case changing the operative clauses would be a better option than changing the definition.

It is therefore advisable to leave the definitions alone and make changes as appropriate in the operative clauses. Similarly, when reviewing the definitions, it is important to review them in each context in which they are used, as the definition may be appropriate in some circumstances but may require adjustment in others.

Circularity

It is not unusual to find that a defined term itself refers to another defined term. This, if carried to extremes, can make the definitions very difficult for readers to understand. In some cases, it might make the definitions meaningless (see Box 1.6). 1.006

> **Box 1.6**
> An example of a meaningless definition is, '"*Outstanding Indebtedness*" means all moneys outstanding under the Security Documents' while '"*Security Documents*" means all documents executed as security for the Outstanding Indebtedness'.

Operative provisions

The definitions are there to explain what particular expressions mean. They should not include any operative provisions, such as positive or negative undertakings or conditions. The main hazard of including operative provisions in the definitions is that they are harder to find there. At the extreme they may also be ineffective. 1.007

CLAUSE 1: DEFINITIONS AND INTERPRETATION – SECTION 2 – THE LMA DEFINITIONS

Clause 1.1 Some definitions

The following definitions in the LMA Term Loan deserve particular attention.

Base Currency Amount

1.008 This definition is used in a multicurrency facility as a reference point for the lenders to determine from time to time what the amount of the loan would have been had it always been drawn in a single currency and remained in that currency.[4]

Break Costs

1.009 'Break Costs' means the amount (if any) by which:

(a) the interest which a Lender should have received for the period from the date of receipt of all or any part of its participation in a Loan or Unpaid Sum to the last day of the current Interest Period in respect of that Loan or Unpaid Sum, had the principal amount or Unpaid Sum received been paid on the last day of that Interest Period;

exceeds:

(b) the amount which that Lender would be able to obtain by placing an amount equal to the principal amount or Unpaid Sum received by it on deposit with a leading bank in the Relevant Interbank Market for a period starting on the Business Day following receipt or recovery and ending on the last day of the current Interest Period.

1.010 Floating rate loans are generally drafted on the basis that the borrower will have the ability to choose the interest periods from time to time[5] but that the borrower must take the reinvestment risk[6] if any payment is made by the borrower in the middle of an interest period. This is achieved by clause 11.4 discussed at 5.040, which requires the borrower to pay the lenders' 'Break Costs' if payments are made in the middle of an interest period.

1.011 *Comment* In the context of large loans, some borrowers may request that the definition be adjusted to reflect the time value of money and hence ask that it is the **net present value** (the issue then being at what interest rate to make this calculation) of the amount set out in this definition which should be paid (see Box 1.7 on page 55).

---

[4] See the commentary on clause 6 at 3.013 onwards.
[5] See commentary on clause 10 at 5.012 onwards.
[6] The reinvestment risk is the risk that the amount which the lenders can earn on moneys received may be less than the rate which the lenders are obliged to pay (or would have been obliged to pay if they had match funded) on that sum for the remainder of the Interest Period.

> **Box 1.7**
> For example, assume a **prepayment** of $12 million is received one month after the start of a six-month Interest Period relating to that $12 million. Assume that the interest rate payable by the borrower for the six-month period is 5% while LIBOR at the date of receipt of the $12 million is 4%.
>
> Break Costs, in accordance with the definition would be the amount by which:
>
> (a) the interest which the lenders would have received for the rest of the **Interest Period** (i.e. $12 million X 5% X 5/12[7] ($250,000); exceeds
>
> (b) the amount the lenders can recover by investing the sum received for the balance of the Interest Period (i.e. $12 million X 4% X 5/12 ($200,000).
>
> That is, Break Costs would be $50,000.
>
> However, the lenders will not suffer the loss of $50,000 until the end of the six months, since that is when it will receive interest on the sum reinvested and would have received interest from the borrower had the $12 million not been paid early. Therefore, a payment of $50,000 on the date of prepayment of the $12 million will overcompensate the lenders by the amount of interest which will be earned on that sum during the rest of the Interest Period. This can be corrected by requiring payment of the net present value of the relevant sum.

Comment The definition as stated in the LMA Term Loan looks at the total interest (including Margin) which the lenders would have received had the relevant payment not been made and compares that with interest (LIBOR) which can be earned on the payment received.[8] In this way, the calculation compensates the lenders not only for the cost of breaking their funding but also requires the borrower to pay the lenders' Margin for the balance of the Interest Period. The borrower may wish to resist on the basis that the Margin for the rest of the Interest Period is not an expense suffered by the lenders, but a lost profit.

1.012

Lenders may argue that the inclusion of the Margin is correct since the borrower should compensate them for the fact that Margins generally available at the time of prepayment may be lower than that charged to the borrower[9] and that compensation for lost Margin for the balance of the Interest Period is the compromise position required for charging no prepayment fee.

1.013

They may also argue that the Margin is not just profit, but also contains an element of cost because the lender is not actually funding at LIBOR and part of the Margin compensates it for its actual funding cost, part for liquidity cost and only the balance is profit.

1.014

---

[7] In the interests of simplicity, this calculation simply calculates five months of interest as equalling five-twelfths of one year's interest, rather than calculating on the basis of the number of days elapsed and a 360-day year as would happen in practice.

[8] Note the definition assumes moneys received will not be reinvested until the day following receipt.

[9] See also commentary on clause 11.4 at 5.040.

Business Day

1.015

'Business Day' means a day (other than a Saturday or Sunday) on which banks are open for general business in London and [];[10]and:

(a) (in relation to any date for payment or purchase of a currency other than euro) the principal financial centre of the country of that currency; or

(b) (in relation to any date for payment or purchase of euro) any TARGET Day.

There are often a number of different definitions addressing the concept of **Business Day**. A distinction needs to be drawn between business days for the purpose of

- making payments and calculating periods such as grace periods relating to payments; and
- determining the effectiveness of notices and calculating periods such as grace periods in relation to matters which do not involve payments.

Where no payments are involved, paragraphs (a) and (b) of the definition are not relevant.

For the purpose of payments, the principal financial centre for the relevant currency[11] will need to be open as well. This is addressed by paragraphs (a) and (b) of the definition in the LMA Term Loan.

1.016 The LMA Term Loan does not explicitly state whether references to a number of Business Days is intended to mean 'clear' days, that is, excluding the first and last day, or periods of 24 hours (see Box 1.8). General principles of interpretation will treat it as clear days.[12]

> **Box 1.8**
> For example, if three Business Days' notice of drawdown is required and notice is given on Monday at 10 a.m. when will that notice expire? If the intention is to refer to 'clear' days, it will expire on Thursday at midnight (so that drawing will be available on Friday). If it is to periods of 24 hours then it will expire at 10 a.m. on Thursday (so that drawing will be available on Thursday). This example assumes that Monday to Friday are all Business Days.

---

[10] Beware of unnecessarily increasing the cities which need to be open for business for a day to count as a Business Day and thereby potentially having significantly extended notice periods. It should normally be sufficient if the Agent's and borrower's places of business are open since the loan is structured so that communications and payments can be made through the Agent.

[11] For this purpose, see the commentary on **TARGET days** in the discussion of the definition of 'Quotation Day' at 1.056.

[12] This is because a 'day' is treated as meaning a calendar day and a period of days after an event occurs excludes the day on which the event occurred. Lester v Garland (1808) 15 Ves 248.

Compliance Certificate

Generally, financial covenants are tested by requiring periodic certificates confirming compliance.

1.017

The LMA precedent gives the draftsperson a choice here of attaching the form or referring to a form 'satisfactory to the Agent'. Attaching the form is preferable for both parties (and syndicate members) for the certainty it gives as to precisely what will be required. Some flexibility is introduced by saying the document is to be 'substantially' in the form attached, allowing for minor modifications which may prove to be necessary between the date of signing the loan agreement and the date of production of the relevant document.

A third alternative which is sometimes used is to require the document to be substantially in '*agreed form*' and define '*agreed form*' as referring to the forms of documents attached to a particular letter, for example. This has the advantage of keeping the loan agreement itself shorter, and is particularly useful for items which will only be required to be produced once at the start of the loan period.

Default

> '*Default*' *means an Event of Default or any event or circumstance specified in clause 23 (Events of Default) which would (with the expiry of a grace period, the giving of notice, the making of any determination under the Finance Documents or any combination of any of the foregoing) be an Event of Default.*

1.018

The term 'Default' is used to mean the occurrence of any event which might mature into an Event of Default. An example is a breach of covenant which, if not remedied within any applicable grace period, would become an Event of Default. The breach of covenant would be a 'Default'. Some loan agreements use the concept of 'Potential Event of Default' to describe this.

1.019

The concept is used throughout the agreement and in the security documents. It is not the same as an Event of Default, in that occurrence of a Default does not give the lenders the ability to accelerate the loan. However, the existence of a Default causes concern for the lenders and therefore the borrower's rights after a Default and before an Event of Default will be more restricted than they were previously. For example, a lender will usually require that its commitment to lend new money (in a term loan) or to increase the amount outstanding (in a revolving credit) is suspended while there is a Default. It will also often place restrictions on things which would otherwise be permitted (e.g. payment of dividends, or application of insurance moneys or earnings may be prevented after a Default and before an Event of Default) (see Box 1.9 on page 58).

It is important to look carefully at the words in brackets in the definition. The LMA Term Loan provides for three possibilities: expiry of grace periods; making determinations; and giving of notice, or any combination of these.

1.020

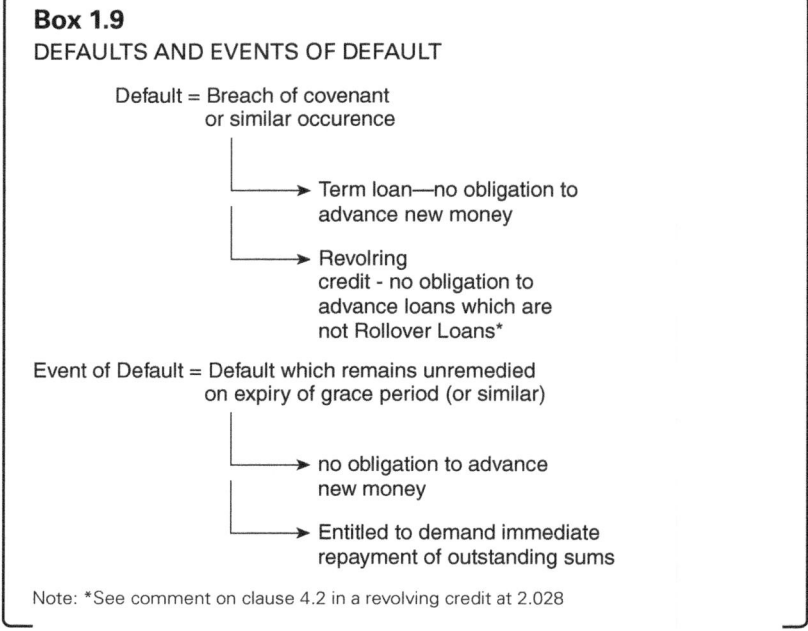

1.021 • *Expiry of grace periods* This part of the definition is to cover circumstances (e.g. a breach of certain undertakings) which will become Events of Default if those circumstances still exist when a **grace period** expires.

1.022 *Comment* The question might arise as to whether an event which is about to be remedied is a 'Default' as defined in the LMA Term Loan (see Box 1.10).

> **Box 1.10**
> For example, assume that a particular loan agreement states that it is an Event of Default if there is a judgement against the borrower in an amount in excess of $1 million and that judgement is not satisfied within 30 days. Assume also that a judgement has been made against the borrower in an amount of $2 million, and the borrower is making arrangements to pay it. It will take the borrower ten days to access the necessary funds. Until the payment has been made, the intention behind the drafting of the LMA Term Loan is that these events should constitute a 'Default'. The borrower might argue that in these circumstances there is no 'Default' because a Default is defined as an event that 'would', on expiry of a grace period, constitute an Event of Default. The judgement will not result in an Event of Default because it will be paid.
>
> Given that, if the borrower's argument succeeded, it would render the definition of 'Default' meaningless, it is reasonably clear that Defaults which are about to be remedied remain Defaults until they have actually been remedied.

- *Making a determination*   This is to cover those circumstances that will become an Event of Default if a party makes an adverse decision. An example is where it is an Event of Default if circumstances occur which, in the opinion of the Majority Lenders, are material. While they consider materiality there is a Default.

1.023

Comment   As discussed in relation to the Events of Default,[13] one issue of concern to the borrower is to avoid subjective Events of Default as far as possible. If Events of Default are included which are to be determined in the opinion of some or all of the lenders, the impact of this definition should be considered. Payments (such as further drawings) are generally frozen on a Default and lenders may well be more willing to exercise their rights to freeze drawings than to exercise their rights of acceleration. By virtue of the definition of 'Default' their right to freeze drawings would arise whenever circumstances occur which *might* fall within the Event of Default, even if, on consideration, it would not do so. However strongly the wording of the Event of Default may be drafted, the ability to freeze future drawings is slightly more easily triggered because of the definition of 'Default' (see Box 1.11). As a result, some borrowers might want to request deletion of the words 'making a determination'. Nevertheless, lenders will want to resist this as they will not want to be obliged to advance further funds while there is any uncertainty as to whether an Event of Default is imminent or not. This is particularly important in the context of financial ratios as discussed in Chapter 8 at 8.116.

1.024

> **Box 1.11**
> For example, there may be an Event of Default if there is '*litigation against the Borrower which, in the opinion of the Majority Lenders, would have a Material Adverse Effect*'. The word 'would' in that Event of Default makes it very difficult for the lenders to use the Event of Default because a high degree of certainty is necessary. Nevertheless, if litigation arises which *might* have a Material Adverse Effect, by virtue of the definition of 'Default,' the lenders will be entitled to freeze drawings while they consider whether or not the circumstances fall within the wording of the Event of Default.

- *Giving of notice*   This wording is to cover any Events of Default that are triggered by the giving of notice. It is unusual for Events of Default to be triggered by notice alone, but often notice is required in addition to the expiry of a grace period or the making of a determination. For example, some breaches of covenant (in the LMA Term Loan, those specified at

1.025

---

[13] See Section 1 of the discussion of clause 23 at 8.216.

clause 23.3(b)[14]) may only be Events of Default if a certain period of time expires after the lenders give notice to the borrower of the existence of a breach. The definition of 'Default' therefore includes the three issues outlined here *and* any combination of them.

> Some definitions of 'Default' or 'Potential Event of Default' include words such as 'or any other occurrence'. This should be resisted as too broad. It could, for example, include the occurrence of a breach of covenant.

Defaulting Lenders

1.026 A Defaulting Lender is a lender which fails to lend, rescinds the agreement, or in respect of which an Insolvency Event occurs. There is a similar concept of 'Impaired Agent' to deal with an Agent in financial difficulty. The consequences of being a Defaulting Lender or Impaired Agent are discussed in Section 5 of the Introduction at 0.155.

It is worth noting that in practice the insolvency limb of these definitions may not work as stated since the authorities may be able to disapply these provisions (as would be the case under the Banking Act 2009 in England) in the event of a bank stabilization or similar procedure.

Euribor

1.027 This definition will be necessary if the loan is to be available in Euros and those Euros are to be funded in the domestic market[15] for Euros (or treated as being funded there for the purpose of the calculation of interest). If they are not to be funded in the domestic market for Euros, but in London instead, the relevant rate will be Euro LIBOR. The choice as to whether Euros are to be funded (or treated as funded) in their domestic market or in London will depend on the wishes of the lenders (or most of them) at the time of negotiating the agreement.

Facility Office

1.028
> 'Facility Office' means the office or offices notified by a Lender to the Agent in writing on or before the date it becomes a Lender (or, following that date, by not less than five Business Days' written notice) as the office or offices through which it will perform its obligations under this Agreement.

The plural ('office or offices' in the first line of the definition) is deliberate so as to allow any lender to service loans from different Facility Offices.[16]

---

[14] 23.3(b) No Event of Default ... will occur if the failure to comply is capable of remedy and is remedied within ... in relation to [Clause] [ ] Business Days ... of the Agent giving notice to the Company ... of the failure to comply.

[15] See Box 0.7 on page 16.

[16] The borrower is concerned to ensure it does not have to gross-up payments. Given the gross-up obligation only applies to the extent that any advance is funded by a 'Qualifying Lender' (see 6.018)

Finance Document

> *'Finance Document'* means this Agreement, any Fee Letter, any Accession Letter, any Resignation Letter and any other document designated as such by the Agent and the Company.

1.029

Many of the borrower's undertakings and representations relate to the Finance Documents. These should not be extended to include lenders' documents such as any document used to transfer interests in the loan to new lenders. Such documents are solely a concern for the lenders and, for example, the obligation of the borrower to pay any stamp duty in relation to the Finance Documents should not extend to these transfer documents.

Financial Indebtedness

The purpose of this definition is to distinguish between ordinary trade debts (e.g. debts to suppliers and employees) and debts in the nature of a financing. The definition needs to be broad to pick up activities having the commercial effect of borrowing, such as repos (short for repurchase agreements) or selling receivables on recourse terms.[17]

1.030

The definition is used in the negative pledge (clause 22.3) and in the cross default clause (clause 23.5) in the LMA Term Loan and may be used elsewhere in any given loan agreement. In the negative pledge the definition is used to distinguish between permitted and prohibited transactions.[18] In the cross default clause only defaults under arrangements that constitute Financial Indebtedness are Events of Default.[19] The LMA Term Loan does not include a covenant to incur no Financial Indebtedness although the relative level of Financial Indebtedness (or something akin to Financial Indebtedness) may well be regulated by the financial ratios.

Commonly, borrowers will want to exclude derivatives, trade instruments (such as performance bonds) and intercompany debts from this definition. Lenders need to be cautious here as they may have different concerns about such debts in the different places where the definition is used. For example, if there is a prohibition on the borrower incurring Financial Indebtedness, the lenders may be happy to allow an exception so as to allow derivatives, but they may still want the definition of Financial Indebtedness to include derivatives for the purpose of the negative pledge and cross default clause.

1.031

> *'Financial Indebtedness'* means any indebtedness for or in respect of: ...

1.032

---

the ability of the lenders to specify different Facility Offices does not cause an issue for the borrower as long as those Qualifying Lender provisions are retained.

[17] See 0.234 for a discussion of transactions having the commercial effect of borrowing and giving security.

[18] See commentary on clause 22.3(b) at 8.144.

[19] See commentary on clause 23.5(a) at 8.233.

1.033 *Comment* It might be sensible to add the words 'without double counting' at the start of this definition. This ensures that there is no duplication for the purpose of the thresholds.

1.034
(a) *moneys borrowed;*

(b) *any amount raised by acceptance under any acceptance credit facility or dematerialised equivalent;*

(c) *any amount raised pursuant to any note purchase facility or the issue of bonds, notes, debentures, loan stock or any similar instrument;*

(d) *the amount of any liability in respect of any lease or hire purchase contract which would, in accordance with GAAP, be treated as a finance or capital lease;*

1.035 Note here that there are proposals to end the different accounting treatment of finance and operating leases. In view of this it may be sensible to change this definition so that it clarifies that the reference to GAAP here (see also 1.040) is intended to refer to GAAP as it existed at the date of signing the loan agreement (as distinct from its use in other clauses – particularly in clause 20.3, discussed at 8.083, where it is intended to refer to changing GAAP).

1.036
(e) *receivables sold or discounted (other than any receivables to the extent they are sold on a non-recourse basis);*

(f) *any amount raised under any other transaction (including any forward sale or purchase agreement) of a type not referred to in any other paragraph of this definition having the commercial effect of a borrowing;*

(g) *any derivative transaction entered into in connection with protection against or benefit from fluctuation in any rate or price (and, when calculating the value of any derivative transaction, only the marked to market value ... shall be taken into account);*

1.037 Lenders want the definition to include derivatives for two reasons. Firstly, for the purpose of the negative pledge, lenders want to be sure that credit support arrangements are prohibited (see the discussion on the negative pledge at 8.152). Under the standard drafting, arrangements which fall short of 'Security' are only prohibited if they are entered into primarily for the purpose of raising 'Financial Indebtedness'. Therefore, in order to prohibit credit support arrangements, Financial Indebtedness needs to include derivatives. Secondly, for the purpose of the cross default clause, non-payment of a derivative can trigger a large unexpected payment in the same way as non-payment of financial debt can. Therefore lenders want to ensure that the borrower's breach of a derivative is an Event of Default.

1.038 However there are three difficulties for the borrower:

- First, because derivative values fluctuate, including them in thresholds, such as the amount of debt which can be secured, makes compliance with those thresholds difficult.

- Second if, as is common, ability to borrow is restricted, derivatives will use up the cap and reduce the amount available for borrowing, even though they are not borrowing.
- Third, for the purpose of the cross default clause, the current drafting has the effect that early termination of the derivative due to default of the swap counterparty is an Event of Default under the loan – which ought not to be the case.

The simplest solution may be to exclude derivatives from the definition of Financial Indebtedness but deal with them separately in each place where the expression 'Financial Indebtedness' is used (see Box 1.12).

> **Box 1.12**
> If derivatives are to be dealt with separately from Financial Indebtedness then one way to reconcile the concerns of both parties could be as follows
> - The negative pledge could prohibit giving security for Financial Indebtedness or for Derivatives
> - Any prohibition on incurring Financial Indebtedness would relate only to Financial Indebtedness not Derivatives (or perhaps would only prohibit speculative derivatives and have the threshold calculated only with reference to Financial Indebtedness, not Derivatives)
> - The cross default clause could be triggered by breach relating to Financial Indebtedness and Borrower breach in relation to Derivatives, perhaps with counterparty breach of a Derivative dealt with as an early prepayment event.

(h) any counter-indemnity obligation in respect of a guarantee, indemnity, bond, standby or documentary letter of credit or any other instrument issued by a bank or financial institution; and

(j) the amount of any liability in respect of any guarantee or indemnity for any of the items referred to in paragraphs (a) to (h) above.

Comment Borrowers may wish to exclude Non-Recourse Indebtedness if any company in the group[20] has or is likely to have any limited recourse indebtedness, since failure to pay such debt should not trigger the cross default clause and security over the project assets for such indebtedness should not cause a breach of the negative pledge.

1.039

GAAP

'GAAP' means generally accepted accounting principles in [ ] [(including IFRS)].

1.040

---

[20] Which is not a limited recourse company excluded from the provisions of the loan agreement as discussed at 0.141.

Some, but not all, companies are required to produce accounts in accordance with International Financial Reporting Standards ('IFRS'). Even where this is the case, they must also comply with local legal requirements (GAAP) in their own jurisdiction. That is why the reference is not solely to IFRS, but to GAAP, including, '*if applicable*', IFRS. IFRS is itself defined to mean IFRS to the extent it is applicable to the relevant company. This is because the extent to which IFRS is applicable differs in different jurisdictions. If the company is not required to comply with IFRS, lenders need to be satisfied that they have sufficient understanding of local GAAP in the relevant country to be able to interpret the accounts correctly.

1.041 It is also worth noting that the intention appears to be to refer to GAAP as it is in operation at the date the relevant accounts are prepared, as opposed to GAAP at the date of the Loan Agreement. This is consistent with the the provisions of clause 20.3 discussed at 8.083 (but see also the discussion of the interpretation provisions at 1.066). However, this may give rise to problems in relation to finance leases as discussed in relation to the definition of Financial Indebtedness at 1.035.

Group

See the discussion on the scope of the agreement in the Introduction at 0.121 onwards

LIBOR

1.042 '**LIBOR**' *means, in relation to any Loan:*

(a) the applicable Screen Rate;

(b) (if no Screen Rate is available for the Interest Period of that Loan) the Interpolated Screen Rate for that Loan; or

(c) if:

  (i) no Screen Rate is available for the currency of that Loan; or

  (ii) no Screen Rate is available for the Interest Period of that Loan and it is not possible to calculate an Interpolated Screen Rate for that Loan,

the Reference Bank Rate,

as of, in the case of paragraphs (a) and (c) above, the Specified Time on the Quotation Day for the currency of that Loan and for a period equal in length to the Interest Period of that Loan [and if that rate is less than zero, LIBOR shall be deemed to be zero].

See 0.111 for a summary of the interest rate provisions in the loan agreement.

1.043 In the case of both LIBOR and Euribor the rate is defined as the applicable Screen Rate or, if none, the rate supplied by the Reference Banks, (or an interpolated rate if there is a Screen Rate for the relevant currency but not for the specified duration of the Interest Period) in each case at the Specified Time on the Quotation Day for the relevant amounts (see Box 1.13 for an alternative to Screen Rate).

> **Box 1.13**
> One of the optional provisions which the LMA issued during the financial crisis of 2008, as part of their 'kits' dealing with Defaulting Lenders and the like, was an alternative definition of LIBOR – not using the Screen Rate, but instead using the rate quoted by the Reference Banks. As many lenders at that time were unable to fund at the Screen Rate, the alternative was put forward, which, if used in the documentation, would result in the interest rate being determined by reference to the funding cost of the named Reference Banks in the relevant interbank market, as opposed to the Screen Rate. It may also be used as an alternative for currencies for which there is no Screen Rate of LIBOR. The alternative was not popular with borrowers, who clearly preferred to use the Screen Rate where it exists – despite its deficiencies – or the local equivalent such as STIBOR, so as to impose at least some market standard on the rate payable, albeit subject to the market disruption clause.

1.044 The **Screen Rate** is defined as the relevant rate specified on the Telerate or Reuters screen. Rates are specified on those screens for different currencies for the most common Interest Periods. See the discussion of Screen Rate at 1.060.

In 2013, LIBOR was discontinued for certain maturities, and as a result, a new concept of 'Interpolated Screen Rate' was introduced. The idea behind this is that if an Interest Period is chosen for which there is no LIBOR quote, the appropriate rate will be interpolated from the rates which are quoted. The Reference Banks are to be used as a fallback if there is no published Screen Rate as discussed in the definition of 'Reference Bank Rate' at 1.057.

The definitions of Specified Time and Quotation Day allow for the definitions to match the different market practices for different currencies and markets. The Specified Time is set out in Schedule 12 to the LMA Term Loan.

1.045 Also note the optional last sentence of the definition of LIBOR quoted at 1.042 which provides that LIBOR will never be below zero for the purposes of the loan agreement. This addresses the rather peculiar situation which happened with Swiss francs in 2011 during the Euro crisis. Negative interest rates were seen for Swiss francs as investors saw it as a safe haven during the crisis.[21]

---

[21] If there is an interest rate hedge in place for the loan then of course there will also need to be a zero floor in the definition of LIBOR in the hedge if it is to be effective – this may add to the cost of the hedge.

Majority Lenders

1.046 *'Majority Lenders' means a Lender or Lenders whose Commitments aggregate more than $[66^2/_3]\%$ of the Total Commitments (or, if the Total Commitments have been reduced to zero, aggregated more than $[66^2/_3]\%$ of the Total Commitments immediately prior to the reduction).*

One of the basic principles of a syndicated loan is that the lenders will be treated equally and that the syndicate will act in accordance with the wishes of a 'Majority'. The lenders need to decide what they mean by a Majority. Commonly, the level is set at 66.66% of the loan by contribution. A different level may be appropriate in a club deal, particularly if the usual level would give one lender (e.g. the Agent) a blocking vote.[22]

1.047 It is worth noting that this definition has changed over time. Originally, the definition looked at the amounts actually outstanding (ignoring amounts committed but not yet lent). It is now calculated with reference to the total of amounts advanced and committed to be advanced. In a loan where all lenders share all parts of the facility in the same proportion, the distinction makes no difference. However, commonly, loan facilities provide for a number of different facilities, with lenders able to have a different level of participation in the different parts of the facility. So, for example, there may be a facility agreement which provides for both a term loan and a revolving credit, with some lenders only participating in the term loan and not the revolver, and vice versa. In this case, the new formulation of the definition is preferable, because with the previous formulation, lenders under the revolving credit may be effectively disenfranchised if their facility was undrawn at the time consent was sought.

Definition of Majority Lenders in the LMA recommended form for a combined facility for a term loan and revolving credit

1.048 Because the LMA recommended form allows the facilities to be syndicated separately, care is needed in considering voting rights of syndicate members. It may be appropriate to have two separate definitions for a majority of Facility A lenders and a majority of Facility B lenders and, in certain circumstances, to require consent of a majority relating to each facility.

1.049 Areas which are likely to need consideration include:

- amendments and waivers (can provisions for one facility be amended without consent of a majority for that facility, and/or can a Default be waived for the purpose of allowing a drawing under one facility, or

---

[22] See also the commentary on this definition in the context of a combined term loan and revolving credit at 1.048.

preventing acceleration of it, without the consent of the majority of that facility's providers?[23]);
- prepayments and cancellations (do these need to be made pro rata between facilities?);
- pro rata sharing (should the facilities be treated separately or should any surplus recoveries by one lender be shared among lenders to both facilities?);
- the partial payments clause (clause 29.5), which allows the order of payments to be varied by the Majority Lenders. Should this require a majority in relation to each facility?
- Changes to any of these clauses

Margin

If the Margin is adjusted with reference to the performance of the borrower (e.g. by reference to financial ratios or the rating of the borrower[24]) there may be

- an implication that the lender is a partner in the business[25]
- tax issues to consider (e.g. might the payment be treated as a distribution of profits of the company, as opposed to a payment of interest?) and/or
- issues as to the priority of the loan in an insolvency of the borrower (see Box 1.14 on page 68).

These will be issues for due diligence in the country or countries in which the borrower conducts business and in which an insolvency of the borrower may occur. This sort of arrangement is referred to as a 'Margin ratchet' or 'pricing grid'.

1.050

Where, as is common, the Margin changes with reference to financial ratios, a question arises as to the date on which the revised Margin will take effect. The lenders will want any increased Margin to take effect retrospectively, from the date the ratios were tested, rather than from the (later) date on which any Compliance Certificate is delivered. Borrowers are likely to also want downward adjustments to the Margin to be retrospective although

1.051

---

[23] These special provisions need to be reflected in clause 35 discussed at 11.023, as well as in the clause concerned (such as conditions for drawing the facility) so as to ensure that provisions which have been added to protect one group of lenders can only be amended with consent of the appropriate 'Majority' of that group of lenders.
[24] It is worth noting that contractual provisions such as Margin ratchets which are triggered by changes in ratings have been the subject of numerous investigations over the years, as concerns arise over the consequences of over-reliance on corporate ratings. For example, in 2013, EU regulation 462/2013 required public authorities which supervise certain financial institutions to 'encourage the supervised entities to ... reduce automatic reliance on ratings issued by recognised agencies'.
[25] Under English law, entitlement to a share in the profits is not conclusive as to the existence of a partnership – s2 Partnership Act 1890.

lenders are likely to resist that so as to incentivize the borrower to produce the Compliance Certificate (and hence get the benefit of the reduced Margin) as quickly as possible.

> **Box 1.14**
> s3 Partnership Act 1890[26] states *In the event of any person to whom money has been advanced by way of loan upon such a contract as is mentioned in the last foregoing section.*
> [this reference is to s2(3)(d) Partnership Act which reads 'the advance of money by way of loan to a person engaged...in any business on a contract with that person that the lender shall receive a rate of interest varying with the profits...arising from carrying on that business']
> *being adjudged bankrupt...the lender of the loan shall not be entitled to recover anything in respect of his loan...until the claims of the other creditors of the borrower...have been satisfied.*
> This English provision does not, however, affect a lender's right to recover under any security held for the loan.[27]

Sometimes the Margin is stated to increase if a Default occurs. The effect, of course, is to allow a higher interest rate to be charged even for Defaults which are not related to non-payment. This may be a useful provision, especially for minor Defaults.

Material Adverse Effect

1.052 This definition is used as a qualifier to undertakings, representations and Events of Default (see Box 1.15), as well as in the material adverse change Event of Default itself (if there is one).[28]

> **Box 1.15**
> For example there may be a representation that
> *No Environmental Claim has been commenced...where that claim would be reasonably likely...to have a Material Adverse Effect*
> The relevant Event of Default could say that it is an Event of Default if
> *any event or circumstances occurs which is reasonably likely to give rise to a Material Adverse Effect.*

---

[26] This section of the Partnership Act probably applies to companies as well as to persons by virtue of Rule 12.3(2A) Insolvency Rules 1986. The Law Commission (in its paper No 283 on partnership law, issued in November 2003) has recommended repeal of this section of the Partnership Act.

[27] Re Lonergan, ex p Sheil (1876–77) LR 4 Ch D 789 and Badeley v Consolidated Bank (1888) LR 38 Ch D 238.

[28] See the commentary on clause 23.12 at 8.267 for further discussion of the material adverse change Event of Default.

There is an example definition taken from the Leveraged LMA in Box 1.16. 1.053

> **Box 1.16**
> 'Material Adverse Effect' means [in the reasonable opinion of the Majority Lenders] a material adverse effect on
> a) [the business, operations, property, condition (financial or otherwise), or prospects of the Group taken as a whole;
> b) [the ability of an Obligor to perform [its obligations under the Finance Documents]/[its payment obligations under the Finance Documents and/or its obligations under clause [ ](Financial condition) of this Agreement]]/[the ability of the Obligors (taken as a whole[29]) to perform [their obligations under the Finance Documents]/[their payment obligations under the Finance Documents and/or their obligations under clause [ ] (financial condition) of this Agreement]]; or
> c) the validity or enforceability of, or the effectiveness or ranking of any Security granted or purporting to be granted pursuant to any of, the Finance Documents or the rights or remedies of any Finance Party under any of the Finance Documents].

Month

The definition of 'month' is intended to reflect the practice in the Interbank Markets. The normal practice in the London markets is for rates which are quoted on the last day of a month to end on the last day of the month in which they end. So, a two-month period starting on 28 February will end on 30 April, not 28 April. If the document is to reflect that market practice, paragraph (c) of the definition of 'month' in the LMA Term Loan should be included which reads 1.054

> *[(c) if an Interest Period begins on the last Business Day of a calendar month, that Interest Period shall end on the last Business Day in the calendar month in which that Interest Period is to end.].*

Optional Currency

> *'Optional Currency' means a currency (other than the Base Currency) which complies with the conditions set out in clause 4.3 (Conditions relating to Optional Currencies).* 1.055

In the LMA Term Loan every new currency not agreed in the original loan agreement must be approved by every lender.

---

[29] See 0.149.

Original Financial Statements

Consolidated statements are required from the Company as the ultimate holding company. Given that the lenders do not have recourse to assets which are in group members which are not Obligors, it may be that financial covenants will be tested with reference to the Obligors as opposed to (or as well as) the entire group.[30] In this case the lenders will need a method to assess the financial position of each Obligor, in addition to that of the group as a whole. For this reason (and also because lender policy generally requires this) audited statements are usually required from each Obligor in addition to the consolidated statements.

Quotation Day

1.056 The Quotation Day for each currency takes into account the amount of notice required to book funds in that currency. Where the currencies are to be funded in the London Interbank Market, two days' notice is required and each of those days must be a business day in the principal financial centre for that currency. In the case of Euros, two days' notice is required and each such day must be a TARGET Day (a day when the Trans-European Automated Real-time Gross Settlement Express Transfer payment system is open for payments of euro).

There is general wording at the end of the definition which prevents the definition from having the effect of requiring places to be open for business that are not relevant for rate fixing for the relevant currency. That general wording reads:

> *unless market practice differs in the Relevant Interbank Market for a currency, in which case the Quotation Day for that currency will be determined by the Agent in accordance with market practice in the Relevant Interbank Market (and if quotations would normally be given by leading banks in the Relevant Interbank Market on more than one day, the Quotation Day will be the last of those days).*

Reference Banks

1.057 The Reference Banks are used to determine LIBOR if a Screen Rate is unavailable. The definition reads:

> '**Reference Bank Rate**' *means the arithmetic mean of the rates (rounded upwards to four decimal places) as supplied to the Agent at its request by the Reference Banks:*
>
> (a) *in relation to LIBOR, as the rate at which the relevant Reference Bank could borrow funds in the London interbank market[; or*
>
> (b) *in relation to EURIBOR, as the rate at which the relevant Reference Bank could borrow funds in the European interbank market],*

---

[30] See discussion on scope of the agreement at 0.151.

in the relevant currency and for the relevant period, were it to do so by asking for and then accepting interbank offers for deposits in reasonable market size in that currency and for that period.

This Reference Bank mechanism proved useful when the Screen Rate was abolished for some currencies. The wording of the definition of Reference Bank Rate reflects the wording used in calculating the Screen Rate (see Box 1.18 on page 72). Following the litigation over LIBOR quotes and the overhaul of LIBOR in 2013, banks became reluctant to act as Reference Banks, or, if already named as Reference Banks in documents, they became reluctant to provide quotes as envisaged by this definition (see Box 1.17). In the event that no Banks agree to be named as Reference Banks, it may be necessary to provide that the Reference Banks are simply appointed by the Agent, in consultation with the Borrower, at the time when the fallback rate needs to be determined. If no Reference Banks provide quotes when a fallback rate is needed, the market disruption clause will come into effect and lenders will be entitled to charge their 'cost of funds'.

1.058

Box 1.17
The main concerns are potential liability to the Borrower or other lenders arising from the Reference Bank role and the regulatory obligations of panel banks to keep their LIBOR submissions confidential. Some banks may therefore be prepared to agree to be named as Reference Banks provided they are satisfied that there are adequate exclusion clauses, limiting their liability, and confidentiality clauses enabling them to comply with their regulatory obligations.

Repeating Representations

It is important that the Repeating Representations should consist only of those which are not already covered by an undertaking or an Event of Default.[31]

1.059

Screen Rate

This is defined as follows

1.060

Screen Rate means:

(a) *in relation to LIBOR, the London interbank offered rate administered by ICE Benchmark Administration Limited (or any other person which takes over the administration of that rate) for the relevant currency and period displayed on pages LIBOR01 or LIBOR02 of the Reuters screen (or any replacement Reuters page which displays that rate)[and*

---

[31] See commentary on clause 19 at 8.010 onwards.

(b) in relation to EURIBOR, the euro interbank offered rate administered by the Banking Federation of the European Union (or any other person which takes over the administration of that rate) for the relevant period displayed on page EURIBOR01 of the Reuters screen (or any replacement Reuters page which displays that rate),]

or [,in each case,] on the appropriate page of such other information service which publishes that rate from time to time in place of Reuters. If such page or service ceases to be available, the Agent may specify another page or service displaying the relevant rate after consultation with the Company.

The Screen Rate is intended to reflect the rate at which prime banks ought to be able to borrow the relevant currency in the interbank markets for the duration of the Interest Period (see Box 1.18).

Box 1.18

The Screen Rate was invented by the British Bankers Association. It is calculated by asking a panel of banks to specify the rate which they believe they can borrow in the London Interbank markets at the relevant time; discarding some at the top and bottom of the quotes and averaging the rest. The rate came under scrutiny during the 2007–2008 financial crisis when a lack of liquidity in the market and rigging of the figures quoted in some cases, led to a lack of confidence in the rate. A comprehensive review followed and rates for some currencies and maturities were abolished as a result – due to the lack of liquidity for those currencies and maturities. Numerous other changes were made, including making the quoting of rates a regulated activity, delaying publication of rates quoted, requiring the rate quoted to be supported by transaction data and transferring the responsibility for the rate away from the British Bankers Association and to ICE Benchmark Administration Limited.

1.061 Borrowers (but not necessarily lenders – see Box 1.19 on page 73) prefer a Screen Rate definition rather than have a definition which reflects the lenders' actual cost of funds for two main reasons. First, it is transparent.[32] Second (subject to the comments made on clause 11.2 in 5.028 onwards) it protects them from having to pay a higher interest rate simply because a lender cannot obtain funds at as fine a rate as a prime bank.

Subsidiary

1.062 The draftsperson may choose whether to define 'Subsidiary' with reference to subsidiary undertakings or to subsidiaries (see Box 1.20 on page 73). Lenders may wish to include subsidiary undertakings because they will have been included in the consolidated accounts. Depending on the

---

[32] That is, the borrower is able to check the rate by looking at published sources. This is not the case with a personal rate of LIBOR.

Group, borrowers may wish to exclude them from the undertakings and other provisions if the borrower does not have full control over them.

> **Box 1.19**
> There are of course risks for the lenders in agreeing to a screen rate, since this does not accurately reflect their own cost of funds. If, as happened with many Japanese banks in the early 1990s, the lenders' costs of funds increase substantially, the result may (subject to the issues discussed at 5.028 onwards in the context of the market disruption clause) be that the rate they are able to charge the borrower (Screen Rate plus Margin) is less than their actual costs. In order to avoid the continuing losses involved, the lenders may need to sell their interest in the loan if they are unable to trigger the market disruption clause.

> **Box 1.20**
> A is a subsidiary undertaking of B if, effectively, B has the right to exercise, or actually exercises, a dominant influence or control over it, or the right to remove or appoint a majority of the board of directors or if it may exercise the majority of the voting rights, or if the two companies are managed on a unified basis, regardless of the fact that B may not own the majority of the shares in A.

It is also worth noting the decision in Enviroco Ltd v Farstad Supply [2011] 1 W.L.R. 921, in which the Supreme Court held that a company ceased to be a subsidiary of its parent when its shares were subject to a legal mortgage (because, technically, the effect of a legal mortgage is to transfer ownership of the mortgaged asset to the mortgagee for the duration of the security, see A1.042). It might therefore be sensible to amend the definition of Subsidiary to include companies which would be subsidiaries were it not for any security on their shares.

Clause 1.2 Construction

Clause 1.2(a)(vii)

This clause sets out some rules of interpretation (not quite the same as definitions, contained in clause 1.1) Of note is the following, broad statement about the interpretation of the word 'regulation' 1.063

> 1.2 *Construction*[33]
>
> *(vii) a 'regulation' includes any regulation, rule, official directive, request or guideline (whether or not having the force of law) of any governmental, intergovernmental or supranational body, agency, department or of any regulatory, self-regulatory or other authority or organization.*

---

[33] See 1.004.

1.064   This broad meaning is principally due to the use of the word 'regulation' in the increased cost clause (clause 14) and in the context of capital adequacy rules.[34]

1.065   *Comment*   Some like to add the words 'but compliance with which is customary' after the words 'whether or not having the force of law', so as to introduce some level of objectivity.

Clause 1.2(a)(viii)

1.066   The rule in (viii) says that a reference to a law is intended to refer to that law as it may be amended from time to time. This rule needs to be considered whenever a reference to a statute or other legal reference is made in the agreement since it may not be appropriate in each case to have the reference treated as a reference to the **statute** as amended from time to time. For example, a reference to a particular tax provision would often be intended to refer to that particular provision, not that provision as it may change from time to time.

It is worth noting that this clause only applies to references to a 'provision of law' and so does not apply to the definition of 'GAAP' even though, as discussed at 1.041 in relation to that definition, it appears to be the intention that GAAP should be interpreted to be a reference to the relevant accounting principles as they change from time to time.

Clauses 1.2(d)

> (d) A Default (other than an Event of Default) is 'continuing' if it has not been remedied or waived and an Event of Default is 'continuing' if it has not been [remedied or waived][waived]

1.067   Particularly important is the definition given to the word 'continuing'. A Default continues until remedied or waived. Under the LMA Term Loan, two alternatives are provided in relation to an Event of Default. The first alternative is that the Event of Default is continuing unless 'remedied or waived'. So, following an Event of Default, the lenders lose their rights of acceleration not only if they waive them, but also if the Borrower remedies the Event of Default before the loan is accelerated. In the second alternative the Event of Default will continue unless waived (i.e. the remedy of it will not terminate the lenders' acceleration rights). The reason some lenders require this is that they take the view that the Default should have been remedied while it was a Default and before it became an Event of Default. Moreover, if the borrower could unilaterally cure Events of Default it would reduce the borrower's incentive to inform the lender of them (see Box 1.21 on page 75).

---

[34] See 0.096.

> **Box 1.21**
> For example, assume that the loan agreement provides that the existence of a potential environmental liability against the borrower is an Event of Default. Assume that such a **liability** arises. The borrower may feel that, if they can deal with the issue (e.g. by arranging for the clean up or whatever else is necessary to discharge the liability) the best course for them would be not to notify the lenders, but simply to satisfy the liability, thereby remedying the Event of Default.
>
> If this clause provides that an Event of Default is continuing unless 'waived' (as opposed to saying that it is continuing unless 'remedied or waived') then if the borrower were to pursue their proposed course of action in this case, they would run the risk that the lenders subsequently might discover what had happened, and, since the Event of Default had not been 'waived', the intention is that the lenders would be entitled to accelerate the loan even though the Event of Default had been remedied. In other words, if the clause specifies that an Event of Default is continuing unless waived, this gives the borrower an incentive to advise the lenders of Events of Default so as to obtain waivers.
>
> This is particularly important in the context of the obligation to notify of a Default. If that can be remedied at any time prior to acceleration, the obligation has no teeth.

Clause 1.3 Currency symbols and definitions

1.068 These currency definitions are one of the areas which came into focus during the crisis over the Euro during 2011. Concerns arose that some countries might exit the Euro, and that payments denominated in Euros might, as a result, be 'redenominated' into whatever new currency the departing country adopted in place of the Euro. A related concern was that countries might impose Exchange Control restrictions (as both Iceland and Cyprus did following their currency crises) which might prevent the borrower from fulfilling its repayment obligations in the due currency.

1.069 To protect against these risks, amendments were made to the LMA Term Loan to clarify that the expression 'Euro' meant the common currency of the participating member states. Lenders also focused on their ability to take legal and enforcement action in some countries other than the 'departing' country. So they focused on the choice of law clause and the jurisdiction clause, in particular

- trying to ensure that the courts hearing the dispute would not be Euro countries and that they would apply a law other than the law of one of the Euro countries
- making the change of these clauses require unanimous lender approval (as opposed to Majority Lender)[35]

---

[35] See 11.023.

- ensuring that they had the ability to require payment in a country other than one of the Euro countries[36]
- trying to ensure they also had recourse to assets and companies which were located outside the Euro area (in the form of guarantees or other security), including an indemnity specifically addressing any loss arising from redenomination.
- In some cases lenders required the documents to include an option allowing the lender to redenominate the loan in a different currency (i.e. not the Euro) – with the aim of protecting against the redenomination risk, although the exchange control risk would remain.

1.4 Third party rights

1.070 Clause 1.4 deals with the position of third parties. It is intended to clarify the intention of the parties in relation to the rights that third parties may acquire as a result of the agreement, as envisaged by the <u>Contracts (Rights of Third Parties) Act 1999</u>. The LMA Term Loan provides for two options. First, the parties may elect that no third parties[37] are intended to have enforceable rights under the agreement. Alternatively, they may select that enforceable rights will arise where specifically stated – this choice will be made if it is preferred to have the Act regulate the position in relation to the exclusion clause in clause 26.10, rather than rely on the common law (see Box 1.22 on page 77).

---

[36] See 11.001.
[37] Meaning, in the context of the LMA Term Loan, by virtue of the definition of 'Party' in clause 1.2(a)(i), persons who are not assignees or transferees – see Box 1.22 on page 77.

Box 1.22

The Contracts (Rights of Third Parties) Act 1999 was introduced to remove some of the difficulties which the common law doctrine of **privity** of contract had given rise to. That doctrine has the effect that no person is entitled to enforce a contract or to take a benefit under it unless that person is a party to the contract. There are a number of exceptions to the doctrine, notably the law relating to assignments of contracts and the law in relation to the taking of the benefit of exclusion clauses.[38] The Act did not abolish the doctrine of privity but it did supplement it, allowing third parties to enforce terms of a contract and to take the benefit of those terms if the contract intended (expressly or by its proper construction) that those third parties should have the benefit of the relevant terms of the contract. The Act expressly preserved the rights of persons who could take the benefit of exceptions to the privity rule (such as assignees) under the common law. However, how the common law and the Act interrelate in such circumstances is a complex issue.[39] Given this uncertainty, some prefer to provide that no third parties (other than assignees and transferees, who will become 'Lenders' as defined in the agreement when the assignment or transfer is effected) are intended to take the benefit of the contract. Others prefer to specifically provide that employees may take the benefit of the exclusion clause in clause 26.10 in accordance with the Act (rather than under an exception to the privity rule), in order to avoid the complexities of the common law in this area.[40]

---

[38] Treitel *The Law of Contract*, 13th edn, at 14.077 onwards.
[39] Treitel *The Law of Contract*, 13th edn, at 14.118 onwards.
[40] If any third party is intended to have the benefit of any provision of the contract, the Act (s2) also allows that third party to prevent amendment of the contract to their detriment in certain circumstances. This right is subject to any express term of the contract to the contrary. This is the reasoning behind clause 1.3(b) – to ensure that third parties cannot object to amendment of the loan agreement.

2 The Facility

CLAUSE 2: THE FACILITY

Clause 2.1 The facility

2.001 Clause 2.1 contains the lenders' agreement to provide the facility.

> ### Clause 2.1 in a Revolving Credit Facility
>
> **2.002** It is worth considering the mechanics by which a revolving credit based on LIBOR operate, in order to understand the documentation properly. As we saw in the discussion on LIBOR funding in the Introduction, LIBOR is a market driven rate which changes constantly. Therefore, in order to offer a LIBOR interest rate, the lenders need to fix their notional LIBOR funding for a period of time (an Interest Period) as otherwise it would be impractical to calculate the interest rate given these constant changes in LIBOR. In the context of a revolving credit, the way in which this is done is to require the borrower to choose the Interest Period for an advance on the date the advance is made. The borrower will then (subject to the cashless rollover provisions which we look at in Box 2.1 on page 79) repay the advance at the end of its Interest Period.
>
> The flexibility which the borrower wants in terms of having the ability to draw and repay as and when their commercial requirements merit doing that is achieved by the fact that the borrower can prepay an advance in the middle of an Interest Period if it wants to (but note the discussion on the definition of Break Costs at 1.009) and the borrower can draw additional advances while the first is outstanding (but note clause 4.4 discussed at 2.032).

Optional Clause 2.2 LMA (Increase)

2.003 Next comes an optional clause which is part of the Defaulting Lender provisions. It deals with the situation where the borrower has cancelled the Commitment of a Defaulting Lender or cancelled or prepaid a lender which requires additional payments under the gross-up, increased cost or tax indemnity, or which requires to be prepaid as a result of illegality. It allows for the borrower to bring in another lender to lend the missing part. This clause is in addition to the borrower's rights to require the relevant lender to transfer its interests to another lender nominated by the borrower. It is discussed further in the comments on Clause 8.5 at 4.023.

> **BOX 2.1**
> In practice of course, often at the end of an Interest Period for an advance, the borrower will want to keep the funds for a further period rather than repay them. So, on the date of repayment of the first advance, the borrower will redraw a new advance, possibly in a different amount from the maturing advance – that is, the funds will be 'rolled over'. In practice then, instead of repaying the first advance and drawing the second, the borrower will simply pay (or receive, depending on which of the two advances is larger) the difference. This commercial practice of simply paying the net amount is included in the 'cashless rollover provisions' in the repayment provisions discussed in relation to clause 7.
> So the 'repayment' of an advance at the end of its Interest Period is simply a drafting mechanism for allowing interest periods to be fixed so that the loan can be offered on the basis of LIBOR without undue administrative costs in calculating the interest rate. That is why the conditions for advance of a 'Rollover Loan', (that is, one where no extra funds are being advanced) are less onerous than for other advances (see the discussion on the conditions precedent at 2.028).

Clause 2.2 Finance parties' rights and obligations

Clause 2.2(a) provides that the rights and obligations of the lenders are several.[1] The lenders are not underwriting each other and, if one lender fails to advance funds when due, the others are not responsible. This is so even if, at the time the syndicate was being put together, one or more lenders underwrote the syndication. That underwriting related to the syndication process only – that is the ability to obtain sufficient take up of the loan – and not to the creditworthiness of the participants.

2.004

The borrower is not, of course, at the complete mercy of the Arranger in terms of the identity of lenders to be invited into the syndicate (and therefore, whose credit risk the borrower will be exposed to). The borrower and Arranger will have agreed principles relating to the syndication process, and the types of lenders who can be invited to join the syndicate, at an early stage in the syndication process.

The Defaulting Lender provisions referred to in the Introduction at 0.155 are the usual way to mitigate the problems which would arise if a lender defaulted. Those provisions do not reduce the possibility of a lender

2.005

---

[1] For a discussion of the difference between several, joint, and joint and several obligations, see A1.016.

default, but simply provide a mechanism to ameliorate the results for the borrower, provided a substitute lender can be found. If the borrower wants to avoid taking credit risk on persons other than the original underwriting bank(s) other options are:

- In a term loan with a short drawdown period, the borrower may request that the loan be advanced by the underwriters and only syndicated after full drawdown. This would, however, limit the amount that could be financed,[2] and would not be possible at all in a revolving credit.
- The borrower may request that, if one or more of the non-defaulting lenders would have had undrawn commitments still available to the borrower after the date of the drawing in which another lender defaulted, those other lenders should commit in advance to permit their undrawn commitments to be used to fund the defaulted sum.

2.006 Clauses 2.2(b) and (c) provide that the rights of the lenders are separate and they may take independent action to enforce their rights (subject as otherwise stated) (see Box 2.2).

> **Box 2.2**
> Generally, the loan agreement will state that acceleration and enforcement of security given for the loan require Majority Lender consent. Those rights therefore cannot be exercised independently as envisaged by this clause. The most likely enforcement action available to be exercised independently pursuant to this clause is the right of set off and/or the ultimate sanction which unsecured creditors generally have, which is to petition for the winding up of the company.

2.007 This may seem an unusual provision, inconsistent with two basic concepts in a syndicated loan:

- that all lenders are equal and will achieve equal levels of return (subject to fees etc.);
- that the syndicate will be run in accordance with the wishes of the 'Majority'.

Clause 2.2(c) represents one of the limits on these concepts of joint action in a syndicated term loan.[3] Its effect in a fully drawn term loan is that, even though Majority Lender approval is needed for acceleration of the loan and enforcement of security, and even though it is not possible for a single lender to accelerate its portion of the loan independently of the rest; nevertheless

---

[2] It would often also limit the amount which they would be prepared to underwrite in the first place.
[3] See below at 2.009 for revolving credits.

there will come a time when the loan advanced by each lender will fall due, regardless of the views of the rest of the syndicate. If the borrower fails to pay any amount which has fallen due this clause ensures that each lender has the same rights as any other unsecured creditor in relation to its share in that instalment.

This can be a useful right in a workout if some lenders do not want to go ahead with a **rescheduling** which the Majority are pursuing, but would prefer to enforce their rights. Clause 2.2(c) gives the individual lenders at least some leverage in that situation (but see Box 2.3).

2.008

> **Box 2.3**
> For this right to be effective, lenders must ensure that
>
> - any recovery they make is not required to be shared with the syndicate under clause 28 (pro rata sharing);[4] and
> - the due date for payments cannot be altered by the Majority Lenders.[5]
>
> The right to petition to wind up the company may well turn out only to be a temporary advantage since in many countries, creditors can be forced to agree to restructuring and rescheduling proposals in a potential winding up, if those proposals are approved by a certain percentage of the creditors, with the aim of allowing the company to continue as a going concern. Depending on the percentages involved, the creditor which initiated the process may find itself bound by a rescheduling in any event.

In the case of a term loan which is not fully drawn (or a revolving credit), clause 2.2(c) gives little comfort to lenders because, although an individual lender can take action to enforce amounts due, they can also be forced by the Majority Lenders to advance further funds, despite the existence of a Default or an Event of Default. See commentary on clause 4.2(a)(i) at 2.027.

2.009

In some circumstances the borrower or the lenders may wish to negotiate amendment of this clause precisely to protect themselves against being held to ransom by individual 'rogue' lenders. In this case deletion of clause 2.2(c) may not be sufficient. It would be sensible to expressly exclude individual lenders' rights to petition to wind up the borrower as, in the absence of clause 2.2(c), it is likely in many jurisdictions that courts would interpret the loan agreement as establishing several (as opposed to joint) debts due from the borrower to each lender. The result would be that each lender would have its own right to take action against the borrower (principally the right of set off and the right to petition for winding up) for its own portion of the debt even if the agreement did not specifically provide for this.

2.010

---

[4] This is achieved by clause 28.5 of the LMA Term Loan. See 10.025.
[5] This is achieved by clause 35.2 of the LMA Term Loan. See 11.024.

CLAUSE 3: PURPOSE

Clause 3.1   Purpose

2.011 The borrower undertakes to use the loan for the specified purpose. This does not, of itself, provide a great deal of protection for the lenders for three reasons:

- first, the borrower may disregard the clause, using the money for unauthorized purposes (and putting the lenders in the position of, at best, having assumed a different credit risk from that intended);
- second, the loan may be used for the purpose intended (e.g. general corporate purposes), but its availability results in other moneys being able to be diverted to a purpose which the lenders would not have funded; and
- third, the purpose stated is often quite vague, for example, 'general corporate purposes', leaving a lot of room for interpretation.

Nevertheless, the purpose clause is of some value. It may assist in good faith arguments by the lenders (e.g. to demonstrate their lack of awareness of any illegal use or use in contravention of a regulation). It will, in most cases, be likely to trigger discussions about intended use of the facility, which may then be more specifically detailed. It can, in the worst cases, assist in establishing a claim in fraud if the borrower uses the funds for an unauthorized purpose.

2.012 In some cases the purpose clause may also give rise to a 'Quistclose trust' so that the moneys can only be used for the specified purpose and if that purpose fails (for example, if the loan was to finance construction of a factory but the borrower became insolvent before construction was completed) then any loan proceeds which were still in the hands of the borrower would be held on trust for the lenders (and therefore would not fall into the insolvency of the borrower). This can only be achieved if it is clear (both in the document and commercially) that the loan is to be used exclusively for the specified purpose.[6]

Some lenders use the clause to specify prohibited uses, for example, to say that it is not available for any purpose which would constitute (illegal) financial assistance in England.[7]

It is also worth noting that under Basel III regulations, facilities which may be used for liquidity purposes attract a different (more onerous) regulatory treatment for the purpose of the liquidity coverage ratio (see clause

---

[6] See Barclays Bank v Quistclose [1968] UKHL 4, Twinsectra Ltd v Yardley [2002] UKHL 12 and Gabriel v Little and others [2013] EWCA Civ 1513.

[7] If it were to be used for such a purpose, the clause would not protect the lenders from the consequences, so this is no substitute for proper due diligence including investigating any debt which is to be refinanced.

14 at 6.040) than other facilities. Lenders may therefore want to prohibit the use of the loan to refinance debt.

Clause 3.1 in other commercial circumstances

In an asset finance transaction (or indeed a corporate loan in some instances such as a refinancing), the loan agreement will provide that advances will be made to a specified account (e.g. the account of the seller of the asset or the lender to be refinanced) and that that will be treated as an advance to the borrower. In a project finance transaction, the agreement will provide for the loan to be advanced to a disbursement account (charged to the lenders) with provisions for drawings on that account against invoices and/or other certification.

2.013

Clause 3.2 Monitoring

Clause 3.2 provides that the lenders are not required to verify the application of moneys lent under the agreement.

2.014

CLAUSE 4: CONDITIONS OF UTILIZATION

Clause 4.1 Initial conditions precedent

Clause 4.1 reads *No Borrower may deliver a Utilization Request unless the Agent has received all of the documents and other evidence listed in Part I of Schedule 2 (Conditions precedent) in form and substance satisfactory to the Agent. The Agent shall notify the Company and the Lenders promptly upon being so satisfied.*

Before the loan can be advanced, the borrower must provide certain documentary conditions precedent as listed in Schedule 2 of the LMA Term Loan and discussed in relation to that schedule at 13.002 onwards. Satisfaction of these conditions precedent supplements the lenders' own due diligence procedures and the borrower's representations set out in clause 19, so that, before the loan is advanced, the lenders have three independent checks on each important issue: the borrower's statement in the representations; the lenders' independent review (encapsulated, in the case of legal issues, in its lawyer's legal opinion); and the evidence presented in satisfaction of the conditions precedent. As a drafting matter, changes negotiated in any one of these areas of the document may need to be reflected in the others.

2.015

Comment Borrowers need to review the list of conditions precedent to ensure that they are able to satisfy them. They will need to be particularly careful with any conditions which are not within their control, such as consents and licences, particularly if there is a reasonable risk that they will not be

2.016

forthcoming (for example, acknowledgements of notices of assignment, if a contract is being assigned).

2.017 One issue here is what instructions (if any) the Agent needs from the lenders to approve the conditions precedent. Clause 4.1 requires the conditions precedent to be met to the satisfaction of the Agent, while clause 35 requires the consent of the Majority Lenders (or, in the case of matters covered by clause 35.2, all the lenders) for waivers and amendments. The Agent therefore needs to differentiate between

- making a decision as to whether a particular document does or does not satisfy the condition precedent (which is a decision which, under clause 4.1, is delegated to the Agent[8]); and
- deciding that a particular document does not satisfy the condition precedent but deciding to waive that condition precedent (which, because of clause 35.1,[9] the Agent can only do with the consent of the Majority Lenders, or, if the effect of the waiver is to change those entrenched provisions listed in clause 35.2,[10] with the consent of *all* the lenders) (see Box 2.4).

> **Box 2.4**
> For example, assume that it is a condition precedent that the borrower delivers an acceptance by the borrower's agent for receipt of service of process in the UK. That document is duly delivered but the agent appointed was an individual. Generally, lenders do not want individuals appointed as they may leave the country or die, leaving no properly appointed agent for service of proceedings. The Agent will have a discretion on whether to accept this or not since the document delivered satisfies the description set out in the conditions precedent, so no waiver or amendment is needed and clause 35 will therefore not be relevant.

2.018 In exercising its discretion as to whether to approve a condition precedent or not, the Agent is entitled to rely on its lawyers' advice on legal issues (see clause 26.2 and 26.7(e), discussed at 10.005) and will often require the lawyer to confirm satisfaction of those conditions precedent in writing. For other issues, such as satisfactory reports from experts (surveyors,

---

[8] In making its decision on this issue, the Agent will rely on advice from its lawyers and, if there is any doubt, in practice will be likely to seek the views of the syndicate, partly because the distinction between approving a document and waiving a condition is often unclear, and partly to minimize its potential liability in relation to breach of fiduciary duty.

[9] '35.1(a) Subject to Clause 35.2 (All Lender Matters) and clause 35.3 (Other exceptions) any term of the Finance Documents may be amended or waived only with the consent of the Majority Lenders ...'

[10] Such as the Margin, and which, in a secured loan, is often extended to include the existence of the security.

environmental experts and the like) or, as in legal opinions, or reports on title, where the lawyer gives advice but the lenders need to assess that advice, the Agent is well advised to circulate drafts round the syndicate in advance, for their approval, rather than taking that decision on its own shoulders. Taking the decision without involving the syndicate would go beyond the 'purely mechanical and administrative' role of the Agent described in clause 26.3(a) and discussed at 10.006 and, while it is authorized to take such decisions, doing so could expose the Agent to liability as discussed in 10.003. See also Box 2.5.

> **Box 2.5**
> To avoid potential liability relating to conditions precedent, an addition was made to the agreement in 2014. A new paragraph (b) was added, with the intention of excluding liability for the Agent arising in relation to satisfaction of the conditions precedent. The clause reads
> *Other than to the extent that the Majority Lenders notify the Agent in writing to the contrary before the Agent gives the notification described in paragraph (a) above, the Lenders authorize (but do not require) the Agent to give that notification. The Agent shall not be liable for any damages, costs or losses whatsoever as a result of giving any such notification.*

2.019

Changes sometimes suggested in relation to Clause 4.1 include

2.020

- 'No Utilisation Request may be given until the Agent has received documents and evidence **appearing to comply with**...'. The problem here of course is that the lenders are obliged to lend if the documents delivered **appear** to comply (e.g. board minutes) even if the Agent is not satisfied that they do in fact comply or even if he knows they do not (e.g. perhaps he was aware that insufficient notice of the meeting was given);
- Sometimes borrowers ask for the condition to refer to the items being 'reasonably satisfactory' to the lenders. This is similar to referring to someone as being 'somewhat pregnant' – the items delivered are either satisfactory or they are not.

Clause 4.1 in other commercial circumstances

The following commentary looks at clause 4.1 in certain situations not covered by the LMA Term Loan.

Asset finance transactions

2.021 For transactions where the loan is to finance the purchase of an asset and security is to be taken over that asset, the conditions precedent will fall into two categories: those required before notice of drawdown can be given; and those (the conditions related to the establishment of the security) which are required on drawdown. There will be practical difficulties in satisfying the conditions precedent to drawdown.[11] In particular, given that the lenders will have arranged their funding in advance, but will need to be advised of satisfaction of conditions precedent in order to actually advance funds, the agreement should specify a time of day by which the conditions precedent need to be satisfied, so as to ensure that the Agent is in a position to notify lenders of satisfaction of conditions precedent in sufficient time for payments to be effected.

Multiple drawdown facilities

2.022 The conditions precedent in clause 4.1 will require adjustment where there is a term loan with multiple drawdowns (and possibly an extended drawdown period). There will be different conditions precedent for the first drawdown from those which apply to subsequent drawings.

Documentary conditions precedent to subsequent drawdowns clearly need to reflect the purpose of the drawdown. So, for example, a loan for construction of a given project, such as an airport, may provide for drawdowns matching stages of construction – in which case the conditions precedent will relate to evidence of achievement of the relevant stage of the project. Often the lenders are also concerned that the ratio of debt to **equity** is maintained and will therefore require evidence that the relevant amount of equity has been injected.

Revolving credit

2.023 In a revolving credit facility, it would be highly unusual to require additional documentary conditions precedent on each drawdown.

Backstop Facilities

2.024 Some loans are intended to be a backstop only – it is not intended that they be drawn except in exceptional circumstances. For these, unless the conditions precedent are satisfied before the loan agreement is signed (in which case no condition precedent clause is necessary) it will be sensible to have key conditions precedent (such as board resolutions and legal opinions) satisfied as a condition precedent to the lenders' commitment to lend (as opposed to being a condition precedent to the actual advance of funds, as would normally be the case) and perhaps to require those conditions precedent to be satisfied within a fairly short period after signing

---

[11] See Box 13.1 on page 297.

the facility. There may then be a separate clause with any other conditions precedent required for an advance to be made (such as, perhaps, a condition precedent that there is no Default).

Clause 4.2   Further conditions precedent

Clause 4.2 requires certain factual conditions precedent to be satisfied in addition to the documentary conditions precedent referred to in clause 4.1. These are a requirement that there be no 'Default'[12] and a requirement that the Repeating Representations are true.

2.025

The reason for the requirement that there should be no 'Default' is that, if circumstances exist which may mature into an Event of Default, the lenders should not be obliged to advance additional money (even though, of course, the lenders would not yet be entitled to require immediate repayment of money already advanced, as that right would not arise unless the relevant circumstances did, in fact, mature into an Event of Default).

2.026

The condition is that no Default is 'continuing'. This requirement should be read together with clause 1.2(d) (which defines 'continuing') and clause 34 (which sets out the level of consent required to grant a waiver of a Default). The result is that, for most Defaults, it is a decision for the Majority Lenders as to whether or not to advance the loan, despite the existence of a Default. In certain cases (see, e.g. the options in relation to clause 8.2 relating to change of control) this decision not to advance funds can be taken by individual lenders, independently of the Majority.[13] See also the discussion on clause 1.2(d) at 1.067.

2.027

Clause 4.2 in a revolving credit

The concept of 'Default' involves drawing a distinction between the lenders' right to require repayment of moneys already advanced (which arises on an Event of Default) and their right to be relieved of their obligation to lend new money (which arises on a Default). This distinction is more difficult to make in a revolving credit facility. The mechanics of a revolving credit facility are that a loan is advanced for a relatively short period, for example, three months. It is repaid in full at the end of that period and the borrower may then redraw whatever available amount it requires for a new period. The new advance on a **rollover** may technically be regarded as 'new money', but in commercial terms, it is only any additional money over and

2.028

---

[12] See commentary on the definition of 'Default' at 1.018.
[13] Note that change of control does not constitute a Default because the clause is drafted as a compulsory prepayment – see clause 8. Therefore, to be accurate, Clause 4.2(a) ought to cross refer to clause 8.2 so as to clarify that even if the requirements of clause 4.2 are met (that is, there is no Default and the Repeating Representations are true) there are additional circumstances in which some lenders are not obliged to lend.

above the amount outstanding immediately prior to the rollover, which is really new (see comments on Clause 2.1 at 2.002).

For this reason, clause 4.2 of the LMA recommended form for revolving credits specifies that, in relation to 'Rollover Loans' (where the amount of the new loan does not exceed the old loan and the new loan is in the same currency as the old loan) the condition precedent is that no 'Event of Default' exists. For loans which are not 'Rollover Loans' the condition precedent is that no 'Default' exists (see Box 2.6).

Box 2.6

Clause 4.2   in the LMA Recommended Form for a Revolving Credit

4.2 Further conditions precedent

The Lenders will only be obliged to comply with Clause 5.4 (Lenders' participation) if on the date of the Utilisation Request and on the proposed Utilisation Date:

(a) in the case of a Rollover Loan, no Event of Default is continuing or would result from the proposed Loan and, in the case of any other Loan, no Default is continuing or would result from the proposed Loan; and
(b) the Repeating Representations to be made by each Obligor are true in all material respects.

'Rollover Loan' means one or more Loans:

(a) made or to be made on the same day that a maturing loan is to be repaid;
(b) the aggregate amount of which is equal to or less than the maturing loan;
(c) in the same currency as the maturing Loan (unless it arose as a result of the operation of Clause 6.2 (unavailability of a currency)); and
(d) made or to be made to the same Borrower for the purpose of refinancing a maturing Loan.

2.029 In addition, clause 4.2(a)(ii) requires all Repeating Representations to be true (and this applies to all advances of a term loan and to all rollovers of a revolving credit – whether or not they are simply 'Rollover Loans'). The reason is to ensure that certain very basic issues (such as the ability to borrow the loan) remain as they originally were. It is up to the draftsperson to specify which of the representations are to be 'Repeating Representations' and are therefore to be conditions precedent to advances. This is a complex area, discussed in detail at 8.007 onwards in relation to clause 19 (Representations).

Clause 4.3   Conditions relating to optional currencies

Clause 4.3 sets out additional **conditions** for drawing in a currency other than the Base Currency. These include a requirement that the currency has been approved, is freely convertible to the Base Currency, and is readily available in the amount required. Once a currency is agreed the Agent must notify minimum drawing amounts.

2.030

Comment   It may be helpful for borrowers to have a list of pre-approved Optional Currencies, not least to avoid delay if the borrower wants to draw or convert the Loan into a currency other than the Base Currency. The lenders have the protection of Clause 6.2 which provides that if the relevant currency is not available to that lender or it is illegal to fund in that currency, they can fund in the Base Currency instead.

2.031

Of course if any of the Base Currency or the agreed Optional Currencies is a currency for which LIBOR is not quoted, alternative interest rate mechanisms will need to be included.

Clause 4.4   Maximum number of loans

Clause 4.4 limits the number of loans that may be outstanding. This limits the administrative requirements in servicing the loan for the lenders. In the case of a loan such as the LMA Term Loan, which allows for different loans to different group members, the number of loans allowed must of course be sufficient for the anticipated number of borrowers.

2.032

Where the loan is to a single borrower, a number of different loans or tranches may also be desirable to enable the borrower to divide the loan into different parts with different interest periods. This will enable the borrower to use the loan to manage its interest rate exposure.

In a revolving credit, clause 4.4 raises different concerns for the borrower as the maximum number of loans needs to be set at a high enough number to ensure that the borrower is not effectively unable to borrow any balance of the commitment (while still paying a commitment fee on it) until the end of the then current Interest Period (see Box 2.7).

2.033

> **Box 2.7**
> So, for example, assume that a revolving credit facility for $50 million provides that only one loan at a time is available under it. Assume that the borrower has borrowed a loan of $20 million for a six-month Interest Period under the facility. The result is that, during that six-month period, the borrower will be paying a commitment fee on the unused facility ($30 million) but will be unable to draw any of that commitment. Clearly, a limit of one loan at a time is therefore too restrictive in a revolving credit.

Other conditions precedent

2.034 Conditions precedent relating to any other items which were important to the credit decision need to be added. These might include conditions precedent as to execution and registration of security and guarantees, and conditions precedent as to key assets and contracts.[14]

There is also often an additional clause permitting the lenders to request such further favourable certificates as the lenders may reasonably request. This is intended to cover things which subsequent events show to be advisable. Borrowers often object to this clause, particularly in a revolving credit facility or a term loan with a long **availability period**, as giving too much discretion to the lenders and too little certainty to the borrower.

---

[14] See the commentary on clause 22 (undertakings) at 8.190 onwards and the commentary on Schedule 2 at 13.002 onwards.

3 Utilization

CLAUSE 5: UTILIZATION

Clause 5.1 Delivery of a utilization request

Clause 5.1 requires a drawdown notice to be given at a 'Specified Time'. The precise period of time required for notice of drawdown depends on the currency, and on the market in which the loan is being funded, and is set out in a schedule. The drawdown must be made within the Availability Period. This prevents an open-ended commitment arising. **3.001**

There are requirements as to the minimum amounts of any drawdown. This is for the administrative convenience of the lenders. Sometimes, there will be requirements as to frequency of drawdowns.

In the LMA Term Loan there are no restrictions on how many utilizations may be made on the same day (hence a number of currencies may be drawn).

Comment Lenders may wish to impose not only a minimum amount on the drawing but also require drawings to be in integral multiples of a given figure to prevent themselves from being required to fund odd amounts which may not be readily available in the market. **3.002**

Clause 5.2 Completion of a utilization request

Clause 5.2 requires the borrower to deliver a utilization request specifying the amount required, the date on which it is required, and the Interest Period, for any loan. **3.003**

Clause 5.3 Currency and amount

Clause 5.3 specifies the minimum amounts in which drawings must be made. **3.004**

Clause 5.4 Lenders' participation

3.005 Clause 5.4 requires the lenders to lend through their Facility Office.[1]

Clause 5 in other commercial circumstances

3.006 Since 2011, the LMA has published variations of its loan agreements containing swingline facilities options. In addition they have published a version of the agreement which includes a letter of credit facility.

Swingline facility

3.007 This is a facility available in immediately available funds (the LMA form provides for Dollars or Euros) to support the borrower's liquidity, see Box 3.1.

Drawings under the facility may only be made for a period of five days at most and cannot be applied in repayment of another swingline facility (re-emphasizing the role of the facility as a **backstop facility**).

> **Box 3.1**
> A swingline may be used for general liquidity purposes and/or to support a commercial paper programme. It can assist with the rating of the commercial paper, as it will give the market and the rating agencies comfort that the swingline will be available to be drawn on if the commercial paper cannot be repaid on the due date as a result of a failure (caused by a market disruption) to raise new finance by the issue of a new commercial paper.

3.008 One key characteristic of a swingline facility is that the lenders make available immediately available funds. For this reason, unlike in other facilities, one or two days' notice of drawing cannot be given, as the facility is designed to cover short-term liquidity issues, of which notice is not possible (e.g. there will be no advance notice of a problem in refinancing existing commercial paper). The questions then are:
- which lenders should fund the facility (not all will have access to immediately available funds); and
- which lenders should share in the risk.

3.009 As to funding, under the LMA recommended forms, the facility may be provided by all lenders of the revolving credit or by a sub-group of those lenders, with utilizations under it reducing the amounts of their commitments to the revolving credit.

As to the risk, either the risk lies only with the lenders which fund the swingline (in which case the issues relating to the definition of 'Majority

---

[1] See however the definition of 'Facility Office' discussed at 1.028.

Lenders' discussed at 1.048 in the context of the term and revolving credit facility will apply[2]) or, alternatively, there is an option for loss sharing by all revolving credit lenders on losses suffered by swingline lenders.

Note also that Basel III will increase the cost to the lenders of providing swingline facilities, because liquidity facilities are treated more onerously than other loans under the liquidity coverage ratio discussed at 6.040.

Letter of credit option

3.010 The borrower may request the facility to be made available by the issue of **letters of credit**. The LMA recommended forms provide for these to be issued by a single lender (the 'Issuing Bank') relying on indemnities from all lenders who participate in the revolving credit. Unlike the swingline option, it is not contemplated that lenders' sharing of the risk in this option might be any different from their shares in the revolving credit facility.

Once payment under the Letter of Credit is made by the Issuing Bank, it will require contributions from the syndicate and then those contributions will form part of the loan, repayable by instalments over time.

If an Event of Default occurs prior to the date on which payment is due from the Issuing Bank under the letter of credit, the borrower is required to provide cash security to the Issuing Bank in an amount equal to the potential liability of the Issuing Bank under the letter of credit.

The standard form contemplates that letters of credit may be issued in a currency other than the Base Currency, in which event there are provisions for valuation from time to time in the Base Currency.

3.011 From the perspective of the Issuing Bank, it is relying on the borrower's credit risk, to the extent of that lender's participation in the letter of credit facility, but also, to the extent that other lenders have committed to share the risks in the facility, the lender is relying on the credit risk of those other lenders – that is, will they make payment when due under their indemnities?

3.012 The Defaulting Lender provisions provide some optional clauses which can be added to the facility to address this issue. Where a lender gets into financial difficulties AFTER the Issuing Bank has issued a Letter of Credit, these provisions provide that the 'Unacceptable Lender' must give the Issuing Bank cash to cover its share of the letter of credit; failing which, the borrower must provide the cash.

Where a lender gets into difficulty BEFORE the Issuing Bank issues the letter of credit, the unacceptable lender must provide cash for its share, failing which the borrower has the option of either providing the cash itself, or reducing the amount of the Letter of credit by that bank's share. This is discussed further in the Introduction at 0.096 onwards.

---

[2] Although with less practical problems, given the backstop nature and short duration of swingline loans.

CLAUSE 6: OPTIONAL CURRENCIES

3.013 All companies need to ensure, as part of their normal financial management, that the currencies in which their income is denominated matches the currencies in which their liabilities are denominated or that they have resources available to manage any exposure which they have, resulting from a mismatch. The currencies which borrowers decide to borrow in will therefore normally (but not necessarily – e.g. see Box 3.2) be chosen to match the currencies in which they generate income.

> **Box 3.2**
> The borrower may also own assets which have a worldwide market and which are generally bought and sold in a specific currency. Examples are ships and aircraft, which are normally traded in Dollars. Here, the borrower, or the lenders, may wish to see the loan denominated in the currency in which the assets are normally bought and sold (even if income is earned in a different currency), so as to ensure the relative value of the security is maintained.

Multicurrency loans may be drawn in one or more specified currencies, or switched from one specified currency to another after drawdown. This ability to draw in and convert into different currencies assists the borrower in matching income and liabilities (particularly in a revolving credit), and can also be used as a tool to access the interest rate applicable for borrowings in different currencies.

3.014 Whatever the borrower's reason for wanting to have the ability to switch currencies, it needs to consider also the questions of how its repayment obligations will be calculated and how the amount of the available facility will be calculated. They need to consider, for example, whether it is better for them to have

- a Dollar-based loan which is available for drawing in, or conversion into, Euro or Yen;
- a Euro-based loan which is available for drawing in, or conversion into, Dollars or Yen; or
- three separate facilities, one in Dollars, one in Euros, and one in Yen.

The first two examples would normally be described as multicurrency loans and the mechanisms for providing such facilities are included in the LMA recommended forms for multicurrency loans. The third example is not normally described as a multicurrency loan.

The different impact of the three options depends on whether the facility in question is a term loan or a revolving credit facility.

Revolving credit

3.015 The key differences between the three examples, in the case of a revolving credit, relates to the calculation of how much remains for drawing. If the borrower had three separate facilities in different currencies, it has the security that those facilities will remain available, in their specified amounts, regardless of exchange rates. If, on the other hand, the borrower relied on a Dollar-based loan to finance its need for Euros, it would be exposed to the possibility that the available Euros would be reduced, due to their appreciation against the Dollar – because the amount available at a given drawdown date would be fixed at a Dollar sum. If that sum afforded fewer Euros than at the start, that risk is for the borrower.

Term loan

3.016 In the case of a term loan, the principal difference relates to calculation of repayments. In the first example (a Dollar-based loan), repayment will be required to be made in amounts which keep the value of the loan, in Dollar terms, in line with a schedule fixed at the start of the loan (see Box 3.3). If income is in a currency other than Dollars, the risk is that exchange rates will move such that there will be insufficient income to fund the repayment instalments. In the second case (a Euro-based loan), fixed Euro repayments will be required. Again, the borrower will take the exchange rate risk in relation to the currency outstanding. In the third case, repayment of every facility will be in its outstanding currency, regardless of any movement of exchange rates relating to that currency.

> **Box 3.3**
> Taking a simple example. Assume a multicurrency loan of $10 million is available in Dollars or Euros and has a Base Currency of Dollars. It is repayable by 20 equal instalments, one every six months. It is drawn in Euros at a time when exchange rates are 1 : 1. Hence, 10 million Euros are drawn. On the first repayment date, the exchange rate has moved to 1 : 1.5. The borrower must repay 10 million Euros (i.e. the full amount it has drawn, in the currency in which it has drawn it) and redraw the then equivalent of $9.5 million (the 'Base Currency Amount' at that time, that is, the amount which would have been outstanding if the loan had always been denominated in Dollars). The amount the borrower can redraw is therefore 9.5 X 1.5 (the current exchange rate) = 14.25 million Euros. The borrower repays 10 million Euros and redraws 14.25 million Euros (but is still treated as having made a repayment of $0.5 million). On the next repayment date, exchange rates have returned to 1 : 1. The borrower must now repay 14.25 million Euros and can redraw the then equivalent of $9 million (the Base Currency Amount at that time). The then equivalent of $9 million is 9 X 1 = 9 million Euros. The borrower repays 14.25 million Euros and redraws 9 million Euros.[3] A multicurrency loan therefore involves an exchange rate risk for the borrower.

---

[3] The agreement may include provisions allowing these amounts to be netted so that only the difference between the two amounts is paid.

3.017 Multicurrency facilities can give numerous different options, for example, as to which currencies are permitted (in the case of the LMA Term Loan, those currencies will be specified in the agreement and may only be added to if all lenders agree) and whether more than one currency is available at any one time.

Note that in a revolving credit, the mechanics are straightforward since each advance will be made in a particular currency and repaid in that currency. In a term loan it is more complex since the loan can be converted from one currency to another while it is still outstanding.

Clause 6.1 Selection of currency

3.018 Clause 6.1 allows the Borrower to choose the currency of the loan on drawdown or at the start of an Interest period, in each case from the pre-agreed Optional Currencies

Each loan under the LMA Term Loan must be in a single currency. However, borrowers may request more than one loan at the same time, each of which may be in different currencies.

There are provisions (clause 6.1(c)) dealing with what happens if a borrower asks to convert the loan from one currency to another on a day which is not a Business Day for both currencies concerned (the loan remains in the existing currency and is rolled over on a daily basis until a day which is a Business Day for both currencies). There are also provisions (clause 6.2) dealing with the situation where some syndicate members are unable to fund in the requested currency (they are required to fund in the Base Currency).

Clause 6.3 Change of currency

3.019 Clause 6.3 deals with the situation if a loan is to be converted from one currency to another at the end of an Interest Period.

A multicurrency facility has a Base Currency, with reference to which the amount of the loan available in any given currency will be calculated. This is the concept of the 'Base Currency Amount' in the LMA Term Loan. It is the amount that would have been outstanding in the Base Currency if the loan had always been denominated in that currency. The loan may be drawn in a different currency – in which case the amount advanced will be the equivalent of the Base Currency Amount on the drawdown date. Clause 6.3 of the LMA Term Loan provides that, if a loan is to change currency, then, at the end of the Interest Period when that change is to occur, the amount drawn, in the currency originally drawn, will be repaid in full. The borrower will redraw (in whatever currency is permitted) the Base Currency Amount (or its then equivalent in the new relevant currency).

Clause 6.4

Clause 6.4 applies a similar procedure (without the repayment and re-advance) for interest periods where there is no change of currency (see Box 3.3 on page 95).

There are often provisions (clause 6.4(b) of the LMA Term Loan) that if there is no change of currency and the difference between the amount due to be repaid and the amount due to be re-advanced is minimal then no adjustment will be needed.

These mechanics mean that the lenders may be required to advance further funds even when the loan is being repaid.[4]

The mechanics of repayment and re-advance of the loan can cause difficulties with secured loans as it may inadvertently have the effect of repaying the loan which the security secures.[5]

3.020

---

[4] This has implications for the method of transfer of a multicurrency loan – see 9.014.
[5] See further A1.069.

4 Repayment, Prepayment and Cancellation

CLAUSE 7: REPAYMENT
Clause 7.1 Repayment of loans

4.001 This clause specifies (in a term loan) the repayment schedule.

Clause 7.2 Reborrowing

4.002 This clause states that moneys repaid are not available for reborrowing.

> **Clause 7 in different commercial circumstances**
>
> In a revolving credit the repayment clause reads ...
>
> **4.003**
> *7.1 ... Each Borrower which has drawn a Loan shall repay that Loan on the last day of its Interest Period.*
>
> A revolving credit involves the advance of a loan for a chosen Interest Period, with the loan being repaid in full at the end of its Interest Period. Additional loans may be advanced from time to time (up to a maximum number of loans at any one time). In a revolving credit, if the amount of the lenders' commitment to lend reduces over time, a provision will be included which will specify the applicable limits on the facility during its term.
>
> The LMA revolving credit wording also includes optional 'cashless rollover' provisions, as discussed at Box 2.1 on page 79.
>
> **4.004** There is also an optional LMA Defaulting Lender provision (see Box 4.1 on page 99) dealing with the issue of the repayment of monies to a Defaulting Lender in a revolving credit.
>
> **4.005** The issue is that a Defaulting Lender is unlikely to be able to fulfil its commitment to lend under the revolving credit. This optional clause is designed to ensure that, if at the time a lender becomes a Defaulting Lender it has already advanced funds under the Revolving Credit,

the borrower is not obliged to repay those monies until the end of the Commitment Period – that is, those moneys will be 'termed out' (or effectively, converted into a term loan).

> **BOX 4.1**
> The optional wording reads 'At any time when a Lender becomes a Defaulting Lender, the maturity date of each of the participations of that Lender in the Loans then outstanding will be automatically extended to the Termination Date and will be treated as separate Loans ('the Separate Loans') denominated in the currency in which the relevant participations are outstanding'

CLAUSE 8: PREPAYMENT AND CANCELLATION

Clause 8 deals with **prepayment** and cancellation. It falls into three sections: compulsory prepayment (clauses 8.1 and 8.2 dealing with illegality and change of control); voluntary cancellation and/or prepayment (clauses 8.3 and 8.4); and voluntary prepayment of a single lender (clause 8.5). 4.006

Clause 8.1 Illegality

Clause 8.1 requires compulsory prepayment and termination of the commitment in relation to a single lender if it becomes illegal for that lender to continue to fund the loan. This covers not only illegality due to political events but also illegality due to imposition of exchange control regulations (for example). This clause is intended to deal with situations such as outbreak of war and to allow a mechanism for the lenders to comply with any relevant law. While it may be wishful thinking to expect the participation in the loan to be prepaid in these circumstances, the right not to advance new moneys will be effective and the right to require repayment may enable enforcement action to be taken if the borrower has assets in jurisdictions which are not tainted by the illegality. 4.007

Comment   A borrower may, in certain circumstances, argue that 4.008

- the obligation to fund the loan should be suspended during the period of the illegality, but not cancelled;
- the obligation to prepay should not arise if the situation is capable of remedy, for example, by obtaining necessary licences or exemptions; and/or
- the relevant lender should have an obligation to try to obtain any permits etc. which may be available to cure the problem (although they probably already have this obligation under clause 16 discussed at 6.051).

Sanctions and Anti-Corruption Laws

4.009 Lenders are also increasingly concerned to ensure that the loan specifically addresses anti-bribery, sanctions and money laundering, in addition to this general clause dealing with illegality. Example clauses are in Box 4.2.

> **Box 4.2**
>
> **An example is the LMA loan for use in developing markets which contains the following undertaking:**
>
> a) *No Obligor shall, (and the Company shall ensure that no other member of the Group will) directly or indirectly use the proceeds of the Facility for any purpose which would breach the Bribery Act 2010, the United States Foreign Corrupt Practices Act of 1977 or other similar legislation in other jurisdictions.*
> b) *Each Obligor shall (and the Company shall ensure that each other member of the Group will)*
>   i) *conduct its businesses in compliance with applicable anti-corruption laws and*
>   ii) *maintain policies and procedures designed to promote and achieve compliance with such laws.*
>
> No provisions are included addressing sanctions.

4.010 The lenders' concerns are to ensure that:

- They are not financing an activity which will be tainted by bribery or money laundering;
- They are not financing an activity which breaches sanctions legislation (e.g. purchase of goods from a country which is the subject of sanctions);
- They are not lending (directly or indirectly) to someone they are prohibited from lending to as a result of the sanctions legislation; and
- Even if the relevant legislation does not make it illegal for the lenders to continue to provide the finance, in many cases they will want to disassociate themselves from any company which is the subject of sanctions or tainted by bribery or money laundering, not least, for reputational reasons.

It is common to supplement the illegality clause with specific clauses addressing these issues so as to ensure that the lenders have an exit even if there is no illegality, and also because having specific provisions may help demonstrate that the lender has policies designed to promote compliance with the legislation

4.011 Where the borrower and the lender are subject to the same regulatory regime, this is usually unobjectionable. However difficulties arise where the borrower is in a different jurisdiction from the lenders. Here a practical problem arises, in that the borrower will need advice on the scope of the relevant laws in the lenders' jurisdiction. If the Lenders want the borrower to undertake to comply with the US Patriot Act, for example, this will involve extra expense for the borrower in obtaining (ongoing?) advice on the provisions of that Act. A second problem is that in some cases compliance with the sanctions regime of one country may be prohibited by the laws of a second country – for example in the EU, compliance with US sanctions against Cuba may be prohibited. Borrowers are therefore likely to want to restrict these provisions.

Clause 8.2   Change of control

4.012 Clause 8.2 requires compulsory prepayment of the whole loan and release of all lenders from their obligation to fund if there is a change of control in relation to the borrower and the Majority Lenders require prepayment. The argument is that they have relied on continuity of ownership and management in their credit decision. The commercial effect of this is the equivalent of an Event of Default but it is framed as a compulsory prepayment to avoid triggering cross default clauses.[1] See Box 4.3.

> **Box 4.3**
> There may also be a concern that some countries would regard a provision which gives one party a right to terminate a contract early even when the other party is not in breach of any obligation under the agreement, as being repugnant to local law either because of its one sided nature or because it is seen as an unfair forfeiture. By framing the clause as an obligation to prepay in certain circumstances, failure to pay when required will be a breach, and this may reduce the legal risks.

4.013 There is an option for compulsory prepayment of individual lenders (as opposed to having the decision made by Majority Lenders and relate to prepayment of the **whole** loan). Many lenders will require this option, enabling them to require prepayment regardless of the views of the Majority in those cases where the identity of the shareholder is critical to their lending decision, even though a guarantee may not have been sought from the shareholder.

4.014 A key issue is what constitutes a change of control. Commonly it is defined to mean the power to control more than a stated percentage

---

[1] See commentary on clause 23.5 at 8.250 'Compulsory prepayment events'.

(usually 50%) of the company, either through shares or through control of the board of directors.

The directors of the borrower need to have regard to their duties in agreeing this clause – such as duties of directors of a listed company to disclose details of any significant agreement which can be terminated on a change of control, and the directors' duties to act in the best interests of the company and to promote the best interests of the company.[2]

Borrowers will want to negotiate a long period for prepayment to give time to arrange alternative funding.

Lenders will want to ensure that the clause relates to the ultimate control of the holding company.

4.015 *Comment*   The borrower may wish to ask for compulsory negotiation and/or a grace period.

4.016 Some loans contain other circumstances in which a compulsory prepayment is required. These may include cash sweeps if results for a given period are better than expected, prepayment with the proceeds of permitted disposals, or prepayment out of insurance proceeds in an asset finance, or out of post-completion price adjustments, or on flotation in an acquisition finance.

The borrower may want to ensure that the prepayment need only be made at the end of the next Interest Period so as to avoid broken funding costs.

Other issues which arise in relation to prepayments out of disposal proceeds are discussed in 8.176.

4.017 The LMA version of the clause allows the right to require prepayment to be exercised independently from the right not to lend new money. It may be that lenders will be reluctant to call for prepayment of moneys already advanced but will want to stop future drawings.

Clause 8.3   Voluntary cancellation

4.018 Clause 8.3 gives the borrower the right to reduce the amount of the facility. This right to reduce the **commitment** is a useful additional right to the right to prepay, particularly in a revolving credit or a term loan with a long drawdown period, as in these cases the **commitment fee** will be payable

---

[2] For example it is clear that agreeing a 'poison pill' (i.e. a provision which triggers adverse consequences for the company in the event of a takeover) is a breach of the directors' duties if it was only agreed by the directors in order to entrench themselves or to deny the shareholders the right to consider the merits of a takeover offer see Criterion Properties v Stratford UK Properties LLC [2004] UKHL 28, [2004] 1 W.L.R. 1846 at [29], where the directors adopted a poison pill in order to frustrate a potential takeover.

during the whole drawdown period and cancellation allows the borrower a method to bring these fees to an end.

Lenders often require the minimum amount for cancellation to be significant. They may also require (both in this clause and the voluntary prepayment clause) that the right be exercised in relation to integral multiples of the specified amount to ensure that lenders are not left with odd amounts to fund in the markets.

Comment The notice period for cancellation should be short so as to bring the commitment fee to an end as soon as possible. **4.019**

Clause 8.4 Voluntary prepayment of loans

Clause 8.4 gives the borrower the right to prepay the loan.[3] Prepayment must be in minimum amounts. Generally, the prepayment will be applied against the last instalments of the loan – to reduce its life. The lenders prefer this, not least as it is easier to assess risk over the shorter term. **4.020**

Comment Borrowers may wish to have prepayments applied pro rata against repayment instalments in certain circumstances so as to see immediate benefit from any prepayment. This would be particularly important in an asset finance where the prepayment was made from the sale of an asset which would otherwise have generated part of the income required for the loan repayment. **4.021**

Sometimes lenders will impose a prepayment fee. This is uncommon in unsecured loans but becomes more common in more complex transactions or in local markets. If a prepayment fee is provided for, then the borrower should consider whether that fee is appropriate in circumstances where there is a compulsory prepayment or a voluntary prepayment of part of the loan under clause 8.5. The case for a prepayment fee is, of course, different from the arguments relating to Break Costs. The fee is to compensate for lost profit while Break Costs represent an expense.[4] **4.022**

Some agreements provide that prepayment may only be made on the last day of an Interest Period. Provided the borrower agrees to pay Break Costs, there is no need for this limitation on prepayment.

In a revolving credit, given that the loan period is relatively short and any prepayment would result in broken funding, the right of prepayment is often not included.

---

[3] Without this express right, the borrower would probably not be entitled to prepay. See Hooper v Western Counties and South Wales Telephone Co Ltd (1892) 68 LT 78.
[4] See the discussion at 1.009 on the definition of Break Costs.

Clause 8.5 Right of repayment and cancellation in relation to a single lender

4.023 Clause 8.5 allows voluntary prepayment of an individual lender in circumstances where it is costing the borrower additional moneys to fund that lender. The circumstances in which this is allowed are:

- where a gross-up applies to that lender;
- where that lender is entitled to payment under the increased cost clause or the tax indemnity.

> In a project finance or a structured or other complex financing, the option of prepayment by the borrower is often impractical and other solutions may need to be negotiated if additional costs arise.

Rights to prepay and or replace individual lenders

4.024 There are a number of different situations in which it is common to give borrowers the right to prepay and/or replace individual lenders. Some of these are contained in the LMA Term Loan, some in the optional 'kits' dealing with Defaulting Lenders and some appear in the Leveraged LMA but do not appear in the LMA Term Loan. For convenience, the provisions are summarized here.

The circumstances in which it is common to give borrowers rights to cancel/prepay/replace individual lenders are:

4.025
- Where the lender is a Defaulting Lender. These rights are part of the optional 'kit' dealing with Defaulting Lenders referred to in the Introduction and are inserted at Clauses 8 and 35 of the LMA Term Loan. They are invariably included in the documents;

4.026
- Where the lender votes against granting a waiver or consent required where a certain specified minimum percentage of lenders have given approval. This is the so-called 'yank the bank' provision which is not included in the LMA Term Loan but is included in the Leveraged LMA;

4.027
- Where there is an extra cost attached to that lender's share of the loan, under the increased cost clause, gross-up clause or tax indemnity;

4.028
- Where a lender is entitled to be prepaid as a result of the illegality clause.

The standard LMA terms give the borrower somewhat less rights in relation to Defaulting Lenders than in relation to the other circumstances listed as discussed in Box 4.4 on page 105.

> **Box 4.4**
> In relation to Defaulting Lenders, the borrower cannot simply prepay the Defaulting Lender. The options are:
>
> - To require the Defaulting Lender to transfer its participation in the loan to another lender nominated by the borrower; or
> - To cancel the undrawn Commitment of the Defaulting Lender and ask another lender to increase its Commitment to make up the shortfall.
>
> In the other circumstances in which the borrower has the right to remove an individual lender in the LMA Term Loan (additional costs and illegality), the standard provisions give the borrower the option of either prepaying or substituting a new lender.
>
> Note also that the borrower cannot remove the Agent. There are separate provisions dealing with Agents in difficulty and Agents affected by FATCA withholding. These give the power of removal to the syndicate as it is they who take the credit risk on the Agent. Note however that this provision refers to the Agent in its capacity as Agent – it does not prevent the borrower from prepaying the Agent in its capacity as lender.

Comment Other circumstances in which borrowers may want to have rights of prepayment and/or cancellation include: 4.029

- if one lender requires to be prepaid on a change of ownership,
- if a lender makes a claim under the market disruption clause,[5]
- if one lender requires prepayment under a clause which is specific to that lender, for example, due to sanctions issues or other issues only relevant to that lender, such as social policies.

Comment In those cases where the borrower has the right to require a lender to transfer some or all its Commitment to another lender, the borrower does not have the right to use a Group company to purchase the loan, even if that would normally be allowed. 4.030

Comment Sometimes there are time limits within which these various rights must be exercised. Borrowers should bear in mind that of course it can take some time to negotiate a transferee. 4.031

Clause 8.6 Restrictions

Clause 8.6 provides for notice of cancellation and prepayment to be irrevocable and for payment to be accompanied by payment of interest and **broken funding costs**. 4.032

---

[5] However in this third case, lenders are likely to resist strongly since in those circumstances they will not want the Agent to disclose the identity of the lenders in question, to avoid reputational issues.

5 Costs of Utilization

CLAUSE 9: CALCULATION OF INTEREST
Clause 9.1 Calculation of interest

5.001 See 0.111 for a summary of the interest provisions in the LMA Term Loan.

5.002 Clause 9.1 provides for the borrower to pay interest at LIBOR[1] plus Margin plus (optionally, see Box 5.1) the Mandatory Costs. The Mandatory Costs are the costs to the lenders of contributing to the running costs of banking regulators, insofar as that cost is attributable to their participation in the loan.[2] The costs depends on the nationality and lending office of each lender.

> **Box 5.1**
> Historically, English banks charged Mandatory Costs in addition to the Margin, while this was unusual outside England. It is increasingly common for English Banks not to charge the Mandatory Costs in addition to the Margin. In 2013, LMA withdrew the schedule which it had previously provided which had set out the calculation of Mandatory Costs for lenders with their lending office in the UK, partly as a result of the diversity of lenders (and therefore the differing amount of Mandatory Costs for each lender) which had led to complexity in calculating the Mandatory Costs and administrative inconvenience for the Agent in distributing the payment. Commonly lenders now simply absorb the cost in the Margin, as has previously been the case in other markets.

Where the loan may be outstanding in Euros, the interest rate specified may refer to Euribor or to LIBOR, depending on the wishes of the syndicate. If most of the lenders are planning to fund the loan in London, they will fund at Euro LIBOR and the reference to Euribor will not be necessary.

---

[1] See the discussion of 'LIBOR' at 1.042.
[2] See 0.101.

If they plan to fund in the domestic markets for the Euro they are likely to want the interest rate calculated with reference to Euribor.[3]

Clause 9.2   Payment of interest

Clause 9.2 deals with the timing of payment of interest. As a general principle, interest is required to be paid on the same dates (the last day of each Interest Period) as interest would be due on the lenders' underlying funding assuming the lenders completely match funded.[4] However, as a credit issue, the lenders normally require regular interest payment and therefore will not want to allow interest to accrue for longer periods than six months. This is the reason for the provision in the LMA Term Loan requiring six-monthly interest payments when longer Interest Periods are chosen.

5.003

Clause 9.3   Default interest

Clause 9.3 provides that if any amount is not paid on its due date, the rate of interest applicable to it will be increased to a default rate. This is usually LIBOR plus Margin (plus any Mandatory Costs if applicable) plus an uplift. This is intended partly to give the borrower an incentive to pay in full and on time and partly to compensate the lenders for the additional credit risk and for the additional management time involved in lending to a borrower which is in default. The increase in the interest rate must be such that the overall default interest rate is higher than the rate a borrower could normally expect to have to pay if their financial fortunes reversed and obtaining funds was difficult, so as to make non-payment an unattractive form of financing in those circumstances.

5.004

The obligation to pay default interest arises whenever a payment is overdue, regardless of whether or not that non-payment constitutes an Event of Default. So, for example, if (as in the LMA Term Loan) the agreement provides that failure to pay **principal** is not an Event of Default if caused by technical error and remedied within a given period of time, nevertheless, default interest will start to accrue on the date of non-payment. Default interest is normally[5] only charged when payment is overdue. Hence, if there is an Event of Default other than as a result of non-payment, default interest will only start to accrue if the loan is accelerated.

5.005

Clause 9.3(a) provides for the default interest to be paid both before and after judgement. This is because many jurisdictions specify a statutory

5.006

---

[3] See the discussion of 'Euribor' at 1.027.
[4] See clause 10.1 at 5.012 for further discussion of Interest Periods and match funding.
[5] In some cases, lenders choose to require the loan agreement to allow them to charge default interest on the occurrence of any Event of Default, even if there are no moneys overdue, as an added encouragement to the borrower to avoid Events of Default, particularly those which are minor where the lenders may be thought unlikely to exercise their right to accelerate. This would usually be achieved in the definition of 'Margin'.

rate of interest to apply to amounts that the court has determined to be due and has issued a judgement for. That rate would apply from the date of the judgement until the judgement had been enforced, but often only applies if no other rate has been agreed. Given that the statutory rate is not regularly updated, the lenders prefer to know that, during that period, default interest will still be LIBOR-based.[6]

5.007 *Comment* The wording of clause 9.3 allows the lenders to choose their funding periods for overdue amounts (and the interest will be compounded at the end of each such funding period). Some borrowers will ask that, if the borrower fails to make a payment on its due date, the lenders fix daily Interest Periods for the overdue sums. This is in the belief that any such failure to pay will quickly be remedied and the choice of short interest periods will minimize broken funding costs.[7]

5.008 Default interest is one of the areas that can cause difficulty in a number of jurisdictions. In some jurisdictions there is a limit on the duration for which such interest can be charged, or secured. In some there is a limit on the amount which can be charged, or secured. In others, **compound interest** (charging interest on interest) is not permitted. In England the provision will be void and unenforceable if it is a **penalty**. A 'penalty' is a provision that seeks to penalize (or punish) someone for being in default under an agreement, as opposed to a provision that seeks to compensate the other party for the consequences of the default. If the provision is a genuine pre-estimate of loss then it is interpreted as being compensatory and not penal in nature. The lenders' argument is that the additional 1 or 2% is compensatory in nature and is not intended as a punishment, since it costs the lenders more to manage a loan which is in default than one which is not.[8]

Clause 9.3(b) reads as follows

5.009 *9.3(b) If any overdue amount consists of all or part of a Loan which became due on a day which was not the last day of an Interest Period relating to that Loan:*

(i) the first Interest Period for that overdue amount shall have a duration equal to the unexpired portion of the current Interest Period relating to that Loan; and

(ii) the rate of interest applying to the overdue amount during that first Interest Period shall be [one] per cent higher than the rate which would have applied if the overdue amount had not become due.

---

[6] A contractual choice of interest rate post-judgement is effective under English law. See Director General of Fair Trading v First National Bank Plc 2002 1 AC 481. Such a provision may not be effective in the place of enforcement of a judgement.

[7] See also commentary on clause 11.4 (break costs) at 1.009.

[8] Lordsvale Finance plc v Bank of Zambia (1996) QB 752 considered an increase of 1% on a default and found it enforceable in the circumstances of the case.

Clause 9.3 draws a distinction between principal and other sums. **5.010**

Sums that are not already being funded by the lender (e.g. overdue interest or principal unpaid at the end of the Interest Period relating to it) are dealt with under clause 9.3(a) which provides for the lender to charge interest at LIBOR on the due date plus the Margin and additional percentage.

Clause 9.3(b) deals with overdue principal, where the principal in question falls due *during* an Interest Period – for example, as a result of compulsory prepayment or as a result of an acceleration following an Event of Default. It provides for the Margin plus additional percentage to be added to the LIBOR *already applying* to that payment of principal – that is, the LIBOR applicable to the then current Interest Period. This is because the lender is deemed to be already funding these sums at that rate and committed to carrying on doing so until the end of the current Interest Period.

Clause 9.4 Notification of rates of interest

This clause provides for the Agent to notify all parties of interest rates when they are determined. **5.011**

CLAUSE 10: INTEREST PERIODS

Clause 10.1 Selection of interest periods

It would be extremely unlikely, post the financial crisis of 2007–2008, for lenders to actually fund themselves for the loan in the interbank market specified in the loan agreement and for the Interest Periods stated or chosen; (i.e. to 'match fund'), nevertheless, in a LIBOR-based loan, provisions for calculation of interest remain drafted on the assumption that the lenders match fund.[9] **5.012**

Clause 10.1 gives the borrower the option during the course of the loan to choose the period for which LIBOR is quoted (and thus charged to the borrower) within certain limits set down by the clause. This is to give the borrower the ability to use the choice of Interest Periods as a way to manage its interest rate exposure. (Both the duration of funding and the timing of funding will impact on the rate of LIBOR.) The borrower will choose the duration of the first Interest Period prior to drawdown and, for each subsequent Interest Period, shortly before it is due to start. Hence, in a floating rate loan based on LIBOR, the interest rate is effectively fixed at the start of each Interest Period and paid at the end of it,[10] with a new interest rate being fixed for a new period each time an Interest Period comes to an end. **5.013**

---

[9] See further 0.106 onwards.
[10] Subject to clause 9.2 dealing with interest periods of over six months.

5.014 It is normal to give the borrower the choice between one-, three-, and six-month periods, (see Box 5.2) sometimes also allowing 12 months, as these maturities are more readily available in the markets. Other durations may be available but at a premium or with difficulty. Also, of course, only certain durations have a Screen Rate so that interest rates for other periods will be calculated on the basis of the various fallback provisions discussed at 0.111. Under the LMA Term Loan, the Agent may only agree to periods other than those specified if all lenders agree.

> **Box 5.2**
> Many lenders have also removed the option for a one month Interest Period, as this option would result in more onerous treatment under Basel III. Put simply, Basel III imposes various obligations on banks to handle their liquidity risks (see the discussion at 6.038). If the lender agrees one month interest periods it will be exposed to liquidity risk (i.e. the risk of being unable to refinance in the interbank markets) twelve times a year, whereas if it agrees three month Interest Periods, the liquidity risk only occurs four times a year.

5.015 In some markets, such as aircraft finance, and with some lenders such as supranational agencies, or lenders in local markets, the practice is not to give borrowers the flexibility to choose Interest Periods. In such cases, Interest Periods are often set in advance to coincide with repayment dates (e.g. to be three-monthly) and are not changeable. This gives the borrower less flexibility to use its choice of Interest Periods as a way of managing its interest rate exposure as it will be unable to influence the timing of approaches to the market to fix LIBOR.

5.016 The optional part of Clause 10.1(d) (which is quoted in Box 5.3) may be included to allow the borrower to choose Interest Periods of unusual durations so as to coincide with repayment dates and avoid broken funding costs.[11]

> **Box 5.3**
> [In addition a Borrower (or the Company on its behalf) may select an Interest Period of: a period of less than [one] Month, if necessary to ensure that there are sufficient Loans (with an aggregate Base Currency Amount equal to or greater than the Repayment Instalment) which have an Interest Period ending on a Repayment Date for the Borrowers to make the Repayment Instalment due on that date].

---

[11] See the discussion of 'Break Costs' at 1.009.

Where the agreement provides for a small number of loans, or there is a single loan, borrowers will usually want the ability to split the loan into parts with different interest periods, to ensure that they are not restricted in their choice of interest periods with reference to repayment dates (see Box 5.4). This provision is not needed in the LMA Term Loan because that document allows a number of different loans to be advanced so that in effect the whole facility has already been split into parts which can have different Interest Periods.

5.017

> **Box 5.4**
> An example of appropriate wording follows,
> *Where an Interest Period would otherwise overrun one or more Repayment Dates, the Loan will be split into parts, with one part in the amount of each Repayment Instalment falling due during that Interest Period and another part in an amount equal to the balance of the Loan. Each such part shall have a separate Interest Period ending, in the case of each amounts equal to a Repayment Instalment, on the Repayment Date for that Repayment Instalment, and, in the case of the balance of the Loan, on the date complying with the other requirements of this clause [].*

Clause 10.1 in a revolving credit facility

5.018

In a revolving credit facility Clause 10.1 reads as follows

Selection of Interest Periods
a. A Borrower may select an Interest Period for a Loan in the Utilization Request for that Loan
b. Subject to this Clause 10 and [...], a Borrower may select an Interest Period of one, three or six Months or any other period agreed between the relevant Borrower and the Agent (acting on the instructions of all the Lenders)
c. An Interest Period for a Loan shall not extend beyond the Termination Date
d. Each Interest Period for a Loan shall start on the Utilization Date
e. A Loan has one Interest Period only

5.019

The principle relating to Interest Periods is the same whether the loan is a term loan or a revolving credit. The mechanics are different. In a revolving credit which is based on LIBOR, the borrower will request an advance, specify an Interest Period, and become obliged to repay the advance on expiry of that Interest Period. A couple of days before expiry it will request a new advance (which it will use to repay the old one) and specify the Interest Period for that new advance. As a result, the borrower cannot alter the amount outstanding on a daily basis, but only at intervals corresponding to Interest Periods. In other words, if, on drawdown, the borrower wishes to take advantage of six-month LIBOR, by doing that, it

5.020

loses its ability (subject to any rights of prepayment it may have) to reduce the amount of the loan during that six-month period.

Hence in a revolving credit it is important for the borrower to have the right to draw further loans while a loan is outstanding so as to be able to access the undrawn commitment.[12]

Clause 10.1 in a loan advanced by instalments

5.021 In loans advanced by instalments lenders will require the amounts of instalments to be significant to avoid administrative inconvenience, if necessary having drawdowns to a disbursement account to achieve this.[13] Generally, the lenders will also require Interest Periods for the advances to 'consolidate'. In other words, they will require that any Interest Period for a second or third or later advance should end on the same day as the Interest Period for the first advance, rather than giving the borrower full choice of Interest Periods for each advance separately. This is simply a matter of administrative convenience for the lenders.

Clause 10.2   Changes to interest periods

5.022 Clause 10.2 allows the Agent to shorten Interest Periods to coincide with repayment dates and so avoid broken funding costs.

Clause 10.3   Non-business days

5.023 Clause 10.3 deals with the position if an Interest Period ends on a non-business day.

Clause 10.4   Consolidation and division of loans

5.024 Clause 10.4 allows loans to be consolidated if they are in the same currency, with the same **maturity** and to the same borrower. It also allows loans to be split into parts on the borrower's request.

CLAUSE 11: CHANGES TO CALCULATION OF INTEREST

11.1   Absence of quotations

5.025 Clause 11.1 provides that if any Reference Bank does not provide a quote for LIBOR when needed, the calculation will be made on the basis of the quotes of the other Reference Banks.

---

[12] See clause 4.4 at 2.032.
[13] See clause 3.1 at 2.013.

Clause 11.2   Market disruption

This clause states that in the event of a Market Disruption Event, the interest rate charged will be the Margin plus, for each lender, its cost of funds, instead of LIBOR. The definition of Market Disruption Event reads: 5.026

(i) *at or about noon on the Quotation Day for the relevant Interest Period LIBOR [or, if applicable, EURIBOR] is to be determined by reference to the Reference Banks and none or only one of the Reference Banks supplies a rate to the Agent to determine LIBOR [or, if applicable, EURIBOR] for the relevant currency and Interest Period; or*

(ii) *before close of business in London on the Quotation Day for the relevant Interest Period, the Agent receives notifications from a Lender or Lenders (whose participations in a Loan exceed [35] per cent of that Loan) that the cost to it of obtaining matching deposits in the Relevant Interbank Market would be in excess of LIBOR or, if applicable, EURIBOR.*

This clause was originally introduced out of concerns that the Eurodollar markets may be interrupted and lenders in general may be unable to fund in those markets. It retains this function as defined in clause 11.2(b)(i). No LIBOR rate will be available in those circumstances. 5.027

This aspect of the clause has become of increased significance as a result of the reforms of LIBOR made during 2013. One impact of these reforms was to abolish LIBOR in relation to some currencies, and to make the traditional fallback to Reference Banks more problematic, as discussed in the definition of the Reference Bank Rate at 1.057. Where there is no LIBOR for the relevant currency or period and the Reference Banks fail to quote – the market disruption clause takes effect (through clause 11.2(b)(i)) and performs a valuable role.

Clause 11.2(b)(ii) on the other hand, extends the function of the clause so that it will also apply where the cost to the lenders, (or to a specified proportion of the lenders) of funding themselves in the interbank market exceeds LIBOR (i.e. the Screen Rate). This protects the lenders against a differential arising between the Screen Rate and their personal funding costs in the London Interbank markets. (See Box 5.5 on page 114) Of course, there is still likely to be a difference between their actual funding costs and their personal funding costs in the London Interbank Markets since they will not, in practice, fund in the London interbank market. 5.028

One difficulty with this clause is that it does not differentiate between the situation where there is an increase in the cost of a lender's funds in the interbank markets caused by that lender's own credit position and the situation where the problem arises from market problems. Lenders argue that if the percentage of lenders needed to trigger the clause is reasonably high, that is sufficient to ensure that the clause only operates in times of real market problems. This is not always the case, depending on the make 5.029

up of the syndicate[14] and, in any event, is of little assistance to borrowers in bilateral facilities or club deals.

> **Box 5.5**
> During the 1990s, Japanese banks had numerous loans on which they were charging a screen rate of LIBOR plus a Margin. The definition of Market Disruption Event at that time was limited to the circumstances set out in clause 11.2(b)(i). The fall in credit standing of the Japanese banks at that time resulted in an increase in their costs of funding themselves in the London Interbank Market, such that their LIBOR exceeded their return from their loans. They had no option but to sell the loans (at a loss) to banks which were still able to fund at a rate at or near to the Screen Rate. If the current wording of this clause from the LMA Term Loan had been included in their loans, they may have succeeded in charging the additional cost to the borrower, leaving the borrower with the burden of arranging a refinancing. This event was the reason for the introduction of para (ii) – to ensure that if the Screen Rate of LIBOR was not representative of lenders' funding costs in the interbank market, they could charge their actual funding costs instead.

5.030 In practice, if the market disruption clause were to be triggered by a credit problem of the lenders, then the borrower would be likely to exercise its right to prepay and arrange a refinancing by lenders which continued to be able to finance at the Screen Rate of LIBOR. Nevertheless, the result would be that the borrower would have to

- pay the additional rate of interest until the prepayment occurred
- incur further time and expense in arranging the refinancing, and
- bear the risk of not being able to obtain the same Margin at that time as applied to the original loan.

All of these would be due to a change in the lender's credit position.

So, the borrower will want the proportion of lenders who need to be affected to be as high as possible.

5.031 In a bilateral facility or club deal, a different mechanism will be needed to ensure that the clause can only be invoked in the case of a market problem. One option could be to use an accepted measure of the degree of market stress in the Interbank Markets, being the spread between LIBOR and the Overnight Swaps Rate ('OSR'). In normal circumstances, LIBOR and OSR track each other, with the OSR usually being 10 to 15 basis

---

[14] For example if the syndicate has a disproportionate number of lenders from a country which experiences credit problems then the clause may be triggered even though lenders in all other countries are unaffected.

> points above LIBOR. If the difference exceeds that level, this is widely accepted as evidence of market stress and lack of liquidity in the Interbank Markets. In 2008 the spread reached 364 basis points. So borrowers under a bilateral facility or a club deal might suggest that para (ii) of the clause can only be used at a time when the differential is above say 30 to 40 basis points, so as to ensure it could only be used in times of market stress.

A very strong borrower may argue that clause 11.2(b)(ii) should be deleted completely. There are two reasons to suggest this. **5.032**

The first is that the costs which the lender is seeking to pass on here have already been included in the Margin as a result of the Basel III requirement[15] for lenders to include liquidity risk in their pricing. The liquidity premium which is included in the Margin is the price which the lender has calculated as being an appropriate price for the lender's liquidity risk – that is, its risk of not being able to access funds in the interbank markets when needed or only being able to access them at a premium – that is, exactly the situation covered by the market disruption clause. So, having charged the borrower a fee for the lender taking this risk, they then seek to pass the risk to the borrower through this clause. **5.033**

The second reason for deleting para (ii) is that the lenders were aware that their funding costs would be different from the Screen Rate of LIBOR when they agreed the interest rate, and yet they still decided to quote on the basis of a Screen Rate of LIBOR. Lenders are clearly taking the risk of the difference between funding costs and the Screen Rate. They are probably only funding a small portion of the loan in the interbank markets, so why should the rate for the whole loan be changed entirely if there is an extra cost for the lender in funding the small portion of the loan funded in the Interbank Markets? **5.034**

Nevertheless, as a result of the experiences of the financial crisis, when lenders sought refuge in the clause to protect them against the problems with the Screen Rate of LIBOR, lenders are very keen to keep the clause, see Box 5.6 on page 116. Although the safeguards put in place during 2013 following the Wheatley review of LIBOR should improve confidence in the Screen Rate, lenders are reluctant to step out of line with market practice and abandon a clause which has been useful to them in the past. They may also argue that the calculation of the liquidity premium to include in the Margin was made on the assumption that loan agreements would retain a market disruption clause and that deleting it might require a recalculation of that premium. Borrowers may well feel that the lower Margin compensates them for the risks they take by accepting the clause.

---

[15] The requirement is contained in the guidelines issued by the Committee of European Banking Supervisors – (the 'Guidelines on Liquidity Cost Benefit Allocation'). These guidelines specifically refer (among other things) to the need to include in the pricing the cost of keeping a liquidity buffer to cover funding problems. See http://www.eba.europa.eu/documents/10180/16094/cebs18_Guidelines.pdf.

5.035   This is an example of the tensions in the documents (discussed at 0.107) caused by the increasing divergence between the assumption which the document makes as to lenders' funding costs (LIBOR) and the reality.

> **Box 5.6**
> This clause became particularly significant during the financial crisis of 2007–2008. Many lenders found themselves unable to fund in the London interbank markets at the Screen Rate. Lenders started to suspect that there might be an issue with the Screen Rate itself, and that it might not be an accurate benchmark for Interbank Market funding costs in the extraordinary circumstances prevailing at that time. History proved them correct. The Wheatley review highlighted a number of defects in LIBOR including:
>
> - The fact that, during periods of inactivity in the markets, there was a lack of data on which to base quotes;
> - The fact that quotes given to the British Bankers Association for the purpose of calculating the Screen Rate were public so that those quoting might wish to put a good spin on things rather than give the impression that the market perceived them to be more risky than other lenders and;
> - The fact that there was no regulation surrounding the submission of quotes – no evidence was required to support the quotes and the quotes did not need to be linked to any real transactions.
>
> A substantial overhaul of LIBOR resulted as discussed at Box 1.18 on page 72.
>
> Having concluded that the Screen Rate was not an accurate benchmark, lenders turned to the market disruption clause (and in particular, para (ii) of the definition of Market Disruption Event) to protect them and to ensure that they could continue to charge a 'fair' rate of LIBOR plus the Margin.

5.036   *Comment*   If the clause is retained as it stands, borrowers should place some restrictions on loan transfers. At present the clause can be triggered if lenders who have lent the specified percentage of the loan cannot fund at the Screen Rate in the interbank markets, even if the reason for that is the creditworthiness of the lenders. If that is the commercial agreement then the borrower needs to be able to prevent the loan being sold to less creditworthy lenders.

Borrowers can, of course, take some comfort in the fact that lenders will be reluctant to use the market disruption clause because of reputational concerns.

Alternative version of the clause

5.037   One of the optional LMA provisions referred to in the Introduction provides an alternative market disruption clause which is designed to make it less likely that the borrower will find itself paying each lender their 'cost of funds' plus Margin and to deal with some of the practical problems arising under the standard clause, see Box 5.7. The alternative version introduces a second requirement before resorting to 'cost of funds'. Essentially, if a market disruption occurs under the wording of the usual clause, instead of each lender charging its cost of funds plus Margin, a single rate will apply to all lenders, based on quotes supplied by a named group of lenders (referred to as the Alternative Reference Banks). There is then a provision that if a set percentage of lenders cannot fund at that rate in the interbank markets (with the percentage required being larger than the percentage required to trigger the application to the Alternative Reference Banks) the usual cost of funds mechanism will kick in.

> **Box 5.7**
> Numerous problems arose with the clause in practice during the credit crunch. These included:
>
> - Lenders being reluctant to use the clause for fear of the effect on their reputation;
> - Problems in lenders determining their 'cost of funds';
> - Competition law problems in disclosing 'cost of funds';
> - Lack of transparency for borrowers who simply have to rely on the lenders' statement of their 'cost of funds';
> - Absence of a mechanism for the Agent to be required to consult lenders if any lender wants to discuss the possibility of triggering the clause;
> - If the clause is triggered then a different interest rate is due to each lender.

Clause 11.3   Alternative basis of interest or funding

Clause 11.3 requires the Agent and borrower to try to agree a substitute rate of interest if a Market Disruption Event occurs (but the borrower will continue to have to pay the cost of funds until a substitute basis is agreed). Any substitute rate must be agreed by *all* the lenders under clause 11.3(b). This forces the borrower in effect to cater to the demands of the weakest member of the syndicate.   **5.038**

Comment   Some borrowers may be keen to require as much transparency as possible, for example, a certificate from the relevant lender confirming that it has taken similar action in other loans and certifying the disruption and attempted solutions.   **5.039**

Clause 16 requires the lenders to try to avoid additional costs under this clause (and other similar clauses).

Clause 11.4 Break costs

5.040 The borrower agrees to pay to each lender '*its Break Costs attributable to all or any part of a Loan or Unpaid Sum being paid ... on a day other than the last day of an Interest Period for that Loan or Unpaid Sum*'.

Clause 11.4 is the obligation to pay broken funding costs. The obligation arises wherever a sum is paid on a date other than the last day of the relevant Interest Period for the sum in question. So this obligation may arise on prepayment or if a repayment date falls during an Interest Period.

In the LMA Term Loan this requirement and (almost) all other requirements to make payments other than principal and interest are expressed to be payable within three Business Days of demand. Hence, no further grace period is appropriate in the Events of Default.

5.041 The obligation is to pay a specified amount in respect of Break Costs as opposed to an indemnity. So the lender does not actually need to incur any broken funding costs to be entitled to claim. As with LIBOR itself, the calculation of Break Costs is simply a proxy for the cost to the lender of breaking its funding.[16]

Broken funding may also be incurred as a result of failure to draw on the specified date. This is because the practice in the London Interbank Market is for the lenders to commit to borrow two days before the funds are drawn. If the funds are not advanced on the date anticipated, the lenders will need to reinvest the moneys borrowed and will face a reinvestment risk. The loan agreement includes an indemnity (in clause 15.2) from the borrower for these costs (see Box 5.8).

> **Box 5.8**
> This is the reason the loan agreement needs to be signed and drawdown notice given before the lenders fix their funding. In some instances administrative convenience may suggest that the agreement should be signed at the same time as funds are advanced. One issue which will need to be dealt with in such a case is to ensure that a valid indemnity is given (with consideration) by the borrower, in respect of any broken funding costs, before the funding is booked in the market.

5.042 *Comment* It may be that interest rates have moved such that the lenders will make a profit on moneys paid in the middle of a funding period. The borrower may ask the lenders to agree to pay any broken funding profits to the borrower. Lenders may resist this given that they do not in fact fund the whole loan in the interbank market, and so they will not actually make the specified profit.

---

[16] See also the definition of Break Costs at 1.009.

5.043 The provisions of clause 11.4 dealing with Break Costs are appropriate only for a floating rate loan. In the case of long-term fixed rate funding, the practice is that if the loan is repaid early, the borrower must also pay the mark to market value[17] of the loan at the date of prepayment.

Box 5.9 briefly summarizes the principal ways in which fixed rate funding may be made available to borrowers.

> **Box 5.9**
> There are many different methods by which fixed rate funding may be made available to a borrower. The basic options are:
> - the lenders fund themselves on a fixed rate basis (e.g. by issue of commercial paper) and pass the costs (including any early termination costs, usually calculated on a mark to market basis) on to the borrower;
> - the lenders fund themselves on a floating rate basis but enter into a swap under which they swap fixed interest due from the borrower under the loan agreement for the floating rate required for the lenders' funding. Again, termination costs relating to the swap will be passed through to the borrower;
> - the lenders fund themselves on a floating rate basis and lend moneys to the borrower on the same basis, leaving the borrower to effect a swap. This is the most popular route as it leaves the borrower taking the credit risk of the swap counterparty rather than the lenders.

CLAUSE 12: FEES

5.044 This clause provides for a commitment fee, an arrangement fee, and an agency fee. The commitment fee is payable to all lenders in relation to the amount the lenders are committed to lend but which has not been drawn. It is calculated on a daily basis and payable at regular intervals during the drawdown period. The LMA Term Loan suggests that the fee should only start to accrue once the loan agreement is signed and the lenders are legally committed. Some lenders (particularly in club deals) will charge this fee from the date of the acceptance of the offer letter. Some borrowers request it should only start to accrue once the conditions precedent are satisfied.[18] This is an issue for the offer letter.

5.045 There is also an optional provision here which is part of the Defaulting Lender provisions and which provides that no commitment fee is due to a Defaulting Lender in relation to its undrawn commitment.

---

[17] See Appendix 2.
[18] This argument might be made if there are conditions to the lender's commitment, as opposed to the drawing (and the amount of the loan is sufficiently high to justify the point). See commentary on conditions precedent to backstop facilities at 2.024.

5.046 The agency fee and arrangement fee are stated to be as specified in a fees letter. The amount of these fees is confidential to the Agent/Arranger. Their existence needs to be disclosed to ensure that the obligation to pay them is secured by any security, that non-payment would constitute an Event of Default, and to ensure that the Agent/Arranger is under no obligation to share those fees with participants on the basis that they are undisclosed profits.

6 Additional Payment Obligations

CLAUSE 13: TAX GROSS-UP AND INDEMNITIES
SECTION 1 – INTRODUCTION

Withholding tax

Many countries (including England) require that, if a payment of interest (or other payments, such as rent under a lease, or payments of royalties) is paid by a resident of that country, the resident must, in certain circumstances, first deduct tax from that payment and account for that tax to the appropriate tax authorities. Any obligation to deduct tax in this way is referred to as 'withholding tax'. The tax is a tax on the recipient and the payer of interest is, in effect, acting as a tax collector on behalf of the tax authority. See Box 6.1.   **6.001**

> **Box 6.1**
> So, for example, if the withholding tax rate was 20% and the resident was due to pay 100, then the resident would only pay 80, paying the other 20 to the tax authorities. This 20 is tax on the recipient, in the country of the resident.

Double tax treaties

The result of the imposition of a withholding tax in relation to a cross-border payment may be that the recipient is taxed twice on the same income: once in the country of the source of the income and again in the country of the recipient. This may be avoided if the recipient is a resident of a country with which the payer's country has a **double taxation treaty**. Broadly speaking, (but see 6.018), such a recipient is referred to in the LMA Term Loan as a 'Treaty Lender'. Such treaties may either remove or reduce the requirement to withhold tax on payments to residents of the country concerned (see Box 6.2 on page 122). It may also be the case that, if tax is deducted at source, the country of the recipient will grant a tax credit in respect of tax paid in the country where tax has been deducted.   **6.002**

> **Box 6.2**
> Usually, in deciding which double tax treaties might be relevant, the countries concerned are those in which the income from which the interest is paid is earned – being the relevant place of business of the borrower (which is not necessarily the same as its place of incorporation) and the country of residence of the lender which is beneficially entitled to the interest – that is, entitled to use it as its own money and not simply as an agent for someone else.[1] Often there are administrative requirements which need to be complied with to get the benefit of the treaty.

6.003 However, it is worth noting that even if there is a double tax treaty, which removes the need to withhold tax on payments to the relevant lender, the borrower often needs to deduct tax pending receipt of authorization from the local tax authorities, permitting payment to be made without deduction, and that can be a very slow process. This would be the case in the UK for example, unless the lender uses the DTTP Scheme discussed at 6.011.

Gross-up

6.004 Lenders need to receive their full interest without deduction, not least in order to fund their payment obligations in respect of their corresponding cost of funds (LIBOR). In a cross-border case, absent a double tax treaty, the lender's obligation to pay tax in the borrower's jurisdiction is not part of the lender's ordinary corporation tax bill but is an additional cost incurred by the lender as a result of the location of the residence of the borrower. The LMA Term Loan (at Clause 13.2(c)) therefore states that if any withholding tax has to be paid in relation to payments under the loan, (other than in relation to FATCA, as discussed at 6.030 onwards) then, in certain circumstances,[2] the amount of the payment will be increased to whatever amount as, after deduction of the withholding tax, will leave the lender with the amount of interest originally due. This is referred to as 'grossing-up'. See Box 6.3.

> **Box 6.3**
> So, taking the example from Box 6.1 on page 121, if the borrower is obliged to gross-up, they must ensure that, after taking tax off the payment, the net sum received by the recipient will be 100. Assuming the withholding tax rate is 20%, that will require a total payment of 125, with 25 going to the tax authorities and 100 to the recipient

---

[1] Nevertheless, there may be tax consequences in the country of the Agent simply as collecting and/or distributing agent.

[2] Essentially, the borrower does not have to gross-up if the lender was not entitled to receive payment without deduction in the first place or if the reason for the deduction was an issue relating to the lender's circumstances, acts or omissions.

Note that the arguments in relation to the gross-up obligation will be different if the borrower and lender are located in the same jurisdiction and the local law imposes a withholding tax on the payments. In this case the borrower is in effect simply acting as a tax collector, ensuring that the lender pays the tax which the lender is in any event due to pay in the local country.[3] The difference from a cross-border payment is that, in the case of a cross-border payment, the tax on the lender in the country of the borrower is an additional tax on the lender incurred solely because of the location of the borrower.

6.005

It is also worth bearing in mind that there is a personal obligation on the borrower to make the tax deduction and pay it to the relevant tax authorities. This means that if the borrower is unaware of the fact that they should have deducted tax (e.g. because the borrower incorrectly believes that the recipient is entitled to receive the funds without deduction), then the borrower still has to make payment of the tax. Unless the document provides for the borrower to have a claim against the lender in those circumstances (which it usually doesn't), then that cost will need to be borne by the borrower. See Box 6.4. This is discussed further at 6.023.

6.006

> **Box 6.4**
> So, taking the example at Box 6.1 on page 121, if the resident failed to make any deduction and paid the full 100 of interest to the recipient, then the resident would have a personal obligation to pay tax (still tax on the recipient) of 25.

Categories of lenders

There are three basic categories of lender to consider, and the provisions of the LMA Term Loan for each category are broadly summarized here.

6.007

- Those entitled to receive payment without deduction. Here the LMA requires the borrower to gross-up payments if withholding occurs.[4] The main consequence is that if the law changes so as to require a deduction, the borrower will be obliged to gross-up.

6.008

- Those entitled to receive payment without deduction once approval has been obtained from the relevant tax authorities. The LMA makes no distinction between these (who are Treaty Lenders) and the first

6.009

---

[3] It is just the same as the withholding tax which employers are usually required to apply on payments to their employees – the employer is simply helping to ensure that the employee pays its tax. The employee would in most cases be unlikely to succeed in a request that their employer 'gross up' their salary.

[4] Unless the withholding results from a change of facts or failure to submit relevant forms.

6.010

category, so that the borrower has to gross-up to this category of lender, pending receipt of the approval.[5]

- Those not entitled to receive payment without deduction. The intention behind the LMA drafting is that there should be no obligation for the borrower to gross-up to this category except where the position has changed since the loan agreement was signed and that change falls to the borrower under the first category above. (But see the discussion at 6.018 on the definition of 'Treaty Lenders'.)

Double Tax Treaty Passport Scheme ('DTTP Scheme')

6.011

Before turning to the clause itself it is worth mentioning the DTTP scheme in the UK. This was introduced to try to alleviate some of the problems which arise in relation to Treaty Lenders, where borrowers have to withhold tax on payments until they receive authorization from the tax authorities allowing them to make payment without deduction.

The DTTP Scheme is an arrangement in the UK under which lenders may apply for a passport, which is valid for five years, confirming their eligibility for treaty relief. Use of this passport significantly speeds up the process for obtaining clearance to pay without deduction. If a lender holds a passport and wants to use the passport for this loan then if it gives the borrower its scheme reference number and the borrower submits the relevant form to the UK authorities within 30 working days of the lender joining the loan then clearance to pay without deduction can be obtained more speedily.

The LMA Term Loan requires the original lenders to confirm the relevant DTTP information in the original agreement (in the schedule of lenders), and transferees to give the DTTP information in the form of a transfer certificate under which they purchase the loans, if they wish to use the scheme.

Documentation

6.012

In the context of withholding tax, the provisions of the LMA Term Loan are highly jurisdiction specific. The standard provisions include wording (e.g. in the definition of 'Qualifying Lender'), which reflect the requirements of the UK tax authorities relating to withholding tax. They assume that, as at signing, all lenders are eligible to receive interest without tax deduction (albeit, in some cases, only after receipt of a direction from the tax authorities), or, if not, that the borrower will not be obliged to gross-up.

---

[5] This is the case despite the fact that (in the UK at least) the lender will be entitled to recover the tax withheld by the tax authorities. The LMA Term Loan simply includes limited assurances by the lenders that it will co-operate in the process for obtaining permission to pay without deduction.

Significant changes will be needed dependent on the tax residence of the borrowers and the lenders, the provisions of any relevant double tax treaty, and the risk allocation as between the parties. Therefore, this discussion does not look at the wording in detail but, rather, highlights the general principles which the clause seeks to address. Thorough review of the LMA provisions is very instructive, despite their jurisdiction specific nature, as it highlights issues which need to be dealt with whatever jurisdictions are involved. It is worth noting that many loan agreements designed for use outside the UK have much simpler tax provisions than those we discuss here. Superficially, that may seem attractive to borrowers, but they will usually find that the simplicity in the wording results in significant tax risks being taken by the borrower which ought more appropriately to be borne by the lenders.[6]

CLAUSE 13: TAX GROSS-UP AND INDEMNITIES – SECTION 2 – THE CLAUSE

Clause 13.1 Definitions

Clause 13.1 sets out some definitions used in the tax **gross-up** clause. 6.013

Clause 13.2 Tax gross-up

Clause 13.2 is the clause dealing with tax gross-up. 6.014
Clause 13.2(a) and (b) require the borrower to advise the Agent if it becomes obliged to make tax deductions from payments and to make payments free of such deductions unless it is obliged to make deductions by law. Clause 13.2(b) also requires a lender to notify the Agent if it becomes aware that the borrower must withhold tax on a payment to it.
Clause 13.2(c) is the gross-up clause. It reads: 6.015

> 13.2(c) If a Tax Deduction is required by law to be made by an Obligor, the amount of the payment due from that Obligor shall be increased to an amount which (after making any Tax Deduction) leaves an amount equal to the payment which would have been due if no Tax Deduction had been required.

> 'Tax Deduction' means a deduction or withholding for or on account of Tax from a payment under a Finance Document, other than a FATCA Deduction.

In some countries there are doubts as to the enforceability of this clause on the basis that an agreement by one person to pay another person's tax is unenforceable and this is a mandatory principle of public policy which cannot be avoided by a choice of law.[7] This is an issue for due diligence (see Box 6.5 on page 126).

---

[6] For example the LMA template for use in developing market jurisdictions requires the borrower to gross-up in all circumstances – regardless of whether the gross-up results from the lenders' acts or omissions or not. There is a footnote highlighting the fact that the clause should be considered on a case-by-case basis.
[7] Enforcement of judgements which included payments of another's tax may also therefore be affected.

> **Box 6.5**
> If a gross-up clause is unenforceable then, if there is an actual withholding tax issue on commencement of the transaction, the Margin will need to be higher to enable the transaction to proceed.

The grossing-up clause is generally included in the loan agreement even where there is no withholding tax obligation on payments between the relevant parties – so as to ensure that, if withholding tax is subsequently imposed, the lenders will be protected. The borrower's escape route in this event is the right to prepay the affected lender (see clause 8.5 at 4.023).

Clause 13.2(d) Limitations on the gross-up obligation.

6.016 For the borrower, the obligation to gross-up clearly makes a significant difference to the cost of the loan. The borrower will therefore wish to limit its gross-up obligations. As far as practical they will wish to ensure that they do not borrow money from lenders in respect of whom there would be an obligation to withhold. This will be achieved by agreement with the Arranger on the types of lenders to be invited into the syndicate in the first place, and by clause 24.2(f), discussed at 9.046, which limits the borrower's gross-up obligations in the event of a change in Facility Office or a change in lender. In addition, clause 13.2(d) sets out some other common limitations on the gross-up obligation. See Box 6.6.

> **Box 6.6**
> Clause 13.2(d) reads:
> *13.2(d) A payment shall not be increased under paragraph (c) above for a Tax Deduction in respect of tax imposed by the United Kingdom from a payment of interest on a Loan, if on the date on which the payment falls due:*
> *(i) the payment could have been made to the relevant Lender without a Tax Deduction if the Lender had been a Qualifying Lender but on that date that Lender is not or has ceased to be a Qualifying Lender other than as a result of any change after the date it became a Lender under this Agreement in (or in the interpretation, administration, or application of) any law or Treaty, or any published practice or concession of any relevant taxing authority*
> *(ii)*
> *(A) the relevant Lender is [a non-bank lender]; and*
> *(B) an officer of HM Revenue and Customs has given (and not revoked) a direction (a 'Direction') under section 931 of the ITA which relates to the payment and that Lender has received from the Obligor making the payment or from the Company a certified copy of that Direction; and*
> *(C) the payment could have been made to the Lender without any Tax Deduction if that Direction had not been made.*

Comment The first thing to notice about this limitation is that it only applies to United Kingdom withholding tax (the wording reads – '*A payment shall not be increased ... for a Tax Deduction in respect of tax **imposed by the United Kingdom**'...*). If any likely Obligor is resident outside the UK and may be required to pay withholding tax in a different jurisdiction, the parties will need to consider whether there should be similar restrictions on the gross-up obligations of that Obligor in addition to the provisions of clause 13.2(d). In other words, where Obligors may be from different tax jurisdictions, there may need to be a number of clauses dealing with withholdings imposed by different countries. In the case of the LMA Term Loan, the group needs to consider not only the jurisdictions of the original Obligors, but also of any likely future Obligors.

6.017

The limitations in clause 13.2(d) can then be roughly summarized as follows. There is no gross-up obligation if:

(a) (by virtue of clause 13.2(d)(i) see Box 6.6 on page 126) the lender is not a 'Qualifying Lender' in the first place. The definition of 'Qualifying Lender' consists of Treaty Lenders and local lenders and is intended to reflect the circumstances in which the UK tax authorities will allow payments without withholding. The difficulty here is that in relation to Treaty Lenders, double tax treaties do not come in one standard form, so, depending on the location of the lenders, there may be different requirements which need to be fulfilled in order for payment to be made without deduction and the LMA Term Loan leaves that issue to be addressed on a case-by-case basis. The Association of Corporate Treasurers provides two sets of suggested wording[8] to include in the definition of Treaty Lenders to address this. The relevant part of the simpler version is set out in Box 6.7.

6.018

Box 6.7
'Treaty Lender' means a lender which...

(i)...

(ii)...; and

(iii) meets all other conditions in the Treaty for full exemption from United Kingdom taxation on interest which relate to the Lender (including its tax or other status, the manner in which or the period for which it holds any rights under this Agreement, the reasons or purposes for its acquisition of such rights and the nature of any arrangements by which it disposes of or otherwise turns to account such rights)

---

[8] In its 'ACT Borrower's Guide to LMA Loan Documentation for Investment Grade Borrowers', available from the website of the Association of Corporate Treasurers at www.treasurers.org.

6.019 If Treaty Lenders are included in the definition of Qualifying Lenders, the borrower should be aware that, in the UK, they will be obliged to deduct tax on interest payments until they receive a direction from the UK tax authorities allowing them to make payment without deduction. Unless the DTTP Scheme is used the procedure can be slow so that gross-up may well be triggered at least on the first interest payment, or, if the loan is transferred, on the first interest payment following transfer.

Even though lenders (in the UK at least) will be able to obtain a refund for tax withheld pending receipt of the permission to pay without deduction, it is normal for lenders to require the borrower to gross-up these interim payments. See Box 6.8.

> **Box 6.8**
> The borrower's position may be alleviated by
>
> - trying to ensure that the first payment of interest falls due as late as possible so as to give time to complete the process for the initial lenders
> - use of the DTTP Scheme (although the LMA Term Loan provides that that is the lenders' choice)
> - relying on the clause dealing with tax credits discussed at 6.028 – although, as mentioned there, that clause is not very borrower friendly; and
> - historically, in relation to transferees, relying on the provision in clause 24.2(f) discussed at 9.046, to the effect that a transferee could not claim a payment under the gross-up clause unless the transferor could have done so. However, since the introduction of the DTTP Scheme an exception has been made to that clause, to the effect that the borrower cannot claim the benefit of the protection if their delay resulted in the expedited procedure being unavailable. See further the discussion at 9.048.

6.020 (b) (by virtue of clause 13.2(d)(i) see Box 6.6 on page 126) the lender ceased to be a lender to which payment could be made without deduction (other than as a result of a change of law or similar). In other words, if a change of facts (e.g. tax residence of the lender) results in a change of its status for the purpose of withholding tax this will not fall to the borrower.

6.021 (c) (by virtue of clauses 13.2(d)(ii) see Box 6.6 on page 126) the tax authorities have required payment to be made subject to deduction of tax where the lender is resident or taxable in the United Kingdom but not a bank. (The tax authorities may do this if they believe that the payment in question is not actually eligible to be paid without deduction)

6.022 (d) (by virtue of clause 13.2(d)(iii) and (iv)) payment could have been made without deduction to the lender if it had delivered a Tax Confirmation or complied with certain necessary administrative requirements – See Box 6.9 on page 129.

> **Box 6.9**
> - In the case of non-bank lenders – borrowers can only make payment gross to non-bank lenders if they 'reasonably believe' that the payment is exempt. So this clause says that the borrower does not have to gross-up to non-bank lenders unless they have delivered a 'Tax Confirmation' to the borrower, so as to enable the borrowers to reach that reasonable belief.
> - In the case of Treaty Lenders, borrowers can only make payment without deduction if the lender is entitled to, and elects to, use the DTTP passport scheme or the borrower receives approval from the tax authorities allowing them to pay without deduction. In each case this will require the co-operation of the lender. So this clause says that the borrower does not have to gross-up to a Treaty Lender which has not complied with its (limited) obligations to co-operate.

Confirmation of Tax Status

Clauses 13.2(k) and (l) require UK lenders which are not banks and which are party to the loan agreement at the start, to confirm their tax status. A similar provision is included in the transfer certificates signed by incoming lenders, but in this case there is an express provision preventing the borrower from relying on the confirmation.

Comment Borrowers may wish to extend this provision (and the definition of 'Tax Confirmation') to all original lenders and to require a similar confirmation (and the ability to rely on that confirmation) from buyers in the secondary market, as well as undertakings to advise the borrower if the position changes. This is because the borrower may not be able to identify whether any particular lender is entitled to receive payment without deduction or not because this depends on issues which are only within the knowledge of the lender (such as whether the lender is 'beneficially entitled' to the interest and whether it is liable to UK tax on the interest). If the borrower pays the lender without deduction when it should have made a deduction, the borrower will be liable to pay tax on the interest. Under the LMA Term Loan the borrower will have no recourse to the lenders except for those who have been required to give a confirmation under this clause or in the transfer certificates.

Clause 13.3 General tax indemnity

Clause 13.3(a) Tax Indemnity

The tax indemnity reads as follows

> (a) *The Company shall (within three Business Days of demand by the Agent) pay to a Protected Party an amount equal to the loss, liability or cost which that Protected Party determines will be or has been (directly or indirectly) suffered for or on account of Tax by that Protected Party in respect of a Finance Document.*

6.023

6.024

6.025

6.026 *Comment* Some borrowers may request removal of the words 'which that Protected Party determines' to make this indemnity less one-sided.

Clause 13.3(b)   Exceptions

6.027 There are exceptions to the tax indemnity (contained in paragraph 13.3(b) of the LMA Term Loan) which effectively ensure that the borrower does not compensate the lenders for ordinary income tax on their profits in their countries of normal tax residence or with respect to FATCA claims (as discussed at 6.030).

Clause 13.4   Tax credit

6.028 Clause 13.4 provides that, if a lender receives a tax credit as a result of the tax withheld, the benefit of this tax credit will be passed back to the borrower. This is commonly referred to as the '**clawback clause**'. This clause should be read in conjunction with clause 27 which provides that the lenders can arrange their tax affairs as they see fit; they are not obliged to investigate or claim any relevant tax reliefs; and they are not obliged to disclose their financial affairs or tax computations to the borrower.

6.029 The existence of a tax credit and a clawback clause is of limited value to the borrower because:

- the timing of any payment under clause 13.4 could well be some years after the gross-up payment was made. It will take some time for the financial year to end and then for the tax position for that financial year to be finally settled;
- a tax credit is not usually specifically attributed to any particular loan;
- clause 13.2 itself only applies if the lender *decides that* there has been an applicable tax benefit;
- the lender must have *used* and *retained* the benefit (i.e. it depends on the lender being profitable); and
- the clause provides that the borrower will be given whatever amount *the lender decides* will result in the lender being in the same after tax position as if there had been no gross-up.

Despite these limitations there is little improvement that a borrower can realistically hope to achieve through negotiation in most cases. Lenders cannot permit borrowers to get involved in the lenders' tax affairs. Nevertheless, where the parties enter into the loan knowing that a gross-up will apply and perhaps that the effects of that will be lessened by an applicable double tax treaty, these standard provisions will not necessarily be applicable and the document will need to be adjusted to reflect each party's responsibilities in relation to claiming, and making use of, whatever relief is available.

CLAUSE 13: TAX GROSS-UP AND INDEMNITIES – SECTION 3 – FATCA

What is FATCA?

6.030 Potential withholding tax issues also arise as a result of the US legislation commonly referred to as 'FATCA'.[9] This stands for the Foreign Account Tax Compliance Act. This legislation enacted in 2010 is designed to assist US tax authorities in ensuring that its citizens disclose (and pay tax on) all their worldwide income. The purpose of the legislation therefore is to gather information about the foreign investments of US citizens. It achieves this purpose by requiring foreign financial institutions (commonly referred to as 'FFIs') which receive US source income to provide information on their US customers to the US tax authorities or face a 30% withholding on their US source income. Interest under a loan agreement would be US source income if it comes from a US borrower (or a subsidiary of a US borrower) or from an agent on behalf of a US borrower or its subsidiary. This causes three problems for lenders:

- First the administrative burden of compliance (the information required is extensive and regular);
- Second how to reconcile this with bank confidentiality laws in many of the countries in which they are operating; and
- Third, uncertainty as to which payments are affected.

Confidentiality

6.031 On the issue of confidentiality, a number of countries have entered into intergovernmental agreements with the US (referred to as 'IGAs') which are designed to enable financial institutions in those countries to receive US source income in full, without the deduction, and without breaching local bank confidentiality laws. The UK version of this agreement requires financial institutions in the UK (and UK branches of financial institutions elsewhere) to provide the requisite information to the UK tax authorities (which will then pass it on to the US), and, provided they do so, they will be treated as being 'FATCA compliant'. It is anticipated that many countries will enter into intergovernmental agreements with the US along similar lines.

Which payments are affected?

6.032 On the issue of uncertainty as to which payments will be affected, the difficulty arises because of the concept of 'passthru payments' including 'foreign passthru payments' which FATCA has introduced. The concept of foreign passthru payments will not come into effect until 2017 if at all, but it has caused concern partly because the concept is vague – covering foreign

---

[9] More information on the regulations is available from the US tax authorities website at www.irs.gov.

(i.e. non-US) payments to the extent they are 'attributable' to US source payments. There are two facts which make this issue of foreign passthru payments less problematic than originally feared.

First, the UK intergovernmental agreement (which is an example of a 'Model 1' agreement) provides that the obligation to withhold on 'foreign passthru payments' will not apply to those institutions which are deemed to be FATCA compliant as a result of the IGA. Similar provisions will apply in other countries which adopt a Model 1 Intergovernmental agreement. See Box 6.10.

> **Box 6.10**
> It is worth noting that there is another model of intergovernmental agreement, referred to as 'Model 2'. Under this model, the financial institution deals direct with the US tax authorities and is not relieved of its obligation to withhold on 'Foreign passthru payments', but the financial institution does agree only to accept new accounts which consent to disclosure.

Second, the rules on foreign passthru payments will not come into effect until 2017 at the earliest, and obligations in existence before the date falling six months after the date of publication of the regulations will not be affected.

What FATCA provisions are needed?

6.033 Turning then to the loan agreement – the question is – how should FATCA withholding be dealt with? FATCA risk arises if there is US source income and may arise under the foreign passthru payments concept if there is an FFI in the borrower group and that FFI is not in a country with a Model 1 Intergovernmental agreement.

Within the US, market practice is that the borrower does not bear FATCA risk as FATCA compliance is not within the control of the borrower. Outside the US the position is less clear-cut. This is mostly because when FATCA was first introduced, compliance was also outside the control of many lenders – they simply could not comply as things stood because of bank secrecy laws. Now that the intergovernmental agreements have removed this obstacle in many countries, market practice in Europe has also settled into the position that the borrower does not bear FATCA risk, because it is hard to see why borrowers should bear the burden of the failure of banks to comply with their Model 1 IGA obligations, or the cost of decisions made by the banks in other countries as to whether to comply with FATCA or not.

6.034 If there is no FFI in the borrower group and the income is not US source income then FATCA should not arise.[10] The LMA originally provided a

---

[10] More information on FATCA and its implications for loan agreements is available from the website of the Association of Corporate Treasurers at www.treasurers.org.

number of riders, with different options depending on the commercial agreement, and subsequently (in June 2014) incorporated borrower friendly FATCA provisions in their recommended form documents. The original riders may still be helpful in countries where FATCA compliance is illegal.

The FATCA provisions now included in the recommended forms assume that the Agent is in a country with a Model 1 IGA and provide that:

6.035

- All parties can make any FATCA withholding which is required and no party will be obliged to gross-up for that (nor will any claim be made under any of the general indemnities);
- Any information which needs to be disclosed in order to comply with FATCA may be disclosed; and
- The Agent may be replaced if there is a risk that payments to it may be subject to a FATCA withholding.

CLAUSE 14: INCREASED COSTS – SECTION 1 – INTRODUCTION

As mentioned in the Introduction, Euro currency loan agreements have always provided that any change in regulation which increases the lenders' costs or reduces their profits, must be compensated for by the borrower. The regulations which are most likely to result in a claim under this Clause are Basel II and Basel III,[11] so we start with a very brief description of these regulations.

6.036

BASEL II

Basel II is the capital adequacy regime agreed in 2004. One main purpose of Basel II was to make the regulatory requirements for capital reflect market perception of risk more accurately than was the case under Basel I. The previous system was recognized as a blunt instrument that required more capital than generally thought necessary for some risks and less than necessary for others. The Basel II system relies on three elements (known as the three 'pillars').

6.037

Pillar 1 is similar to Basel I rules in that it requires banks' capital to be at least 8% of risk-weighted assets but operating risk (the risk of mistakes and wrongdoing) was added to the risks to be taken into account, in addition to credit risk and market risk included under Basel I. In measuring credit

---

[11] It should be noted that 'Basel III' is not a single set of rules but comprises a number of documents issued by the Basel Committee on Banking Supervision, which, in the EU, was implemented into law via the Fourth Capital Requirements Directive and the Capital Requirements Regulation ('CRD IV') in July 2013. Some parts of Basel III take effect as amendments to Basel II. Therefore if the intention is to exclude Basel II costs but allow Basel III costs, careful drafting is needed to ensure the exclusion does not go too far. The LMA publishes appropriate wording in the footnotes to this clause.

risk, banks were also given an option to use their own internal methods of risk assessment as the basis of the weighting.

Pillar 2 of the Basel II framework allowed national regulators the discretion to adjust the requirements of Pillar 1 to reflect the different track record of different banks in recovering losses.

Pillar 3 required greater disclosure of the risks to banks' profitability so as to expose them to the discipline of market reaction.

BASEL III

6.038 Shortly after Basel II became effective the financial crisis of 2007–2008 hit. The sudden demise of Northern Rock in England highlighted the dangers of the model they used, of funding themselves mostly in the London interbank markets. It was clear that the existing bank regulatory framework was not sufficiently robust and in particular, that liquidity risks were not sufficiently regulated.

Basel III ensued. It contains a number of new provisions including the 'Net Stable Funding Ratio' and the 'Liquidity Coverage Ratio', as well as requiring affected banks to maintain countercyclical buffers (putting funds aside in good times which can be used to absorb losses in difficult times) and capital conservation buffers (which will be imposed if a bank is in difficulty, so as to prevent payment of dividends) and imposing more stringent rules on what counts as capital for the purpose of the existing capital adequacy rules. It also introduced a new leverage ratio which compares the bank's assets (without any risk weighting) to its Tier 1 capital (essentially, the core capital).

It is worth focusing a little on the two new funding and liquidity ratios, as these have had a significant effect on banks' funding models.

Net Stable Funding Ratio

6.039 The net stable funding ratio requires banks to ensure they have a sufficiently stable mix of funding sources to fund the types of assets they have invested in. So for example, if the bank kept all its funds in cash, there would be no restrictions on its funding sources because, (unlike long-term loans to customers) cash can be liquidated easily, so if the bank's funding disappeared, the bank could simply use its cash to repay the funding. Clearly banks do not keep all their assets in cash, so the amount of stable funding required will depend on the bank's particular mix of assets, with long-term loans to customers requiring more stable funding than say, stocks and shares. Different sources of funds for the bank are then treated differently, for the purposes of the ratio, depending on how 'stable' that funding source is deemed to be. So for example, deposits from the public are treated as relatively stable, while funding in the London Interbank market is less stable.

Equity is treated as about twice as stable as funding in the interbank markets. So, if banks relied only on the interbank markets, they would need twice as much funding to meet this ratio as if they used shareholders' funds.

Liquidity Coverage Ratio

The second ratio which is of interest for our purposes is the liquidity coverage ratio which requires the bank to keep sufficient high quality liquid assets to see it through periods of stress. This ratio looks at how much of the bank's funding would be expected to flow out during a crisis (again, with funding in the interbank markets being expected to flow out faster than customer deposits) and then requires the bank to have sufficient high quality liquid assets, such as bonds and gilts, to cover that outflow. So again, funding in the interbank markets will require the banks to maintain a higher level of liquid assets, compared to funding from customer deposits.

6.040

These two new ratios are therefore a powerful incentive to lenders to reduce the proportion of their funds raised in the interbank markets.

CLAUSE 14: INCREASED COSTS – SECTION 2 – THE CLAUSE

14.1 Increased costs

The increased costs clause reads as follows

> (a) *Subject to Clause 14.3 (Exceptions) the Company shall, within three Business Days of a demand by the Agent, pay for the account of a Finance Party the amount of any Increased Costs incurred by that Finance Party or any of its Affiliates as a result of (i) the introduction of or any change in (or in the interpretation, administration or application of) any law or regulation or (ii) compliance with any law or regulation made after the date of this Agreement.*

6.041

Clause 14.1 is one of the 'yield protection' clauses in a LIBOR-based loan designed to ensure that the lenders pass on to the borrower all their costs attributable to the loan and recover a pre-agreed level of pre-tax profit (the Margin) on top of their costs incurred in providing the loan. The main costs which a lender incurs in providing a loan are its funding cost (assumed to be LIBOR for the purpose of the loan agreement) and the cost of complying with the capital adequacy and liquidity requirements applicable to the loan. The document then treats existing (known) costs differently from future (changed) costs.

- Generally lenders are expected to fix their Margin at a rate that covers them for the cost of complying with *existing capital adequacy and liquidity requirements*.[12]

---

[12] See 0.091 onwards.

- The practice differs in relation to *existing regulatory fees*.[13] The LMA Term Loan optionally provides for the borrower to pay the Mandatory Costs in addition to LIBOR plus Margin (see 5.002).
- Clause 14.1 deals with the possibility of a regulatory *change*, after the date of signing, in these capital adequacy, liquidity and regulatory costs and of any other costs, and passes these on to the borrower (which also has the right to prepay affected lenders under clause 8.5).

Under this clause the borrower agrees to compensate the lenders for any additional costs or lost profits (for any lender or any member of a lender's group of companies) attributable to the loan, resulting from changes in the regulatory[14] environment. The clause applies to increased costs arising as a result of regulations made after the loan agreement is signed and also as a result of existing regulations where a change occurs (such as a change in interpretation or a compliance date) after the loan agreement is signed.

6.042 In relation to Basel II, arguably, this can now be ignored since the regulations are already in place in most jurisdictions (and the clause only covers changes in 'regulations'). However, given that the clause also covers changes in the 'application' of regulations, it may be sensible to exclude Basel II specifically, to ensure that issues such as changes in facts or changes in lenders' internal risk assessment procedures cannot trigger a claim.

6.043 As for Basel III, once again, the regulations are now in place – the CRD IV package[15] which transposes – via a Regulation and a Directive – the Basel III standards on bank capital into the EU legal framework entered into force in July 2013. So there is no change of regulation.

However, the increased costs clause extends beyond introduction of regulations, extending also to change in the 'application' of a regulation. Basel III is unusual in that it is being implemented over a long timeframe and with the details (such as how stable different types of moneys are treated as being for the purpose of the net stable funding ratio) being adjusted along the way. For example, the leverage ratio, although finalized in early 2014, is subject to adjustment and 'calibration' which is not expected to be completed until 2017. Therefore during the interim period it is impossible for lenders to gauge costs of compliance precisely and they will wish to retain the ability to pass on changes in anticipated Basel III costs under this clause at least until Basel III is fully settled in its details.

Many lenders will therefore want to specifically clarify that they have the right under this clause to pass on costs arising from any changes in the details of Basel III from the details currently published, and to specifically clarify that

---

[13] See 0.091 onwards.

[14] The word 'regulation' in this context needs to be read in the light of clause 1.2(a)(vii) discussed at 1.063.

[15] The fourth Capital Requirements Directive (Directive 2013/36/EU) and the Capital Requirements Regulation (Regulation 575/2013).

they are entitled to make claims resulting from Basel III even if there is no change in regulation. A common solution is to limit recoverable costs to those which are not reasonably foreseeable at the time the agreement is signed

The situation in relation to Basel II and III leads to a lack of transparency for borrowers who cannot be clear on what assumptions about Basel III have been built into the pricing and what aspects might result in an additional claim under this clause. Nevertheless, the clause may prove difficult for lenders to implement in relation to Basel III for two reasons. 6.044

- the lenders will only be able to claim compensation from the borrower if the additional cost results from the introduction of Basel III or any part of it, or from a change in its operation or application. Proving this causation may be difficult – what changes in the bank's funding structure or capital base have been made as a result of the new regulations, and what changes happened as a result of prudent banking practice?
- the clause only allows lenders to pass on those additional costs or lost profits which are attributable to this loan – but in many cases it would be hard to allocate costs to particular loans.

This clause will, of course, not be appropriate in a loan agreement based on an inclusive rate of interest such as the base rate or prime rate. It is also not always appropriate in a LIBOR-based loan – in certain more complex transactions where allocation of *all* risks needs to be agreed it may be appropriate for the lenders to take the risks of future regulatory change or perhaps of regulatory change in a given jurisdiction. 6.045

Clause 14.2   Increased cost claims

Clause 14.2 provides for the affected lender to notify the Agent, which will then notify the borrower, before making a claim. 6.046

Clause 14.3   Exceptions

The Increased Cost clause does not deal solely with capital adequacy rules: it compensates the lenders for any reduction in their anticipated profits resulting from a change in regulation. Clause 14.3 cuts back the scope of the clause to ensure that it does not compensate the lenders for ordinary tax on their profits (clause 14.3(a)(iii)), FATCA deductions, or for issues such as withholding tax and Mandatory Costs which are covered elsewhere in the agreement. 6.047

CLAUSE 15: INDEMNITIES

Clause 15.1   Currency indemnity

Clause 15.1 is the **judgement currency indemnity**. This deals with the situation which may arise if, in order to make a claim against the borrower 6.048

or any of its assets in a particular country, the claim needs to be denominated in the local currency. In this event, the final judgement will be for an amount which, when converted back to the currency of the debt, will give a profit or a loss. This clause provides for the borrower to indemnify the lenders for any loss in this situation. This provision may not be enforceable in some countries and is an area for due diligence.

Clause 15.2 Other indemnities

6.049   Clause 15.2 is a general indemnity to the lenders in respect of the occurrence of any Event of Default and in respect of funding costs. This indemnity applies whether or not the lenders exercise their right to accelerate. Note also that clause 15.3 indemnifies the Agent for expenses incurred in investigating a Default. Clause 15.3(d) also indemnifies the Agent for the cost of instructing professional advisers, even where there is no Default.

6.050   *Comment* Borrowers may want to restrict their obligations to pay for the Agent's professional advice contained in 15.3(d) so as to only apply where the Agent reasonably believes that there is a Default or where the borrower has requested a waiver or amendment.

CLAUSE 16: MITIGATION

6.051   To some extent, the increased cost clause is a blank cheque in favour of the lenders – the borrower cannot be clear in advance as to how much it may become liable to pay under the clause. Its effect is mitigated by this clause 16.1 (and, of course, by the borrower's right to prepay the lender in question in these circumstances[16]).

Under clause 16.1 the lenders agree to try to minimize any additional costs to the borrower under the illegality, gross-up and increased costs clauses and under the provisions dealing with Mandatory Costs. They need not, however, take steps which, in their opinion acting reasonably, might be prejudicial to them. One possible way of mitigating these additional costs and other difficulties might, in certain circumstances, be to lend through a different branch.[17]

CLAUSE 17: COSTS AND EXPENSES

6.052   Clause 17 deals with costs of putting the transaction together, costs of amendments, and costs of enforcement. In the first two cases, the borrower pays only the costs of the Agent and the Arranger, while in the case of enforcement expenses, the expenses of all lenders are to be covered. At the

---
[16] See commentary on clause 8.5 at 4.023.
[17] See commentary on clause 24.2(f) at 9.046.

enforcement stage, lenders may well wish to have independent advice and even to take independent action;[18] whereas at the transaction stage, lenders are largely content to rely on the advice given to the Agent supplemented by the individual participant lenders' in-house lawyer's views, since, at this point, the interests of all the lenders are (almost) identical. This is often not the case on enforcement.

A number of comments may be made on this clause.

Comment   Commonly borrowers ask for a **cap** on transaction expenses. It is unlikely that lenders would agree to any such cap or other restriction in relation to enforcement expenses in most cases. However, perhaps in a workout loan, a borrower may argue that they should only pay the expenses of the Agent in relation to any enforcement. The argument would be that the risk of multiple actions by different lenders could be reduced if only the Agent's legal expenses were covered, and that this would effectively help protect all parties from 'rogue lenders'. **6.053**

Comment   In relation to clause 17.2 lenders may argue that all lenders' expenses should be covered, not just the Agent's as they may wish to be advised separately from the other lenders. On the other hand the borrower may want to delete clause 17.2 entirely to prevent unnecessary reference to lawyers. **6.054**

Comment   The requirement in clause 17.1 is to pay 'promptly'; while in most other cases (including clauses 17.2 and 17.3) payment is required within three Business Days of demand. A borrower may wish to clarify the timing of the obligation in clause 17.1 to ensure they have a reasonable period to consider, and if appropriate, challenge any particular expense before default interest starts to be chargeable. Lenders may also prefer greater certainty on the timing of this obligation. **6.055**

---

[18] See commentary on clause 2.2 at 2.006 onwards.

PART II
GUARANTEE, REPRESENTATIONS, UNDERTAKINGS AND EVENTS OF DEFAULT

This Part deals with the guarantee (if there is one, and if it is included in the loan agreement); representations; undertakings; and Events of Default. These provisions are in clauses 18–23 of the LMA Term Loan. This is the part of the agreement that regulates the working relationship between the lenders and the borrower, and hence is often the most heavily negotiated part of the document.

7 Guarantee

CLAUSE 18: GUARANTEE AND INDEMNITY

Clause 18.1 Guarantee and indemnity[1]

The guarantee itself is contained in three separate provisions. First comes Clause 18.1(a) which reads as follows

> Each Guarantor irrevocably and unconditionally jointly and severally:[2]
>
> (a) guarantees to each Finance Party punctual performance by each Borrower of all that Borrower's obligations under the Finance Documents;

7.001

This paragraph (a) is sometimes referred to as a 'see to it' guarantee. It is a promise that each borrower will fulfil its obligations. If the borrower fails to fulfil its obligations, the guarantor is immediately in breach of this 'see to it' promise and will be liable in damages. A **guarantee** may be an 'all moneys' guarantee – guaranteeing whatever the borrower owes the lenders from time to time; or it may relate to a specific transaction. In the context of major financings, all moneys guarantees are unusual.

Next comes clause Clause 18.1(b) which reads:

> (b) undertakes with each Finance Party that whenever a Borrower does not pay any amount when due under or in connection with any Finance Document, that Guarantor shall immediately on demand pay that amount as if it was the principal Obligor; and

7.002

This paragraph (b) is a conditional payment obligation. It is a promise to pay if the underlying debtor fails to pay. This gives the beneficiary of the guarantee a claim in debt against the guarantor (as opposed to the claim in damages under paragraph (a))

---

[1] See A1.071 onwards for a brief commentary on some important aspects of English law on guarantees.
[2] See A1.016.

The third part of the guarantee clause is Clause 18.1 (c) which reads

7.003

(c) *agrees with each Finance Party that if any obligation guaranteed by it is or becomes unenforceable, invalid or illegal, it will, as an independent and primary obligation, indemnify that Finance Party immediately on demand against any cost, loss or liability it incurs as a result of a Borrower not paying any amount which would, but for such unenforceability, invalidity or illegality, have been payable by it under any Finance Document on the date when it would have been due. The amount payable by a Guarantor under this indemnity will not exceed the amount it would have had to pay under this Clause 18 if the amount had been recoverable on the basis of a guarantee.*

Clause 18.1(c) constitutes a primary obligation[3] on the guarantor to pay sums expressed to be due under the loan agreement if unpaid by the borrower. The intention is to ensure that any difficulties with the underlying debt (e.g. invalidity, illegality, or release by variation) do not affect the guarantor's liability.[4]

Clause 18.2   Continuing guarantee[5]

7.004

This guarantee is a continuing guarantee and will extend to the ultimate balance of sums payable by any Obligor under the Finance Documents, regardless of any intermediate payment or discharge in whole or in part.

Clause 18.2 is particularly important in a revolving credit, but is often also necessary in a term loan if, for example in a multicurrency loan, it is treated as being repaid in full and re-advanced from time to time.[6] The intention is to clarify that the guarantee relates not only to the original loan (which may well have been repaid[7]) but also to the re-advanced loans from time to time. The clause is also useful even in a single currency term loan, in order to clarify that the guarantee is not limited to moneys advanced at the start of the transaction but also includes future moneys under the loan such as interest and indemnities.

Clause 18.3   Reinstatement

7.005

If any discharge, release or arrangement (whether in respect of the obligations of any Obligor or any security for those obligations or otherwise) is made by a Finance

---

[3] See A1.074.
[4] In McGuinness v Norwich and Peterborough Building Society [2010] EWHC 2989 (Ch); the court held that a single guarantee could create different rights for the beneficiary with one clause giving rise to a claim in damages and another giving rise to a separate (and more valuable) claim in debt.
[5] See A1.078.
[6] See comments on clause 6.3 at 3.019.
[7] Or treated as repaid by virtue of the rule in Clayton's case (Devagnes v Noble 1816 1 Mer 572).

Party in whole or in part on the basis of any payment, security or other disposition which is avoided or must be restored in insolvency, liquidation, administration or otherwise, without limitation, then the liability of each Guarantor under this Clause 18 will continue or be reinstated as if the discharge, release or arrangement had not occurred.

Clause 18.3 deals with the possibility of clawbacks. Most jurisdictions allow for certain transactions[8] which a company has entered into, to be 'clawed back' or reversed, if the company becomes insolvent within a certain period (commonly referred to as the 'hardening period' or the 'suspect period') after the transaction occurred, subject to various criteria. Clause 18.3 provides that if the loan is repaid, but the lenders subsequently have to reimburse that payment because it is clawed back in an insolvency, the liability of the borrowers and guarantors shall remain in place as though there had been no repayment of the loan in the first place.

Comment This issue is not too contentious in an unsecured guarantee. However, if the guarantor has given security for their guarantee obligations, and that security had been discharged on repayment of the loan, such a provision would not be effective to reinstate the security. Therefore, secured guarantees often allow the lenders to retain the security for a period (matching the longest hardening period) after repayment of the loan. This, of course, can be commercially difficult for a guarantor. They are likely to want to be sure that, when the loan is repaid, any security they have given for the guarantee will be released. Any right to retain the security may have the effect of preventing a refinancing (see Box 7.1).

7.006

Box 7.1
It can be hard to find a compromise between the position of the lenders and the guarantor on this point. Ideally, the likelihood of a clawback occurring might need to be assessed and, if the lenders perceive this as a real risk, provisions may need to be included in the original documents to the effect that security will only be released if evidence is provided, at the time of the repayment and requested release of the security for the guarantee, that there is no risk of clawback given the law in relevant jurisdictions (e.g. because the person making payment of the loan is not insolvent therefore no question of clawback arises).[9]

---

[8] Under English law, these include preferences, transactions at an undervalue and floating charges. In some countries, set offs exercised shortly before winding up may also be clawed back.
[9] This clearly depends on the relevant jurisdiction of potential insolvency. If proof of solvency is a solution, it should not be sought lightly. It would be time consuming and expensive on any given date to prove solvency.

Clause 18.4 Waiver of defences

7.007 Clause 18.4 is designed to ensure that acts or omissions which might otherwise discharge the guarantee or reduce the amount of the lenders' claim under it do not have that effect. It states that the guarantee will remain effective despite any amendments or waivers granted by the lenders, despite any release of security held by the lenders and despite any failure to enforce other rights or any problems with the borrowers' authorization of the loan.

Clause 18.4(e) states that the guarantee shall remain valid despite

> (e) any amendment, novation, supplement, extension, restatement (however fundamental and whether or not more onerous) or replacement of a Finance Document or any other document or security including without limitation any change in the purpose of, any extension of or increase in any facility or the addition of any new facility under any Finance Document or other document or security;

7.008 *Comment* This clause 18.4(e) provides that the guarantee will extend to increases in the facility, new facilities and more onerous obligations assumed by the borrower without the need for the guarantor to give its consent to those changes. The wording of this clause results from the series of cases on amendments discussed in Box 7.3 on page 147 and is intended to avoid the need to obtain guarantor's consent even for significant variations. Even though in practice lenders remain likely to request guarantor consent to significant amendments, because of the legal uncertainties in this area, guarantors may wish to restrict paragraph (e) so as to only give pre-approval of changes which are not more onerous and are not for a different purpose than the original loan.

7.009 Under English law, guarantors can raise numerous defences to a claim under the guarantee. The rationale for most of these defences comes from the guarantor's right of **subrogation**. This is the right of the guarantor, when they have paid under the guarantee, to stand in the shoes of the lenders and take over their rights against the borrower. If lenders alter their rights and thereby change the rights which the guarantor will obtain through subrogation, in certain cases, unless the guarantor has agreed otherwise, this will be a good defence for the guarantor to a claim for payment under the guarantee. In some cases it will completely release the guarantor from liability, while in others it will reduce their liability (see Box 7.2 on page 147).

7.010 This is the reason for clause 18.4, which provides that the guarantors' liability will remain unaffected. In practice and as a matter of risk avoidance, lenders should not rely on this clause to be effective. There is always a risk that, on the facts of the case, what has happened is construed as not falling within the clause (e.g. a variation of the loan may be held to be so substantial as to result in a new loan, not the subject of the original guarantee. See Box 7.3). Therefore, in practice, whenever amending a guaranteed loan (or one where any party other than the borrower has given security, where the same principles apply) consent of the guarantor and third party security providers should be sought, together with their written confirmation, before the change is made, that the guarantee and security will remain effective following the change.

Box 7.2

Cases include where

- the lenders give time to pay;[10]
- the lenders alter or release their rights against, or any security given by, the debtor;[11]
- the lenders negligently fail to protect the value of their security, for example, by non-registration;[12]
- the loan terms are amended (see Box 7.3)
- the lenders sell their security without taking proper care to obtain the current market value.[13]

Box 7.3

There have been a number of cases on the effect of these clauses where the guaranteed obligation is amended. The basic principle (absent these clauses) was set out in Holme v Brunskill (1877) 3 QBD 495. That case held that amendments to the guaranteed debt would discharge the guarantee unless the guarantor consented to the variation or the variation is patently insubstantial. A later case[14] held that a clause consenting to future amendments of the guaranteed debt would be effective to allow changes as long as those changes did not amount to a replacement debt and as long as the amended agreement was within the general scope of the original contract. Unsurprisingly, there have been a number of cases[15] on what amounts to a variation, and what is a new loan. Each case is decided on its facts, so, if in doubt, the sensible approach remains to obtain the written approval of the guarantor before effecting amendments.

---

[10] Associated British Ports v Ferryways NV & anor (2009) EWCA Civ 189.
[11] Polak v Everett (1875–76) LR 1 QB 669 and Holme v Brunskill (1877–78) LR 3 QBD 495.
[12] Wulff v Jay (1871–72) LR 7 QB 756.
[13] Although (in the absence of bad faith) there is no positive duty to maximize the price obtained. See comments in China & South Seas Bank Ltd. v Tan (1990) 1 AC 536.
[14] Triodos Bank v Dobbs (2005) EWCA Civ 630.
[15] See for example North Shore Ventures Ltd v Anstead Holdings (2011) EWCA Civ 230; Bank of Scotland Plc v Constantine Makris and Ben O'Sullivan (2009) EWHC 3869; Aviva Insurance Ltd v Hackney Empire Ltd (2012) EWCA Civ 1716; and Close Brothers Ltd v Ridsdale (2012) EWHC 3090.

Clause 18.5 Immediate recourse

7.011 Clause 18.5 allows the lenders to claim against the guarantor without first having to take action against any other party. It is, in any event, the case under English law that claims against a borrower do not need to be exhausted before a claim can be made on a guarantor,[16] but this express clause clarifies that position.

Clause 18.6 Appropriations

7.012 Clause 18.6(a) allows the lenders to apply all proceeds they have available for the loan in whatever order they choose. This freedom can significantly affect recoveries.

7.013 Clause 18.6(b) allows the lenders to recover money from the guarantor and not apply it in reduction of the debt. Instead the money can be placed in an interest bearing account, allowing the lenders to claim in the insolvency of the borrower for the full debt and only apply the guarantee proceeds after the winding up has been completed. This will benefit the lender if the payment from the guarantor is less than the debt outstanding. In those circumstances, after payment under the guarantee, the lender is left with a claim against the borrower. The ability to put the guarantee payment in a suspense account increases the amount the lenders can claim for in an insolvency, which, in turn, increases their recovery in the insolvency.

Clause 18.7 Deferral of guarantors' rights

7.014 Clause 18.7 provides that the guarantor will not exercise its rights of subrogation and reimbursement until the lenders have been paid in full because lenders do not wish to have to share their security, or face competing claims with the guarantor in the insolvency of the borrower, or of any other guarantor, if the lenders have not been paid in full.

7.015 There are three separate rights that are being deferred here:

- first, the right of subrogation;
- second, the right of reimbursement (including its enforcement rights such as set off and insolvency proof in relation to the right of reimbursement); and
- third, the right of contribution from other guarantors (again, including enforcement rights).

---

[16] The Court of Appeal confirmed in White v Davenham Trust Ltd (2011) EWCA Civ 747, that a beneficiary can enforce a guarantee even where they have security for the same loan from the principal debtor.

Lenders are concerned to ensure that, until they are repaid, guarantors do not compete with them, whether in the insolvency of the borrower or in the insolvency of other guarantors, to the extent that guarantors have a claim in any insolvency arising by virtue of payment under the guarantee. See Box 7.4.

7.016

> **Box 7.4**
> The effectiveness of clauses deferring the right of reimbursement and non-competition clauses was considered in a number of cases between 2009 and 2011.[17] Such clauses have been upheld as not being contrary to public policy.[18] For a while there were concerns that the wording at the time did not go far enough and left the guarantor able to exercise rights under a rather obscure legal rule known as the rule in Cherry v Boultbee.[19] As a result, the LMA added paragraphs (d) onwards to the clause to try to clarify that that rule was also being excluded. The conclusion of the cases was that as long as the guarantee is of the whole loan, the guarantor would not be entitled to claim in the insolvency under the rule in Cherry v Boultbee anyway,[20] even without the clauses. Nevertheless the practice is to retain the clauses, and this is particularly important in the case of partial guarantees.

Subordination

Some guarantees go considerably further than clause 18.7. An example follows (Box 7.5).

7.017

> **Box 7.5**
> *Until all the Guaranteed Liabilities have been paid, discharged or satisfied in full ... the Guarantor agrees that it will not*
> *a) exercise its rights of subrogation, reimbursement and indemnity against any Obligor;*
> *b) demand or accept repayment in whole or in part of any Indebtedness due to the Guarantor from any Obligor ...;*
> *c) claim any set off or counterclaim against any Obligor or prove in competition with the Lender in the liquidation of any Obligor ... but so that, if so directed by the Lender, it will prove for the whole or part of its claim in such liquidation and hold all recoveries in trust for the Lender.*

---

[17] Mills and others v HSBC Trustee (C.I) Ltd and others [2009] EWHC 3377 (Ch).
[18] See Re SSSL Realisations (2002) Ltd [2006] EWCA Civ 7.
[19] See Cherry v Boultbee (1839) 4 My & Cr 442.
[20] See Cattles plc v Welcome Financial Services and others [2009] EWHC 3027 (Ch).

Subordination before winding up

7.018 In this (not uncommon) example, the guarantor is being asked to agree to make *no claim whatsoever* against the borrower (or any other guarantor) until the loan is repaid. All sums due to the guarantor from time to time are being subordinated to the loan. This clearly depends on the commercial position and what cashflows exist within the group. In many cases the guarantor and borrower (and other Obligors) have trading relationships which require inter-company payments to be made and should not therefore agree to such a broad subordination. It may well be that free flow of moneys between the debtor and the guarantor should be permitted prior to winding up.

Subordination on winding up

7.019 A separate issue is subordination on a winding up. This is achieved by clause (c) in the example. This prohibits the guarantor from putting in a claim in the insolvency of the borrower (or other Obligor such as a co-guarantor) in competition with the lenders. Alternatively, if the lenders direct, they may require the guarantor to claim in the insolvency and hold the proceeds on trust for the lenders. The argument for inclusion of this provision is that the guarantor should be supporting the borrower and not doing anything that would reduce the lenders' recovery. If the guarantor does not claim in insolvency, or holds its claim in trust for the lenders, the lenders' recovery will be greater.

7.020 Guarantors should be wary of agreeing such a clause. The difficulty is that the guarantor cannot agree two such clauses in different guarantees with different lenders to the same borrower. One lender may direct them to make no claim in the insolvency while the other directs them to claim and hold the claim in trust for them. The guarantor cannot comply with both directions. In most cases therefore, the agreement of the guarantor not to claim in the insolvency either of the borrower or of any other Obligor should apply only (as in the LMA Term Loan) to any claim which the guarantor has which arises from payment under the guarantee in question.

Interest[21]

7.021 When moneys have been paid under the guarantee and not applied against the debt (in accordance with clause 18.6(b)) the guarantee should provide for that money to be placed in an interest bearing account (see Box 7.6 on page 151).

---

[21] See *The Modern Contract of Guarantee*, 2nd English edition 2010, at 5–75 onwards.

Box 7.6
Some guarantors, where the amounts at stake are high, may wish to specify in the guarantee that where moneys are placed on deposit as envisaged by clause 18.6(b), any additional claim for interest accruing under the loan will be limited to an amount equal to the interest accruing on the suspense account. This would be most likely to be an issue in cases where a guarantor provides a guarantee for less than the full amount of the loan. If the guarantor guarantees the whole loan, the suspense account issue will not arise since, assuming the guarantor pays in full, there will be no need for money to be applied otherwise than in immediate satisfaction of the debt.

8 Representations, Undertakings and Events of Default

CLAUSE 19: REPRESENTATIONS – SECTION 1 – AN INTRODUCTION

1 Purpose

8.001   The loan agreement contains representations which are required to be made on the date of the agreement. It also often contains representations which are required to be made on other dates (typically, on each drawing and on the first day of each Interest Period). The purpose of the representations is:

- in the case of representations required to be made on the date of the agreement, to trigger disclosure of information; and
- in all cases, to give the lenders the contractual right not to advance additional monies (i.e. to act as a drawstop) and/or to accelerate the loan if the specified statements are untrue on the date they are made.

There may also be liability in misrepresentation (as opposed to liability in contract) for the borrower if the statement is untrue.

We look at each of these functions of the representations in more detail here.

Disclosure

8.002   The representations form a checklist of basic propositions which the lenders expect to be true. The borrower and their lawyer, in commenting on the draft agreement, will read through the representations and disclose further information on any which are not accurate. They form part of the three sets of checks which the lenders make before advancing the loan (representations, due diligence and conditions precedent[1]).

Drawstop/acceleration

8.003   The representations ensure that the lenders have a remedy against the borrower (drawstop and/or **acceleration**) if any of the stated facts are

---

[1] See commentary on clause 4.1 at 2.015.

untrue when the representation was made. They ensure that it is the borrower, not the lenders, who take the risk of any of them being untrue on that date (see Box 8.1).

> **Box 8.1**
> Take, for example, the representation at clause 19.12 which states:
>
> *Its payment obligations under the Finance Documents rank at least pari passu with the claims of all its other unsecured and unsubordinated creditors, except for obligations mandatorily preferred by law applying to companies generally.*
>
> The borrower may not know whether this statement is true or not, and may object to being asked to make it, on the grounds that it is not something which the borrower should be expected to know and, in any event, the lenders should rely on advice from their lawyers on this point.[2] Nevertheless, in most cases, the representation should usually be retained to ensure that, if the statement is not true and the loan does not rank pari passu, the lenders have the right not to advance the funds. Similarly the lender would not want this representation qualified with reference to the borrower's belief. What matters is not the state of the borrower's knowledge, but rather, what remedy the lender has if the statement is untrue.

8.004 It is therefore important to focus on the risk allocation role of the representations in any negotiation of them, and to focus on the question 'Should the lenders have the right not to advance the loan if this statement is not true?'(i.e. who should take the risk of the statement being untrue?) and not on the question 'Is it reasonable to ask the borrower to represent that?' (see Box 8.2 on page 154). Sometimes borrowers' lawyers object to this because of their client's potential liability for misrepresentation. In practice this ought not to be a concern for two reasons. First, as noted shortly, lenders are rarely interested in suing borrowers for misrepresentation – they simply want to rely on their contractual right to be repaid. Second, in order to have a claim in misrepresentation (certainly under English law, at least), the lender needs to have relied on the representation which they will not have done in those circumstances where the borrower is making this argument.

Nevertheless, sometimes borrowers' lawyers remain uncomfortable with the concept of representations being used for risk allocation. In this case an alternative approach is to recast the issue in question as an Event of Default. So, for example, if the borrower is uncomfortable with making the pari passu representation, an alternative, which would avoid the borrower having potential liability for misrepresentation, would be to recast it as an

---

[2] There are a number of other clauses in relation to which a similar point could be made, including clause 19.6 (Governing law) and 19.8 (no filing), leading some borrowers to make a broad objection that they should not be required to make representations on matters of law.

Event of Default. The disadvantage of this alternative approach is that it is more cumbersome and involves more drafting, so that it is more expensive in terms of legal fees.

> **Box 8.2**
> The answer to the question of who should take the risk of a particular representation being untrue will depend (as always) on the nature of the transaction. In straightforward situations, the borrower is expected to take all risks including the risk that the initial legal situation is not as it had been expected. In complex cases, for example where the transaction is structured to take advantage of particular tax, accounting, or regulatory rules in different jurisdictions, it is not necessarily the case that the borrower should take risks relating to the existing or future legal position. In these cases certain representations on matters of law may need to be deleted to reflect the agreed risk allocation. See also the discussion at Box 8.8 on page 163.

Liability in misrepresentation

8.005 The contractual rights which the agreement contains (the right not to lend if any representation is untrue, and the right to demand early repayment of the loan) are in addition to the remedies for misrepresentation and breach of warranty given by English law (see Box 8.3).

> **Box 8.3**
> Under English law, a person may be liable if he makes an incorrect statement which another relies on and which induces that other to enter into a contract.[3] That statement may be written or verbal and liability may arise even if the person making the statement was simply negligent in doing so. So, statements made by the borrower during negotiation of the loan could give rise to subsequent liability for the borrower, independently of any claim under the loan agreement itself. The lender will need to show, among other things, that the lender relied on the representation in deciding to advance the funds.

8.006 The lenders may be able to make an independent claim for misrepresentation in relation to the representations contained in the agreement. However, in many cases there will be little point in doing so. If any of the representations are untrue, there will often be no need to make a claim in misrepresentation as the contractual remedies (acceleration, default interest and the **indemnity** in clause 15.2(a)) should normally be sufficient.

---

[3] See Goode, *Commercial Law*, 4th edn, 2009, p. 119 et seq.

The most likely circumstances in which these contractual claims will be insufficient is where, for some reason, they are unenforceable against the borrower. This may arise either because the entire agreement is not binding (e.g. because of a problem with due authorization of it), or because a particular provision (e.g. the provision for compound interest) is unenforceable. In these circumstances, the lenders may be tempted to make a claim in misrepresentation in relation to the borrower's statement that the agreement is valid and binding. In the circumstances where the problem arises in relation to a particular provision, as opposed to the agreement as a whole, this can be a useful additional remedy. However, if the problem relates to invalidity of the agreement as a whole, it is likely that, if the agreement is not validly authorized, neither is the representation. Additionally, of course, it is unlikely that the lenders will have relied on many of the representations. In many areas they will have done their own due diligence so that one of the requirements of a claim in misrepresentation is likely to be missing.

Hence, although it is possible that the representations could give rise to an independent claim in misrepresentation, in most cases this will be of little benefit.

2 Repetition of representations

Many loan agreements require certain of the representations to be repeated after the date of the agreement. This is usually required as a condition precedent to drawdown (clause 4.2(a)(ii) of the LMA Term Loan, often also confirmed in the drawdown notice itself) and at the beginning of Interest Periods (clause 19.14 of the LMA Term Loan). The LMA Term Loan also requires repetition as a condition to the addition of a new Obligor. 8.007

Introduction – purpose of repetition

Clause 19.14 reads as follows 8.008

> *The Repeating Representations are deemed to be made by each Obligor by reference to the facts and circumstances then existing on:*
>
> *(a) the date of each Utilisation Request and the first day of each Interest Period; and*
> *(b) in the case of an Additional Obligor, the day on which the company becomes (or it is proposed that the company becomes) an Additional Obligor.*

Clause 19.14 states that the 'Repeating Representations' are deemed repeated on (among other dates) the date of each new drawing and the first day of each Interest Period. The purpose of this is to ensure that, if any of the Repeating Representations become untrue, the lenders may refuse to advance new money and demand immediate repayment of moneys already advanced. The LMA Term Loan does not define 'Repeating Representations' and there may be much negotiation over which representations should fall into this category.

Hazards of repetition of representations

8.009 The effect of repeating representations is far reaching, particularly when considered in conjunction with other provisions of the agreement. The main problems which this simple clause creates are:

- it makes it hard to avoid inconsistencies in the document which will lead to uncertainty in its application; and
- it makes it difficult (particularly for the principals involved) to understand the precise implications of the document.

Given these drawbacks, the simplest solution, for the person reading the loan agreement, is to avoid repetition of representations (at least after the first drawdown) and to deal with the relevant issues by specific conditions precedent, undertakings, compulsory prepayment events, and events of default, as discussed in the summary to this introduction at 8.015. Nevertheless, it is often not possible, or worthwhile in terms of legal fees, to make such a change to the structure of the agreement, so all concerned need to be alive to the difficulties which repeating representations create and take extra care in reviewing these provisions. These main difficulties with repeating representations are therefore discussed in more detail here.

Inconsistencies

8.010 What the lenders want to achieve by the repetition is to ensure that if one of the specified representations is no longer true on one of the specified dates, then the lenders will be entitled to accelerate the loan. However, if a Repeating Representation covers a topic which is also covered by an undertaking or an Event of Default, any difference in the wording of the provisions will create uncertainty (see Box 8. 4 on page 157).

8.011 It is important to ensure that the agreement does not contain conflicting provisions. Some of the practical difficulties which such inconsistencies give rise to are:

- Neither party will be certain as to the real intention. Did the parties really intend, in the above example, to have the right to accelerate the loan even if the default in question clearly would not give rise to a material adverse effect?
- The Agent may feel that the inconsistency is unintentional and that there is simply a 'technical' Event of Default but not one which any of the lenders really intended to amount to a real Event of Default. However, if the Agent is to avoid potential liability for breach of **fiduciary duty**, it may need to advise the syndicate nevertheless and obtain instructions.

- As a result, unnecessary time and expense will be incurred in debating the issue.
- The need to obtain consent is something better avoided as, if circumstances have changed (including change in market conditions generally or change in lender's policies), the lenders may have incentives to withhold consent, or they may want to link consent to other issues.[4]
- The syndicate may be influenced by concerns about the reaction of other lenders to the borrower. Assuming that other loans include a cross default clause, other lenders will have the right to accelerate their loans as a result of the fact that the syndicate has the right to accelerate this loan (whether or not that right was included intentionally).

> **Box 8.4**
> An example may illuminate the problem. Assume that a loan agreement includes the following Event of Default:
>
> '[It is an Event of Default if] the Borrower defaults under any material contract by which it is bound and such default could reasonably be expected to have a Material Adverse Effect.'
>
> Assume the agreement also contains a representation, which is repeated on the first day of each Interest Period, as follows:
>
> 'The Borrower is not in default under any material agreement by which it is bound'
>
> Given that it is invariably expressed to be an Event of Default if a representation is untrue when made or repeated, the effect of repeating that particular representation would be to remove the Material Adverse Effect carve-out which had been negotiated into the Event of Default.
>   In practice, were the borrower to default under a material contract in circumstances where the result was unlikely to have a Material Adverse Effect the borrower would be likely to contest the right of the lenders to demand immediate repayment of the loan because the Event of Default and the repeating representation are in conflict.

8.012 The simplest way to avoid inconsistencies between the Repeating Representations and other parts of the agreement, and the problems which such inconsistencies cause, is to ensure that those representations which deal with issues which are commercially significant (e.g. default under other contracts, or litigation) are not repeated, but that the relevant issue is dealt with instead by the undertakings and events of default. This will usually result in those representations which relate to matters of law being the ones which will be repeated (see commentary on the individual representations from 8.021 onwards).

---

[4] See Box 0.5 on page 12.

8.013 However, in different markets where there is a significant cross-border element such as in structured or project finance, it may not always be appropriate that a change in law which results in representations becoming untrue should result in an Event of Default. It may be better for them to result in a positive obligation on some party (perhaps a lender) to seek necessary consents or licences to cure the problem, and, if not curable, it may result in compulsory prepayment. The simplest way to achieve these objectives is not to repeat the representations, but instead, to ensure that the undertakings, conditions precedent, events of default and compulsory prepayment events deal with all issues as necessary.

Comprehensibility

8.014 As might be apparent from the discussion on this topic, another difficulty with repeating representations is that it makes the document hard to understand (and to draft correctly). Extra care must be taken in reviewing the Repeating Representations and it is often not immediately obvious to the borrower what the effect of the repetition is. For example, will repeating a given representation detract from what has been discussed in relation to the Events of Default? Or will it result in a difference in relation to the opportunity which the borrower has to cure the problem? In the LMA Term Loan, the borrower has no ability to remedy an Event of Default which is triggered by a misrepresentation while it may be given the possibility of curing other events of default.[5]

Summary

8.015 If any representations are to be repeated on dates after the first advance of the loan, some guidelines may help to reduce the difficulties that this concept can give rise to. Some suggested guidelines (bearing in mind that there is no consensus on this issue) are:

- Whichever representations are to be repeated, they should be the same ones for the purpose of drawdown and for Interest Periods (see Box 8.5 on page 159).
- No representation should be repeated if it covers a topic which has been dealt with in the undertakings or the events of default, or if it deals with a commercially significant issue which should more appropriately be dealt with by the undertakings or events of default.
- A representation should not be repeated if the risk which that representation addresses should not fall on the borrower or should not constitute an Event of Default (e.g. if the risk of change of law should fall on the lender or if the relevant issue should give rise to a compulsory prepayment event instead of an Event of Default).
- Consider grace periods in relation to the misrepresentation Event of Default – see clause 23.4 at 8.225.

---

[5] See clause 23.4 at 8.225.

> **Box 8.5**
> Some argue that certain representations should be repeated in relation to new money advanced by the lender but not at any other time because the circumstances in which the lenders are relieved of their obligations to advance new money should be more stringent than the circumstances in which they are entitled to demand immediate repayment of moneys already advanced. This objective cannot be achieved by stating that Repeating Representations are only to be repeated on dates on which new drawings are to be made and not at any other time (e.g. by requiring repetition on drawdown dates but not on the first day of all Interest Periods). This is because, if on such repetition on a proposed drawdown date, the representation were to be untrue, it would result not only in a right not to advance additional money, but also in a right to accelerate the outstanding debt. A rather peculiar situation would result in which the lenders would be entitled to accelerate outstanding sums if certain circumstances (the facts specified in a Repeating Representation being untrue) happened to coincide with an attempted drawdown, but not if the same circumstances occurred at any other time.
>
> If lenders do want to draw a distinction between the obligation to advance additional funds and the right to accelerate existing moneys, this can be done by including a condition precedent that the Repeating Representations are true, but without actually requiring them to be repeated in clause 19.14.[6] However in many cases lenders will not want to find themselves in a position where they are not obliged to advance further funds but cannot demand repayment of sums already advanced. They will usually prefer to have a complete exit route if problems arise.
>
> For this reason it is unusual[7] to draw a distinction between the representations which are required to be true for the purpose of the lenders' obligation to advance funds and those which are required to be true for the purpose of giving rise to their right to accelerate.

3 Qualifications

Commonly, borrowers seek to qualify the representations in important respects. We look at some of the most common qualifications requested below:

Who is making the representations about whom?

See comments at 0.126 onwards for a discussion of whether provisions should extend to Group members who are not Obligors and the concept of 'Material Subsidiaries'. Additionally, in some cases, borrowers may want to resist having to make representations relating to companies over which

---

[6] This is the approach taken with a 'Default'. Existence of a Default allows lenders not to advance funds but does not give rise to the right to accelerate.
[7] At least, it is unusual outside project finance, where the limited recourse nature of the loan makes a significant difference.

they have no control – that is, companies higher up the corporate structure or subsidiary undertakings (see the discussion on the definition of 'Subsidiary' at 1.062).

Inclusion of materiality thresholds

8.018 Borrowers are likely to want certain representations, for example, representations relating to compliance with laws, such as environmental laws, to be limited so as to represent that they are in compliance 'in all material respects'. Alternatively they may request that the qualification says they are not in breach in a way which could be expected to have a 'Material Adverse Effect'. Note, except for very strong credits, lenders will want to restrict the second formulation. Some issues will be important to lenders for reasons other than credit risk. For example, lenders may require their borrowers to have sound environmental policies simply as part of the lenders' own internal policies, regardless of the credit risks involved.

Limitations with reference to knowledge

8.019 Borrowers commonly request the insertion of words such as 'to the best of their knowledge'. There are issues here for both lenders and borrowers. Borrowers need to consider precisely whose knowledge would be relevant. There may be people in the company who have the relevant knowledge, but if management does not, they will not want that to trigger the clause. It is common to specify that the reference is to the actual knowledge of specified persons, such as the board of directors. Lenders, if they agree to a qualification with reference to knowledge, frequently require the addition of the expression 'having made due enquiry'. Lenders also need to ensure, whenever they agree a limitation with reference to the knowledge of the borrower, that they accept that the given set of circumstances is not an Event of Default if the borrower was not aware of it at the time the representation was made. See the discussion at Box 8.1 on page 153.

Geographical limitations

8.020 Some of the representations relate to specified countries, defined in the Leveraged LMA as 'Relevant Jurisdictions'. In an unsecured transaction such as the LMA Term Loan the representations are usually restricted to the place of incorporation of the borrowers. In a secured transaction 'Relevant Jurisdictions' usually include the countries where the security is located and anywhere any Obligor conducts business. So, for example, the representation in Clause 19.5 to the effect that the borrowers have all desirable authorizations is often extended to give that confirmation in 'all Relevant Jurisdictions'; similarly with the representations as to stamp duties and registration requirements in clause 19.8. For international groups this may be impossible to ascertain and borrowers may therefore want to restrict the representation to their countries of incorporation or to request a materiality qualification.

CLAUSE 19: REPRESENTATIONS – SECTION 2 – THE LMA TERM LOAN REPRESENTATIONS

19. Representations

Each Obligor makes the representations and warranties set out in this Clause 19 to each Finance Party on the date of this Agreement (see Box 8.6).

8.021

> **Box 8.6**
> There is a technical difference between a representation and a warranty. The remedies for breach of the two types of provision are different and there are different requirements before a claim for breach can be founded. For most practical purposes, if any of the statements listed in this clause is untrue, the lenders will rely on their contractual rights (not to lend and/or to accelerate) which arise as a result. These rights are the same for a misrepresentation as for a breach of warranty.

Turning then to the content of the representations. The LMA Term Loan contains certain fairly standard representations relating to legal issues such as the power and authority of the borrower. It also contains a few representations relating to the borrower's business. It is likely that these business-related representations will need to be supplemented in many cases by additional representations relating to the business issues of concern to the lenders.[8]

8.022

This section reviews each representation in turn, first with reference to the statement required to be made on the date of the loan agreement, and second in the context of its potential inclusion in the definition of 'Repeating Representation'. In this second context it should be emphasized that there is no consensus on which representations should be defined as 'Repeating Representations' and the suggestions made here are designed to help readers to identify and avoid conflicts between different parts of the document. In most cases, where this book suggests that a particular representation should not be a Repeating Representation, an alternative (but more cumbersome) approach would be for that representation to be a Repeating Representation, but also to identify any undertaking or Event of Default which deals with the same issue and ensure that these various provisions do not conflict.

8.023

Clause 19.1 Status

Clause 19.1 is a representation that the company exists, is a limited liability company and has power to carry on its business.

8.024

---

[8] See Section 2 of the commentary on clause 22 at 8.190 onwards.

Sometimes the words 'in goodstanding' are added. This will be relevant when the borrower is incorporated in a jurisdiction (such as the US) which requires annual payments or filings to maintain **goodstanding**, lack of which may result in fines or restrictions on business activities.

The representation will of course need adjusting if any relevant Obligor is not in fact a company (e.g. if there are limited partnerships in the Group).

Should clause 19.1 repeat?

8.025 It is possible (if not likely in most cases) that the borrower could cease to be duly incorporated, validly existing, or to have power to carry on its business. Licences to conduct the relevant business may be withdrawn or taxes unpaid may lead to the company being struck off the register. If it did so, the lenders would wish to have the right to accelerate the loan. Given the unlikelihood of this occurrence, any potential conflict with other provisions of the agreement is usually commercially insignificant. Therefore, if the concept of repeating representations after the first drawdown is to be used, this representation is one which can be repeated in normal circumstances.

> In a more complex transaction, if the risk of change of law is not to fall simply on the borrower, it might be appropriate to recast this (or at least to ensure that the Event of Default relating to misrepresentations is not an automatic Event of Default but allows a period for remedy as discussed in the context of clause 23.4) to give appropriate possibilities to the borrower to remedy the situation.

Clause 19.2 Binding obligations.

8.026 In clause 19.2 the borrower represents that the agreements are *valid, binding and enforceable* obligations subject to principles of law specifically referred to in the legal opinion (see Box 8.7).

> **Box 8.7**
> There is an issue here as to whether the lenders' legal opinion should be disclosed to the borrower. The main argument against disclosure is that disclosure will highlight any areas of perceived legal risk, which the borrower may take advantage of at a later date. This is most likely to be a real issue for the lenders in circumstances where the opinions in question would not readily be apparent to the borrower or their advisers. This may be the case in innovative transactions involving legal issues on which lawyers may have differing opinions. It is less likely to be a significant issue in a straightforward unsecured loan. It would be hard for the borrower to make the representation as drafted here if they had not seen the legal opinion!
>
> An alternative way of dealing with this which is used in some of the other LMA documents, such as the agreement for use in developing markets, is to make certain of the representations subject to the 'Legal Reservations' and to define these.

The limitation on the representation with reference to a legal opinion (or to 'Legal Reservations') is necessary because, of course, there are circumstances (administration or a **Chapter 11** for example) which would freeze enforceability. Any such issues should have been addressed in the legal opinion and accepted by the lenders. The question, as discussed at 8.003, is which risks should fall on the borrower, and which on the lender? See Box 8.8.

8.027

> **Box 8.8**
> Most of the reservations will be issues which lenders accept – such as the impact of insolvency on the enforceability of the borrower's obligations. There may occasionally be others that highlight areas of legal uncertainty, of which lenders are aware but will want to ensure that they have the right to exit the transaction if they materialize; an example might be the issue of the effectiveness of the parallel debt structure discussed at 9.029. Lenders may be aware of the issue, still, if it were to become clear that the parallel debt structure was ineffective, lenders would want the right to accelerate the loan. To achieve this, if the representation is expressed to be subject to legal reservations then lenders need to ensure that the 'Legal Reservations' are limited and only include those legal issues in respect of which it is agreed that the risk should fall on the lender, not the borrower. An example would be the limits on enforceability of foreign judgements.

Comment If security is given, the representation may also need adjusting to refer to the need for registration, notice to third parties or similar requirements.

8.028

Should clause 19.2 repeat?

It is possible (if not likely in most cases) that the borrower's obligations under the loan agreement could cease to be binding and enforceable. There may be a change of law which has this effect. The same arguments apply as in relation to clause 19.1.[9] Therefore, again, this is a representation which can be repeated after drawdown in normal situations.

8.029

> In a more complex transaction, if the risk of change of law is not to fall simply on the borrower it might be appropriate to recast this[10] to give appropriate possibilities to the borrower to remedy the situation.

Clause 19.3   Non-conflict with other obligations

In clause 19.3 the borrower represents that performance of their obligations does not breach (a) any applicable regulation; (b) its constitutional documents or (c) any agreement it (or its Subsidiaries) has signed.

8.030

---

[9] That is, (a) if these events occurred the lenders should be entitled to accelerate and (b) commercial insignificance of this issue.
[10] Or at least to ensure that the Event of Default relating to misrepresentations is not an automatic Event of Default but allows a period for remedy as discussed in the context of clause 23.4.

Borrowers may be restricted in their activities by law or regulation (e.g. if they belong to a regulated industry such as banking or insurance, or if they are public bodies), or by virtue of a general regulation affecting particular types of borrowing such as financial assistance. Clause 19.3(a) is designed to address these issues.

8.031 Clause 19.3(b) is intended to address the question of whether the borrower has power (capacity) to borrow the loan – some companies have limited borrowing powers in their constitutional documents.

8.032 Clause 19.3(c) will confirm that this borrowing is not in breach of contractual provisions, such as a restriction on borrowing, or a negative pledge, given in a different loan agreement. The terms of these prior agreements (unlike the borrower's constitutional documents, which are often a matter of public record) are not generally available for inspection by the lenders on any public register, so there is little independent due diligence which the lenders can do to ensure that clause 19.3(c) is correct. Including this representation can assist in a good faith defence by the lenders to any claim by a third party, for example, that this loan agreement caused a breach of their existing contract and that the lenders were guilty of the tort of inducing a breach of contract.

Should clause 19.3 repeat?

8.033 It is possible that regulations may be introduced after the date of the agreement which would be breached by continued performance of the borrower's obligations under the loan agreement or associated transaction. If this occurred, the lenders would want the right to accelerate the loan and therefore, given the commercial unlikelihood of such an event, this is a representation which can be repeated after drawdown in normal situations.

> In a more complex transaction, if the risk of change of law is not to fall simply on the borrower it might be appropriate to recast this[11] (at least in the case of clause 19.3(a)) to give appropriate possibilities to the borrower to remedy the situation.

Clause 19.4 Power and authority

8.034 In 19.4 the borrower represents that it has power to perform its obligations under the documents and that they have been validly authorized.

This issue is a mixture of fact and law. The borrower may make the comment that they should not be required to give representations on matters of law (because that is not something on which they are competent to comment) to the extent that the representation is one of law. Nevertheless, as discussed at 8.004 onwards, lenders are likely to want to

---

[11] Or at least to ensure that the Event of Default relating to misrepresentations is not an automatic Event of Default but allows a period for remedy.

retain this representation to ensure that they have the right not to lend (or to accelerate) if the representation is untrue.

Should clause 19.4 repeat?

It is not inconceivable that continued performance of the borrower's obligations under the loan agreement could subsequently become subject to some additional authorization. The same comments apply as in relation to clause 19.1.[12] Therefore, again, this is a representation which can be repeated after drawdown in normal situations.

8.035

> In a more complex transaction, if the risk of change of law is not to fall simply on the borrower it might be appropriate to recast this[13] to give appropriate possibilities to the borrower to remedy the situation.

Clause 19.5 Validity and admissibility in evidence

Clause 19.5 is a representation that the borrowers have all necessary 'Authorizations' to enable them to comply with their obligations under the documents and to make the documents admissible in evidence. This representation refers not only to corporate authorizations but also consents (such as exchange control consent) licences, notarizations and registrations.[14]

8.036

This representation is one which the borrower might object to, on the basis that it is a matter of law on which they have no expertise.[15] Nevertheless, it should normally be retained to ensure that, if untrue, the lenders have the right to accelerate and/or not lend if relevant authorizations are not in place. Of course, the lenders will also be taking advice from their lawyers on this issue and on the other matters of law referred to in the representations.

Should clause 19.5 repeat?

It is possible that further authorizations may become necessary for the loan agreement to continue to be performed and admissible in evidence in the borrower's country of incorporation. The same comments apply as in relation to clause 19.1.[16] Therefore, again, this is a representation which can be repeated after drawdown in normal situations.

8.037

> In a more complex transaction, if the risk of change of law is not to fall simply on the borrower it might be appropriate to recast this[17] to give appropriate possibilities to the borrower to remedy the situation.

---

[12] That is, (a) if these events occurred the lenders should be entitled to accelerate and (b) commercial insignificance of this issue.
[13] Or at least to ensure that the Event of Default relating to misrepresentations is not an automatic Event of Default but allows a period for remedy.
[14] If any filings are required it may be appropriate to cross refer to clause 19.8 discussed at 8.042.
[15] See comments at 8.003 onwards.
[16] That is, (a) if these events occurred the lenders should be entitled to accelerate and (b) commercial insignificance of this issue.
[17] Or at least to ensure that the Event of Default relating to misrepresentations is not an automatic Event of Default but allows a period for remedy.

Clause 19.6 Governing law and enforcement

8.038 In clause 19.6 the borrower confirms that the choice of law is valid and that an English judgement would be enforced in its place of incorporation.

Once again,[18] this representation should be retained to ensure the lenders have the contractual rights they need if the statement is untrue. It is also a key point for the lenders' due diligence. These issues will be addressed by any legal opinion issued and borrowers ought to request that the representation is restricted with reference to any relevant qualification in the legal opinion.

Should clause 19.6 repeat?

8.039 It is possible that the borrower's jurisdiction of incorporation will cease to recognize judgements obtained in the law of the country chosen to have jurisdiction. The same comments apply as in relation to clause 19.1.[19] Therefore, again, this is a representation which can be repeated after drawdown in normal situations.

> In a more complex transaction, if the risk of change of law is not to fall simply on the borrower it might be appropriate to recast this to give appropriate possibilities to the borrower to remedy the situation.

Clause 19.7   Deduction of Tax

8.040 Clause 19.7 confirms that the borrower is not required by law to make deductions on payments to Qualifying Lenders (once they have received any relevant approvals and, for non bank lenders, as long as the tax authorities have not directed otherwise). Note that in an earlier version of the LMA Term Loan this clause read as follows '*It is not required to make any deduction for or on account of Tax from any payment it may make under the Finance Documents*' This wording was changed because it resulted in an Event of Default in ANY circumstances where a tax deduction is required even if this is due to issues which are agreed commercially should not result in a gross-up (e.g. if the lender was not a Qualifying Lender in the first place).

If the borrower is not English this representation is likely to need to be amended to reflect the tax law in the borrower's country as to whom a payment can be made to without deduction for Tax.

Should clause 19.7 repeat?

8.041 It is possible that a withholding tax will be imposed which did not exist on the day the loan agreement was signed. However, in this case, the lenders will not need the right to accelerate the loan. They have the protection of

---
[18] See comments on clause 19.5 at 8.036.
[19] That is, (a) if these events occurred the lenders should be entitled to accelerate and (b) commercial insignificance of this issue.

the gross-up clause (clause 13.2(c)). Therefore this representation should not be repeated.

Clause 19.8 No filing or stamp taxes

Clause 19.8 confirms that no registrations or other filings are required in relation to the documents.[20]

8.042

Clearly this clause needs to be amended (and corresponding conditions inserted to require the relevant filing etc. to take place) if it is incorrect.

This clause is another area where the borrower may argue that it should not be required to make statements on matters of law,[21] but where the lenders will usually want the representation in any event.

Should clause 19.8 repeat?

It is possible that a filing requirement may arise in the future. The same comments apply as in relation to clause 19.1.[22] Therefore, again, this is a representation which can be repeated after drawdown in normal situations.

8.043

In a more complex transaction, however, it may be appropriate to recast this to give the borrower the opportunity to effect the relevant filing etc. without its giving rise to an Event of Default.

Clause 19.9 No default

Clause 19.9 reads

8.044

(a) No Event of Default is continuing or might reasonably be expected to result from the making of any Utilization.

(b) No other event or circumstance is outstanding which constitutes a default under any other agreement or instrument which is binding on it or any of its Subsidiaries or to which its (or its Subsidiaries') assets are subject which might have a Material Adverse Effect.

The impact of this representation depends on the definition of 'Material Adverse Effect' and in particular on whether that definition looks on the effect on the group as a whole, or on individual Obligors, or on individual group companies.

Assuming for the moment that the representation is not a 'Repeating Representation',[23] borrowers' comments on it will be made in light of the circumstances which exist at or about the time the representation is being

---

[20] See comment on clause 19.5 at 8.036.
[21] See comments at 8.003 onwards.
[22] That is, (a) if these events occurred the lenders should be entitled to accelerate and (b) commercial insignificance of this issue.
[23] See discussion at 8.045 for issues which arise if this representation is repeated.

negotiated. In these circumstances, the word 'might' in clause 19.9(b), even though it would be objectionable in the material adverse change Event of Default,[24] may well be a reasonable standard for the lenders to insist on – they want to be advised of all adverse possibilities before becoming obliged to lend.

Should clause 19.9 repeat?

8.045 Clause 19.9(a) is a representation that there is no Event of Default and that none might reasonably be expected to result from the making of any Utilization. This is perhaps worth repeating in relation to new drawings so that, if a drawing is likely to result in an Event of Default (e.g. if it would result in a breach of a financial covenant) this representation would be incorrect, giving rise to an Event of Default and so enabling the lender not to advance the funds.

8.046 Clause 19.9(b) is different. This is a representation that there is no default (see Box 8.9) under any agreement which might have a material adverse effect. There is a hazard in repeating this representation, which is that there is a danger of a conflict between this and the cross default clause.[25] The cross default clause (clause 23.5 of the LMA Term Loan) deals with the circumstances where, if the borrower is in breach of a contract with a third party, that should give rise to a right for these lenders to accelerate. If lenders wish to provide that default under an agreement which does not relate to Financial Indebtedness should be an Event of Default in certain circumstances[26] then the simplest way to deal with that clearly and without risking a conflict between Repeating Representations and the Events of Default is to deal with the issue directly as an Event of Default and not to repeat this representation (see Box 8.4 on page 157).

Box 8.9

This representation relates to Events of Default and 'defaults' as opposed to 'Defaults'. The difference is significant. The borrower should not repeat a representation that no Default has occurred. The effect of this is that, if a Default has occurred (but it is not yet an Event of Default as, for example, the grace period is running) then the representation is untrue. Making an untrue representation is itself an Event of Default (without a grace period generally). The result of repeating a representation that no Default exists is therefore to potentially lose the benefit of the grace periods. Note this is different from having a condition precedent that there is no Default. In that case, if there is a Default, it is not a misrepresentation and therefore not an Event of Default. Instead it simply relieves the lenders of the obligation to lend.

---

[24] See comments on clause 23.12 at 8.274.
[25] See the example referred to in Box 8.4 on page 157.
[26] As to which, see the commentary on clause 23.5 at 8.233.

Clause 19.10 No misleading information

Clause 19.10 is a representation that the information provided to the lenders was accurate when given; that financial projections made were based on reasonable assumptions; and that nothing has happened since the information was provided and nothing has been omitted from the information provided, which makes it misleading.

8.047

Comment How contentious this representation is depends on the degree and type of information which has been provided to the lenders during the negotiation of the loan. For example, if the loan is to finance a new project, the borrower will not want there to be an Event of Default if the projections they made prove to have been optimistic. Rather than representing that the figures were based on reasonable assumptions, they will want to restrict the representation so that they are only saying that they believed the assumptions to be reasonable at the time the figures were provided.

8.048

It is common for borrowers to ask for the representation to be restricted to 'written' information provided. It is also sensible to keep a record of the information which has been provided.

Should clause 19.10 repeat?

This clause should not be repeated. It simply states that previous statements (in the **information memorandum**) were true when made and that nothing has happened which makes that document misleading. Once the lenders have signed the loan agreement they no longer rely on the information memorandum for their information (but rather on the updates from the borrower from time to time) nor do they expect that the facts stated in it will not change from time to time. Therefore, it is not intended that any changes from the position set out in the information memorandum which occur after the date of the agreement should give rise to an Event of Default. Therefore, this representation should not be repeated.

8.049

Clause 19.11 Financial statements

Clause 19.11 contains confirmation by the borrower that

8.050

- (Under clause 19.11(a),) the Original Financial Statements were prepared in accordance with GAAP,
- (Under clause 19.11(b),) they fairly represent the financial position of the relevant company in relation to the period covered, and
- (Under clause 19.11(c),) there has been no material adverse change in the position of the Group or of the relevant company since those statements were prepared.

Clauses 19.10 (c) and 19.11(c) are intended to update the Information Memorandum and financial statements to the date of the signing of the agreement.

The representation in clause 19.11(c) is set with reference to the consolidated financial position of the Group as a whole and also with reference to each Obligor.[27]

Should clause 19.11 repeat?

8.051 The comments made on clause 19.10 apply equally here. This representation simply updates the financial information provided up to the date of signing. Paragraphs a) and b) are statements relating to the Original Financial Statements – which are a specified set of statements which never change – so, if those statements were true on the date the agreement was signed, they will always be true, so that repeating the representation is pointless. As for paragraph c) – if that were to be repeated, it would duplicate the function of the material adverse change Event of Default (and probably conflict with it). This representation should therefore not be repeated.

Clause 19.12 Pari passu ranking

Clause 19.12 reads

8.052 *Its payment obligations under the Finance Documents rank at least pari passu with the claims of all its other unsecured and unsubordinated creditors, except for obligations mandatorily preferred by law applying to companies generally.*[28]

8.053 Clause 19.12 is one of three clauses (with the negative pledge (clause 22.3) and cross default clause (clause 23.5)) which are important to an unsecured lender to ensure that they are equal with other lenders to the borrower outside the syndicate. The intention is to ensure that the syndicate of lenders for this loan is at least equal with all other unsecured creditors, or, if not, that they know what creditors have priority.

The pari passu clause simply requires this loan to be of at least equal ranking with other unsecured debts (see Box 8.10).

> **Box 8.10**
> In other words, it requires the borrower to confirm that, on a winding up, to the extent that the lenders have an unsecured claim, they will share the assets which are available to unsecured creditors, pro rata with such other creditors, subject to the exceptions set out in the clause.

---

[27] See the discussion on clause 21 at 8.112 and on the scope of the agreement at 0.121 onwards.
[28] The lenders might like to consider what obligations are mandatorily preferred by law.

It does not prevent the borrower from 8.054

- giving security for other debts – that is the purpose of the negative pledge;
- agreeing different, more favourable, terms in any loan agreements with other creditors – again, a specific covenant is needed to achieve this;[29]
- paying other debts before making payment on the loan – if lenders want to achieve this, an undertaking not to prepay those other debts will be necessary (although a recent case in the US has cast some doubt on this proposition – see Box 8.11).

Box 8.11

During 2012/2013 the conventional understanding of the pari passu clause was successfully challenged by the US decision in the case of <u>NML Capital v Argentina</u>. In that case, Argentina had issued bonds which contained a pari passu clause which stated that

'1. The Securities will constitute…unsubordinated obligations of the Republic and
2. The payment obligations of the Republic under the Securities shall at all times rank at least equally with all its other…[indebtedness]'.

The court held that these two sentences addressed different issues, with the first being an agreement about the legal ranking of the debt (i.e. having the meaning which the pari passu clause in a loan agreement has conventionally been understood to mean). The second paragraph (which is very similar to the LMA wording) was held to be an undertaking to make payment on its debts rateably – that is, not to give preference to some debts over others when choosing which to pay.

The court was influenced by a number of facts

- the fact that the clause appeared in a sovereign debt instrument – therefore the conventional interpretation of the clause as being a description of the legal status of debts on a winding up cannot have been the purpose of the clause since sovereign states cannot be wound up;
- the fact that Argentina passed a law (the 'Lock Law') prohibiting the Argentinian state from making payment on the Securities; and
- the existence of the two separate limbs of the clause noted earlier.

The court was at pains to point out that it was not deciding on the meaning of the clause in general, but only on its application in the specific facts of the case.

In the context of sovereign debt, the function of the clause is debateable although the general opinion in the UK at least has been strongly 8.055

---

[29] Although, to an extent, the cross default clause has this effect, in relation to undertakings, if not in relation to fees and Margin. See discussion on clause 23.5(d) at 8.244.

opposed to the 'rateable payment' interpretation[30] given to the clause in the case discussed at Box 8.11 on page 171. Outside sovereign debt the rateable payment interpretation is even more suspect. It is hard to see how any borrower could comply with such an obligation unless it were limited to debts which originally fell due on the same day. In any event, outside sovereign debt, lenders have no need of the clause since they are protected by insolvency laws dealing with preferential payments.

Nevertheless, in view of the uncertainties created by the case quoted at Box 8.11 on page 171, borrowers would be well advised to clarify the drafting, particularly in the (not uncommon) cases where there is not only a pari passu representation, but an undertaking as well.

8.056 The clause itself, on investigation, might look puzzling. It states that the obligations under the loan are at least pari passu with other creditors except (a) secured creditors; (b) subordinated creditors; and (c) creditors preferred by laws applying to companies generally.

In most countries these three specified circumstances are the main ways in which one claim may have a different priority to others and therefore it might be thought that the clause was unnecessary as it simply states the obvious truth. However, the clause is included because, although those are the three *main* ways in which two debts may have different priority in insolvency, there are sometimes other, exceptional ways, which the lenders wish to be advised of (and not to be obliged to lend, if the position is that their loan will be junior to other, ordinary creditors without security).

For example, it may be that the law in the borrower's country,

8.057 • allows one claim to be preferred over another without giving security and without consent of the creditor who is effectively subordinated;[31]

8.058 • provides that loans with certain attributes will be subordinate to others – as in the case of the English position on loans where the return to the lender varies with the profits of the borrower.[32]

The representation is helpful, therefore, in ensuring that the lawyers involved consider whether any such subordination may be applicable.

8.059 However, the pari passu clause gives the lenders little comfort unless they also know what claims may be preferred by operation of law applying to companies generally. Common examples are tax and employee payments as well as, sometimes, payments to certain companies such as public utility companies. This is an area for the lenders' due diligence. Having established

---

[30] See Lachlan Burn, 'Pari Passu Clauses – English Law after NML v Argentina', *Capital Markets Law Journal*, 2014, 9(1). See also the report of the Financial Market Law Committee on pari passu clauses in sovereign debt obligations, issued in March 2005 and available from their web site www.fmlc.org

[31] As was the case in Spain until 2003, (and may still be the case in Spanish law-based jurisdictions) where execution of a debt instrument as an 'escritura publica' gave this priority.

[32] See discussion on the definition of 'Margin' at 1.050.

what claims may have priority by operation of law, the lenders may want to include undertakings by the borrower not to allow indebtedness to those creditors to exceed a given amount.

Should clause 19.12 repeat?

It is possible for the loan to cease to be pari passu with other creditors, for example, if there were a change in the law of the relevant jurisdiction. Therefore this representation can be repeated after first drawdown in normal circumstances.

8.060

> In a more complex transaction, if the risk of change of law is not to fall simply on the borrower it might be appropriate to recast this[33] to give appropriate possibilities to the borrower to remedy the situation.

Clause 19.13 No proceedings pending or threatened

Clause 19.13 reads

8.061

> *No litigation, arbitration or administrative proceedings of or before any court, arbitral body or agency which, if adversely determined, might reasonably be expected to have a Material Adverse Effect have (to the best of its knowledge and belief) been started or threatened against it or any of its Subsidiaries.*

The reference to administrative proceedings is intended to pick up references to competition authorities and the like. Sometimes lenders extend this representation so as to also confirm that there is no litigation against the directors of any Obligor.

Comment The impact of this clause depends on whether the definition of 'Material Adverse Effect' relates to the effect on the group as a whole, or on any individual Obligor, or on any individual member of the group.

8.062

Assuming for the moment that this representation is not a 'Repeating Representation', borrowers' comments on it will be made in light of the circumstances which exist at or about the time the representation is being discussed.

8.063

Comment The borrower may wish to request removal of the words 'if adversely determined' (or the addition of the words 'is reasonably likely to be adversely determined and which') particularly if the representation is to be repeated after the initial drawdown. These words have the effect that *any* proceedings taking place that could have a material adverse effect could trigger the clause and prevent drawing (or worse, result in acceleration if the representation is repeated) even though the proceedings in question are highly unlikely to

8.064

---

[33] Or at least to ensure that the Event of Default relating to misrepresentations is not an automatic Event of Default but allows a period for remedy.

8.065 *Comment* have that result because the case in question is unlikely to succeed against the borrower.

Comment This representation has an important caveat – only litigation which might reasonably be expected to have a material adverse effect (if it were to be adversely determined) is relevant. The lenders may wish, in certain circumstances, to remove this carve-out at least for the initial representation, to ensure it has full details of all litigation at the time the loan agreement is signed.

Should clause 19.13 repeat?

8.066 This representation should not repeat in its current form, since the effect is that the existence of major litigation would give lenders the right to accelerate, regardless of the merits of the case – see 8.064. Provided the words 'if adversely affected' are deleted then the representation may be repeated but there is a danger of a conflict arising between this Repeating Representation and any Events of Default dealing with litigation or judgements. There is no Event of Default relating to litigation in the LMA Term Loan. The nearest is clause 23.8, dealing with execution of judgements. This may lead the borrower to assume that litigation against it will not give rise to an Event of Default unless the circumstances in clause 23.8 occur. If lenders intend litigation to give rise to an Event of Default in circumstances which fall short of those referred to in clause 23.8 then the clearest way to achieve this is to include an Event of Default to this effect and not to repeat this representation.

Representations in different circumstances

8.067 The representations as to validity and admissibility in evidence (clause 19.5(b)), governing law and enforcement (clause 19.6), withholding tax (clause 19.7), and no filing or stamp tax (clause 19.8) are not usually required of an English borrower in a straightforward unsecured loan, since, in those circumstances, these issues are a matter of English law on which the lenders, by common practice, are content to rely on their own lawyers.

The LMA Term Loan includes only very basic representations which will be applicable in all cases, covering issues such as power and authority. Additional representations will be necessary to reflect the specific transaction and the requirements of the lenders' credit decision.[34]

Clause 19.14 Repetition

8.068 Clause 19.14 is the clause which deems certain representations to be repeated on certain dates during the life of the loan. It reads

---

[34] See Section 2 of the comments on clause 22 at 8.190 onwards.

19.14 The Repeating Representations are deemed to be made by each Obligor by reference to the facts and circumstances then existing on

(a) the date of each Utilisation Request and the first day of each Interest Period **8.069**

For comments on clause 19.14 see 8.007 onwards and see also the commentary on each individual representation at 8.021 onwards.

CLAUSES 20–22: UNDERTAKINGS – AN INTRODUCTION

1 Purpose

The purposes of the undertakings are to ensure the lenders have the information they need; to ensure good housekeeping by the borrower; to give the lenders' leverage; and to protect the borrower's assets.   **8.070**

The undertakings in the LMA Term Loan cover:

- provision of information (clause 20);
- financial ratios (clause 21); and
- positive and negative undertakings relating to protection of assets (clause 22).

Other undertakings are likely to be required in any given case as discussed in Section 2 of the comments on clause 22 at 8.190 onwards.

2 Shadow directors

One issue which lenders should be aware of when exercising their rights under a loan agreement is the concept of 'shadow directors'.[35] A shadow director is a person in accordance with whose instructions the directors of a company are accustomed to act. There are similar concepts of de facto directors in many jurisdictions. The risk for the lenders is that, in times of financial difficulty, the lenders may step in and start to take an active role in the management of the borrower's business, thereby potentially becoming a shadow director and assuming the responsibilities of directors. The particular concern is that the lenders may then take on liability for issues like wrongful trading (under English law) or negligent mismanagement (under some other laws) under the local law in the place where the borrower is trading.[36] Whether a lender is a shadow director is a question of fact.[37] Monitoring and suggesting is one thing, but giving the borrower directions, under threat of enforcement action if those directions are not followed, is more likely to be a problem.   **8.071**

---

[35] s251 Companies Act 2006.
[36] See comments on clause 23.13 at 8.285.
[37] In Re PFTZM Ltd [1995] BCC 280, the lenders held weekly management meetings with a borrower in financial difficulties, monitoring the business. The court held that they were not a shadow director.

The undertakings are expressed to cease to be effective once there is no longer any loan outstanding.[38]

3 Qualifications

8.072 Borrowers are likely to want to reduce the impact of the undertakings in a number of ways. The most common types of restrictions are:

- only prohibiting the relevant action if it is material or could have a material adverse effect;
- introduction of some reasonableness standard (e.g. 'reasonable' expenses, expenses 'reasonably incurred', 'reasonable' opinion, not to be 'unreasonably withheld', 'reasonably likely' etc.);
- requiring a greater degree of certainty or a closer link, for example, by replacing 'desirable' with 'necessary' or replacing 'could' with 'is likely to' or limiting indemnities to losses 'directly' caused by the relevant act;
- limiting the companies whose acts are restricted (see 0.121 onwards);
- baskets, allowing the prohibited act (such as the creation of security) in limited amounts (see Box 8.12).

Box 8.12
Issues to consider here are:

- whether the amount allowed is an annual figure or an absolute cap (or perhaps an annual figure plus a limit on the total allowed during the whole loan)
- if it is an annual figure, whether unused amounts can be carried forwards or backwards
- whether the figure is a fixed amount or a formula (such as 5% of Tangible Net Worth)
- the size of the basket – generally lenders will want to impose very modest baskets[39] on the negative pledge and on any prohibitions on incurring debt
- whether each 'basket' is independent of the others (for example, if the borrower is permitted to dispose of fixed assets up to a value of $10 million, and is also allowed to give security up to an amount of $10 million, could an unused allowance on sale of assets be used to increase the amount of permitted security, so that the borrower could give security for $15 million provided its disposals of fixed assets were no higher than $5 million?).

---

[38] It is important to be clear that other provisions such as indemnities and undertakings to reimburse the lenders are not limited in this way. A claim under these other clauses may need to be made after the loan has been fully repaid, or before it is advanced.

[39] In a report in 2006, ('Request for Comment on Moody's Indenture Covenant Research and Investment Framework') Moody's stated that the basket 'should not exceed a modest percentage of consolidated net tangible assets'.

- permissions for intra group transactions
- permissions for transactions in the ordinary course of business (see Box 8.28 on page 205)
- requiring only 'reasonable endeavours' to perform the undertaking (see Box 8.13).

> **Box 8.13**
> There is a difference between 'reasonable endeavours', 'all reasonable endeavours' and 'best endeavours', with 'reasonable endeavours' being at the lowest end of the scale and 'best endeavours' at the top end. Although interpretation of a contract will always depend on the circumstances, there is case law which suggests that 'reasonable endeavours' requires the person to follow ONE reasonable course of action to achieve the result, but allows him to take into account his own commercial interests. 'All reasonable endeavours' requires the party to explore ALL avenues reasonably available – that is, to leave no stone unturned – although again he need not disregard his own commercial interests. 'Best endeavours' has been described as an obligation to take steps 'which a prudent, determined and reasonable [person], acting in his own interests and designed to achieve that result would take'. But it does not include actions which would not be likely to succeed, and, depending on the context, it does not require the person to disregard its own financial interests entirely.[40]

4 Covenant lite loans

8.073 It is also worth mentioning that for some borrowers in the leveraged market it is sometimes possible to negotiate significant loosening of the undertakings which would normally be seen (see Box 8.14 on page 178), particularly in the US market. This arose before the financial crisis of 2008 and again, in 2013, as investors sought yield. The loosening became so widespread that it led Moody's to warn of the formation of a 'covenant bubble'.[41]

5 Duplication

8.074 Another issue which the borrower needs to consider is duplication. That is, the borrower may find that an act which is permitted under one provision may be prohibited under another provision. There are numerous examples:

- the borrower may have negotiated a provision which has the effect that material litigation is not an Event of Default if it is being contested and

---

[40] See Jet2.Com Limited v Blackpool Airport Limited [2012] EWCA Civ 417, where a number of cases were reviewed.
[41] 'Signs of a Covenant Bubble', Moody's Investor Service, May 2013.

> **Box 8.14**
> Some of the features of these 'covenant lite' loans include:
> - incurrence, rather than maintenance financial covenants (see 8.113)
> - very loose financial ratios (so that breaches only occur if results are up to 50% off projections, as opposed to traditional cushions of 15% or so)
> - equity cure rights (see 8.119)
> - More unrestricted subsidiaries
> - Ability to pay dividends and repay subordinated debt provided financial ratios are met (as opposed to, traditionally, only out of that part of excess cashflow not required to be used to prepay the loan)
> - Long (say 60 day) grace periods on the events of default, misrepresentation not leading to Events of Default, and cross acceleration rather than cross default (see 8.244) and
> - Ability to borrow money and make acquisitions provided certain financial ratios are met.

reserves have been made for it, but they may find that if they have to pay money into court in relation to the litigation – that causes a breach of the negative pledge;
- the borrower may be complying with its financial ratios but the lenders may still claim that there has been a material adverse change in its financial condition, triggering the material adverse change Event of Default;
- the borrower may have negotiated equity cure rights but it may find that they cannot exercise them because they have also undertaken not to issue new shares;
- the borrower may have negotiated the right to enter into certain types of derivatives in the undertaking relating to derivatives but may find that that is prohibited by the undertaking relating to Financial Indebtedness;
- the borrower may have the right to enter into cash pooling arrangements in certain circumstances under the negative pledge but may still find that cash pooling results in a breach of undertakings, for example, not to lend money; or
- The borrower may believe they have the right to change the group structure; buy new companies and sell existing companies, but they may find that although this is not expressly prohibited, they have not negotiated appropriate carve-outs from any 'no disposals' or 'no acquisitions' undertakings to enable them to do this.

The list is endless.

8.075 Some borrowers try to deal with this by having a concept that if a transaction is specifically permitted by one clause, it is permitted for all purposes in the document. This causes two problems:

- First, it only works where transactions are specifically permitted, as opposed to falling outside the clause.

- Second, more importantly, the various prohibitions in the document are cumulative. So for example, lenders may be happy to agree that litigation is not an Event of Default if it is being contested and reserves have been made for it. However, quite separately from that, they have concerns about the provision of security, so that if the litigation in question requires the posting of security, that may well make a difference to the lenders' position.

In practice therefore, whenever borrowers negotiate carve-outs to one provision, they need to consider what other provisions are relevant and request corresponding changes to those provisions as well.

CLAUSE 20: INFORMATION UNDERTAKINGS
Clause 20.1   Financial statements

In Clause 20.1 the Company agrees to provide financial statements to the lenders

8.076

There are a number of issues here.

- Which companies should the accounts relate to? This needs to reflect the credit decision and the basis on which financial ratios are tested.[42] The LMA Term Loan requires consolidated statements for the Company (the highest level in the group to which the lenders have recourse, which thus gives financial information for the whole of the group below the Company), and individual statements for each Obligor (thus ensuring that the lenders have financial information relating to those companies against which they have direct claims).

  8.077

- How much time is allowed for preparation of the statements?

  8.078

- Which types of financial statements are required? Normally, the lenders require annual audited statements plus half-yearly unaudited statements. This is what the LMA Term Loan provides for. In the case of sub-investment grade borrowers, lenders, not uncommonly, require additional financial statements such as monthly management accounts. In view of the possibility that some lenders may also be involved in trading in shares, there may be concerns that some information they receive under the loan agreement could constitute inside information which could restrict their ability to trade in the relevant shares. To protect against this risk the LMA added a provision (clause 26.14(c)) allowing lenders who do not want to receive non-public information to nominate a third party to receive information on their behalf. That third party can then filter the information as appropriate. Borrowers would be reluctant to take this role of filtering the information on

  8.079

---

[42] See discussion of financial ratios at 8.112.

Clause 20.2   Compliance Certificate

8.080 Clause 20.2 will be required where there are financial ratios. It requires the Company to deliver a Compliance Certificate (in the form attached as a schedule) signed by two directors of the company, with each set of financial statements, confirming that the ratios have been met and setting out their calculations of the figures. The Compliance Certificate also requires the directors to confirm that there is no Default.

The clause provides, as an option, for an auditor's certificate to be produced with the audited annual statements confirming compliance with the financial ratios. The auditor's willingness to do this needs their prior approval. They are only likely to agree to this if the form of report is agreed in advance and the lenders engage them directly to issue these reports.

8.081 If there are no financial ratios then lenders may decide to delete the requirement for Compliance Certificates. However, caution is needed here because the Certificates also have the important function of requiring the borrower to consider the question of whether there is a Default on a regular basis. If the Certificates are not required, it would be sensible to add a confirmation as to whether there is a Default or not into the Selection Notice (where borrowers select the next Interest Period).

Sometimes borrowers argue that regular confirmation of the position in relation to Defaults is unnecessary because the agreement contains an obligation to notify of a Default in any event. Lenders are likely to resist that because often it is not readily apparent that a Default exists, so it is useful to impose an obligation on the borrower, requiring them to pro-actively consider the question on a regular basis.

Clause 20.3   Requirements as to financial statements

8.082 Clause 20.3 establishes certain requirements in relation to the financial statements. It

- requires a director to certify that each set of financial statements fairly reflects the financial position of the company; and
- requires each set of financial statements to be prepared using GAAP (and note that the definition of GAAP includes IFRS if applicable as discussed at 1.040).

8.083 The clause gives the draftsperson two choices: either (i) the accounts are to be prepared in accordance with the relevant GAAP as it changes from time to time; or (ii) it gives the borrower the option to prepare the statements in accordance with the original GAAP, or to use changing GAAP with a reconciliation of what the figures would have looked like if the original GAAP had been used.

The second is known as a 'frozen GAAP' provision and is usually used to facilitate the working and testing of financial ratios.

As a practical matter, if the clause provides for a frozen GAAP provision then, if GAAP changes, there will be an additional administrative burden for the borrower in the production of ALL subsequent sets of accounts, during the whole life of the loan. For this reason, borrowers might like to require lenders to commit in advance to agree on appropriate changes to the financial ratios to reflect the change in GAAP going forward, and so remove the need to continue to provide these reconciliations to original GAAP. See Box 8.15 for appropriate wording to achieve this.

> **Box 8.15**
> The following wording, which was agreed between the Association of Corporate Treasurers and the LMA in the context of the move to IFRS in the UK, would also be suitable to deal with any other changes in GAAP:
>
> If the Company notifies the Agent in accordance with [para] (requirements as to financial statements) the Company and the Agent shall enter into negotiations in good faith with a view to agreeing any amendments to this Agreement which are necessary as a result of the change. To the extent practicable these amendments will be such as to ensure that the change does not result in any material alteration in the commercial effect of the obligations in this Agreement. If any amendments are agreed they shall take effect and be binding on each of the Parties in accordance with their terms.

Clause 20.4   Information: miscellaneous

Clause 20.4(a) requires the borrower to give the lenders copies of all documents which the borrower sends to its shareholders.

Comment   Paragraph (a) is intended to ensure that those events that are significant enough to be notified to shareholders and/or creditors are, at the same time, notified to the lenders. However, in the case of private companies, it may be appropriate to limit the requirement to apply only to information which the borrower delivers to creditors or *is required by law* to deliver to its shareholders, since shareholders of private companies are often intimately involved in the day-to-day management and may receive more information than would be appropriate for a lender.

Clause 20.4(b) requires the borrower to give the lenders details of any significant litigation against them. It reflects the wording of the representation on litigation contained in clause 19.13.

8.087 *Comment* This clause ought to reflect any changes agreed to in clause 19.13 discussed at 8.061 onwards.[43]

8.088 *Comment* If (as suggested in relation to clause 19.13) clause 19.13 is not repeated then, under the LMA Term Loan, the lenders will be entitled to be advised of litigation which falls within this clause but will not have any rights to take action as a result of such litigation unless the circumstances also constitute an Event of Default under, for example, the material adverse change Event of Default or the cross default clause. Lenders may wish to consider whether they want significant litigation to be an Event of Default[44] and, if not, whether they wish to be advised of it.

8.089 Clause 20.4(c) requires the borrower to supply such further information about its business (or that of any group member) as any lender may reasonably request.

8.090 *Comment* The borrower may want to restrict clause 20.4(c) to exclude certain group members or to include only Obligors.[45] They may also want to restrict the generality of the clause[46] so as to discourage frequent unwarranted requests, particularly as the clause relates to the requirements of 'any Finance Party' so exposing the borrower to the requirements of every lender. Nevertheless, borrowers should bear in mind that provision of information to lenders is often as much in the interests of the borrowers as the lenders, because it facilitates well-informed decisions by lenders.

Clause 20.5   Notification of default

8.091 Clause 20.5 requires the borrower to notify the lenders of a Default, and, if requested, to confirm that there is no Default or, if there is a Default, to advise how it is being dealt with. One might query what incentive there is for the borrower to comply with this undertaking since, if there is a Default, then failure to notify the lenders of that fact will constitute another Default but will not make the borrower's legal position any worse.[47] See also the comments on Compliance Certificates at 8.081.

For this reason, it is important that the drafting ensures that failure to notify of a Default does indeed make the borrower's position worse. This is achieved by ensuring (in clause 23.3) that this undertaking either has no grace period or has only a very short grace period before it becomes an Event of Default. As a result, breach of this undertaking results in an Event of Default (not just a Default) even though the grace period for the underlying Default may not have expired (see Box 8.16 on page 183).

---

[43] Such as any removal of the presumption that litigation will be adversely determined, and any restriction of the scope of the clause, for example, to relate to Obligors only.
[44] See further commentary on clause 19.13 at 8.061 and on clause 23.8 at 8.261.
[45] See the discussion of the scope of the agreement at 0.121 onwards.
[46] Although they already have the benefit of the word 'reasonably'.
[47] Since the lenders have no more rights if there are two Defaults than if there is only one.

> **Box 8.16**
> So, for example, the borrower may be in breach of the undertaking in clause 22.1 to maintain all necessary authorizations for performance of its obligations. Under clause 23.3(b), assume that a grace period of ten days has been given for this particular undertaking. Once the borrower realizes that a necessary authorization is missing, that is a Default but not an Event of Default. If the borrower fails to notify the lenders 'promptly' of the fact that an authorization is missing, that failure to notify is a breach of clause 20.5 and a Default in its own right. As long as no grace period has been given in relation to clause 20.5, it is also an immediate Event of Default, so failure to notify has the result of depriving the borrower of the grace period they would otherwise have had in respect of the original Default.

Comment   Lenders may prefer to replace the word 'promptly' with a specific time period.   8.092

Clause 20.6   Use of websites

Clause 20.6 contains provisions which allow for communication by the Company by posting information on their website, but only in relation to those syndicate members who have agreed to that form of communication and with a requirement to inform the syndicate if information which is required under the Loan Agreement is posted onto the website.   8.093

Clause 20.7   'Know your customer' checks

This clause contains provisions requiring delivery of information as necessary to allow the Agent and the lenders to comply with any applicable 'know your customer' regulations.[48]   8.094

These checks need to be carried out before signing. This clause requires additional information to be delivered in the event of a change of law, a change of status of an Obligor (e.g. de-listing), or a proposed secondary market purchase.

CLAUSE 21: FINANCIAL COVENANTS

1   Purpose

Lenders use financial covenants for a number of reasons –   8.095

- Firstly they help to impose discipline on the borrower and to focus the attention of management on key financial goals.

---

[48] Which, in England, arise under the Money Laundering Regulations 2007 (as amended)

- Secondly, they provide a mechanism by which the lenders can monitor the performance of the borrower's business and get early warning of any deterioration.
- Next, they can also be used to provide incentives for the borrower to achieve certain financial targets. For example, it is common to have provisions by which the Margin reduces or dividends are permitted, when targets are met.
- Lastly, at the end of the day, the financial covenants operate as a stop loss. That is, if the desired financial results cannot be met, the financial covenants give the lenders the right to accelerate the loan and exit the transaction.

8.096 The main questions which need to be considered in relation to the ratios are:

- which aspects of the borrower's financial condition should be tested?
- at which level of the Group should the tests be run?
- in respect of what periods should the the tests be run?
- what the consequences of breach of a ratio be?
- can a breach be cured? and
- how should the various words used in the tests be defined?

2   Which aspects of the borrower's financial condition should be tested?

8.097 A number of different ratios may be used, each of which is designed to highlight different types of financial difficulty, before these problems become entrenched. Precisely which ratios to test clearly depends on the identity of the borrower – with significantly fewer, and simpler, tests being used for investment grade borrowers than in other situations. Ratios which may be tested include

- interest cover
- cashflow
- leverage
- liquidity
- gearing and
- tangible net worth.

8.098 In addition, financial tests may be used

- to restrict capital expenditure
- to give rise to a requirement for prepayment (a 'cash sweep') and
- sometimes, only to restrict taking on additional debt – that is, they are used on an 'incurrence' as opposed to a 'maintenance' basis (see 8.113)

8.099 and finally,

- it is because of certain limitations in the ratios that lenders will often include a 'clean down period' in a revolving credit.

We will look at these issues in turn, starting with interest cover.

Interest Cover

8.100 This ratio looks at the financial period just ended and compares income earned during that period (net of expenses) with the interest payable on loans during that period. The purpose of this ratio is to identify how easy it is for the borrower to service its loans out of current income and without having recourse, for example, to sale of assets, past income, or currency exchange gains. The concept of EBITDA is used to define income earned. See Box 8.17

Box 8.17

EBITDA stands for Earnings before Interest, Tax, Depreciation and Amortization. It also excludes profits and losses from unusual items. It represents the total profit of the company for the period in question, disregarding the effect of

- unusual items such as major asset sales, currency losses and currency profits – because what we are trying to get at is the core income of the company, to the extent that it can be earned again and again – it is **maintainable** earnings which are being measured,
- tax and interest, – because these are not indicators of the health of the underlying business so they 'muddy the water',
- depreciation and amortization – because these are notional figures reflecting the price paid for assets (in the case of depreciation) or goodwill (in the case of amortization) and the decision of the finance director about how long that asset would have value – again, nothing to do with the health of the company.

Cashflow

8.101 The second income related ratio looks at cashflow. This ratio looks at actual cash received in a given period (net of cash paid out) and compares it with total scheduled loan payments during that period.

The point to focus on here is the distinction between earnings and cash. The difference is explained by the accruals concept, which is used in preparing a company's profit and loss accounts. That concept requires income and expenses to be allocated to the period in which they were earned or accrued even if payment is not made until some time later (or at all). So for example, if services are provided during December but not billed till January, the accounts will nevertheless show the price of those services in the December figures. So the accounts (and EBITDA) will recognize income before that income is actually received. Indeed, that income may never be received. So the cashflow ratio looks at cash actually received rather than money earned which may not be received. See Box 8.18 on page 186.

> **Box 8.18**
> Both the interest cover ratio and the cashflow ratio are necessary because there are two ways in which a company may find that it doesn't have enough income to pay its debts – it either didn't earn enough in the first place (the interest cover ratio will reveal this) or it earned the income but for some reason did not get paid (the cashflow test is designed to reveal this). An example may help. Assume a company has interest payments to make each month in the amount of $250,000.
>
> In scenario 1 the company earns $1,000,000 in January but does not get paid until March, meaning that there is a potential problem paying the interest due in February. If the only test made in January was the interest cover ratio then there is no apparent cause for alarm – the company has earned plenty of money with which to pay the interest – but it has not received the cash yet. A cashflow cover test in January and February will reveal whether this is a problem building up or not.
>
> Similarly in scenario 2 assume the company earns nothing in January but receives payment for work done in the previous year. The fact of having earned nothing in January may give rise to a problem paying the interest due in February and March. A cashflow test in January will not reveal any problem as the company has received plenty of cash with which to pay the January interest. An interest cover test in January would reveal the potential problem.

8.102 The cashflow ratio is different from the interest cover ratio in that

- it is concerned with all loan payments, not just interest, and
- it focuses on actual cash receipts and payments as opposed to income earned (but not received yet) and expenses accrued.

Hence it is useful to have tests based on cash actually received – that is, the cashflow test. But it is also useful to have a test (the interest cover ratio) based on income earned (EBITDA) in order to give advance warning of future cashflow problems.

Leverage

8.103 This looks at the relationship between EBITDA for a period and the total amount of the borrower's debts. The purpose of the ratio is to look at the longer term – the whole life of the loan, and examine how easy it is for the borrower to pay off their total debts out of core maintainable earnings. It is similar to the income multiple used in consumer mortgages.

It is also worth noting that both the cashflow ratio and the interest cover ratio just look at payments of principal and interest which are scheduled to be made during the current period. They ignore future debt repayments and unscheduled repayments such as payments under a revolving credit. They also do not take into account debts on which no interest is due (such as PIK[49] notes – where interest may be capitalized). So, to take an extreme example, if the borrower's only financing was a loan which capitalized interest and had a bullet repayment after seven years, the company could earn practically nothing but neither the interest cover ratio nor the cashflow ratio would reveal a problem because those ratios are only looking at the ability to service the interest and principal which is scheduled to be paid in the period in question. So those tests would not highlight the issue ahead as to whether the company had enough to pay the final payments and capitalized interest.

This leverage ratio is therefore useful to address the total borrowing, regardless of maturities

Liquidity

Another important ratio is the liquidity ratio, or 'quick' ratio. This is a test of solvency and compares current assets to current liabilities. It is somewhat unusual to see this ratio in a loan agreement, but, if it is included, the drafting will need to deal with how to value contingent liabilities such as guarantees (since those liabilities may never fall due) and how to value stock (since ultimately it may not be sold at the anticipated price). **8.104**

This test is perhaps not as useful as the cashflow test or the interest cover test since it does not identify the time at which the assets were generated. So, for example, the company may be able to meet the liquidity ratio even if it earns no income for years, as long as it has cash in the bank generated by a single good piece of business some time in the past.

However the liquidity cover ratio is a useful supplement to the other ratios because, at the end of the day, the issue is whether the borrower has liquid assets with which to pay its current debts. This ratio looks at ALL current debts so it will include payments to suppliers, employees, tax and the like.

Gearing

The gearing ratio looks at the amount borrowed and compares it with the balance sheet value of the company to see if the company has over-borrowed against its assets. The relationship between the amount of borrowing and the amount invested in the company by shareholders will have a significant impact on the resilience of the company in times of financial stress. See Box 8.19 on page 188. **8.105**

For this purpose, borrowings will include the various items (other than derivatives, and with liabilities under guarantees being a debatable item) included in the definition of Financial Indebtedness so as to catch transactions having the same commercial effect as borrowings. Subordinated debt will be an item for discussion with its treatment depending on the level of subordination.[50] **8.106**

---

[49] Standing for 'payment in kind', see 0.034.
[50] See discussion of subordination at A1.033.

> **Box 8.19**
>
> GEARING
>
> Take the example of an investment trust. Investment trusts can borrow money to invest. This is called gearing. Gearing improves an investment trust's performance when its investments are doing well. On the other hand, if its investments do not do as well as expected, gearing lowers performance.
>
> Example
>
> If the investment trust is made up of £50m of investors' money and £50m of borrowing then the total fund available for investment is £100m. Say the value of the fund goes down by 10% as a result of losses in the stockmarket – the value of the overall fund falls from £100m to £90m. However, bear in mind that the borrowing is still £50m, therefore the remaining £40m belongs to the investors.
>
> So, although the overall fund went down by 10%, the investors' money has actually gone down by 20% (i.e. from £50m to £40m). Gearing boosts gains, but it also magnifies losses. Not all investment trusts are geared and deciding whether to borrow and when to borrow, is a judgement the investment manager makes. An investment trust that is geared is a higher-risk investment than one which is not geared (assuming the same underlying investments).

Tangible Net Worth

8.107 This test simply looks at the book value of the company's assets, less the amount of its liabilities. For this purpose, lenders generally exclude the value of intangible assets such as goodwill, looking instead at the value of tangible assets which can be sold. The company's assets are represented in its balance sheet by the figure shown in respect of 'shareholders funds', and therefore the starting point of the definition is the amount of shareholders' funds less items such as goodwill, which are intangible. Nevertheless, it is worth noting that the book value of the company's assets is no guide to their real value. The book value represents the price paid for assets and the assumed rate of depreciation, but that is not the same as the price at which they can be sold. Therefore the Tangible Net Worth covenant is one of the less common financial covenants.

Summary

8.108 So, in summary, there are ratios which can test whether the company

- has earned enough recently to pay its debts (the interest cover ratio)
- Has been paid enough recently to pay its debts (the cashflow ratio)
- Has borrowed too much compared to its income (the leverage ratio)
- Has borrowed too much compared with the amount invested by shareholders (the gearing ratio)

- Can pay its debts as they fall due (the liquidity or quick ratio); and
- Has enough assets (the Tangible Net Worth test).

In addition to these tests, lenders often impose restrictions on what the company can do with its profits. These are described next.

Restriction on Capex

Lenders will often want to restrict the extent to which the borrower is allowed to make capital expenditure for two reasons. Firstly they want to prevent earnings, which are otherwise available for debt service, being used for other things. Secondly, they prefer the borrower to develop steadily rather than in spurts. Heavy capital expenditure will usually result in increased operating costs, often with the return on the investment taking a little while to materialize. Firm and steady is therefore the preference.

8.109

Cash Sweeps

Lenders often want to ensure that if profits are high in a given period, those profits are used to prepay debt rather than being used for capital expenditure or being paid out to shareholders by way of dividend. This is particularly important in a cyclical industry.

8.110

Clean Down Period

As noted earlier, the cashflow ratio only measures the availability of cash to meet scheduled repayments. It does not address the ability to make repayments under a revolving credit. This is one reason why lenders often require a 'clean down period' in a revolving credit. That is, they require the borrower to repay the revolving credit and leave it undrawn for a given period each year. This clean down is also intended to ensure that the borrower only uses the revolving credits to fund working capital needs, not as part of their permanent capital.

8.111

3 At which level of the group should the tests be run?

This clearly needs to reflect the credit decision. Lenders may be concerned with the financial condition of the group as a whole and/or with the condition of specific companies (most likely the Obligors) within the group.[51] They may therefore wish to impose certain financial covenants on the Obligors in addition to any covenants for the group as a whole. If any specific companies (such as subsidiary undertakings or non-recourse companies[52]) have been excluded from the definition of 'Group' then the

8.112

---

[51] See the discussion of the scope of the agreement at 0.126 onwards.
[52] See 0.126 onwards.

lenders will probably want to have the ratios tested against the financial position of the group excluding those companies.[53]

4 In respect of what periods should the tests be run?

'Incurrence' tests

8.113 In large transactions, non-bank lenders and lenders active in the US market often accept that the financial covenants will apply on an 'incurrence' rather than a 'maintenance' basis. That is, instead of requiring the various ratios to be met in relation to successive financial periods throughout the life of the loan, they are only used to prohibit the borrowing of further funds if they are not met. Once additional funds have been borrowed, the tests will only become relevant again if the borrower wants to borrow further monies.

The rationale for this is that these lenders do not want to be consulted with requests for consent and the like, both because of manpower constraints and also because they do not wish to receive the non-public information which would go with such requests as this would hamper their freedom to invest. The size of the loan and its liquidity also enables them to take a less restrictive view than might be the case in smaller loans.

8.114 An incurrence basis for testing significantly devalues the financial ratios. Where they are tested on a 'maintenance' basis, they operate to give the lenders a steady stream of information about the business, and to forewarn the lenders if difficulties start to emerge. If the undertakings only apply on an 'incurrence' basis, this regular information flow will not occur.

'Maintenance' tests

8.115 Most financial ratios are drafted on a 'maintenance' basis. That is, the borrower is required to meet the ratio in each successive financial period. One drawback with these financial ratios is that there is often a mismatch between the timing of any problem and the occurrence of the Event of Default. By the time a breach becomes apparent, the accounting period in which it occurred will have come to an end and the particular issue may have been resolved.[54] On the other hand, it may be evident that there is a problem and that once the accounts for the relevant period are produced, they will show a breach, but until the accounts are produced, there is nothing the lenders can do about it. It is for this reason that lenders often require to have an Event of Default relating to material adverse change in financial condition notwithstanding the existence of financial ratios. See

---

[53] With corresponding adjustment needed to the undertaking in clause 20 to provide financial information.

[54] Nevertheless, depending on the drafting of the financial ratios, the Event of Default may have occurred and, subject to anything agreed on equity cure rights, will not be capable of being cured (see 8.223).

comments at 8.278 onwards on the interrelation of the material adverse change clause and the financial ratios.[55]

8.116 It is also worth noting here that the material adverse change Event of Default will, of necessity, be subjective – that is – it is always a question of opinion as to whether any given change is 'material' or not. So, if there is a deterioration in the financial condition of the borrower between test dates, unless the change is extreme, then lenders are likely to want to wait until there is a clearer Event of Default to rely on, rather than accelerate on the basis of the material adverse change Event of Default itself. This is in line with the general advice on use of the material adverse change Event of Default. Nevertheless, the lenders will want the ability not to advance further funds and, if applicable, to freeze payment of dividends and the like. This is where the definition of 'Default' comes in. As long as the definition of Default is in the LMA standard form and the words 'the making of any determination' have not been excluded,[56] then the deterioration in financial condition should constitute a 'Default', enabling the lenders to freeze the loan until the situation becomes clearer.

5 What should the consequences of breach of a ratio be?

8.117 These ratios are particularly important because, unlike many of the other undertakings and events of default, breach of them does not necessarily mean there is a problem, simply that the credit risk has changed somewhat. They give advance warning of changes and are able to be graded subtly as opposed to the black or white nature of other provisions. For this reason, breach of a financial ratio need not be drafted to have the effect of an Event of Default. It is possible (and not uncommon) to provide that, within certain limits (breach of which will be an Event of Default) failure to meet a particular ratio simply affects the Margin.

8.118 Finance directors in established companies need to be sure that the numbers specified in the ratios are reasonable and will not give rise to an Event of Default too readily. The borrowers' argument is that, assuming the borrower is a reasonably well-established company, they need a robust loan agreement which will see them not only through good times but also through downturns. All companies have ups and downs, so setting ambitious ratios, or even ratios reflecting the current situation, if breach of those ratios is an Event of Default, leads to a fragile position in which any deterioration in the borrower's condition will give the lenders the right to accelerate. This, in turn (through the cross default clauses), will result in its other lenders having the same right. The threat to their liquidity which this may

---

[55] Lenders might also seek to make the tests predictive as well as historic, based on the predictions within the company's management accounts.
[56] See the discussion of 'Default' at 1.023 onwards.

cause (regardless of the overall financial stability of the company) could be sufficient to precipitate its collapse. If breach resulted in a change in Margin, this risk would disappear.

6 Can a breach be cured?

8.119 It is often agreed that if there is a breach of the financial covenants, this can be cured by an injection of equity. This is referred to as the 'equity cure right'. Lenders will usually put a limit on the number of times the equity cure rights can be exercised during the life of the loan.

8.120 A number of other issues arise here

- First, how long does the borrower have to inject the equity? Often, borrowers will not know that there has been a breach of a ratio until after the end of the financial period in question, when the accounts are being prepared. In order to avoid triggering cross default clauses it is important that the cure period does not start until the borrower knows there is a breach – that is, until the date on which the Compliance Certificate is (or is required to be) delivered.
- Second, what should happen to the additional funds which are injected by way of equity? Lenders will probably want the moneys to be used to prepay debt to reduce the risk of the problem recurring. Borrowers may request that it be simply deposited in an account and released if the ratio is met the next time around. Regardless of what happens to the money in practice, a separate issue arises as to what its effect should be on the various ratios. Is it treated as
  ○ extra cash just for the cashflow covenant
  ○ extra profit earned (i.e. an increase in EBITDA) for the interest cover ratio, and/or as
  ○ A reduction in debt for the interest cover ratio?
- Also, given that other issues may be driven off these figures – such as the amount of the Margin and permitted capital expenditure, will the injection have any effect for these purposes or will it only be effective in relation to ensuring there is no Event of Default? These are issues for negotiation.

8.121 Another issue sometimes agreed is a 'Mulligan' clause. This takes one of two forms. It may provide that there is only an Event of Default if the ratios are breached twice in a row. Alternatively, it may provide that the lender loses its right to accelerate for a breach of financial covenant if it does not exercise the right and, on a subsequent test date, the borrower meets the ratios.

7 How should the words used in the tests be defined?

8.122 This is an area where the accountants will need to be involved. There are a number of detailed issues to consider, which are beyond the scope of this book. A useful source of suggestions on this can be found in the Association of Corporate Treasurers guide to the LMA facilities agreement for leveraged transactions, which is available on the Association of Corporate Treasurers website at www.treasurers.org. It is also worth noting the comment made by the Association of Corporate Treasurers in their commentary on the Investment Grade Loan Agreement to the effect that 'Financial covenants in leveraged loans are complex because they are crafted to benchmark the base case financial model, and tailored closely to the assumptions used in it. In contrast, in corporate deals, in particular in investment grade deals, the Borrower's financial condition is measured by reference to its Original Financial Statements. Covenants may be phrased much more simply, by reference to accounting concepts used by the Group without such detailed definition.'

8 Financial covenants in an asset finance transaction

An asset finance transaction will often include a security cover ratio (see Box 8.20).

8.123

This will specify that the value of the security must always equal at least a given percentage of the loan outstanding. The percentage varies

---

Box 8.20
EXAMPLE SECURITY COVER RATIO
If at any time the Security Value is less than the Security Requirement then the Borrower shall, within 10 Business Days, either

(a) prepay the Loan in such amount as shall be required to ensure that, after such prepayment, the Security Value is not less than the Security Requirement; or

(b) provide additional security for the Loan having a value, as determined by the Majority Lenders in their absolute discretion, equal to the difference between the Security Value and the Security Requirement.

'Security Requirement' means, at any relevant time, an amount equal to one hundred and fifty percent of the amount of the Loan[1] at that time;
 'Security Value' means, at any relevant time, the value of the Security at such time as determined by the latest valuation delivered to the Lenders pursuant to Clause {}.

---

[1] If the loan is a multicurrency loan, the ratio will generally be tested with reference to the Base Currency Amount of the loan (see definition of 'Base Currency Amount'). However, this exposes the lenders to an exchange rate risk in between the dates (usually the start of each Interest Period) when the loan needs to be readjusted to match the Base Currency Amount, as discussed in relation to clause 6. So, if the loan may be outstanding in a currency which is not the same as the currency in which the security is likely to be sold (the 'Security Currency'), the lenders may require the ability to test the Security Requirement from time to time during Interest Periods, with reference to the amount of the loan at its then current exchange rate as against the Security Currency.

between 120% and over 200%. The excess over 100% is designed to give the lenders a cushion for

- interest which will accrue between commencement of proceedings and realization of proceeds of security;
- expenses which will be incurred by the lenders in realizing the security;
- the fact that values of assets tend to fall precisely when the lender requires access to them;[57] and
- currency fluctuations, if the loan is a multicurrency loan or if the value of the security may be affected by the value of currencies other than the currency of the loan.

8.124 If the ratio is breached at any time, the borrower generally has the option of providing additional security or prepaying the loan to the extent necessary to bring the ratio back into line.

There are a number of issues that often arise in negotiation of this undertaking:

When and how is the security valued?

8.125 As to when, lenders frequently wish to have the ability to obtain valuations more often than annually. The issue often boils down to one of expense, with the borrower obtaining annual valuations but with a right for the Agent to obtain interim valuations at its own expense.

As to how, there are many options, including:

- each of the Agent and the borrower appoint a valuer, and the value is the average of the two;
- the borrower appoints a valuer but the Agent is able to challenge the valuation and, if it does so, the Agent's valuer's determination is the value;
- each of the Agent and the borrower appoints a valuer and the valuation is the average of the two but the Agent has the ability to appoint a third if he disputes the borrower's valuation. The value will then be the average of the three (or of the Agent's two); and
- as above but the valuations can only be made by a valuer which is on a list of pre-agreed approved valuers.

The lenders may also want to include a fallback provision to deal with the (rare) eventuality that it proves impossible to obtain a valuation of the security. This happened in relation to ships after the credit crunch because certain types of ships were not being traded and therefore values could not be made.

---

[57] The reason for this is twofold. First, the borrower is more likely to have financial difficulties at a time of economic turmoil generally, when asset prices are also likely to have fallen; and second, the markets will often be aware that the sale is a distressed sale, which will always result in lower prices than a voluntary sale.

Should there be any restriction on the types of assets that the lenders must accept?

8.126 Often the lenders will limit additional security to assets which have a public market, for example, stocks and bonds. If other assets may be permitted, lenders often require complete discretion as to how to value them, so as to protect themselves from
- being offered assets of a type which they would not have accepted at the commencement of the loan; and
- the possibility that there may be legal difficulties in relevant countries in creating valid security (such as security over moveable property[58]) or that any security created may be clawed back in an insolvency, for example, because it is a **preference**.[59]

Should the value of additional security be determined by Majority Lenders?

8.127 Lenders may wish to consider whether the requirements as to the valuation of additional security should be determined by all the lenders or by a Majority. Individual lenders may not want to be required to accept security based on the views of the rest of the syndicate. However, the borrower will be likely to object to a requirement that the value should be agreed by all lenders as it exposes the borrower to the views of the most cautious lender.

How to value cash

8.128 If cash is part of the security (e.g. perhaps where moneys are blocked in an account where there is a restriction on distribution of those moneys) then the borrower may request that the Security Requirement should be the relevant percentage of the *loan minus the amount of cash cover*. The effect of this request is to reduce the Security Requirement by more than the cash held, on the basis that the cash should count Dollar for Dollar against the loan. The argument is that, because cash is readily accessible, the justifications discussed above for requiring the Security Value to exceed the amount of the loan do not apply (see Box 8.21 on page 196).

Release of additional security

8.129 The borrower often requests that if, after additional security has been given, the point comes when the ratio would be satisfied without taking into account the value of the additional security, the lenders should release that additional security.

Borrowers may also ask that the clause should not operate if, between the time of the shortfall and the date on which the clause would otherwise require prepayment or additional security, a repayment falls due which will have the effect of bringing the loan down to a figure such that there is no longer any shortfall.

---

[58] See A1.063.
[59] See Appendix 2.

> **Box 8.21**
> For example, assume the loan is $10 million and the security cover ratio is 150%. If the security (excluding cash) is valued at $12 million, there is a shortfall of $3 million in the required Security Value. To cure this, the borrower would need to provide cash se-curity of $3 million. If the borrower succeeds in its argument discussed here, however, then the cash security required will be only $2 million. This is because that $2 million will be counted against the $10 million loan on a dollar for dollar basis. That brings the amount of the loan which is not covered by cash security down from $10 million to $8 million. Security cover of 150% is required for that $8 million, resulting in a re-quirement that the value of non-cash security is at least $12 million and the existing non-cash security covers that requirement.

CLAUSE 22: GENERAL UNDERTAKINGS – SECTION 1 – THE LMA UNDERTAKINGS

8.130   The general positive undertakings in the LMA Term Loan are minimal – to maintain consents and comply with laws affecting the loan.

The negative undertakings in the LMA Term Loan consist of the nega-tive pledge clause, a no disposals clause, and a clause prohibiting merger or change of business. See Box 8.22.

> **Box 8.22**
> It is interesting to compare the standard LMA Term Loan undertakings with those used by Moody's in their covenant quality assessment matrix,[60] used to assess the value of undertakings in bond issues. The matrix looks at key undertakings and rates them from strong (e.g. if they have few carve-outs) through weak to non-existent. The undertakings which are in-cluded in the matrix are:
>
> - restricted payments (e.g. restricting dividends);
> - change of control;
> - merger restrictions;
> - restrictions on disposals;
> - limitations on borrowings;
> - negative pledge;
> - limit on sale and leaseback; and
> - limitation on subsidiaries incurring debts.
>
> Note that items which Moody's regard as important but which are miss-ing from the LMA Term Loan are the restriction on payments, the limi-tation on borrowings and the limitation on subsidiaries incurring debts (which is important because of the concept of structural subordination discussed at A1.036).

---

[60] See 'Request for Comment on Moody's Indenture Covenant Research and Assessment Framework' for a detailed discussion of the criteria for assessment.

Clause 22.1   Authorization

Clause 22.1 requires each Obligor to obtain all necessary 'Authorizations' required in the place of their incorporation to enable them to perform their obligations under the agreements and to ensure that the documents are admissible in evidence there.

8.131

Comment   This undertaking relates to corporate authorities and other consents, licences, filings, and registrations required under the laws in the place of incorporation of Obligors. It is somewhat less broad that the corresponding representation in clause 19.5 discussed at 8.036, which, unlike this clause 22.1, is not limited to Authorizations from the Obligors' jurisdiction of incorporation. The two clauses should be reviewed together.

8.132

The clause not only requires the borrower to make sure they have all necessary 'Authorizations' but it also requires them to deliver copies to the Agent – borrowers might like to restrict this so that they are only required to deliver copies of the Authorizations 'on request'.

Where this clause is restricted to the borrower's place of incorporation, (as it is in the LMA Term Loan), compliance ought not to be too onerous. However this is one of the clauses which, particularly in the context of secured transactions, may often be extended to apply to all 'Relevant Jurisdictions', which is likely to include the locations of secured assets and wherever the borrower conducts business. In this case the borrower may need to restrict the clause further, for example, by adding a materiality test.

8.133

Clause 22.2   Compliance with laws

Clause 22.2 is a good housekeeping undertaking, requiring the Obligors to comply with all applicable laws if failure to do so would materially affect their ability to perform their obligations under the documents.

8.134

Clause 22.3   Negative pledge

The negative pledge clause prohibits the borrower from giving security unless that security falls within one of the exceptions to the clause. There are many different reasons for inclusion of a negative pledge and its significance varies from transaction to transaction.

8.135

Purpose

In an unsecured loan, it is one of the three clauses (pari passu, negative pledge, and cross default) which the unsecured creditor will regard as particularly important as they ensure equality with other creditors. Its role here is

8.136

- to preserve equality – as a general requirement that lenders to the borrower (except, perhaps, in special cases such as asset or project financings), lend on the same (unsecured) basis; and/or

- to provide advance warning of a change in financial condition – if the borrower needs to borrow significant amounts on a secured basis this may reflect a change in its condition; and/or
- to protect the lenders' leverage in the event of the borrower's insolvency – the lenders may wish to ensure that there are no secured lenders for fear that a secured lender may be more prepared to take proceedings against a borrower than an unsecured lender; and/or
- to protect the pool of assets which the borrower has at the start of the transaction, from being dissipated.

8.137 In a secured transaction lenders may be equally concerned as in an unsecured transaction to:

- protect their leverage in insolvency and hence prevent existence of any other secured creditors; and
- protect the initial pool of assets from being dissipated.

In addition, if the lenders are taking security over substantially all the company's assets they will want the negative pledge so as to:

- facilitate the lenders' control of the company;
- enable the lenders to sell the company as a going concern should an Event of Default occur;
- reduce the likelihood of other creditors taking action against the company;
- bolster a floating charge;[61] and
- simply as part of the range of undertakings designed to ensure the company does not undertake any other business, if the company is a single purpose company.

Consequences of breach

8.138 One problem with the negative pledge clause relates to the consequences of breach. The clause aims to ensure that if the lenders need to enforce their rights against the borrower, all its assets will be shared pro rata. However, if the borrower breaches the clause, the lenders' remedy is to accelerate. If they do accelerate, they will then be in the situation which the clause was intended to avoid – that is, of having to enforce but not having equal access to the borrower's assets. In other words, the clause does not in fact protect the lenders against a borrower which breaches the clause. The position may be different if the person taking security knew, or should have known, that that security was given in breach of the negative pledge.[62]

One variation on the negative pledge permits security to be given but only if the lenders are equally and rateably secured. This may be difficult to give effect to, given the fluctuating value of security and of the debt concerned, unless there were a formal security sharing agreement.

---

[61] See Box A1.12 on page 330.

[62] This is one reason for the representation at clause 19.3 – to help ensure that if anything done under this loan arrangement is a breach of prior agreements, the lenders can point to the representation and show that they were unaware of the breach.

Content

Generally, it is in all parties' interests to ensure that the clause permits the borrower's day-to-day activities and that it does not have the result of forcing the borrower to regularly request consent under it. The scope of the clause (e.g. does it prohibit title financing?[63]) and of any exceptions (e.g. does the operation of law exception depend on the relevant security also arising in the ordinary course of trading?[64]) needs to be reviewed in the context of the borrower's business and country of operations.

8.139

The negative pledge clause in the LMA Term Loan falls into three sections:

8.140

- First clause 22.3(a) prevents the creation or existence of 'Security';[65]
- Second clause 22.3(b) outlaws quasi security if that takes the form of one of the items specified in the clause and if its primary purpose is to raise Financial Indebtedness;
- Third clause 22.3(c) sets out the exceptions.

Clause 22.3(a)   Prohibition on security

Clause 22.3(a) prevents the creation or existence of 'Security' (see Box 8.23). The clause does not only prohibit the borrower from creating Security but also says the borrower must not *'permit [Security] to subsist'*. This outlaws those security interests which arise at law such as liens.[66] It also has an impact on Security created by companies which initially were not restricted but become restricted at a later stage.[67]

8.141

> **Box 8.23**
> In this clause 22.3(a) (unlike Section (b) relating to certain forms of quasi security) all manner of Security is prohibited, whether or not it is created as security for Financial Indebtedness.[68] For example, security arising in the context of litigation, such as judgement liens, will be prohibited under clause 22.3(a) – subject to any relevant exceptions in clause 22.3.

Comment   The prohibition in this clause relates to all members of the group. The borrower may want to limit the prohibition to Obligors on the basis that lenders have no recourse against members of the group which are not Obligors and therefore should be unconcerned with their assets.[69]

8.142

---

[63] See comments below on clause 22.3(c) at 8.160 onwards.
[64] See comments on clause 22.3(c)(iv) at 8.155.
[65] 'Security' is defined to mean *'a mortgage, charge, pledge, lien or other security interest securing any obligation of any person or any other agreement or arrangement having a similar effect'*.
[66] See the discussion on clause 22.3(c)(iv) at 8.155.
[67] See Box 0.14 on page 29.
[68] See commentary on clause 22.3(b) at 8.144 onwards.
[69] See 0.142.

Clause 22.3(b) Prohibition on quasi security

8.143 (b) No Obligor shall (and the Company shall ensure that no other member of the Group will):
  (i) sell, transfer or otherwise dispose of any of its assets on terms whereby they are or may be leased to or re-acquired by an Obligor [or any other member of the Group];
  (ii) sell, transfer or otherwise dispose of any of its receivables on recourse terms;
  (iii) enter into any arrangement under which money or the benefit of a bank or other account may be applied, set-off or made subject to a combination of accounts; or
  (iv) enter into any other preferential arrangement having a similar effect,

  in circumstances where the arrangement or transaction is entered into primarily as a method of raising Financial Indebtedness or of financing the acquisition of an asset.

8.144 Clause 22.3(b) outlaws quasi security if that takes the form of one of the items specified in the clause. This prohibition on quasi security only applies where it occurs primarily for the purpose of raising Financial Indebtedness. The purpose, of course, is to ensure that, no matter the legal structure, if the commercial effect is equivalent to security, it is prohibited. The qualification relating to Financial Indebtedness is intended to distinguish between quasi security and arrangements which do not amount to raising finance.

8.145 The specific forms of quasi security prohibited by this clause are:

- sale and repurchase or leaseback;
- selling receivables but keeping the risk; and
- set off or similar arrangements with cash.

There is also a provision (clause 22.3(b)(iv)) stating that similar arrangements are also prohibited.

One area which lenders might like to consider is cash pooling because it may result in funds being used for the benefit of non-Obligors and thereby removed from the grasp of the lenders. See Box 8.24 on page 201.

8.146 Cash pooling falls within the scope of paragraph 22.3(b)(iii) – as being *'an arrangement under which money or the benefit of a bank account may be applied, set off or subject to a combination of accounts'* but this is only prohibited if *'the arrangement ... is entered into primarily as a method of raising Financial Indebtedness'* (see the last two lines of clause 22.3(b)). Raising Financial Indebtedness may arguably be one of the purposes of the arrangement, but is rarely the primary purpose, so that cash pooling is unlikely to be prohibited by this clause in most circumstances.[70]

---

[70] But of course it may breach some other clause, for example, there may be restrictions on lending or borrowing money or giving guarantees or it may even breach the no disposals undertaking.

> **Box 8.24**
> Cash pooling is an arrangement which many corporate groups have, which is designed to minimize fees and interest payments and to ensure that all group members, wherever situated, have the benefit of funds held in the pool by other group members. In effect, these arrangements have the commercial effect of treating the group as a single entity, paying interest only on any net debit amount.
>
> There are two principal mechanisms for the operation of the pool: one is physical and the other notional. Under the physical system, cash in the accounts of any individual group member are regularly swept into a 'central' account on which all group members who are members of the cash pool can draw. The transfers have the effect of intercompany loans between group members.
>
> In the notional system, no physical transfers are made but lenders effectively charge interest on a 'net' basis. However, in order to do this, lenders will usually require all pool members to guarantee each others' debts in relation to the pooled accounts so as to enable the bank to use surpluses in one account to offset against debits in another account in the event of insolvency of a pool member.
>
> Therefore, whichever route is used, a lender could find that funds which are earned by its borrower may be on-lent to a different entity (in the case of a physical pool) or set off against debts of a different entity (in the case of a notional pool) and thereby removed from the grasp of the lender.

Even if it were, clause 22.3(c)(ii) expressly allows netting and set off in the ordinary course of banking arrangements so that cash pooling would probably be allowed (although some borrowers ask for clarification of this as noted at 8.149).

Lenders may want to consider whether they want to protect themselves against money leaking from the borrower to other group members via a cash pool. One option could be at least to require guarantees of the loan from all members of the cash pool. Another would be to take security on important bank accounts and prevent those accounts from being used as part of the pool. See Box 8.25.

> **Box 8.25**
> It is worth noting the provisions of the Leveraged LMA in this respect. That agreement permits *'netting or set off entered into by a member of the Group...in the ordinary course of its banking arrangements for the purpose of netting debit and credit balances...but only so long as (i) such arrangement does not permit credit balances of Obligors to be netted or set off against debit balances of members of the Group which are not Obligors and (ii) such arrangement does not give rise to other Security over the assets of Obligors in support of liabilities of members of the Group which are not Obligors...'.*

Borrowers needing to have cash pool arrangements need to consider whether they breach any other provision of the loan agreement such as perhaps restrictions on lending or giving guarantees or on dealings with affiliates.

Clause 22.3(c)   Exceptions to negative pledge

The exceptions are as follows.

Clause 22.3(c)(i) Existing security

8.147   Paragraph c(i) allows security already in place but only to the extent of the amount advanced to date.

8.148   *Comment*   Borrowers sometimes ask that this exception be extended to allow any refinancing of existing secured debt as long as the amount of the debt and the extent of the security are not increased. Some lenders will not agree as they are only happy to allow existing security on the basis that, over time, it will be paid off.

Clause 22.3(c)(ii) Netting or set off in the course of ordinary banking arrangements

8.149   (ii) *any netting or set-off arrangement entered into by any member of the Group in the ordinary course of its banking arrangements for the purpose of netting debit and credit balances;*

Sometimes borrowers ask for additional exceptions to this clause to expressly permit set off arrangements under such things as cash pooling and bank standard terms. These arrangements would not normally be entered into 'primarily for the purpose of raising Financial Indebtedness' and so would not be prohibited by paragraph (b). However paragraph (a) prohibits 'Security' which is defined to include things with the same commercial effect as security. Then the concern arises that cash pooling may not be considered to be merely 'banking arrangements' but something more than that. Similarly, standard terms of banking arrangements may give rise to other security in addition to the right to set off debit and credit balances. See Box 8.27 on page 204. Expressly permitting these items may therefore be helpful.

Clause 22.3(c)(iii)

8.150   *any payment or close out netting or set off arrangement pursuant to any hedging transaction entered into by a member of the Group for the purpose of:*

   A.   *hedging any risk to which any member of the Group is exposed in its ordinary course of trading; or*

   B.   *its interest rate or currency management operations which are carried out in the ordinary course of business and for non speculative purposes only excluding, in each case, any Security or Quasi Security under a credit support arrangement in relation to a hedging transaction.*

This paragraph is designed to allow netting and set off for derivatives as long as those derivatives were not speculative in nature. However it specifically excludes credit support arrangements. These are arrangements under which a party to a derivative which is 'out of the money' is required to set funds aside to settle the termination payment under the derivative if it terminates. See Box 8.26.

8.151

> **Box 8.26**
> Take for example an interest rate swap. The parties to the swap will have agreed that one party will make payments to the other calculated on one basis (for example, they may have agreed to make monthly payments at a fixed rate of say 5% on a notional sum of $100 million, over the next five years, in exchange for the counterparty making payment at LIBOR on the same notional sum on the same dates over the same period.) As interest rates move, one party will become 'out of the money'. If it wanted to terminate the swap at a time when it was out of the money, it would need to compensate the counterparty for the whole future stream of income. This termination payment can get quite high.

Therefore the derivative may include a requirement for a credit support arrangement. This is a requirement that the party which is out of the money transfers a sum of money to the counterparty, with a provision for a transfer back when the derivative terminates, to the extent that the sum transferred exceeds the termination payment.

Although a credit support arrangement is not security, it is intended to have the same commercial effect in that that sum of money will effectively be used to settle the termination payment. Legally, this effect is achieved through a netting arrangement rather than security. See Box A1.16 on page 337. Lenders therefore want to prohibit it in the same way as they prohibit security.

8.152

As long as 'Financial Indebtedness' includes derivatives, credit support arrangements are prohibited, either under 22.3(b)(iii) because it is an '*arrangement under which money or the benefit of a bank account may be applied*', or under clause 22.3(b)(iv) because it is a '*preferential arrangement having a similar effect*' and, in either case, it is also '*entered into primarily as a method of raising Financial Indebtedness*' as required by the last two lines of paragraph (b)[71].

8.153

---

[71] If Financial Indebtedness does not include derivatives, the position is less clear but credit support arrangements may well be prohibited by paragraph (a) since they have the same commercial effect as security so could fall within the defined term 'Security'.

8.154 *Comment* This prohibition may cause difficulties for borrowers since many borrowers will find that counterparties are only willing to enter into a derivative with them if they are prepared to give credit support arrangements

Clause 22.3(c)(iv) Operation of law

8.155 Many security interests arise without being deliberately created by the borrower and, subject to the exceptions in this clause 22.3(c), existence of these forms of security is prohibited, regardless of the fact that they were not created on purpose and they do not secure borrowings. They will be permitted under paragraph (iv) if they arise both by operation of law and in the ordinary course of trading (see Box 8.27).

> **Box 8.27**
> Examples of security which arises by operation of law *or* in the ordinary course of trading may include
> - security over an asset as security for a debt arising from a transaction relating to that asset – for example, in England, if equipment is delivered to a repairer the repairer will be entitled to hold onto the equipment (and will have security over it) until paid;
> - security arising by statute – for example, in some countries, the tax authorities have security over a company's property for any tax owing; or environmental agencies have security over a company's property for clean-up costs of environmental incidents caused by the company;
> - security arising under standard terms of banking arrangements – for example, under such arrangements, banks may have security over property deposited with them for safe keeping;
> - security in favour of unpaid sellers (in some countries, unpaid sellers automatically have security in the assets sold until they have been paid for them);
> - security given or arising automatically in the context of litigation, while proceedings are pursued.

8.156 The exception is cumulative. It requires the security to arise *both* by operation of law *and* in the ordinary course of trading. So, only some of the examples listed in Box 8.27 will be permitted by this exception. For example, security for clean-up costs in some circumstances would not be permitted because, although the security arises by operation of law, the environmental incident may well not have occurred 'in the ordinary course of trading'. Security under standard banking terms does not normally arise by operation of law, even though it is in the ordinary course of trading. To the extent that the relevant security is not permitted under this clause, it would be counted towards the threshold amount in clause 22.3(c)(x).

8.157 *Comment* Sometimes borrowers ask for the exceptions in paragraph (iv) to be independent, not cumulative, so that liens arising by operation of law are permitted (e.g. in respect of taxes) and liens arising in the ordinary course of trading are also permitted. Lenders prefer the cumulative requirement as, without it, the borrower's ability to deliberately create security in the ordinary course of trading is unlimited (see Box 8.28).

Lenders may require that any security permitted under this parapraph must be discharged within a specified period.

> **Box 8.28**
> Despite the frequency of the use of the expressions 'ordinary course of trading' and 'ordinary course of business' in contracts and in legislation, these expressions have no precise, clear meaning.
>
> What is the ordinary course of trading?
>
> It is clear that the 'ordinary course of trading' is a more restrictive expression than the 'ordinary course of business.' It will include activities which the business does, and expects to do, as part of its trading (meaning buying and selling), such as disposals of stock and acquisitions of raw materials. It is unlikely to include acquisitions of fixed assets or businesses.
>
> What is the ordinary course of business?
>
> This expression has a number of possible meanings. For example, if a company commonly enters into a particular type of transaction, that is probably in the ordinary course of business. Less clear would be the case where a company had never entered into a particular type of transaction, but that type of transaction was common in the industry. In one instance,[72] the courts held that even an unprecedented or exceptional transaction could be in the ordinary course of business (although that case involved the interpretation of a statute, not a contract, so that the purpose of the expression was quite different to its purpose in a loan agreement). Given the uncertainty, this expression should be used with caution.

Clause 22.3(c)(v) and (vi) After acquired property/companies

8.158 These clauses allow the borrower to purchase assets or companies which already have security on them provided that security is discharged within a specified period after the acquisition.

8.159 *Comment* The requirement in clauses 22.3(c)(v) and (vi) that the security must be discharged within a period after the acquisition is one which a borrower might seek to resist. Existence of that security does not contain any

---

[72] This case was Ashborder BV v Green Gas Power Ltd (2004) EWHC 1517, which looked at the expression in the context of floating charges. See also 'Defining the "Ordinary Course of Business"', *Journal of International Banking Law and Regulation*, 2004, 19(12), p. 513.

adverse implications as to the borrower's financial position and retention of these restrictions may make acquisitions more difficult. If the lenders view the purpose of the negative pledge as being to protect the borrower's existing pool of assets, this requirement is unnecessary. If, on the other hand, lenders are concerned simply to ensure equality and leverage on a winding up,[73] they will require these provisions to remain as drafted.

Clause 22.3(c)(vii) Under the Finance Documents

8.160 This allows the security created by the documents

Clause 22.3(c) (viii) Under certain title finance arrangements.
This paragraph permits title financing arrangements such as hire purchase arrangements if they are in the ordinary course of trading. This would permit such things as hire purchase of company cars or computers. The permission is important since, without it, it is unclear whether title financing arrangements are prohibited by the negative pledge in the first place.
They are clearly not prohibited by paragraph (a) since the key characteristic of title financing is that the financed asset belongs to the financier, not the user. Paragraph (a) prohibits the borrower from giving Security on its assets but in title financing the borrower's asset would be its contractual rights under the title financing arrangement rather than the asset itself.
Paragraph (b) is unclear, particularly because it prohibits only a sub-category of finance leasing – sale and leaseback.
By permitting title financing in certain circumstances it becomes clear that it is prohibited in all other circumstances.

Clause 22.3(c)(ix) Other
Other common exceptions are,

8.161
- Security created by non recourse subsidiaries (unless non recourse subsidiaries have been excluded from the ambit of the loan altogether)[74]. The argument is that this cannot harm the group except to the extent of the assets to which recourse is available for the limited recourse finance. As long as those assets are disregarded for the purpose of this loan (e.g. excluded in calculations of financial ratios) then existence of security created by non recourse subsidiaries should not concern the lenders.

8.162
- Security over property acquired after the loan agreement is signed, where the security is given to secure financing for purchase of that property. Some lenders may agree to this exception on the basis that giving security in these circumstances is not to the detriment of the existing pool of assets, provided the property being acquired does not replace an asset from the existing pool. On the other hand, lenders may not agree to this

---

[73] See 8.135 onwards.
[74] See 0.141.

exception if they are concerned that the fact that the borrower is raising money on a secured basis might indicate some change in its financial status, or if they want to ensure equality with other lenders.

- Liens in the context of litigation.[75] Even where those liens arise by operation of law (and many, such as payments into court, are not created by operation of law), the litigation may well not be in the ordinary course of trading and therefore these security interests, if permitted at all, would only be permitted if they fell within the threshold set in clause 22.3(c)(x). This could result in a large difference between the negotiated position in relation to litigation[76] and the position in practice. Nevertheless, lenders may justifiably argue that the circumstances in which they are content to see litigation occur will differ depending on whether that litigation involves the creation of security or not.   8.163
- Security given in order to access a particular (advantageous) source of funds only available on secured terms, such as export credit.   8.164
- Security for trade finance such as pledges of goods for the provision of letters of credit   8.165
- Intra group security   8.166
- Rent deposits for leasehold property.   8.167

The lenders should note that there is no cap on the amount of security which can be given under these various exceptions. The only cap is in paragraph (x) and it relates only to security created under paragraph (x). Lenders may prefer to agree a higher cap in paragraph (x) rather than extending the categories of security which can be created without a cap.

Clause 22.3(c)(x) Threshold
This exception reads   8.168

> (x) any Security securing indebtedness the principal amount of which (when aggregated with the principal amount of any other indebtedness which has the benefit of Security given by any member of the Group other than any permitted under paragraphs (i) to (ix) above) does not exceed [] (or its equivalent in another currency or currencies).

Comment   Some borrowers ask for an annual figure to be allowed with carry forward of unused amounts.   8.169

Comment   Another option is to set an aggregate figure at a percentage of Tangible Net Worth.   8.170

---

[75] Examples are payments into court or security for costs in a contested matter. Also see Goode, *Commercial Law*, p. 663 under the heading 'procedural securities' for details of other security interests which may arise in the course of litigation in England.
[76] See clause 23.8 at 8.261.

8.171 In negotiating the threshold amount, the parties need to ensure that it is flexible enough to protect the lenders' interest as well as accommodating the likely commercial needs of the borrower. As with financial ratios,[77] the borrower needs to ensure that the agreement will be robust enough to see it through downturns, up to a point. If on the downturn only minimal secured lending is permitted, the effect of this clause may be to accelerate the downturn which might otherwise have been avoided.

8.172 Lenders often argue that a lower threshold is appropriate because they will give consent under it whenever withholding consent would be detrimental to the borrower's interest. This argument should be treated with caution.[78]

8.173 The amount of the threshold also needs to be set with the other terms of the clause in mind. If title retention is prohibited, the amount of the threshold needs to be higher. Similarly if there were two separate exceptions: one for security arising by operation of law; and a second for security arising in the ordinary course of trading, the threshold could be lower.

It is also worth checking that all the exceptions to the negative pledge are expressed to apply both to 'Security' (i.e. those items prohibited by paragraph (a)) and also 'Quasi Security', that is, those items prohibited by paragraph (b)). Some of the LMA suite of documents (e.g. the Leveraged LMA) are not consistent in this respect.

Clause 22.4   No disposals

8.174 Clause 22.4 reads

(a) *No Obligor shall [(and the Company shall ensure that no other member of the Group will)], enter into a single transaction or a series of transactions (whether related or not) and whether voluntary or involuntary to sell, lease, transfer or otherwise dispose of any asset.*

The lenders may wish to restrict major disposals (even if they are at market value[79]) as they may affect the ability of the borrower to earn income to service the debt; or they may indicate a cashflow problem; or a change in business strategy. In the LMA Term Loan, the clause is *not* only designed solely to ensure that value is maintained in the Company (that would be the role of any Tangible Net Worth covenant and/or restriction on distributions to shareholders), but also to prevent changes in the composition of the Company's major assets ('**asset stripping**'). For the purpose of this clause, assets include cash and future income. See Box 8.29 on page 209. Payment of dividends or sale of receivables in a securitization would therefore both fall foul of this clause (subject to any applicable exception in clause 22.4(b)).

---

[77] See discussion on financial ratios at 8.118 onwards.
[78] See Box 0.5 on page 12.
[79] If so, no exception should be made allowing disposal on arm's length terms nor should the clause be replaced by a Tangible Net Worth covenant.

Comment This clause is almost certainly not intended to prohibit payment of dividends or to prohibit the type of transaction referred to in Box 8.29. Its breadth is mitigated by the exceptions – the first of which allows disposals 'in the ordinary course of trading'. However, given the vagueness of that expression – see Box 8.28 on page 205 – (and the fact that payment of dividends, while probably in 'the ordinary course of business' is certainly not 'in the ordinary course of trading') it might be sensible to restrict the no disposals clause itself so as only to restrict disposal of 'capital assets'.

8.175

> **Box 8.29**
> In fact the scope of this clause may be surprising. In a case in 2006,[80] a company had a contract for the sale of goods to a customer. The company accelerated the payments due from the customer then used the amount paid by the customer to repay a debt of the Company. The court found that there were two 'disposals' here. The debt due from the customer was being 'disposed of' by way of its being accelerated and paid (and thus turned from a debt payable in the future into present cash/bank credit). The proceeds (cash/bank credit) were being 'disposed of' by being applied to repay the Company's debt.

In sub-investment grade loans it is common to allow disposals of capital assets, provided the net proceeds (or a proportion of the proceeds) are used to prepay the loan or are reinvested within a given period of time. In the Leveraged LMA this is achieved by having a definition of 'Permitted Disposals' and then requiring the net proceeds from the disposal to be used to make a compulsory prepayment of the loan, unless those proceeds are 'Excluded Disposal Proceeds'. Some issues here are

8.176

- What deductions to make from proceeds in arriving at the figure for net proceeds – for example, expenses and tax?
- If the proceeds are not to be used to make a prepayment, for example, because they are to be reinvested – how soon must the reinvestment occur?
- Whether all the net proceeds of all assets are required to be used to make a prepayment or whether to restrict the required prepayment so that it only applies to major assets or only requires prepayment if a given leverage ratio is breached, and
- When the prepayment must be made – for example, can the borrower retain the moneys until the end of the next interest period?

---

[80] Marplace (Number 512) Limited v Chaffe Street (a firm) [2006] EWHC 1919 Ch.

8.177 *Comment* The clause may apply only to Obligors or to all members of the group. Borrowers may wish to restrict it to Obligors as lenders have no claims against other group members.[81]

Clause 22.4(b) Exceptions to no disposal clause

8.178 The first exception in paragraph (b) allows disposals in the ordinary course of trading. This allows such day-to-day activities as disposal of cash to pay for goods or services.[82]

Note the difference between the 'ordinary course of business' and the 'ordinary course of trading' discussed at Box 8.28 on page 205.

8.179 This exception also needs to be considered in the context of any security given to the lenders. The extent to which Obligors which have provided security are able to sell the assets which are the subject of that security in the ordinary course of their business may be a determining factor in the characterization of the security as a fixed charge or as a floating charge.[83] Assets which are intended to be subject to a fixed charge must not be able to be sold without consent of the lenders and, if necessary, this clause should be adjusted to reflect that.

8.180 The second exception in paragraph (b) reads

> (ii) *of assets in exchange for other assets comparable or superior as to type, value and quality;*

8.181 *Comment* Borrowers may want to adjust this to allow disposals for cash if the cash is reinvested within a reasonable period in assets which would otherwise have qualified under this paragraph.

8.182 Other exceptions commonly allowed here include:

- disposal of obsolete assets;
- distributions to shareholders;
- intra group disposals (although lenders will need to consider whether disposals to companies which are not Obligors are permissible);
- disposal of cash or cash equivalents;
- disposals of shares in other Group members;
- disposals where the proceeds are used to prepay a part of the loan.

Paragraph (iv) allows disposals up to a maximum threshold amount in any financial year.

---

[81] See 0.142.
[82] It is a moot point whether the disposals referred to at Box 8.29 on page 209 would have been permitted under this exception, depending, in particular, on whether the acceleration of the debt was regarded as being in the ordinary course of trading.
[83] Ashborder BV v Green Gas Power Ltd (2004) EWHC 1517 (Ch D).

The threshold needs to be set at a level which does not confound the normal activities of the borrower and which allows for some flexibility in changing financial circumstances. The borrower may need to sell some significant assets in a downturn and some ability to do this may be necessary. 8.183

Comment Some borrowers ask for an annual figure to be allowed with carry forward of unused amounts. 8.184

Comment Another option is to set an aggregate figure at a percentage of Tangible Net Worth. 8.185

Clause 22.5 Merger

Clause 22.5 prohibits mergers and *'corporate reconstruction'*.[84] This clause addresses the lenders' concerns that: 8.186

- the resultant entity may not take on the liabilities of the borrower;
- it may not benefit from all the rights which the borrower had (e.g. licences) which may be necessary for the conduct of the business; and
- the merger may cause a conflict of interest for the lenders or result in the new borrower being an entity which the lenders do not want to do business with – the decision to do business with a company involves other considerations – not just credit risk.

Comment This clause applies to every individual member of the group. Borrowers may wish to restrict this to Obligors.[85] 8.187

Clause 22.6 Change of business

Clause 22.6 prohibits change of business. This undertaking relates to the general nature of business of (a) the Company (being the top company in the group to which the lenders have access) and (b) the group as a whole. It does not[86] restrict the Company or the group from selling or stopping carrying on any *part* of its business nor from acquiring new businesses, provided the *general nature* of the Company's and group's businesses remain the same. 8.188

Comment Lenders may wish to make this undertaking more restrictive in certain cases, for example, they may want to extend it to also prohibit ceasing to carry on a material part of its business. 8.189

---

[84] There is no clear legal or business meaning for the expression 'corporate reconstruction'. There is some case law (Re Mytravel Group [2004] EWCA Civ 1734) which emphasizes that the key characteristic is that the identity of the shareholders before and after the event is substantially the same.
[85] See 0.142.
[86] But the no disposals covenant probably does restrict this.

CLAUSE 22: GENERAL UNDERTAKINGS – SECTION 2 – OTHER COMMON UNDERTAKINGS

Other undertakings

8.190   Each transaction is likely to require additional conditions precedent, representations, undertakings, and/or Events of Default to reflect the credit decision taken by the lenders. The following are the areas which are often the subject of additional provisions. The headings below are largely taken from the Leveraged LMA (commonly used as a resource in drafting restrictions in loan agreements for sub-investment grade borrowers)[87] with a few additional categories –

- Authorizations and compliance with laws
- Restrictions on business focus
- Restrictions on dealing with assets and security
- Restrictions on movement of cash – cash out
- Restrictions on movement of cash – cash in
- Information
- Granting powers to others
- Reflecting regulatory or legal risks
- Undertakings relating to assets given as security
- Miscellaneous

For the purpose of simplicity, this book deals with these additional issues of concern to lenders all together in relation to the undertakings. Nevertheless, for each additional provision which the lenders include in the undertakings, they are likely to also require a representation and/or a condition precedent addressing that issue. They need also to consider whether the issue is best addressed by an undertaking or by an Event of Default.[88]

Authorizations and compliance with laws

8.191   Some examples are
- environmental undertakings such as:
  - an environmental report as a condition precedent to the loan; and
  - undertakings to comply with environmental regulations (possibly complemented by insurance[89]) (see Box 8.30 on page 213).

---

[87] By their nature, the areas which these additional provisions may need to deal with are endless and no summary of them can be complete. This selection should therefore be viewed as being by way of example only, of some of the more common issues.

[88] See Box 0.4 on page 11.

[89] Where there are no specific environmental concerns, borrowers might argue that specific undertakings are unnecessary as they are covered by the general undertakings to comply with the law. Where undertakings are included borrowers will want to include materiality restrictions.

> **Box 8.30**
> Environmental liabilities may have a significant impact on the borrower's financial position; on the value of its assets (including assets it may have given to the lenders as security); on the priority of the lenders' security, or on the lenders' exposure if it were to take control of the assets over which it has security. It may simply be a matter of lender policy only to lend to companies or projects which can demonstrate compliance with high environmental standards.

- paying tax and other claims which have priority in insolvency or which give rise to liens[90] (see Box 8.31).
- Undertakings in relation to money laundering, anti-bribery and similar regulations (see discussion at 4.009).

> **Box 8.31**
> For example, in the US under **ERISA** (Employee Retirement Income Security Act) liens may arise on a company's assets if it fails to comply with the requirements of the Act. For a US borrower, it is therefore common to include undertakings and Events of Default related to compliance with the requirements of ERISA.

Restrictions on business focus

Some examples (additional to the ones already looked at in the discussion on the LMA Term Loan) are

8.192

- No acquisitions of companies or shares in companies and no joint ventures.[91]
- No acquisitions of other assets. Clearly the degree of restriction which is workable will depend on the transaction. It is worth noting that, rather like the 'no disposals clause', this prohibition has a broader impact than may at first appear. Every time an asset is sold or a debt is collected, the company acquires a new asset – that is, cash. So if a restriction along these lines is included, it will need careful consideration of appropriate exemptions.[92]

---

[90] The borrower may wish to ensure they have the right to contest these claims as long as they make appropriate reserves.

[91] Issues commonly discussed in this context are (i) acquisition of shares in listed companies (sometimes, only if security is given on those shares to the lenders) and (ii) acquisition of businesses similar to that already conducted by the borrower, in countries approved by the lenders and provided certain financial ratios are met.

[92] Borrowers are likely to need the clause to permit acquisition of trading assets and services in the ordinary course of business.

- No new contracts. A similar point arises here as in relation to acquisition of assets.[93]

Restrictions on dealing with assets and security

8.193 Some examples are
- An undertaking to maintain the ranking of the loan as at least pari passu with the borrowers' other unsecured debt except for those debts preferred by law. See the discussion on clause 19.12 at 8.052 onwards. Borrowers might request the deletion of this clause since in most cases the ranking of the debt is an insolvency law issue, outside the control of the borrower. Also, in view of the uncertainties created by the Argentine case discussed at Box 8.11 on page 171, if the undertaking is included, borrowers will want it to be clear that the undertaking relates only to priority of debts and not the order in which they are paid.
- Undertakings to conduct all transactions on an arm's length basis (including perhaps restrictions on transactions with affiliates and on payments to directors and employees).[94]
- Undertakings to maintain adequate insurance
  - in accordance with industry standards;
  - against key risks identified by the lenders such as key man insurance, business interruption insurance, pollution or other liability insurance, political risk insurance or insurance against physical damage to assets
  - with approved insurers (in an asset finance, the lenders are effectively taking a credit risk on the insurers if there is an insured incident) and to
    o provide a regular expert opinion as to acceptability of the insurance – both as to risks covered and as to the identity of the insurers
    o provide regular evidence that the insurance is up to date
    o make mandatory prepayment of the loan (or repair of asset) out of insurance proceeds;
    o ensure the lenders have some protection (insurance?) against the risks of the insurance not paying out, for example, because it is cancelled for non-payment of premiums or because there was a breach of warranty by the insured;
- Undertakings to maintain their assets in good condition;[95]
- Requirements to maintain appropriate hedging arrangements.

Restrictions on movements of cash – cash out

8.194 Some examples are
- No lending money or giving credit;[96]

---

[93] Exclusions for the ordinary course of trading and materiality carve-outs are likely to be needed.
[94] Borrowers will need to consider whether any arrangements they have such as incentive schemes for employees, or cash pooling arrangements, breach this undertaking.
[95] Borrowers are likely to want some materiality concept here.
[96] Issues to consider here include trade credit to customers, intra group lending, advance payments on capital expenditure, deferred consideration for disposals, cash pooling arrangements, and cash deposited at banks.

- No giving guarantees;[97]
- No payment of dividends. Clearly the shareholders want to make a profit so if this restriction is included it will need to reflect the commercial agreement. Often dividends are permitted if certain financial tests are met after the dividend is paid and provided there is no Default;
- No prepayment of debt. There are often transaction specific issues to consider here. If there are shareholder loans, exceptions may be negotiated similar to those for payment of dividends.

Restrictions on movement of cash – cash in

Some examples are 8.195
- No issuing new shares (with an exception for equity cure rights if these are agreed);
- No new borrowing.[98] In this context borrowers may request exceptions for
  - refinancing existing debt
  - intra group borrowings
  - debts in the context of cash pooling
  - derivatives (if the definition of Financial Indebtedness from the LMA Term Loan is used) and
  - subordinated debt, particularly if the shareholder may wish to inject moneys in that way for tax reasons. Lenders' response to this request may depend on the degree of subordination.[99] Subordination which allows payment prior to a winding up may not be acceptable.

Information

Some examples are requirements to 8.196
- provide access to books and accounts;[100]
- provide management reports;
- give access to auditors and sometimes, to use a named firm as its Auditors;[101] and

---

[97] Borrowers are likely to need an exception for the ordinary course of business to cover things like performance bonds, letters of credit and cash pooling, as well as for indemnities included in standard term documents. Materiality thresholds or a basket allowing guarantees up to a specified amount are also commonly requested.

[98] The lenders may be particularly concerned about new borrowing or other indebtedness by a subsidiary which is not an Obligor but whose assets are relevant for the purpose of financial ratios, since the lenders are structurally subordinate to such claims – see A1.036.

[99] See A1.033.

[100] See comments on clause 20.1 (Financial statements) at 8.079 in relation to insider trading.

[101] Note the Competition Commission has decided to ban 'big four' auditor clauses in loan agreements (as being anti-competitive), with the ban expected to come into effect in late 2014. These are clauses which restrict the borrower's freedom of choice of auditor, for example, by requiring them to use auditors from an agreed list or with an 'international reputation'. They do not prevent the parties agreeing on a specific auditor, or on requiring the consent of the lenders to a change of auditor.

- copy the Agent in on major communications (and advise of defaults or disputes) under specific contracts/insurance.

Granting powers to others

8.197 Some examples are
- undertakings not to give a negative pledge to a third party (as that would restrict the lenders' ability to negotiate further security); and
- undertakings not to agree more favourable loan terms with others (sometimes referred to as a 'most favoured nations' clause).

Reflecting regulatory or legal risks

8.198 Where a particular risk is identified in legal due diligence, the lenders may want to include provisions reflecting that risk. An example is the undertaking not to use the loan in contravention of financial assistance regulations. Another would be an undertaking not to establish a place of business in a particular jurisdiction.[102]

Sometimes the loan agreement contains a representation from the borrower as to the location of its 'Centre of Main Interests' (commonly referred to as its 'COMI') and an undertaking not to change its COMI. This reflects the EU regulation on insolvency – which states that a company will be made insolvent in the state where the company has its 'COMI'.[103] See Box 8.32.

Box 8.32

Where is the COMI?

Article 13 of the EU Insolvency regulation 1346/2000 states that the COMI 'should correspond to the place where the debtor conducts the administration of his interests on a regular basis and is therefore ascertainable by third parties'. There is a rebuttable presumption (in article 2) that the COMI is in the country of the company's registered office. Additionally, in a case in 2006[104] the European Court of Justice held that that presumption that the COMI was the place of incorporation could only be rebutted if factors to the contrary exist which are both 'objective and ascertainable by third parties'. The Eurofood case has therefore made it more unlikely[105] that a company's COMI, within the EU will be anywhere other than its place of incorporation. Nevertheless, the location of the COMI is not always clear-cut and depends on the interpretation by the courts of the relevant regulations. It may therefore be difficult for a borrower to make a representation confirming the location of its COMI. An undertaking not to 'knowingly' or 'deliberately' change the COMI would be preferable for the borrowers.

---

[102] Such an undertaking is often included to lessen the risk of the need to effect registrations in those jurisdictions.
[103] This is also reflected in the UNCITRAL Model Law on Cross-Border Insolvency (Model Law).
[104] Re Eurofood IFSC Ltd [2006] EUECJ C-341/04 (Eurofood).
[105] But certainly not impossible – for example, a case in the High Court in England in 2013 held that the COMI of a Luxembourg incorporated company was in England (ARM Asset Backed Securities SA (2013) EWHC 3351 Ch.)

8.199 The lenders' main concern is of course that they will have conducted their insolvency due diligence in the place of incorporation of the borrowers and they want to be sure that that is in fact the place where insolvency may occur. Where a lender is secured, they have substantial protection from the effects of insolvency law as a result of article 5 of the regulation which effectively allows enforcement of security in one jurisdiction in the EU unaffected by insolvency proceedings taking place in a different jurisdiction within the EU.

Undertakings relating to assets given as security[106]

8.200 Asset related undertakings are often contained in the relevant security document. Some borrowers ask for a 'stripped out' security document (which contains no commercial terms, but simply creates the security) with all commercial provisions being contained in the loan agreement. This can assist with compliance and with ensuring the documents are consistent. The following undertakings may be included (either in the security documents or in the loan agreement):

- to repair the asset;
- not to allow anyone to have a lien (e.g. for repair) on the asset or to limit the amount of any such lien to an agreed figure;
- not to make any major changes to the asset;
- not to install equipment belonging to third parties onto the asset;
- to allow inspection of the asset;
- to use the asset responsibly – that is, in accordance with applicable regulations including environmental rules and not to use it for illegal trades;
- to operate the asset itself (not through a third party);
- to notify the Agent of major issues relating to the asset for example, damage or claims; and
- to insure the asset.

8.201 Commonly, the following provisions will also be included:

- a condition precedent as to evidence of value and condition of the asset and constitution of the security; and
- an Event of Default if:
  - any other security over the asset becomes enforceable,
  - the asset is confiscated or nationalized; or
  - a major insurance incident or environmental claim arises in relation to the asset; and[107]
- if the asset which is taken as security is a particular contract or a particular contract is key to the credit decision, the lenders may want

---

[106] See also 0.207.
[107] May be included as a compulsory prepayment event – see commentary on clause 8.2 at 4.012.

- a condition precedent that the contract has become unconditional and the security on it has been constituted;
- a representation that the copy delivered is the complete agreement;
- an undertaking not to amend it and to comply with the obligations under it;
- an Event of Default if it comes to an end;[108]
- agreement (confirmed by the counterparty) that the income from the contract will be paid direct to a specified account;
- restrictions on the use of money in the account;
- a 'waterfall' providing for a series of accounts with different purposes and regular payment into these accounts from income generated;[109]
- no sharing of the income;
- no alteration to the contract (confirmed by the counterparty);
- agreement to perform its obligations under the contract;
- ability (confirmed by counterparty) for the Agent to terminate the contract and/or to step in and perform it;
- confirmation from the counterparty that it will not exercise rights of set off or counterclaim in relation to payments under the contract; and
- if the contract is assigned, a notice of assignment acknowledged by the counterparty to the contract; (see Box 8.33).

Box 8.33
Notice of assignment is frequently given to the counterparty, who is often required to acknowledge the notice and give certain direct confirmations to the lender in that acknowledgement. Additionally, the counterparty may be asked to

- confirm that they have not received any other notice of assignment (because priority of competing assignments depends on the order in which notice of assignment was given to the counterparty); and/or
- undertake to the lender to perform their obligations under the contract.

In many cases, unless the counterparty is related to the borrower or has some incentive for assisting with the financing, they will be unwilling to give all (or any) of the confirmations requested in the acknowledgement, some of which (particularly the waivers of rights of set off and counterclaim) would be detrimental to the counterparty's own interests.

Miscellaneous

8.202 Other miscellaneous undertakings could include:

---

[108] But the borrower will want an opportunity to find an acceptable replacement contract and, by doing so, to avoid occurrence of the Event of Default.
[109] See Box 0.23 on page 43.

- Undertakings in relation to pensions. Many companies have operated 'defined benefit' pension schemes over the years, under which employees, on retirement, were entitled to receive a set income during their retirement. Most have now moved to schemes based on income earned by contributions made by their employees. The defined benefit schemes have put great pressure on the finances of those companies which ran such schemes, and, in the EU, numerous steps have been taken to try to ensure that those companies will be able to meet their pension obligations over the years. In the UK these steps include the establishment (under the Pensions Act 2004) of the office of pensions regulator, who has power to take action in relation to underfunded schemes. Lenders may therefore want the borrower to confirm that it is in compliance with its obligations in relation to pensions and to undertake to continue to be so. 8.203
- Undertakings to give the lenders and their advisers access to the borrowers' premises and records. Borrowers often want this restricted so that access is only available while there is a Default outstanding, access must be with notice and at reasonable times, and perhaps limiting the frequency of access (e.g. to once per year). 8.204
- Undertakings to retain appropriate senior management of the company and not to amend their service contracts in a way which would be prejudicial to the lenders. These undertakings are highly subjective and therefore difficult both to comply with and to enforce. Borrowers are likely to want to remove the undertaking or to add a 'reasonable endeavours' qualification. 8.205
- Undertakings to assert and protect their rights in relation to intellectual property. These undertakings are usually only required if intellectual property is of particular importance to the borrower. Borrowers are likely to want to add materiality carve-outs. 8.206
- Undertakings to keep all bank accounts and do all their derivative transactions with a lender. The acceptability of this depends on the service available from lenders. Borrowers commonly want freedom to enter into derivatives with third parties to enable them to get the best price. 8.207
- Undertakings to restrict the amount of cash balances which Group members have – and transfer those funds by way of intercompany loan to the parent company borrower. 8.208
- A further assurance clause – that is, an undertaking to do whatever may be necessary to keep the security in effect. 8.209
- Undertakings not to make any change in the group structure (or identity of group members). For example, issue of new shares in a subsidiary to a third party will affect the impact of what has been agreed in the undertakings, for example, as to intra group transactions. 8.210
- Undertakings not to make any change in the constitution of the borrowers (and ensure the constitution only allows the existing business). This can bolster the effectiveness of the undertakings relating to change in business. 8.211

8.212 - Limits on short-term borrowings and undertakings to pay off all short-term debt for a minimum period each year. The intention is to ensure the borrower is not using short-term debt for long-term needs.

8.213 - Undertakings to pay its debts as they fall due (unless contested in good faith).

8.214 - Sometimes, separateness undertakings, designed to reduce the risk of 'substantive consolidation' in relation to special purpose vehicles if there is a US connection. See Box 8.34.

> **Box 8.34**
> 'Substantive consolidation' is a principle which applies in the US, which allows a number of companies to be wound up as a single entity, if those companies have been managed as a single entity. In other words, the separate corporate status of the companies will be ineffective if this principle applies. Clearly, lenders who have transacted with one company will not want its assets to be used to settle liabilities of other companies and therefore they will want to try to ensure that their borrower is managed independently of any other companies, so that substantive consolidation will not arise. This is the role of the 'separateness undertakings'. The borrower undertakes to manage its business separately from that of its affiliates – for example, by keeping separate bank accounts, separate headed paper, and only transacting business with affiliates on arm's length terms.

CLAUSE 23: EVENTS OF DEFAULT – SECTION 1 – INTRODUCTION

Purpose

8.215 The purpose of the Events of Default is to give the lenders the contractual right to require early repayment (and not to lend any new money) if certain specified events happen. The existence of these rights gives the lenders leverage to negotiate adjustments to the transaction (such as a change in security or Margin) if any of the specified events occurs. The Events of Default are not[110] concerned with fault, but only with risk – they set out the circumstances in which it is accepted that the level of risk has changed and the lenders should be entitled to renegotiate.

Objective versus subjective

8.216 The Events of Default should be objective, and subjective tests and words (such as 'reasonable' and 'material') should be avoided as far as possible. Objective wording makes it easier for lenders to exercise their rights, and gives the borrower more certainty as to the circumstances in which the loan

---
[110] Subject to the comments made on clause 23.5 (the cross default clause) at 8.250.

may cease to be available.[111] Nevertheless, complete objectivity is not always possible and where recourse to subjective words is necessary, the lenders will want to add 'in the opinion of the Majority Lenders', (see Box 8.35) to make recourse to the Event of Default more predictable in its results, while the borrower will wish to omit those words and thereby impose some more objective standard of reasonableness or materiality.

> **Box 8.35**
> In this context it is interesting to note that the lenders are likely to prefer that it should be the opinion of the Majority Lenders which counts rather than the opinion of the Agent, as a result of the Torre Asset Funding case[112] discussed at 10.002. That case made it clear that the Agent's role under the 'standard' LMA terms is indeed mechanical and administrative and that therefore they have no positive duty to form an opinion on whether an Event of Default has occurred or not, although if they do consider the issue, they cannot be capricious or arbitrary in their conclusions (which is not the same thing at all as saying that they must be reasonable in their conclusions). The lenders may therefore feel more comfortable to have any opinions stated to be those of the Majority Lenders rather than the Agent.

Control over the relevant events

Borrowers are also concerned to ensure that they have the ability to avoid the occurrence of an Event of Default and so to avoid the acceleration of the loan. So they will want to ensure, as far as possible, that Events of Default do not occur automatically, but only after they have had an opportunity to rectify the situation (see Box 8.37 on page 222.) and that the acts of others over which they have no control cannot result in an Event of Default (see Box 8.36). 8.217

> **Box 8.36**
> For example, the borrower will not want termination of an important contract to be an Event of Default. If that contract was key to the lenders' credit decision, the borrower will want to negotiate the possibility of finding a replacement contract and so avoiding an Event of Default.

For similar reasons, borrowers want to restrict the Events of Default to circumstances affecting Obligors (not any group member[113]). They will be particularly keen to avoid Events of Default relating to their **joint venture** partners or other contracting parties.

---

[111] Although some borrowers prefer to see subjective words because it makes it harder for lenders to exercise their rights.

[112] Torre Asset Funding Ltd v The Royal Bank of Scotland (2013) EWHC 2670 Ch.

[113] See 0.142.

8.218 *Comment* In some circumstances where Events of Default are included relating to parties over which the borrower has no control, such as a joint venture partner, the lenders may agree that no Event of Default will occur with reference to events relating solely to that person if either

- that person is replaced in the relevant contract or other relationship by an acceptable substitute; or
- the borrower can show that its ability to service the debt has not suffered; and/or perhaps
- additional security is provided.

From Default to acceleration (see Box 8.38 on page 227)

8.219 A Default (as discussed in the context of the definitions in clause 1 at 1.018) is something which may or may not mature into an Event of Default, such as breach of an undertaking.[114] It automatically results in the release of the lenders from their obligation to lend new money unless the Majority Lenders waive the Default. See the discussion on clause 4.2(a)(i) at 2.026 onwards.

Some Defaults are automatically also Events of Default. An example is the misrepresentation Event of Default, which, in accordance with clause 23.4, (discussed at 8.225) is automatically an Event of Default. There is no grace period or any other requirement (e.g. to give notice) applicable to this particular Event of Default. Many Defaults only become Events of Default after a period of time and/or the giving of notice (e.g. clause 23.3(b)), see Box 8.37.

> **Box 8.37**
> This distinction between automatic Events of Default (such as misrepresentation) and others is important for both the borrower and the lenders. The borrower is keen to have the opportunity to remedy problems before they become Events of Default. Both borrower and lenders will be keen to ensure that Events of Default do not arise too readily because of the rights that they will give to other lenders under their cross default clauses. Hence, only certain events are automatic Events of Default. Automatic Events of Default usually include non-payment; breach of financial ratio (unless equity cure rights have been granted); breach of the obligation to notify of a Default; cross default; insurance undertakings; deliberate wrongdoings such as the breach of the negative pledge; and insolvency related Events of Default. Other events give the borrower an opportunity to remedy.

---

[114] It must not be confused with a 'default' (as opposed to a 'Default'), as that expression is used in clause 19.9(b) as discussed in Box 8.9 on page 168. In clause 19.9(b) the word is being used without a capital letter, and is therefore given its natural meaning as opposed to the meaning given by the definitions in clause 1. The natural meaning of 'default' is simply 'failure' or 'breach'.

Once a Default occurs, the borrower is obliged to notify the lenders. Failure to do so results in a separate (usually automatic) Event of Default.[115]

8.220

Once an Event of Default has occurred, the lenders have the right to accelerate the loan. Acceleration does not happen automatically. The lenders can elect whether or not to exercise that right and the loan will only become repayable early if the lenders make a demand for such payment in accordance with clause 23.13.

The lenders' right to accelerate the loan, or not to lend additional moneys, will cease to be exercisable in certain circumstances if the document (clause 23.13) states that those rights are only exercisable while the Event of Default is 'continuing'.[116]

CLAUSE 23: EVENTS OF DEFAULT – SECTION 2 – THE LMA EVENTS OF DEFAULT

The events which constitute Events of Default in the LMA Term Loan are as follows:

Clause 23.1   Non-payment

It is an Event of Default under Clause 23.1 if the borrower fails to make a payment when due. A grace period is only normally allowed in respect of administrative or technical error or a 'Disruption Event' (defined to mean disruption to the payment system or financial markets or an unavoidable systems error). There are options to allow different grace periods for different reasons for delay. Default interest will nevertheless accrue from the due date.

8.221

Comment   Sometimes a distinction is made between payments (such as principal and interest) which have a due date, and others (such as reimbursement of expenses) which are payable on request and for which a period for payment is often stipulated. This distinction is not made in the LMA Term Loan since, for the most part, the indemnities specify within themselves the period (in most cases within three business days of demand) within which payment is to be made, so no additional grace is required.

8.222

Clause 23.2   Breach of financial covenant

It is an Event of Default under Clause 23.2 if there is a breach of a financial covenant. This is set out separately since no grace period is appropriate

8.223

---
[115] See commentary on clause 20.5 at 8.091.
[116] See commentary on clause 1.2(d) at 1.067 for a discussion of 'continuing'.

as, in general, the breach cannot be remedied except as discussed in the context of equity cure rights in the discussion on clause 21. If equity cure rights are given then it is important to ensure that the drafting, either in this clause 23.2, or in the financial ratio itself, provides that the breach only occurs (and the grace period starts) when the Compliance Certificate is required to be delivered, as opposed to the end of the financial period to which the ratios relate. Otherwise the cure rights may be illusory because the cure period may expire before the Event of Default is discovered – see clause 8.120.

Another reason for its separate treatment is that financial ratios are not promises which may be broken, in the same way as other undertakings, but, instead, they are tests which may be met or not.

Clause 23.3 Breach of other obligations

8.224 Under clause 23.3, breach of any other undertaking is an Event of Default. The clause divides the various undertakings into different types, giving some (but not all) undertakings grace periods so that they are not automatic; and then allowing for those non-automatic Events of Default to have different grace periods.

Some lenders prefer the grace to run from the Default (rather than following the LMA Term Loan, which is to allow it to run from the date the borrower[117] is aware of, or is notified by the lenders of, the Default). However, this approach may make the Event of Default automatic in practice (as the grace period may expire before any party is aware of the Default). As a result, it may prevent the possibility of avoiding the occurrence of an Event of Default (and thus avoiding triggering the rights of other lenders under their cross default clauses).

Breaches which are often included as automatic Events of Default (i.e. with no grace period) include failure to maintain insurance and breach of undertakings which themselves include a grace period, for example, the obligation to notify of a Default.

Clause 23.4 Misrepresentation

8.225 Clause 23.4 provides that it is an Event of Default if a representation is incorrect in a material respect when made or when deemed repeated.

8.226 *Comment* The LMA Term Loan formulation requires the representation to be incorrect in a 'material respect'. Some lenders may object to this in that it introduces a concept of materiality to each representation, which would be

---

[117] Or rather, in the LMA Term Loan, the 'Company'. This gives rise to the possibility that if a borrower is aware of the Default but the Company is not, the grace period will only run from the date the Company is aware of it.

better negotiated in the representations themselves. Nonetheless it is preferable to the position sometimes requested that the misrepresentation should only constitute an Event of Default if it materially affects the borrower's ability to pay.

Comment This Event of Default is not only triggered if any of the representations made in the loan agreement are incorrect but also if any representation in 'any other document delivered by or on behalf of an Obligor under or in connection with any Finance Document' is incorrect. Borrowers may want to restrict the clause to written representations. **8.227**

It is worth noting that default under this clause is automatic. There is no grace period as a misrepresentation cannot be undone. However, this leads to the result that the opportunity to remedy will be different if, for example, **8.228**

- the borrower repeats a representation to the effect that there have been no changes to a particular contract, at a time when changes have been made, or if
- the borrower undertakes not to amend a particular contract, but enters into an amendment nevertheless.

The borrower will have no grace period for the misrepresentation but would have one for the breach of undertaking.

Comment If representations are repeated, borrowers should consider requesting an opportunity to remedy the underlying situation and thus prevent a misrepresentation from automatically being an Event of Default. **8.229**

Comment Beware. Even if the representations are not deemed repeated, the same effect may be achieved if the Event of Default says something along the following lines: '*if any representation was untrue when made or would have been untrue if repeated at any time*'. This has the same effect as clause 19.14 of the LMA Term Loan. **8.230**

Occasionally the same effect is achieved by adding a requirement to a Utilization Request, Selection Notice (choice of Interest Periods) or Compliance Certificate to the effect that the Repeating Representations are true.

Clause 23.5   Cross default

The existence of an Event of Default under a loan facility clearly gives the lenders significant leverage to renegotiate, for example, new Margins and/ **8.231** or security and/or greater control over the borrower's affairs, perhaps even to require some changes in business, such as sale of assets, as a condition to their maintaining the availability of the loan. The purpose of the cross default clause is to ensure that, if any other lenders have this degree of leverage over the borrower, then so does this syndicate. The intention is to ensure that this syndicate is not left out of any such renegotiation and to ensure that their interests are not marginalized. Nevertheless, the effect of the clause, for the borrower, is to change a localized problem, with an individual lender, which may be relatively easy to solve, into a wider problem, affecting all its lenders, which will be more difficult to solve. A borrower will want to restrict the circumstances in which this clause may operate.

Clause 23.5(a)

The first part of this clause reads

8.232
(a) Any Financial Indebtedness of any member of the Group is not paid when due nor within any originally applicable grace period.

Two definitions are key here: 'Financial Indebtedness', and 'Group'.

Financial Indebtedness

8.233 Under the LMA Term Loan, the clause is only triggered by non-payment of 'Financial Indebtedness' and not by non-payment of ordinary commercial debts (e.g. payment for supplies). This is because,

- failure to pay Financial Indebtedness has far more serious consequences (potential for the relevant creditor to accelerate their debt, causing, at the very least, a liquidity crisis) than failure to pay ordinary commercial debts (probably resulting in court action), and
- the loan agreement deals with court action and the like under separate provisions (representation as to proceedings at clause 19.13 and Event of Default as to creditors' process at clause 23.8).

8.234 The definition of Financial Indebtedness includes derivatives (in paragraph (g) of the definition). These are treated in the same way as borrowed money (not ordinary commercial debts) for the purpose of the cross default clause because a failure to pay when due in respect of a derivative can (just as non-payment of a loan can) trigger a large unanticipated payment, resulting in a liquidity problem for the borrower.

8.235 *Comment* Borrowers may want to make adjustments to the cross default clause to ensure that it is not triggered by a default by the counterparty to the derivative (see the discussion on the definition of Financial Indebtedness at 1.037 onwards).

Box 8.38

STAGES OF A DEFAULT FLOW CHART

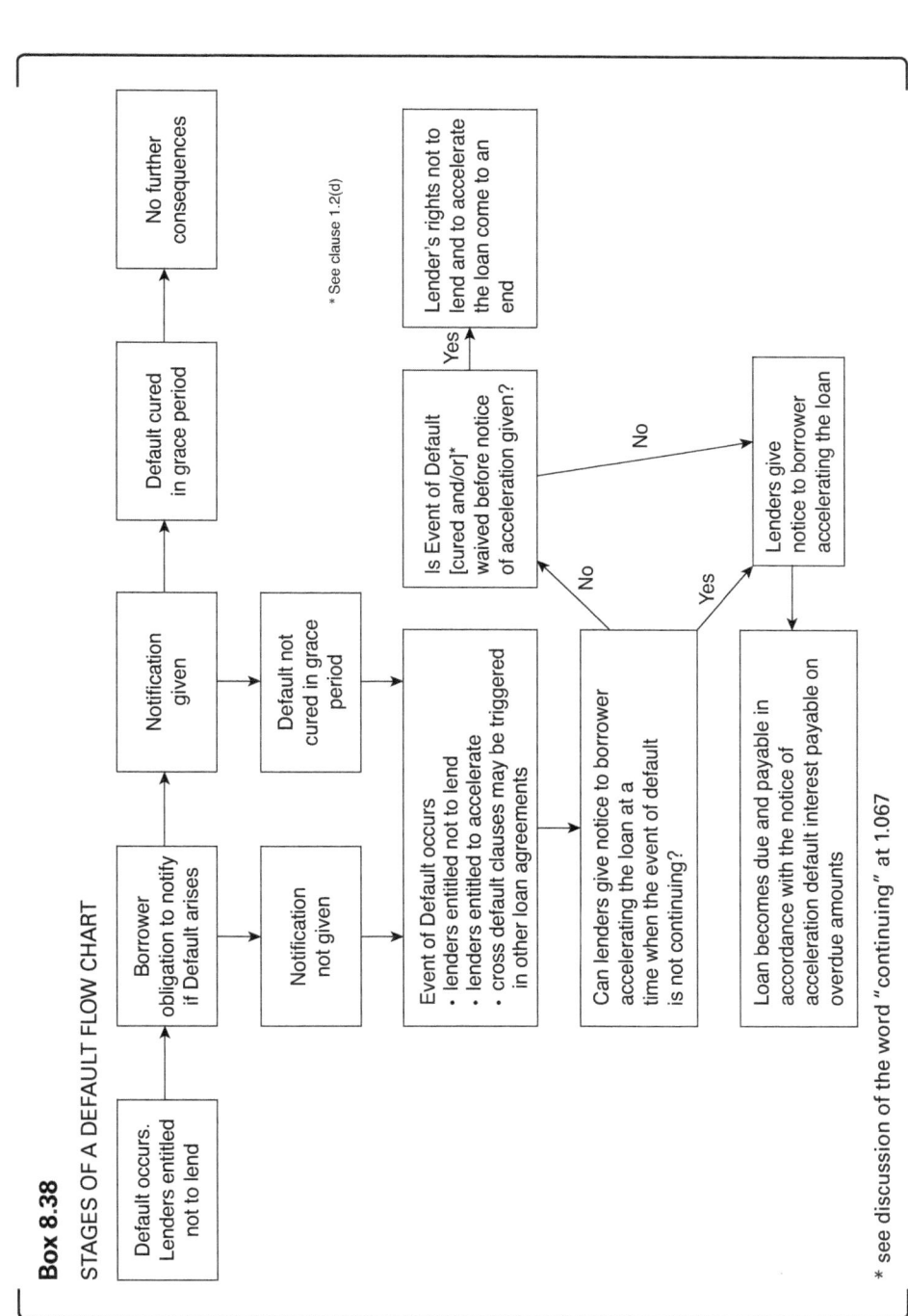

* see discussion of the word "continuing" at 1.067

Group

8.236 The second issue is the definition of 'Group'. Exclusions for non-material subsidiaries and/or non-recourse companies may also be appropriate.[118]

The borrower may ask that the cross default clause should relate only to Obligors, as the lenders have no direct claim against other group members. However this is an instance where, in many cases, the lenders will resist on the basis that problems with other group members may indicate wider problems; could result in reputational problems for the Group; and may result in the Obligors needing to provide support for their group member.

8.237 The clause applies if payment is not made within any '*originally applicable*' grace period. This is intended to prevent the clause being circumvented by other lenders simply extending their grace periods while negotiations proceed.

Clause 23.5(b)

This clause reads as follows

8.238
> (b) Any Financial Indebtedness of any member of the Group is declared to be or otherwise becomes due and payable prior to its specified maturity as a result of an Event of Default (however described).

Paragraph (a) deals with non-payment of a financial debt, and paragraph (b) deals with its acceleration. Where another lender exercises a right to require early payment of a debt, provided that right results from a default, this clause will apply.

The words '*Event of Default (however described)*' are intended to indicate that simply describing an Event of Default as something else (such as a 'Termination Event' in a finance lease) will not circumvent the clause. See also the Box 8.39 on page 229.

8.239 *Comment* Some borrowers may ask for an exception to this clause if the acceleration does not result from a payment obligation and the ability of the borrower to make payment and perform its other obligations under this loan is unaffected. The argument is that where the default is not in payment, it should not concern the lenders unless the acceleration of the loan by the other lender also impacts on the ability of the borrower to service this loan.

8.240 Lenders will be reluctant to agree such an exception because actual acceleration of a loan (unless within the threshold amount allowed in clause 23.5(e)), will change the borrower's financial position, regardless of the reason for the acceleration. Even if the change does not affect the borrower's ability to service this debt, the lenders will want the right (which having

---

[118] See the discussion at 0.126.

the Event of Default gives it) to review the risk involved in the loan and to renegotiate terms appropriate for the altered risk.

Comment Borrowers ought also to ask for an exception to this clause if the declaration that the debt is due is being contested in good faith. As currently worded, the cross default will be triggered even if there has not actually been an Event of Default under another loan agreement if the lender under that loan agreement demands payment early. In other words, all that is required to trigger this clause is for another lender to demand payment early, regardless of whether they are entitled to do that or not. Nevertheless lenders are likely to resist this change as it is not uncommon for borrowers to negotiate and to challenge the existence of the Event of Default at the same time. If the lender had conceded this point they would be frozen out of the negotiations.

8.241

Clause 23.5(c)

This clause reads as follows

> *Any commitment for any Financial Indebtedness of any member of the Group is cancelled or suspended by a creditor of any member of the Group as a result of an Event of Default (however described).*

8.242

This clause deals with the situation which might arise, for example, in the case of a revolving credit, where the lenders may not accelerate the loan, but simply refuse to re-advance it on a rollover as a result of an Event of Default. (see also Box 8.39).

Box 8.39

It is not clear whether suspension of a facility after a 'Default' and before an 'Event of Default' will trigger this clause. The question is, will the fact that a lender is not obliged to advance a loan because of a 'Default' (as opposed to an 'Event of Default') amount to a '*[suspension of the loan] as a result of an Event of Default (however described)*'? Does the fact that we called it a 'Default' prevent it from being an '*Event of Default (however described)*'? There is no definite answer but, given the common practice of making a very important distinction between a 'Default' and an 'Event of Default', it is probable that the suspension of a facility during a 'Default' will not trigger this clause (unless there is also an Event of Default).

A similar point arises in relation to compulsory prepayment events – are they not merely Events of Default by another name? Again there is no clear answer but as long as the concept of compulsory prepayment events is limited to events which happen to a borrower but which do not involve any breach on their part, it is at least arguable that they are different in nature to Events of Default.

8.243 *Comment* A borrower may suggest that if the commitment in question has never been drawn, such as in a backstop facility, the clause should not apply, since the cancellation will not result in the same sort of liquidity crisis (and hence leverage for the provider of the facility) as the requirement for early repayment of a loan.

Clause 23.5(d)

This clause reads as follows

> Any creditor of any member of the Group becomes entitled to declare any Financial Indebtedness of any member of the Group due and payable prior to its specified maturity as a result of an Event of Default (however described).

8.244 This clause applies if another lender *becomes entitled* to declare its debt due early as a result of an Event of Default. In other words, the other lender does not actually accelerate, (which would be caught by clause 23.5(b)) but simply has the right to do so.

Some borrowers request deletion of paragraph (d), (see Box 8.40).

> **Box 8.40**
> If (d) is deleted; the clause is referred to as a *cross acceleration clause* rather than a cross default clause; as it is triggered by *acceleration* rather than default.

The borrower's argument for this is that if the other lender does not actually exercise its right to accelerate, for example, because the borrower persuaded the lender that the default in question was technical and unimportant, then the other syndicates should not be entitled to accelerate. They also argue that giving this right would be to give this syndicate derivative rights which they had not actually required in their own loan agreements (see Box 8.41 on page 231).

8.245 The borrower may also argue that clause 23.5(d) is unnecessary, since, provided the borrower is paying this debt, there is no need for concern.

The difficulty with agreeing to a cross acceleration clause as opposed to a cross default clause is that, in many instances, particularly in unsecured corporate loans, it defeats the main purpose of the clause (which is to ensure that the syndicate's interests are not marginalized in any renegotiation between the borrower and another lender). If the clause is drafted as a cross acceleration clause it does not achieve this objective since the syndicate will have to wait for the results of the negotiation with the lender in question before it has any rights for itself.

> **Box 8.41**
> For example, assume a borrower has two loan agreements. One is for $10 million and is with Bank A and includes an undertaking that the borrower will maintain its Minimum Tangible Net Worth at not less than $30 million. The second agreement is for $5 million and is with Bank B and includes an undertaking that the borrower will maintain its Minimum Tangible Net Worth at not less than $20 million. The borrower's Minimum Tangible Net Worth falls to $25 million and Bank A is <u>entitled to</u> accelerate. The borrower's argument is that Bank B should not also be able to accelerate as otherwise, effectively, he is being given the benefit of A's (more stringent) financial covenant.

8.246 Nevertheless, as in everything, much depends on the credit decision. In the case of a stand alone asset or project finance, if the structure of the loan is such that there is little that any other lender could do which would have an adverse impact on this loan, a cross acceleration clause may be more appropriate than a cross default clause.

Similarly, in an unsecured corporate transaction with a borrower which is financially very strong, a cross acceleration clause may be acceptable if the lenders can be satisfied that all lenders are being (and will be) treated equally in this respect. A consistent policy of agreeing only cross acceleration clauses (if achievable) helps avoid Events of Default having a 'spiralling' effect – that is, turning problems which could be overcome relatively easily into much more intractable problems. Cross acceleration clauses allow the problem to be isolated to the particular creditor.

Clause 23.5(e)

8.247 Paragraph (e) provides a threshold amount so that defaults on debts which are below the threshold will not trigger cross default. This threshold is a cumulative figure applied to all the companies restricted by the clause. Sometimes a threshold is applied separately to different companies in the Group – so, for example, there may be a different, and separate, threshold for the parent company or for an Obligor than the amount which applies to other group companies.

8.248 *Comment* The borrower should try to maintain a consistent position on its cross default clauses, and have, for example, the same thresholds in each of them. This makes compliance easier and prevents weak cross default clauses in one agreement indirectly benefiting other lenders (see Box 8.42 on page 232).

Reducing the impact of the cross default clause

8.249 A borrower should bear in mind that careful drafting of a loan agreement (by including compulsory prepayment events and grace periods, in particular) will reduce the negative impact of cross default clauses in other agreements.

> **Box 8.42**
> An example clarifies this. Assume a borrower has two loan agreements, both for $10 million. In one (Loan A) they have negotiated a cross default clause triggered by financial debts over $1 million. The other (Loan B) has a cross default clause triggered by ordinary debts over $250,000. The borrower fails to pay a creditor $300,000 due to a temporary liquidity problem. This would not be a problem under Loan A alone, but becomes so because of its effect under the cross default clause in Loan B. Loan B is capable of being accelerated because its cross default clause is triggered by the non-payment of the debt of $300,000. Loan A is therefore also capable of being accelerated because Loan B (which is a financial debt in excess of $1 million and is therefore relevant for the cross default clause in Loan A) is capable of being accelerated. The weakest cross default clause has, in effect, benefited both syndicates.

Compulsory prepayment events

8.250   Borrowers should ensure that issues which do not imply any form of failure by the borrower or any of its group members (e.g. change of shareholding or total loss of a secured asset) are not dealt with as events of default, but rather as compulsory prepayment events.[119] For this to achieve its objective, the cross default clauses need to distinguish between early repayment of the loan caused by an Event of Default (which will trigger the cross default clause) and early repayment for other reasons (which will not). See Box 8.39 on page 229.

Grace periods

8.251   The borrower should be negotiating grace periods into its Events of Default. The cross default clause will only be triggered when another lender actually has the right to accelerate (or cancel) the facility. This will not happen until any relevant grace period has expired. In practice therefore, as long as there is, for any given event, a period between its being a Default and its becoming an Event of Default, the borrower will have an opportunity to have negotiations with an individual lender so as to avoid the occurrence of an Event of Default (so long as those negotiations do not include discussion of rescheduling[120] or extension of any original grace period for non-payment[121]) and therefore avoid the triggering of the cross default clauses.

Consents

8.252   It is also worth bearing the cross default clause in mind when requesting or giving consents under the loan agreement. Borrowers will want to ensure that any consent given is comprehensive and does not only relate to the original issue, but also to any consequential breaches of the cross default

---

[119] For example, change of control, dealt with in clause 8.2 at 4.012.
[120] See clause 23.6(a) at 8.254.
[121] See comments on clause 23.5(a) at 8.237.

clause. Lenders on the other hand will not want to waive their rights under the cross default clause until they are sure that no other lenders plan to use their rights under their cross default clauses.

The simplest way to deal with this is to make consents comprehensive but conditional on all other affected lenders waiving their rights under their cross default clauses arising as a result of the original issue.

Clause 23.6   Insolvency

Clause 23.6(a)

The first part of the insolvency Event of Default reads as follows

> 23.6 Insolvency
> (a) A member of the Group:
>   (i) is unable or admits inability to pay its debts as they fall due,
>   (ii) suspends making payments on any of its debts or,
>   (iii) by reason of actual or anticipated financial difficulties, commences negotiations with one or more of its creditors (excluding any Finance Party in its capacity as such) with a view to rescheduling any of its indebtedness.

Clause 23.6(a) covers the cashflow test of insolvency – inability to pay debts as they fall due. It also applies if a group company commences rescheduling negotiations with a creditor. **8.253**

Comment   The borrower may want to restrict this so that it applies only to Obligors.[122] They also want to restrict it so that it only applies if the negotiations are with creditors generally rather than with one or more of its creditors. Although case law gives borrowers some comfort (see Box 8.43), borrowers would be better placed to clarify in the clause itself that it is only intended to catch 'substantial' problems, not, for example short-term cashflow problems which result in it needing to negotiate extra time for payment say of an individual supplier. **8.254**

Box 8.43
In one case[123] the court distinguished between rescheduling discussions in the ordinary course of business and the rescheduling referred to in this clause which must result from 'actual or anticipated financial difficulties' and, because the general thrust of the clause is to deal with insolvency issues, the court's view was that the level of those difficulties would need to be substantial.

---

[122] See 0.142.
[123] Grupo Hotelero Urvasco SA v Carey Value Added SL [2013]EWHC 1039

Clause 23.6(b)

8.255 (b) *The value of the assets of any member of the Group is less than its liabilities (taking into account contingent and prospective liabilities)* (see Box 8.44).

> **Box 8.44**
> The reference to contingent and prospective debts in this clause reflects the test of insolvency contained in s123 Insolvency Act 1986.
>   A 'contingent' debt is a debt (such as that under a guarantee) which may or may not become due depending on the occurrence of an event outside the parties' control. A 'prospective' debt is one which has not yet fallen due. Its precise ambit is unclear but cases on the meaning of the word in the context of tax provisions indicate that it does not include potential liability in respect of sums which may be awarded against a company in an ongoing dispute.[124]

8.256 Clause 23.6(b) deals with the balance sheet test of insolvency. It provides for there to be an Event of Default if assets are less than liabilities. The wording of the clause reflects part of the wording of s123 Insolvency Act 1986, which deems a company unable to pay its debts if the court is satisfied that the value of its assets is less than the value of its liabilities. However, it purports to be a simple test, which, as explained in the Box 8.45 on page 235, is actually open to many different interpretations. The difficulty is that it is not clear on what basis assets and liabilities are to be valued for the purpose of this clause. It might be better to reword the clause to clarify that it is subjective, for example, to provide that it is an Event of Default if

> the company cannot reasonably be expected to meet all its liabilities, looking at the company's assets and making proper allowance for the nature of prospective and contingent liabilities.

This reflects case law on this issue. See Box 8.45 on page 235.

Limited recourse provisions

8.258 It is worth noting the decision of the High Court in a case in 2013[125] which held that even if the debts of a company were limited recourse in nature, that did not prevent those debts from being taken into account for the purpose of the two insolvency tests. The case in question related to a limitation on recourse provision which stated that the creditor could only take legal action

---

[124] See, for example, Customs & Excise Commissioners v Broomco Ltd (1984) formerly Anchor Foods Ltd 2000 WL 1084449.
[125] ARM Asset Backed Securities SA (2013) EWHC 3351 Ch.

for an amount up to the value of the assets of the company. Its purpose was to try to limit the risk of the company becoming insolvent. The case did not relate to the type of non-recourse company discussed at 0.141 but is a good reminder of the need to exclude such companies from the scope of the agreement entirely if there are any such companies in the Group.

> **Box 8.45**
> The value of the company's assets will be significantly different depending on whether they are valued on a going concern basis or a breakup basis. This issue received considerable attention during the credit crunch of 2007–2008, as otherwise viable companies found their prospects threatened as a result of concerns about continued availability of bank funding. This resulted in changes in accounting rules and procedures – requiring companies to report on risks to the 'going concern' basis of preparation of their accounts and to keep those risks under review. For accounting purposes, at least in the UK, departure from the going concern basis of valuation is only required in fairly extreme circumstances.[126]
>
> In relation to contingent liabilities, the question again arises as to how these should be valued depending on the likelihood of a claim under the guarantee. The amount of the liability to be taken into account under a contingent liability is not clear-cut.
>
> In BNY Corporate Trustee Services Ltd v Eurosail – UK- 2007- 3BL Plc [2013] UKSC 28 the court considered an Event of Default in a contract which stated that it was an Event of Default in the event of the borrower
>
> *within the meaning of Section 123(1) or (2)...of the Insolvency Act 1986 being deemed unable to pay its debts;*
>
> The court held that the company would not be deemed unable to pay its debts simply because its assets were less than its liabilities. It was not a simple mathematical exercise but instead required an assessment of whether the company could reasonably be expected to meet all its liabilities, looking at the company's assets and making proper allowance for the nature of prospective and contingent liabilities. (In that case, many of the liabilities were denominated in a different currency from the assets and fell due some time in the future).

Clause 23.7   Insolvency proceedings[127]

This clause makes it an Event of Default if steps are taken for suspension of debt, arrangements with creditors, appointment of a liquidator, enforcement of security or the like.

8.259

---

[126] International Accounting Standard 1 at para 25 requires accounts to be produced on a going concern basis unless 'the directors have no realistic alternative but to liquidate the company or cease trading'.

[127] This Event of Default is intended to allow the lenders to take action before an administration or similar is agreed.

Some may wonder whether an insolvency Event of Default is necessary because, even if the loan is not accelerated on insolvency, the lenders would be able to claim in the insolvency for the whole debt so, arguably, the ability to accelerate has achieved no advantage.

The purpose of this Event of Default is to enable the lenders to accelerate, and claim payment of the whole debt, at an earlier stage of the insolvency process than would otherwise be possible. This may, for example, enable them to exercise rights of set off or enforcement of security prior to a formal winding up.

The clause applies to all companies in the group (but does allow solvent winding up of group members which are not Obligors). Borrowers may seek to restrict the clause to Obligors.[128]

8.260 *Comment* The clause is triggered at an early stage when 'any step is taken'. Borrowers will want to ensure that minor problems do not cause an Event of Default so they may request some carve-outs such as

- an exception for any vexatious action, because creditors may present a winding up petition, based on non-payment of a disputed debt, not because they think the company is unable to pay its debts, but as a tactic to cause maximum disruption for the company and thus persuade it to make early payment;
- Exceptions for disputed items as long as the proceedings are dismissed within a set period of time;
- restricting the clause (which currently catches arrangements with 'any' creditor, and appointment of a receiver to 'any' asset) so that instead it refers to arrangements with 'its creditors generally' or appointments relating to a 'substantial part' of its assets; or
- limiting the clause so that it only operates if an administrator etc. is **actually** appointed.

Clause 23.8   Creditors' process

Clause 23.8 reads

Any expropriation, attachment, sequestration, distress or execution affects any asset or assets of a member of the Group [having an aggregate value of [ ]] [and is not discharged within [ ] days].

8.261 Clause 23.8 deals with distress or execution (i.e. enforcement of court judgements or arbitration awards) as well as expropriation (e.g. nationalization).

---

[128] See 0.142.

The clause allows a number of options. It may be drafted so that,

- any enforcement (without any regard to the amount in question) is an Event of Default;
- it is only an Event of Default if the value of the assets concerned exceeds a threshold amount; or
- it is only an Event of Default if, in addition to the above, the relevant enforcement order remains in place for a given period of time.

8.262 Borrowers will normally ask for all these exceptions to apply so as to allow them time to appeal the enforcement or other action.

8.263 The clause also relates to every group member. The borrower may want to restrict it to Obligors.[129]

There is no other specific Event of Default dealing with litigation or with administrative proceedings in the LMA Term Loan.

8.264 *Comment* In cases other than unsecured corporate loans to investment grade borrowers, lenders may want an additional Event of Default relating to litigation or unpaid judgements. This can be achieved by repetition of the representation as to no litigation in clause 19.13, but a better option (not least because it would be more easily understood) would be to include a specific Event of Default.[130] See also Box 8.46.

Box 8.46

LITIGATION, JUDGEMENT, AND ENFORCEMENT

If a provision is included to the effect that litigation or other proceedings will be an Event of Default, borrowers will normally ask for exceptions relating to litigation which is being contested in good faith by appropriate proceedings, diligently pursued and with reasonable prospects of success, and for which a reserve has been established.

Clause 23.9   Ownership of the Obligors

8.265 Clause 23.9 makes it an Event of Default if an Obligor ceases to be a Group member. This ought not to happen as if the borrower wants to sell an Obligor, it can use the mechanism in clause 25, to allow the Obligor to stop being an Obligor in order to allow the sale to proceed, provided, of course, that the sale does not breach the no disposals undertaking.

---

[129] See 0.142.
[130] See commentary on clause 19.13 at 8.066.

Other Events of Default

8.266 Lenders will usually need to add specific events of default relating to the transaction and credit risk in question. These will follow from the additional undertakings discussed at clause 22 at 8.190.

Clause 23.12   Material adverse change

8.267 The loan agreement will often include some form of material adverse change clause. This clause can be highly contentious. Lenders argue that they cannot be expected to list in advance every circumstance which may arise which could give them cause for concern. This clause is needed as a risk allocation issue to ensure that everything is covered. Borrowers object to the clause principally because of its uncertainty and subjectivity. As with other likely contentious issues, it is sensible to address the issue in the term sheet.

The arguments around the clause fall into two categories: whether to include the clause, and, if included, what it should say.

Should there be a material adverse change Event of Default?

8.268 The borrower's objections to including the clause are:

- The *uncertainty* of the circumstances in which it may be used;
- The fact that lenders *don't use it* (so why have it?);
- The *fragility* it imposes on the borrower's overall business; and
- The fact that it gives *excessive power* and discretion to the lenders.

Uncertainty

8.269 From the borrower's perspective, one of the main issues of concern in the loan agreement is certainty as to the continued availability of funds. If the finance is unexpectedly withdrawn, the consequences are likely to be very difficult for the borrower. For this reason, the borrower wants all Events of Default to be clear and objective, including no element of subjectivity. It is argued that the material adverse change clause, because it is not clear what events can trigger it, causes too much uncertainty as to continued availability of funds.

Lenders may counter this with the reassurance that the very uncertainty of the clause should give the borrower comfort that it is unlikely to be used except in the most extreme circumstances. Lenders who wish to accelerate the loan would always be advised to rely on the objective events of default (e.g. non-payment or breach of undertaking) rather than the subjective ones, since, were the court to disagree with the lenders as to whether or not a particular set of facts fell within the clause, the lenders would be liable in damages for breach of contract if, for example, they failed to advance funds when not entitled to do so.¹³¹ The amounts involved could be significant. In other words, the uncertainty works both ways.¹³²

Lack of use

Borrowers often comment that the clause is rarely used and so must be pointless.¹³³   8.270

The lenders' response is that the existence of the clause is likely to trigger discussions in circumstances where there is cause for concern. Lack of use of the clause as a trigger for acceleration does not make it pointless in its role as prompting discussions and negotiations. Moreover, even though in many cases the clause will not be used to accelerate the loan, either because of uncertainty of application or because of publicity concerns or concerns to avoid precipitating an industry-wide crisis, that does not mean that there will never be cases where those concerns will not apply. See also Box 8.47.

Box 8.47

There are concerns in many jurisdictions as to whether the clause is enforceable or not in any event. These concerns are founded on a number of different legal principles including

- Uncertainty. Is the clause sufficiently clear as to the circumstances in which it will operate or will it be void for uncertainty?
- Unilateral nature of the clause – some jurisdictions, such as France,¹³⁴ have a legal principle that one party cannot reserve to itself unilateral and exclusive control over the implementation of an agreement.¹³⁵
- Might it be contrary to principles of good faith and fair dealing?

In English courts, the clause is not of itself unenforceable, but there may be difficulties in establishing whether any given set of circumstances falls within the circumstances envisaged by the clause. This will be determined with reference to the supposed intention of the parties at the date of the agreement.

---

[131] This must be contrasted with merely serving notice of acceleration incorrectly, when no Event of Default has in fact occurred. Serving such notice may, in some circumstances, of itself, not be a breach of contract and may be simply ineffective. See Concord Trust v The Law Debenture Corp (2005) 1 WLR 1591. The borrower may therefore want the lenders to agree not to serve notice of acceleration unless an Event of Default has occurred.

[132] In fact, some borrowers like to scatter the Events of Default clause with subjective words such as 'material' and 'reasonable', sometimes preferring those over absolute numbers because of the uncertainty this creates and the corresponding caution the lenders will have in enforcing their rights.

[133] Nevertheless, it is used. See BNP Paribas SA v Yukos Oil Co (2005) EWHC 1321 (Ch).

[134] Article 1174 French Civil Code.

[135] Whether a material adverse change clause in loan agreement contravenes this principle is nevertheless a moot point. See 'Material Adverse Change and Syndicated Bank Financing', *Journal of International Banking Law and Regulation* 2004, 19(5), pp. 172–176 and 19(6), pp. 193–198.

Fragility

8.271 Borrowers then argue that including this provision makes the provision of the finance fragile, in that the occurrence of events which could pose a threat to the business can itself cause the loan to be withdrawn. Businesses face new threats regularly. They surmount some and not others and should be given the opportunity to do so. Many businesses are cyclical, making the clause particularly unpalatable if the loan is agreed at the top of the cycle.

Excessive power to the lenders

8.272 There are those who argue[136] that the clause (in some of its varieties) may give so much discretion to the lenders that it, in effect, makes the facility a demand facility and not a long-term commitment at all. The ultimate decision is being given to the lenders as to what threats are acceptable. Lenders counter that the clause contains its own checks and balances against abuse of that power since the consequences to the lenders of using this clause as a justification for failure to advance further funds in circumstances when a court ultimately decides that the circumstances did not entitle the lenders to do so, are likely to be significant.[137]

Nevertheless, lenders will argue strongly for inclusion of the clause, drafted appropriately to address some of the borrower's concerns, so as to ensure that the risk of unforeseen problems would fall on the borrowers, not the lenders and to give the lenders some opportunity to negotiate in such circumstances. The clause is particularly important in relation to the financial ratios, as discussed at 8.116 onwards.

If included, what should the clause say?

See Box 8.48 on page 241.

8.273 The drafting points to be addressed are

- How likely must the material adverse effect be?
- In whose opinion is this to be decided? and
- Material adverse effect on what?

How likely must the material adverse effect be?

8.274 The first question is, how likely must the adverse effect be? The options range from: '*the Lenders believe that a Material Adverse Effect may occur*', at one end of the spectrum to, '*an event occurs which will have*' [or '*has had*']

---

[136] This argument is sometimes made by ratings agencies, particularly in relation to loans needed for liquidity purposes.

[137] However the decision in Concord Trust referred to in note 131 devalues this argument as it appears that in certain circumstances lenders would not have liability to borrowers if they sent notice of acceleration at a time when no Event of Default had actually happened even though that notice may have a significant effect on the borrower as a result of the impact of cross default clauses.

'*a Material Adverse Effect*'; at the other end of the spectrum. Borrowers can be expected to object to words such as 'may', 'might' and 'could', as giving too much of a hair trigger, while lenders are unlikely to agree words such as 'will have' or 'has had' except in very strong credits, as being insufficiently flexible.

Options in between include '... *which could have a Material Adverse Effect*' or '*which could reasonably be expected to*'. This last option provides for a fair degree of objectivity and preserves the clause as one of last resort for the lenders.

Box 8.48

Commonly an Event of Default specifies clearly what is meant by a material adverse effect, as in this definition from the LMA template for use in developing markets:

'Material Adverse Effect' means [in the reasonable opinion of the Majority Lenders] a material adverse effect on:

a) the business, operations, property, condition (financial or otherwise) or prospects of the Group taken as a whole;
b) [the ability of an Obligor to perform [its obligations under the Finance Documents]/ [its payment obligations under the Finance Documents and/or its obligations under [Clause [20.2] (Financial condition)] of this Agreement]]/[the ability of the Obligors (taken as a whole) to perform [their obligations under the Finance Documents]/ [their payment obligations under the Finance Documents and/or their obligations under [Clause [20.2] (Financial condition)] of this Agreement]]; or
c) the validity or enforceability of the Finance Documents or the rights or remedies of any Finance Party under the Finance Documents.

In whose opinion is this to be decided?
If anyone's opinion is to be specified, the lenders would generally require the clause to be tested with reference to their opinion, for example, '*an event occurs which the Lenders reasonably expect to have a Material Adverse Effect*'. This formulation slightly eases the burden of proof in the event the lenders use the clause. They will still need to prove they genuinely held the relevant opinion. The more unreasonable the opinion on the facts, the harder it will be to prove they had that opinion.

8.275

What does there need to be a material adverse effect on?
It is helpful, in the definition of 'Material Adverse Effect' to specify what must be affected. Common options include:

8.276

- prospects (of the company, or the industry it is operating in, or other);
- financial condition;

- ability to perform its [payment] obligations under the loan agreement;
- validity and enforceability of the documents.

1 Prospects

8.277 Borrowers are particularly concerned about clauses which look forward and look at a change in 'prospects' either of the borrower or the industry it is involved in, because

- prospects change regularly, often adversely;
- a change in prospects often does not result in a change in fortunes;
- it is at such times they most need the certainty of finance;
- a clause which is triggered by a change in prospects is too uncertain; and
- all companies face threats to their prospects all the time – there is rarely a situation in which any company can say that there are no circumstances which exist which might cause a material adverse effect on their prospects (see Box 8.49).

Box 8.49

For example, assume a loan is made to a company which runs hotels in Madrid. The Spanish government decides to encourage the tourist industry and introduces a tax credit for construction of new hotels in Madrid. This new tax credit could amount to a material adverse change in the Company's *prospects* as it will presumably result in greater supply of hotel rooms and a possible need for the Company to drop its prices or have more empty rooms.

---

2 Financial condition

8.278 A second option is to provide that the material adverse effect must be on the financial condition of the borrower, see Box 8.52 on page 244. However, the borrower may argue that this would be inappropriate if the agreement also contains financial covenants, because if the borrower is meeting the objective tests which have been set in the financial covenants, the lenders should not be able to accelerate on the basis of a subjective test.

The lenders' response would be that they need the material adverse change clause to deal with a change in financial condition which has not yet been picked up by the ratios. In other words, the material adverse change clause will supplement the ratios and help deal with the timing problem discussed in the commentary on financial ratios, see 8.115. It will permit the lenders to take action immediately when a financial problem becomes apparent, without having to wait until the date on which ratios are next due to be tested (see Box 8.50 on page 243).

> **Box 8.50**
> So, for example, assume ratios are tested every six months, and there is a requirement that the Tangible Net Worth should not fall below $30 million. Assume also that the Tangible Net Worth figure drops to $10 million, one month after the last test date. If the material adverse change Event of Default is triggered by a change in financial condition, the lenders will be able to accelerate (or at least, not advance additional funds) without having to wait until the next date on which the ratios are tested.

Comment Where there are financial ratios, any material adverse change clause which looks at a change in the borrower's financial condition should reflect the agreement on the ratios (see Box 8.51). The simplest way to achieve this would be to provide that a material adverse change in financial condition is only an Event of Default if the lenders have reason to believe that the change is likely to result in a failure to meet a financial ratio when next tested and that such failure would, if not cured (e.g. by exercise of any applicable equity cure rights) be an Event of Default (rather than simply result in a change in Margin). 8.279

> **Box 8.51**
> An example may clarify. Assume the financial ratios require the Tangible Net Worth to be tested six-monthly and, if below $30 million, to be an Event of Default. A drop below $35 million simply changes the Margin. Assume that the Tangible Net Worth on one test date was $40 million, but it falls to $35 million over the next month. This is a material adverse change in financial condition, but should not give the lenders the right to accelerate, because that is contrary to the intention agreed in the financial ratios. The right to accelerate should only apply if the figure drops below £30 million.

3 *Ability to perform obligations under the loan agreement*
A third option is to provide that the material adverse effect must be on the ability of the borrower to perform its obligations under the agreement. Many borrowers prefer this to the formulation which talks of a material adverse effect in financial condition, because, for many borrowers, there is plenty of scope for a change in financial condition before ability to service the debt or perform other obligations are seriously prejudiced. This formulation preserves this clause as one of last resort for the lenders. 8.280

4 *Validity and enforceability of the documents*
Many material adverse change clauses will be expressed to be triggered by any material adverse change in the validity or enforceability of the documents, as well as by change in the various other factors described earlier. 8.281

8.282 *Comment* Other suggestions sometimes made by borrowers to ameliorate the material adverse change clause are

- in a syndicated loan, to require a higher proportion of the lenders than normal (not just Majority Lenders, but introduce a concept of 'Supermajority') to have to agree before this clause can be used;
- require notice to be given to the borrower, and an extended grace period, before the clause can be used – so as to allow an opportunity for discussion and to avoid triggering cross defaults.

> **Box 8.52**
> It is interesting to notice the facts of a case[138] which considered the interpretation of a representation (not an Event of Default) that there had been no material adverse effect in the financial position of the company since a specified date. The lenders argued that the expression 'financial condition' included factors such as changes in market or economic conditions which would affect the financial condition of the borrower, and in particular, a funding shortfall for a planned project. The argument failed with Blair J deciding that
>
> - the first port of call in determining whether there had been a change in financial condition was the financial statements although other facts were relevant. Nevertheless an expected funding gap was not relevant – as that related only to the ability to fund obligations which were as yet uncommitted;
> - in looking at whether a change in financial condition is 'material' it would only be so if it materially affected the borrower's ability to repay the loan;[139]
> - the change must not be temporary; and
> - if the lender knew when signing the agreement that a given set of facts was likely (e.g. a funding shortfall for a planned project) they could not then call an Event of Default under the material adverse change clause if that set of facts materialized.

Clause 23.13 Acceleration

Clause 23.13 reads

8.283 *On and at any time after the occurrence of an Event of Default [which is continuing] the Agent may, and shall if so directed by the Majority Lenders, by notice to the Company:*

---

[138] Grupo Hotelero Urvasco SA v Carey Value Added SL [2013] Bus. L.R. D45.
[139] The judge quoted the following texts with approval. The Encyclopaedia of Banking, where it states: '*if the change would have caused the bank not to lend at all or to lend on significantly more onerous terms, for example, as to margin, maturity or security*'; and Zakrzewski, Law and Financial Markets Review, which considers a change to be material that: '*substantially affects the borrowers' ability to repay, or, more generally, significantly increases the risks assumed by the lender*'.

(a) cancel the Total Commitments whereupon they shall immediately be cancelled;

(b) declare that all or part of the Loans, together with accrued interest, and all other amounts accrued or outstanding under the Finance Documents be immediately due and payable, whereupon they shall become immediately due and payable; and/or

(c) declare that all or part of the Loans be payable on demand, whereupon they shall immediately become payable on demand by the Agent on the instructions of the Majority Lenders.

Clause 23.13 sets out the contractual remedies for an Event of Default. These remedies are to cancel the commitment and/or to accelerate the loan. The wording requires the Agent to exercise the relevant right on behalf of the syndicate and provides that the Agent may act on its own initiative.[140] It also provides that the Agent will exercise the rights if the Majority Lenders so require (subject always to the provisions of clause 26, the agency clause). 8.284

It is also worth noting paragraph (c). This gives the lenders the right to declare that they have the right to demand immediate repayment of the loan (without actually doing so). This can be useful as it avoids the debt actually becoming immediately due. In many jurisdictions, directors must stop trading within a set period of time after the date on which the company is unable to pay its debts (or fails some similar financial test of solvency). See Box 8.53 on page 246. Accelerating the loan will make it immediately due and so can trigger the start of this period. This can make it impossible in practice to negotiate a rescheduling outside the insolvency procedures of the relevant country. 8.285

The option of using paragraph (c) instead can be a useful right for the lenders in these circumstances. The Ideal Standard case[141] considered the effect of this right and concluded that it did not suspend the underlying repayment schedule which continued in effect until demand was made.

An issue which the LMA Term Loan leaves open is whether the contractual remedies disappear at any point after an Event of Default occurs. Borrowers frequently ask for the words 'which is continuing' to be included in the first sentence of 23.13, quoted at 8.283, so that the remedies cannot be exercised after the Event of Default has been remedied. If these words are included, clause 1.2(d) of the LMA Term Loan defines what is meant by 'continuing'.[142] 8.286

---

[140] See clause 26 at 10.001 onwards as to the Agent's liabilities to syndicate members.
[141] Strategic Value Master Fund Ltd v Ideal Standard International Acquisition S.A.R.L. & Ors [2011] EWHC 171 (Ch).
[142] See comment on clause 1.2(d) at 1.067.

Box 8.53

Wrongful trading

Directors' duties on insolvency are an important issue to bear in mind if the lenders start to consider their enforcement/restructuring options following an Event of Default. In some countries directors can be held personally liable if they are found guilty of 'negligent mismanagement' of a company, and the threshold they are required to comply with may be very high. In such countries, directors are likely to want to stop trading at a very early stage, making it difficult to arrange a restructuring. In England the issue is wrongful trading[143] – that is, carrying on trading after the point at which 'that person knew or ought to have concluded that there was no reasonable prospect that the company would avoid going into insolvent liquidation'. However the directors have a defence to any action if they 'took every step with a view to minimizing the potential loss to the company's creditors as...[they] ought to have taken'.[144] The availability of this defence gives directors more scope for having discussions around restructuring than in many countries.

---

[143] Insolvency Act 1986 section 214.
[144] Insolvency Act 1986 s214(3).

PART III
BOILERPLATE AND SCHEDULES

This Part deals with the remainder of the loan agreement (clauses 24–39 in the LMA Term Loan) and with the schedules. These provisions are often referred to as 'boilerplate'. The boilerplate contains important clauses relating to issues such as loan transfers, the agency role, notices and jurisdiction. The schedules are used to attach additional documents and lists, such as the drawdown notice, confidentiality letter and list of conditions precedent.

9 Changes to Parties

CLAUSE 24: CHANGES TO LENDERS – SECTION 1 – METHODS OF TRANSFER

Clause 24 deals with loan transfers. Before looking at the wording of the clause itself, this introduction looks at the methods of transfer available and at issues which arise in relation to transfers of secured loans. 9.001

In summary, the methods by which a new lender can derive an interest in the loan under English law are:

- transfer (see Box 9.1) of rights and obligations (classically, by **novation**);
- assignment of rights;
- sub-participation (which is a contract between selling and buying lender); and
- credit derivatives.

> **Box 9.1**
> The word 'transfers' may be used:
>
> - to indicate a complete transfer of the entire legal relationship (or a specified percentage of it) from one lender to another, for example, by novation, rather than a transfer of some aspects of the legal relationship – for example, rights only but not obligations, as would be achieved by an assignment; or
> - in a less technical sense, to include all the different methods by which a party other than one of the original lenders can either come to be a lender of record or to have an interest in the loan.
>
> Clause 24.2(b) of the LMA Term Loan uses the word 'transfer' in its sense of a transfer of the whole legal relationship. Often the word 'transfer' is used in this sense when making a distinction between the legal effect of a novation and an assignment.

9.002 Within each of these categories there are numerous options available and each has a different regulatory and accounting impact as well as a different impact on the credit risk of the parties and on their rights and obligations. The first two options (novation and assignment) result in the new lender becoming a **lender of record** with direct claims against the borrower. Under the last two options (sub-participation and credit derivatives) the original lender remains the lender of record and the new lender's rights are against the original lender, not the borrower.[1] Generally the loan agreement seeks only to regulate the first two options, since the other options do not involve the borrower, save for the need to obtain the borrower's consent to disclosure of confidential information, which is dealt with in clause 36. However see also the discussion on 'behind the scenes' transfers in clause 24 at 9.035.

9.003 Whichever of the four methods outlined earlier is used, a lender planning to transfer an interest in a loan must ensure that it complies with any relevant **prospectus legislation** in the country in which it is operating and in the countries in which it is inviting participants to consider taking an interest in the loan. It must also ensure that it has authority from the borrower to disclose any confidential information which it may be planning to disclose to potential participants and that the wording of such authority from the borrower covers the circumstances in hand.[2]

The four methods of giving a new party an interest under the loan agreement are discussed here.

1 Novation

9.004 This is the method most commonly used in syndicated loans and provided for in the LMA Term Loan. Novation involves the discharge of the original contract and its replacement by a new contract between the new parties (see Box 9.2 on page 251).

There are two key issues to be considered in relation to a novation, which are:

- mechanics of the novation – what documents need to be signed? and
- effect of novation – what issues does the fact that it creates a new contract give rise to?

---

[1] At least, that is the case initially. The new lender may gain rights against the borrower at a later stage under a risk sub-participation or a credit derivative which is settled by physical settlement.

[2] See discussion of clause 36 of the LMA Term Loan at 11.031.

> **Box 9.2**
> Clause 24.5(c) of the LMA Term Loan creates a novation by the following words:
>   '*On the Transfer Date:*
>
> (i) to the extent that in the Transfer Certificate the Existing Lender seeks to transfer by novation its rights and obligations under the Finance Documents each of the Obligors and the Existing Lender shall be released from further obligations towards one another under the Finance Documents and their respective rights against one another shall be cancelled (being the "Discharged Rights and Obligations");
> (ii) each of the Obligors and the New Lender shall assume obligations towards one another and/or acquire rights against one another which differ from the Discharged Rights and Obligations only insofar as that Obligor and the New Lender have assumed and/or acquired the same in place of that Obligor and the Existing Lender;'

Mechanics

Originally, novation was thought to be a cumbersome method for transfer of syndicated loans as it required all parties to the loan agreement to be party to the novation. The mechanism now included in most syndicated loan documentation avoids this difficulty by providing for the novation to be effected by the selling and buying lender signing a 'Transfer Certificate' which is countersigned by the Agent (and sometimes the borrower), with the result being specified in the agreement to have the effect of novation. This operates on the principle that the lenders which are not party to the transfer certificate make an offer at the time of signing the loan agreement,[3] to accept any person as a lender under the agreement if that person follows the mechanism for novation provided for.[4]

9.005

Effect

The effect of novation is to create a new contract. This may have tax consequences. For example, because novation does not involve a transfer it is unlikely to result in a stamp duty whereas assignment potentially does give rise to a stamp duty subject to applicable exceptions. Secondly the withholding tax treatment of a loan may depend on the identity of the person who made the advance. Novation will involve the making of a new advance, whereas assignment will not. The fact that novation creates a new contract

9.006

---

[3] Which offer is made to the public at large and may be accepted by a person completing the mechanism specified in the offer – being, in this case, the execution of a Transfer Certificate. This idea of an offer to the public at large being established by Carlill v Carbolic Smoke Ball Company (1892) 2QB 484.

[4] The effectiveness of this mechanism was confirmed in Habibsons Bank Ltd v Standard Chartered Bank (Hong Kong) Limited [2010] EWCA Civ 1335, distinguishing an Australian case (Goodridge v Macquarie Bank Limited [2010] FCA 67) which had held that a similar mechanism was simply an agreement to agree.

may also cause difficulty with such things as security, consents and hardening periods, as discussed in the following paragraphs.

Security

9.007 The effect of a novation on any security requires consideration of the law which governs the security as well as the law which applies to the loan agreement.

In many countries, security can only be given for a debt which exists at the time the security is given. So, in such countries, security cannot be given at the time the loan agreement is signed as security for a debt which will or may come into existence (by the novation) at a future date.

In other countries security can be given for future debts but priorities issues may arise (does a creditor who had second priority security and who advanced funds against that security before the new loan was created gain priority over the new loan?) Security problems with a novation can be avoided if the security secures a different debt, such as the covenant to pay in favour of a security trustee contained in the security document, or a parallel debt. This issue is dealt with in this commentary on clause 24 at 9.022 onwards.

Consents

9.008 Any consent given (e.g. exchange control consents) for the loans made by the original lenders will not necessarily also apply to the new loans made by new lenders as a result of novation. If using novation, parties should ensure that, as a matter of construction, all relevant consents apply not only to the original loans made by original lenders, but also to new loans which spring up from novations effected under the loan agreement.

Hardening periods

9.009 In most countries, if a company is wound up, certain transactions that it has entered into within a certain period prior to the winding up (the 'hardening period') may be challenged in certain circumstances. Because novation results in a new contract, any new loans that arise may fall within a relevant hardening period and they, or any security for them, may be open to challenge where the original loans (or loans transferred in a different way) would not. Precisely what transactions may be successfully challenged will depend on the law in the place in which the insolvency of the company concerned occurs.

2 Assignment[5]

9.010 Assignment is an alternative method of transfer which avoids many of the problems of novation as it does not create a new contract. Assignment keeps

---

[5] Often words are not used accurately, and a document may be referred to as an 'assignment' which in fact has the effect of an assignment and assumption agreement discussed at 9.016.

the existing contract in place but has the effect that rights once owned by one lender (principally the right to be repaid and receive interest) will, after the assignment, belong to a different lender (see Box 9.3).

> **Box 9.3**
> So the key differences between this and a novation are that
> - obligations are not transferred; and
> - it is the *original lender's rights* which now belong to the new lender, rather than the new lender owning a *new set of rights*.

Unless the loan agreement says otherwise (which it often does) consent of the borrower is not required.

The principal issues with assignment relate to: 9.011

- effect on indemnities;
- effect on security; and
- effect on obligations.

Effect on indemnities

Personal rights (where one party is only willing to perform in favour of a particular counterparty and it would be unjust to enforce performance in favour of a different party) cannot be assigned[6] (see Box 9.4). 9.012

> **Box 9.4**
> For example, an employer may not assign an employment contract so as to require the employee to work for a different company. A publisher cannot assign the benefit of an author's contract to write a book if the author relied on the publisher's skill as a publisher.[7]

This may not be the case where the contracting party expressly or impliedly contracted with the original counterparty or its assigns.[8]

Arguably, indemnities could be personal rights because it is likely that attributes of the person holding the indemnity will affect the likelihood of a claim being made under it. For this reason any new lender who takes an interest through an assignment ought to ensure that the contractual provisions of the loan agreement (and in particular any indemnities such as the indemnity for broken funding costs) are expressed to benefit not only the

---

[6] British Waggon Co v Lea & Co (1879–80) LR 5 QBD 149.
[7] Griffith v Tower Publishing (1897) 1 Ch 21.
[8] Tolhurst v Associated Portland Cement Manufacturers (1900) Ltd (1903) AC 414.

original lenders, but also assignees, so reinforcing the argument that the indemnities are not personal in the first place.

English law assignments come in many forms (see A1.051 onwards). Usually a lender will be transferring only part of its interest in the agreement and therefore the assignment will be equitable, not statutory. The lenders will usually give notice to the borrower through the Agent. The effect is that, unless the assignor disputes the payment, the borrower must pay the new lender (through the Agent) in order to be discharged from the debt.[9]

Effect on security

9.013   The assignment does not cause the security problems which novation causes because the debt which is secured does not change. That debt still exists but simply belongs to a new party.

In many jurisdictions, an assignment of a debt automatically carries with it (and allows an assignee to benefit from) any security for the debt without the need for that security to be specifically transferred. However, there may be requirements which need to be complied with in the jurisdiction where the security is, for example, for the new lender to be registered on the security register. Such requirements would be fatal to the liquidity of the loan in the secondary market. In such cases, therefore, use of a structure which avoids these additional requirements may be necessary, for example, trustee/parallel debt/guarantee structure. See further 9.022 onwards in relation to transfers of secured loans.

Effect on obligations

9.014   It is not possible to assign obligations under English law (see Box 9.5).

Box 9.5

There is a difference here between assigning and delegating. A person may delegate their obligations to another and the person to whom the obligations are owed may have to accept the performance of those obligations by another if the identity of the person performing the obligation is not critical to the person to whom the obligation is owed. For example, a company which has agreed to deliver cement to a specified place can delegate that obligation, while an architect who has a contract to design a new building for housing the national opera company cannot delegate that obligation because the skills of the person performing the obligation are important to the other party to the contract.

---

[9] If the lenders did not give notice, the assignment would, as a matter of English law, still be effective in a liquidation of the existing lender, but the new lender would not be able to receive payment direct, only through the existing lender.

Lenders under a syndicated loan have obligations (principally to advance funds) as well as rights. The obligation to advance funds to the borrower cannot be delegated, since the identity of the person performing that obligation is relevant for the borrower. So assignment is inappropriate for loans where there are significant ongoing personal obligations on the lenders. This would be the case in a revolving credit, a multicurrency loan, and a term loan which has not yet been fully drawn, for example.

9.015

Nevertheless, a hybrid can be, and often is, used in these situations. This is referred to as an '*Assignment and Assumption Agreement*'. The commercial effect of such an agreement is similar to the novation but without its disadvantages. The assignment and assumption agreement involves three parts:

9.016

- the existing lender assigns its rights to the new lender;
- the new lender agrees with the borrower to perform the obligations owed by the existing lender (to the extent of the amount transferred) and the borrower agrees to accept that performance; and
- the borrower agrees with the existing lender not to pursue it for performance of its obligations (to the extent of the amount being transferred).

The effect is that the new lender has assumed the obligations but there is no discharge of a contract and replacement with a new contract, as in a novation. The security, consents, and hardening period issues which novation gives rise to are therefore avoided. The document has the effect of an assignment coupled with an assumption of obligations by the new lender. Of course, this document is similar to a novation in that it will be necessary for all parties to the loan agreement to be party to it. Therefore, it is usually effected using a transfer certificate mechanism as used for a novation and discussed at 9.005.

3 Sub-participation

A sub-participation is very different from an assignment and a novation because it does not involve the new lender in acquiring a relationship with the borrower. The new lender acquires rights against the existing lender, but not against the borrower. It is sometimes referred to as a 'silent' participation. This can be achieved either by:

9.017

- a risk sub-participation; or
- a funded sub-participation.

Risk sub-participation

For a fee, the sub-participant gives a guarantee to the existing lender in relation to the portion of the loan the risk of which is being transferred. The effect for the existing lender is to change its credit risk from a risk on

9.018

the borrower to a risk on the sub-participant. For the subparticipant, if it is required to make payment, it will be subrogated to the rights of the existing lender in relation to the borrower.[10]

Funded sub-participation

9.019 This is usually achieved through a sub loan. Here the new lender advances funds to the existing lender on the basis that the obligations of the existing lender to repay those sums are limited to amounts received by the existing lender from the borrower. The effect for the existing lender is to reduce the amount of its total credit risk by the amount of the sub-loan. The effect for the new lender is that it takes two credit risks: does the borrower repay the existing lender, and does the existing lender repay the new lender? It may also involve additional tax risk in relation to possible withholding taxes on interest payable under the sub-loan.

4 Credit derivatives

9.020 An alternative method of transferring credit risk is by using credit derivatives. These are highly flexible instruments which can be used to create investments which differ from the underlying debt in many significant ways, such as credit risk and pricing. The documents are in standard form International Swaps and Derivatives Association (ISDA) agreements. Because there is no change in the legal relationship between the lender and borrower, there is no effect on the underlying loan or its security.

There may be issues in some jurisdictions as to whether these derivatives amount to gambling or insurance. ISDA maintains a wealth of legal opinions on these issues in various jurisdictions which are available to ISDA members on their website. Credit derivatives can be very complex although the basic underlying concepts are simple. We focus here on the credit default swap only, as that is the most common form of credit derivative.

Credit default swap

9.021 Under a credit default swap the original lender makes periodic payments to the counterparty of a small percentage of the principal amount due to the original lender from the borrower. These payments are similar in amount to the fee which would be paid in relation to a risk sub-participation. If a Credit Event occurs, the swap will become due for settlement. The swap may provide for cash settlement or for physical settlement. In the case of cash settlement, the counterparty will pay the difference between the face value of the debt (the amount due from the borrower) and its current market value (see Box 9.6 on page 257). In other words, they will compensate the

---

[10] But its rights to be indemnified by the borrower and to be subrogated to the original lender's position will be limited because the guarantee was not given at the request of the debtor – see The Modern Law of Guarantee, Dr John Phillips, 2nd English edn, 2010 at para 12.02.

original lender for the loss in value of the debt. In the case of physical settlement, the counterparty will pay (usually) the full amount of the face value of the loan and the loan will be transferred to it.

> **Box 9.6**
> The Credit Default Swap is very flexible. It may relate to a single payment instalment, or to a single loan agreement, but more commonly it relates to a group of borrowers, a group of loan agreements, a portfolio of debt and so on. The credit protection being purchased may also be limited to particular tranches of risk such as the first 5% of loss suffered. Participants in the CDS market do not even need to hold any of the underlying debt. As discussed in the Introduction at 0.183, these instruments have led to an active market in credit risk, quite separate from the market in the underlying debt. These instruments are most common in the capital markets, but are also used in the loan markets, to a lesser extent.

Since 2009 and the adoption of the so-called 'Big Bang Protocol' the CDS market has become more standardized. Of particular note is

- the development of 'Determination Committees' whose role is to decide, in relation to any given entity, whether a Credit Event has occurred or not, and
- the development of an auction process, following a Credit Event, to determine the market value of the debt in question, and therefore the amounts of the payments due on settlement.

CLAUSE 24: CHANGES TO LENDERS – SECTION 2 – TRANSFERS OF SECURED LOANS

9.022 It will be clear from the previous paragraphs that transferring secured loans gives rise to particular problems. This section looks at the different structures which have developed to allow syndication of secured loans. The first point to make is that the issues discussed in this section relate to syndications, not sub-participation or credit derivatives. Because sub-participation and credit derivatives do not affect the legal relationship between the borrower and its lenders, they also do not affect the security for the loan. The problems addressed in this section arise only when there is a change in the members of the syndicate, that is, under English law, when there is an assignment or novation.

As well as the legal issues discussed in Section 1, syndicating secured loans gives rise to the administrative question of how to avoid the need for signatures from all lenders when security needs to be released or amended. Any requirement (as in some jurisdictions) that any change in identity of a secured party needs to be registered in the registry where the security is registered, can be fatal to the liquidity of the underlying debt. So it is common in secured syndicated loans for security to be given to one of the lenders (often the Agent, or a special Security Agent or Security Trustee) on behalf of all the lenders.

9.023 Two questions therefore need to be addressed in considering the structure for transferring secured loans:

- who should the security be given to? and
- what debt should it secure?

There are three common options, with the choice depending on the jurisdictions of the parties and of any security:

- security given to a trustee for the lenders, as security for the covenant to pay the trustee contained in the security documents;
- security given to an agent for the syndicate as security for the underlying debts to syndicate members[11] or
- security given to an agent for the syndicate as security for a parallel debt or joint creditorship.

1 Security to a trustee for the covenant to pay

9.024 In jurisdictions which recognize the concept of trusts, the security is given to a Security Trustee (normally one of the lenders) as trustee for the lenders from time to time.[12] It will be given to the trustee as security for the covenant, in the security documents, to pay the trustee the amounts due to the lenders from time to time. It is important to take care, in drafting the security, to ensure that it does indeed secure the covenant in favour of the trustee.

In recent years, the concept of trusts in relation to syndicated loans has been obtaining increasing recognition, even in countries which have not ratified the 1985 Hague Convention on recognition of trusts. Trusts created under foreign law have been recognized in the French Belvedere case in 2011 and in Poland in 2009.[13] Japan has also introduced a law recognizing trusts in syndicated loan transactions.

The trust route also has a number of advantages over the other structures described below, notably in that

- changing a trustee is simple and
- the lenders do not take a credit risk on a trustee.

---

[11] Or for the obligation to pay the underlying debts to the Agent on behalf of the syndicate members.
[12] It is not necessary to identify all beneficiaries of a trust at the time the trust is created as long as it is clear enough to be able to identify who the beneficiaries are at any given time.
[13] File IV CSK 145/09.

2 Security to an Agent

In jurisdictions which do not recognize the concept of trust, the security will be held by the Agent as agent for the syndicate members from time to time. In such cases, due diligence will be necessary on the question of what will happen to the security and its proceeds in the event that the Security Agent becomes insolvent when holding proceeds but before they have been distributed.[14] This may also be relevant for regulatory purposes – such as the Basel regulations – where the question arises as to whether the lenders are in fact simply unsecured creditors of the Agent, particularly if the parallel debt structure is used as described below.

9.025

A second disadvantage of an Agent is what happens to the security if the Agent needs to be replaced? Under English law the trust property automatically vests in a new trustee without the need for any transfer. With an Agent, the security may need to be reconstituted in favour of the new Agent.

Thirdly, of course, the lenders' lawyer will need to consider how such security would be enforced in practice – for example, will the Agent be able to claim as secured creditor for the whole debt?

Security to an Agent as security for the underlying debts[15]

This structure is only available if, in the jurisdiction where the security is located, it is possible for security to be given to (and to be enforceable by) one person as security for debts owed to different persons (although payable to the security holder on behalf of those persons) and without the need to make any changes to the registration when there is a change in the members of the syndicate.

9.026

If this structure is to be used, it will be necessary to ensure that the security secures the debts owed to lenders who take an interest in the loan after the date of creation of the security.[16] This involves consideration of the method of transfer.

If interests in the loan are transferred by assignment or by assignment and assumption, the original debts made by the original lenders, which are secured by the security, remain in place throughout, despite any transfers, but are owed to new lenders. Security can be given for the debts existing at

9.027

---

[14] See discussion on trustees versus agents at A1.039.
[15] Or for the obligation to pay the underlying debts to the Agent on behalf of the syndicate members.
[16] Unless under the law which governs the security, and taking account of its conflict of law rules, the obligation to pay the Agent will be regarded as a different debt, independent of the underlying debts, in which case the security may be given for the obligation to pay the Agent and the method of transfer may be disregarded.

9.028 the time the security is created, and that security should remain effective to secure those debts as assigned to new syndicate members (subject to any registration requirements).

If, on the other hand, interests in the loan are transferred by novation, it is important to ensure that the security secures any new debts made by new lenders as a result of the novation as well as the original loans made by the original lenders. It is not sufficient for the security to be given to an agent (or trustee) on behalf of the syndicate from time to time. It must also secure the debts created from time to time. This is an area for due diligence in the country of the security. In most countries it is not possible to create security for future debts which may or may not be advanced by persons unknown. In others, such security may be possible but there may be priority issues if second priority security has been created on the secured assets after the date of the original loan but before the date on which the novation occurred. See Appendix 1 at A1.069.

The same point arises in a multicurrency loan if the original loan is repaid and then readvanced on a change of currency. Does the security secure the new advance, and might there be a loss of priority to other lenders?

Security to an Agent as security for a parallel debt

9.029 This route is often used in those countries in which trusts are not recognized but it is also not possible for security to be given to an agent on behalf of the syndicate because security can only be given in favour of the secured creditors themselves and not to an agent on their behalf. In these countries, syndicates must either accept the administrative inconvenience of registering a change in security holder whenever there is a change in the syndicate (which would severely hamper the liquidity of the loan and therefore the amount of money which could be raised) or use an alternative route.

9.030 The alternative route often used is the so-called 'parallel debt'. Here, security is given to the Agent as security for a 'parallel debt' expressed to be owed to the Agent. This debt is equal to the total amount outstanding under the loan agreement. It is specified that the amount of the parallel debt reduces pro rata with all payments of the underlying debt. It is also specified that any recoveries under the parallel debt must be shared pro rata with the lenders. While this structure has become market standard in some countries, it may be vulnerable to challenge as being a fiction in other jurisdictions. It may also be open to challenge as being a preference in some countries, as the security is granted to an entity which has not advanced all the funds. Nevertheless, the structure is gaining increased acceptance, as evidenced by the fact that it has been held to be effective in France (in the Belvedere case in 2011) and in Poland (file no IV CSK 145/09).

Security to Agent as security for joint creditorship

A similar solution to the parallel debt in some countries involves the concept of 'joint creditorship'. A joint creditorship is rather similar to the more common idea of joint and several debtors. Where there is a group of joint and several debtors owing a sum of money, they must ensure that the sum is paid, on the basis that the person who is owed the debt has the right to sue any one of the debtors for the whole debt. 9.031

Under a joint creditorship – in those countries which have the concept – the sum of money is owed to a group of creditors and any one of those creditors is able to sue, (alone) for the whole amount of the debt on behalf of the group. In this way, the security can be given to the person to whom the debt is owed (if, under local law it can be given to just one of the creditors), and (crucially) that creditor is entitled to sue in its own name for payment of the whole debt. 9.032

An alternative to a parallel debt

An alternative which avoids the fictional element of a parallel debt is for a company (an spc subsidiary of a lender) to guarantee the loan on a limited recourse basis, with recourse limited to its recoveries under security. The security would then be given to the spc as security for the borrower's obligation to indemnify (or cash collateralize) the spc for payments made under the guarantee (see Box 9.7). In this way security is given in favour of the person to whom the debt is owed without the need to create a 'parallel debt'. The method of transfer of the underlying debt then becomes irrelevant as far as the security is concerned. The main disadvantages of this route are the added structural complexity and the need to establish and maintain a special purpose company. Given the increased tendency to recognize both trusts and parallel debts, and the extra expense and complexity of this route, this alternative mechanism is reducing in popularity. 9.033

Box 9.7

An alternative structure to a parallel debt

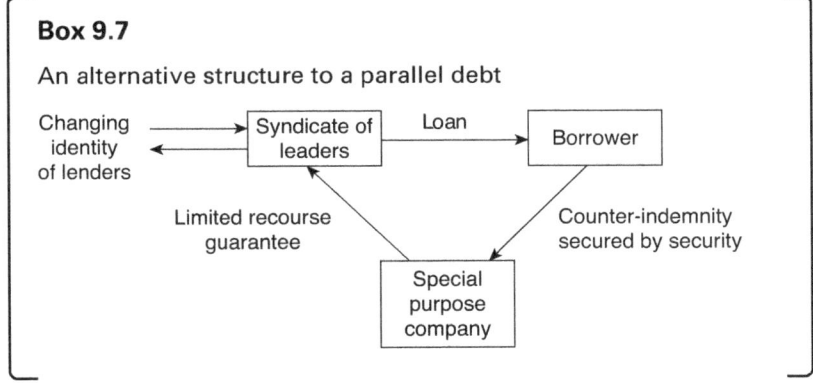

CLAUSE 24: CHANGES TO LENDERS – SECTION 3 – THE LMA TERM LOAN

Consent to transfers

9.034   Clause 24 deals with transfer of the loan. An important question which needs to be addressed is the extent to which the borrower's consent is required for a transfer. There are two separate aspects to this, being

- consent to transfers 'behind the scenes' such as sub-participations and credit derivatives and
- consent to transfers which result in a change in the lender of record.

Consent to transfers 'behind the scenes'

9.035   Traditionally there has been no restriction on the lenders' ability to enter into sub-participations, credit derivatives or other arrangements which do not affect the lender of record. This is the position in the standard LMA Term Loan. The reasoning is that these arrangements do not involve the borrower but are private arrangements entered into by the lender.

However as noted in the Introduction at 0.183, the evolution of active markets for credit risk through the Credit Default Swap market and the distressed debt market can cause significant difficulties for borrowers in trying to negotiate reschedulings because of the lack of transparency as to who is holding the ultimate risk, and the different motivations of different players. For example a lender holding a Credit Default Swap may prefer a Credit Event to occur so as to trigger payment under the swap. A party which has bought into the loan at a discount may also have less motivation than other lenders to try to arrange a turnaround for the company.

9.036   Borrowers may therefore be concerned to try to restrict 'single name' credit derivatives[17] and sub-participations or at least to have the right in certain circumstances to be informed about them. However, lenders would generally be very reluctant, as a matter of policy, to permit any such restrictions as they could have significant impact on the lenders' strategic options in running their own business. Many lenders have strict transfer criteria with which all their loans must comply.

Occasionally a borrower may succeed in including a provision to the effect that lenders cannot enter into arrangements which result in their losing their control over the exercise of their voting rights. Another possibility is to ask lenders to agree to inform them of such arrangements in certain circumstances (e.g. in the event of a refusal of a consent or following an Event of Default).

---

[17] A 'single name' credit derivative is one which relates to the credit risk of a single entity, as opposed to one which relates to a pool of debts.

Consent to transfers which change the lender of record

Changing the lender of record has a much greater impact on the borrower than the 'behind the scenes' arrangements just discussed. For example:

- The credit standing of the lender may be an issue, particularly in a revolving credit, a term loan with a long drawdown period or a multi-currency loan, in all of which the borrower is exposed to the risk that the lender may be unable to advance funds as agreed;
- The credit standing of the lender may also be an issue as a result of the market disruption clause: depending on what has been agreed on that clause, certain lenders may be more likely than others to have a funding problem which could help to trigger the clause;
- The identity and location of the lender can impact the borrower's withholding tax obligations;
- Lenders who have purchased debt at a discount may have different motivations towards rescue than other lenders;
- Certain types of lenders, such as hedge funds may not have the manpower to deal with requests for consent and their motivation may not be transparent;
- Lenders with small amounts of exposure to the borrower may have less motivation to support a turnaround in the event that the company gets into difficulties;
- The lender of record will have access to confidential information about the borrower's business, which could be abused.

9.037

For all these reasons, the borrower would like to ensure that their consent is required for a change in the lender of record. This is the default position in the LMA Term Loan, subject to three provisos –

9.038

- first, such consent must not be unreasonably withheld,
- second, the consent is not required if an Event of Default has occurred, and
- third, consent is not required in the case of a transfer to an Affiliate of a lender.

In many of the other LMA documents, the consent of the borrower is not required for a transfer.

Comment The reason the borrower's consent is not required following an Event of Default is to facilitate sale in the distressed market as well as to allow for physical settlement of derivatives. However as discussed earlier, transfers at such time can cause problems for restructurings so that borrowers may want to restrict this if possible.

9.039

9.040 *Comment* The question of whether or not it is unreasonable to withhold consent is of course subjective. It might be helpful to specify some circumstances in which the parties agreed that it would be reasonable to withhold consent.[18]

9.041 *Comment* If the borrower's consent is not needed for transfer, it should consider specifying certain parameters within which the right to transfer must be exercised (see Box 9.8). However, borrowers need to bear in mind that the more restrictive the transfer provisions, the smaller the pool of money will be for funding the loan. Restrictions on transfer may come at a cost.

Box 9.8

Examples of limits on transfers which a borrower may wish to specify include:

- no transfers such that the amount of the participation of any lender of record is less than a given figure. This will have the effect of limiting the number of lenders of record with whom the borrower needs to deal and also ensuring each of them has a reasonable level of commitment to the borrower;
- no transfers to be made to a competitor (either specified by name or by industry sector) or to a lender to a competitor;
- no transfers to a lender with lower than a certain credit rating (particularly for revolvers or term loans with long drawdown periods);
- no transfers to a lender which is a counterparty to [significant] transactions with the borrower because it will give rise to rights of set off;[19]
- no transfers by the Agent if it would reduce the Agent's participation below a certain figure;
- loan only to be transferred to 'Qualifying Lenders' (see discussions on clause 13);
- no transfers to specific named entities listed in a schedule;
- transfer only allowed to specific named entities listed in a schedule;
- transfers only within the existing syndicate;
- no transfers to lenders which have previously been in a minority refusing consent to a request; and
- transfers only permitted to entities which can provide banking services including fixed term overdraft facilities.

---

[18] For a discussion of the effect of such clauses see 'Restrictions on the transfer of rights in loan contracts' in Butterworths Journal of International Banking and Financial Law, October 2013.

[19] For example, problems may arise if the borrower's debt is being traded at a discount. Assume that a debt of $100 is bought for $70 by a purchaser which owes $100 to the borrower. The purchaser may now, in some jurisdictions, offset its debt to the borrower against the borrower's debt to it. The result is that, for an outlay of $70, the purchaser can avoid a payment of $100. The effect may be to make it more difficult for a company whose loan is being traded at a discount to collect their debts from customers. In the event of liquidation of the company, it will be the company's creditors who will lose out. In some countries, set off exercised shortly before liquidation may be unwound, so the advantage which the customer obtained may not be permanent. (In the UK, under Rule 4.90(2) of the Insolvency Rules 1986, set off is not available against a debt acquired a time when the party knew that insolvency proceedings of the debtor were imminent). Nevertheless, avoiding such sales in the first place would be preferable.

> Sometimes lenders might also like the right to withhold consent to proposed transferees if they are taking significant credit risks on the other lenders. For example, this might be appropriate in a project finance transaction, where there is a long drawdown period, and insufficiency of funds during the construction would be fatal to the viability of the project.

9.042

24.1 Assignments and transfers by the lenders

Clause 24.1 allows a lender to assign its rights or to transfer its rights and obligations (by novation). The clause states that assignment or transfer may only be made to '*an entity regularly engaged in purchasing or investing in loans, securities, or other financial assets*'.[20] Even if it were restricted to 'financial institutions' the court has interpreted this phrase very broadly as discussed earlier at 0.189.

9.043

The wording can also allow transfers to the borrower or its Affiliates. The LMA has included a note in the LMA Term Loan, cross referring to the Leveraged LMA, which contains optional additional wording in two different versions to deal with this. In one version, such transfers are prohibited. In the alternative version they are allowed but the transferee has no voting power and cannot pick and choose which lender to take out – the offer to take a transfer must be made to all lenders pro rata.

9.044

Clause 24.2 Conditions of assignment or transfer

Clause 24.2 requires the borrower's consent to be obtained for an assignment (i.e. of rights only) or transfer (i.e. of rights and obligations) other than to an Affiliate of an existing lender or following an Event of Default. This consent is not to be unreasonably withheld or delayed and is deemed given if not refused within five Business Days of a request.

9.045

Clause 24.2(d) provides that an assignment will only be effective if the new lender confirms it accepts the obligations in the loan towards the rest of the syndicate members and when all applicable 'know your customer' checks are completed.

Clause 24.2(e) provides that the documentation to achieve a transfer (which, under clause 24.1(b), must take the form of a novation) must follow the requirements of clause 24.5. Due diligence is necessary to ensure that novation is a satisfactory method of transfer for the loan in question and that a different method (e.g. assignment and assumption) may not be more suitable.[21] If the parties want to use assignment, clause 24.6 sets out a procedure for that option.

---

[20] This does not, of course, restrict the nature of sub-participants, or of those to whom risk may be sold in a cash settled credit derivative.

[21] See Sections 1 and 2 of the commentary on this clause 24 at 9.001 onwards.

9.046 Clause 24.2(f) ensures that no additional withholding tax or increased cost expense will be borne by the borrower as a result of any transfer or change in Facility Office if that extra cost would arise in the circumstances existing at the time of the transfer.

However there are two exceptions to this principle

9.047 Firstly, this provision only applies after the primary syndication has been completed. The argument is that the question of whether primary syndication predates or post dates loan signature should have no impact on the withholding tax position. It is in relation to Treaty Lenders that this exception is most relevant. If a lender is only eligible to receive payment gross as a result of a double tax treaty, the effect of this exception is that the borrower will have to gross-up payments to that lender until they receive a direction from the tax authorities enabling them to pay without a tax deduction. That would also have been the case if the Treaty Lender had been a signatory to the loan agreement in the first place – although where primary syndication post dates loan signature there is clearly less scope for the borrower to avoid the problem by delaying the due date for the first interest payment as discussed in Box 6.8 on page 128.

9.048 The second exception relates to the 'DTTP Scheme' discussed at 6.011. Under that scheme, in the UK, if a Treaty Lender has a 'passport' confirming its eligibility for relief, and if the borrower submits the necessary forms to the UK tax authorities within 30 days of the lender becoming a lender then the borrower will benefit from a speedy process for obtaining approval from the UK tax authorities to make payment to the lender without deducting tax. This second exception therefore provides that if the lender has provided the necessary information to the borrower to enable them to use the scheme, then the borrower's protection against gross-up is removed. The idea is that it is now within the control of the borrower to submit the forms within the 30 days.

9.049 *Comment*   However the risk remains for the borrower that the Agent may take some time to notify them of the transfer, so the borrower may want to adjust the clause to ensure that they must receive the lender's details in sufficient time to enable it to comply with the 30 day requirement for eligibility for the faster processing.

9.050 *Comment*   Some lenders require an adjustment to this clause to allow transferees or other lending offices to have the benefit of the tax and increased cost indemnity clauses if the change was made for the benefit of the borrower pursuant to clause 16 (the mitigation clause).

9.051 It is also worth noting that in the Leveraged LMA the provision at Clause 24.2(f) only protects the borrower against increased costs resulting from a change of lender, not grossing up payments. This can result in significant additional costs for borrowers. Clearly the question of which costs the borrower should bear is a question of supply and demand. However, in principle, if lenders want to transfer the loan, they should bear the costs and therefore this clause should protect the borrower from gross-up costs as well as increased costs on a transfer. Of course the counterargument is that it is only because of the free transferability of the loan, and hence its liquidity, that lenders are able to provide funds at the price they are charging. Any restriction on transferability (e.g. by giving the borrower the same degree of protection as the LMA Term Loan gives) comes at a price.

Clause 24.3   Assignment or transfer fee

Clause 24.3 provides for the buyer to pay a transfer fee to the Agent. 9.052

Clause 24.4   Limitation of responsibility of existing lenders

Clause 24.4 is an **exclusion clause** limiting the sellers' responsibility to buyers in relation to the borrower. 9.053

Clause 24.5   Procedure for transfer

Clause 24.5 of the LMA Term Loan uses a Transfer Certificate mechanism. This involves seller and buyer of a portion of the loan signing a transfer certificate,[22] with details of the transfer completed, and delivering that to the Agent. The aim of this mechanism is to simplify the trading of interests in the loan and avoid the need for a lengthy new document to be prepared, agreed, and signed by all lenders each time there is a loan transfer. 9.054

Clause 24.5 specifies that the effect of this certificate is to discharge the rights and obligations of the existing lender vis-a-vis the borrower (to the extent they are being transferred) and to substitute the same rights and obligations as between the borrower and the new lender. This is a novation – discharging one contract and replacing it with another contract which is identical except for the parties. The agreement provides for a transfer to be effective on the later of the date proposed in the transfer certificate and the date on which the Agent completes the certificate. There is an obligation on the Agent to complete the certificate as soon as practicable, subject to completion of necessary 'know your customer' checks.

The certificate does not deal with commercial issues which are of no concern to the Agent such as apportionment of interest (if the sale is part way through an interest period and clause 24.9 does not apply). Such matters will already have been dealt with in the document[23] signed by the seller and buyer at the time the trade was agreed and which set out the commercial terms of the trade such as its effective date. 9.055

---

[22] See Section 1 of the commentary on this clause 24 at 9.005.
[23] See, for example, the LMA forms of documentation for loan transfers.

Clause 24.6 Procedure for assignment

9.056 This clause provides an optional procedure to follow if lenders wish to transfer the loan by assignment.

Clause 24.7 Copy of transfer certificate or assignment agreement to Company

9.057 Clause 24.7 requires the Agent to deliver a copy of any transfer certificate or assignment agreement to the Company.

Clause 24.8 Security over lenders' rights

9.058 This optional clause allows lenders to provide this loan to their own financiers in order to secure borrowings by the lenders. Including this type of provision may be necessary in order to enable the lenders to access certain sources of finance such as funding from central banks.

The provision states that the borrower cannot be required to pay anyone other than the lender, nor to pay more than would be due to the lender. They also provide that it will be the lender who remains liable to perform the obligations under the agreement.

Clause 24.9 Pro rata interest settlement

This optional clause provides a mechanism which may be used if the Agent is prepared to arrange for the apportionment of interest payments between sellers and buyers when the transfer date occurs in the middle of an Interest Period.

CLAUSE 25: CHANGES TO THE OBLIGORS

Clause 25.1 Assignments and transfers by Obligors

9.059 Clause 25.1 prohibits the borrowers and guarantors from transferring their rights or obligations under the agreement.

Clause 25.2 Additional borrowers

9.060 Clause 25.2 allows additional group members to become entitled to make drawings under the facility if there is no Default and

- the new party is approved by the lenders (with an option for the draftsperson to require only Majority Lender approval);
- the new party signs an Accession Letter; and

- the new party delivers certain conditions precedent (notably, legal opinions satisfactory to the Agent relating to the relevant country and compliance with any 'know your customer' checks).

In addition, clauses 19.14(b) and 25.5 provide for the Repeating Representations to be repeated by a new borrower on the date it becomes a new borrower, and therefore accession of a new borrower is also conditional on those Repeating Representations being true.

Comment The Company (the top company in the group to which the lenders have recourse) needs to ensure that, when the document is being negotiated, they identify the companies which may be wishing to rely on the availability of funds from the facility and specify them as borrowers in the first instance. They will also want to minimize the requirements which need to be satisfied for other group companies to draw the facility. For this reason, the Company may request:

9.061

- that where the new borrower is from the same country as one of the existing Obligors, they should be entitled to draw the loan without consent of the lenders (because that consent is imposed largely to enable lenders to consider any legal issues which may be highlighted by a legal opinion) and there should be no need for a new legal opinion;[24]
- that addition of borrowers from other jurisdictions should require Majority Lender (not all lender) approval. Nevertheless, many lenders will resist this and require unanimous consent for the addition of such borrowers, so as to enable them to review any relevant legal opinion as a condition of their consent, rather than rely on the Agent (in accordance with clause 25.2(a)(iv)) to determine its acceptability.

Clause 25.3   Resignation of a borrower

Clause 25.3 allows a borrower to cease to be an Obligor once it has repaid its loans and other moneys due from it under the agreement, provided there is no Default at that time. The Company, if it is a borrower, may not resign.

9.062

Clause 25.4   Additional guarantors

Clause 25.4 provides for a mechanism for a new group company to become an additional guarantor. This is likely to be used when other guarantors are resigning. The only prerequisites to addition of guarantors are the same conditions precedent as for an additional borrower (including a legal opinion satisfactory to the Agent) and Repeating Representations.

9.063

---

[24] Lenders may resist this point, particularly if the facility has a long drawdown period, so as to protect against change in law in the intervening period.

Clause 25.5 Repetition of representations

9.064 Clause 25.5 states that the Repeating Representations are repeated on a new Obligor becoming a party to the agreement.

Clause 25.6 Resignation of a guarantor

9.065 Clause 25.6 provides a mechanism for guarantors to resign. The Company, if a guarantor originally, may not resign. Other guarantors may resign but only if all lenders agree and there is no Default.

10 The Finance Parties

CLAUSE 26: ROLE OF THE AGENT AND THE ARRANGER

Clause 26 is the only clause in the agreement where the **Arranger** appears. At the time the loan agreement is signed, the Arranger's task is completed and the main purpose of referring to the Arranger in this clause is to give them the benefit of the **exclusion clause**. However, given that the exclusion clause is effectively retrospective insofar as the Arranger is concerned[1] this clause is no substitute for including an exclusion clause in appropriate pre-loan agreement documentation.

10.001

Clause 26 is concerned with defining the role of the Agent and the Arranger as being that of facilitators of the transaction but not standing in for the lenders nor looking after their interests, nor assuming the fiduciary duties which attach to persons who represent others in a legal matter (see Box 10.1).

Box 10.1
The general English law position is that, where someone represents another in a legal matter, that person has duties (known as 'fiduciary duties') to look after the interests of the person he is representing. However, a fiduciary relationship cannot be superimposed on a contract in such a way as to alter the operation which that contract was intended to have in accordance with its true construction.

Fiduciary duties generally include:[2]

- a duty to act carefully;
- a duty to avoid conflicts of interest and subordinate his own interests to that of his principals;
- a duty not to make a secret profit; and
- a duty not to sub-delegate.

---

[1] See Sumitomo Bank v Banque Bruxelles Lambert (1997) 1 Lloyds Law Reports 487 for a case where an exclusion clause in the loan agreement did not protect the Arranger from liability in respect of its duty of care as Arranger.
[2] See Ross Cranston, *Principles of Banking Law*, 2nd edn, 2002 at p. 187.

10.002 The intention in a syndicated loan is that the Agent should have an administrative role only and should not be obliged to look after the interests of syndicate members nor (as far as practical) to exercise any discretions on their behalf and that therefore, a fiduciary relationship should not arise. Instead, it is intended that it should simply act as a conduit for receipt of money and information with limited ability to take decisions on behalf of lenders. The extent to which other lenders are relying on the Agent is limited as far as possible. In Torre Asset Funding[3] it was held that the agency clause (which was in LMA 'standard' terms) had the effect of limiting the Agent's duties to those set out in the documents. In other words, the case confirmed that no fiduciary duties would be superimposed on the duties set out in the documents.

10.003 The loan agreement does, in certain cases, allow the Agent to take decisions on behalf of the syndicate. Notably, clause 23.13 permits the Agent to exercise the right of acceleration without being directed to do so by the syndicate. Clause 4.1 permits the Agent to decide whether conditions precedent have been met satisfactorily.[4] In Torre Asset Funding, the court highlighted the fact that, where the Agent had discretions such as these, there was an implied term (known as the 'Socimer implied term') that these discretions would not be exercised capriciously or arbitrarily.[5] Therefore in exercising these rights, and in the relationship with the borrower generally, the Agent should be aware that, where in practice it takes decisions on behalf of the syndicate (such as the decisions to approve conditions precedent, or to approve a legal opinion for the purpose of accepting a new Obligor), it must not abuse the power it has been given.

Clause 26 clarifies the administrative function of the Agent. The clause was substantially restructured during 2014, principally in order to clarify that the Agent was not to be liable where it acted on instructions from the lenders or on the advice of professional advisers.

Clause 26.1 Appointment of the Agent

10.004 Clause 26.1 is the appointment of the Agent by the lenders.

Clause 26.2 Instructions

10.005 Clause 26.2 gives control of the loan to the Majority Lenders; provides for all lenders to be bound by the instructions of the Majority Lenders to the Agent; allows the Agent to require security for liabilities before taking action at the direction of the Majority Lenders; and gives the Agent discretion to act on its own initiative. It also permits them to act as they think best in the interests of the lenders and absolves them of liability where they take action with the authority of the lenders or under the advice of professional advisers. See Box 10.2 on page 273.

---

[3] Torre Asset Funding Ltd v Royal Bank of Scotland Plc [2013] EWHC 2670 (Ch) at paras 142–8
[4] See Box 2.5 on page 85.
[5] See paras 35–37 of the judgement. This is referred to as the 'Socimer implied term'.

> **Box 10.2**
> Note here the 'Socimer implied term' referred to in the note at 10.003. That is an implied term to the effect that discretions may not be exercised perversely. In Torre Asset Funding[6] the judge gave an example, saying it may be a breach of the implied term if the Agent failed to notify lenders of an Event of Default which it was aware of, if the only rational action was to notify them. Following that case the LMA made substantial revisions to the text of Clause 26, as well as to other provisions of the Agreement, designed to limit the potential liability of the Agent. The prime example is clause 4.1(b) discussed at Box 2.5 on page 85, relating to satisfaction of conditions precedent. Another example is clause 26.3(g), which states that the Agent only has the duties expressly imposed on it by the documents and 'no others shall be implied'.

Clause 26.3   Duties of the Agent

10.006 The duties of the Agent are specified in clause 26.3. These are to pass on documents received, pass on information received as to existence of a Default, and, if it is aware of a non-payment, to advise the lenders. The duties are stated (at clause 26.3(a)) to be 'purely mechanical and administrative'. See Box 10.3.

> **Box 10.3**
> These duties were considered in the Torre Asset Funding case referred to at 10.002 where the Agent (in its separate capacity as agent for junior lenders) was involved in discussions with the borrower for rescheduling of the junior debt. These discussions constituted an Event of Default under the loan agreement, although the Agent had not realized that. The question arose as to whether the Agent should have notified the lenders of the Event of Default. The court held that because
>
> - the Agent's duties were specified to be 'mechanical and administrative', and
> - the clause stated that the Agent was entitled to assume that no Default had occurred unless it had actual knowledge of a non-payment and was entitled to rely on statements made to it (so that it was entitled to rely on the borrower's statement that no Default had occurred), and
> - the clause provides that the Agent 'may' (not 'shall') notify lenders of information which it receives,
>
> the general scheme was clear and clearly meant that when the Agent received information, it was not obliged to evaluate whether that information constituted an Event of Default or not. The agreement clearly limits the Agent's notification obligations to those specifically set out in the clause.

---

[6] See Box 10.3.

These are in addition to other duties specifically set out in the agreement, such as the duty to distribute moneys received.

Clause 26.4 Role of Arranger

This clause specifies that the Arranger has no obligations except those specifically set out in the documents

Clause 26.5 No fiduciary duties

Clause 26.5 states that the Agent has no fiduciary duties. See Box 10.1 on page 271. Much of clause 26 specifically allows the Agent to do things which would be in breach of their fiduciary duty if they had such a duty – for example, clause 26.6 allowing the Agent to conduct other business with the borrower (even though this may give rise to a conflict)

Clause 26.6 Business with the Group

Clause 26.6 allows the Agent and Arranger to conduct other business with the borrower group.

Clause 26.7 Rights and discretions

10.007

This is the clause referred to at Box 10.3 on page 273, which

- allows the Agent to rely on certificates which it receives as being accurate,
- allows the Agent to assume that no Default has occurred unless it has received notice to the contrary or has actual knowledge of non-payment,
- allows the Agent to assume that requests from the Company are authorized by the borrowers,
- allows the Agent to instruct professional advisers and rely on their advice (specifically stating that they will not have any liability as a result),
- allows lenders to communicate direct with the borrower and not through an Impaired Agent,
- allows the Agent to act through its employees, and
- allows (but does not require) the Agent to pass on information which it reasonably believes it has received in its capacity as Agent.

Clause 26.8 Responsibility for documentation

10.008

Clause 26.8 provides that the Agent is not liable for the accuracy of information supplied in connection with the transaction, or for the effectiveness of the documents. The intention is that the Agent and the Arranger should simply be facilitators but should not assume any responsibility in relation to information circulated to the syndicate or for the effectiveness of the loan documentation. They are simply acting as co-coordinators, not inviting the syndicate to rely on them. The Agent instructs the lawyers and leads the negotiation but

- the syndicate members are not bound by that negotiation – they are given their own opportunity to review the documents and make comments; and
- the Agent is not underwriting the effectiveness of their lawyers – if a mistake is made which impacts on the transaction, the intention is that that risk should be borne equally by all the syndicate members.

Clause 26.9   No duty to monitor

This clause clarifies that the Agent has no duty to monitor whether an Event of Default has occurred, or whether any party is in breach of any of its obligations under the documents

10.009

Clause 26.10   Exclusion of liability

Clause 26.10 states that the Agent is not liable for anything it does or fails to do except in the case of 'gross negligence or wilful misconduct' – that is, liability for negligence is excluded. The gross negligence standard is generally accepted market practice. It supplements the general principle that the Agent is simply an **administrator** and all risks (including the risk of negligence by lender's employees) are shared equally among the syndicate. Nevertheless, it is difficult to specify in advance what circumstances a court might hold to fall within the definition of 'gross negligence',[7] particularly given the general approach which courts take to exclusion clauses.[8] The main protection for the Agent is to exercise its rights with care and to involve the syndicate members in any potentially contentious decisions which have to be taken.

10.010

Clause 26.11   Lenders' indemnity to the Agent

Clause 26.11 requires the lenders to indemnify the Agent for any losses and expenses incurred in its role as Agent.

10.011

---

[7] meaning a serious disregard of or indifference to an obvious risk – see Red Sea Tankers v Papachristidis [1997] 2 Lloyd's Rep. 547.
[8] See A1.027.

Clause 26.12 Resignation of the Agent

10.012 Clause 26.12 allows the Agent to substitute a different group member as Agent without consent of any other party. It also allows the Agent to resign and (in paragraph (h)) allows the Majority Lenders to require the Agent to resign. (See also the discussion at 10.018). If the Agent wants to resign and have its position assumed by a third party, the syndicate (not the borrower) has the right to appoint a substitute, but if they fail to do so within 20 days, the Agent may do so. This right can be useful for an Agent as it may be the only way to resolve a conflict of interest. It is therefore important that the Agent's ability to resign cannot be restricted by other parties (although it may be frustrated if it cannot find a third party willing to take on the role).

10.013 *Comment* Note the clause allows the Agent to impose revised terms unilaterally on the other parties in relation to the agency fees, duties and responsibilities of the Agent in order to induce the replacement Agent to take up its role. The only restrictions are that the Agent must be acting reasonably; the rights and obligations must be 'consistent with then current market practice for the appointment and protection of corporate trustees' and the revised fees must be 'consistent with the successor Agent's normal fee rates'. Borrowers may want to object to the unilateral nature of this clause, particularly where no Default has occurred.

Clause 26.13 Confidentiality

10.014 Clause 26.13 provides that the agency department of the Agent will be treated as a separate entity from the rest of the Agent bank so that information received by the agency department will not be deemed to be known to personnel in other divisions of the Agent bank. This Clause is particularly important in the context of the Agent's duties set out in clause 26.3 discussed at 10.006.

Clause 26.14 Relationship with the lenders

10.015 Clause 26.14 requires the lenders to give the Agent five Business Days' notice of a change in Facility Office or lender and to deliver to the Agent all information necessary to allow the Agent to calculate the Mandatory Costs (if applicable – see 5.002).

10.016 This Clause also allows lenders to appoint a third party to receive information on their behalf. This is to deal with the issue of public and private information as discussed at 0.191.

Clause 26.15 Credit appraisal by lenders

Clause 26.15 contains confirmation by the syndicate members that they have not relied on any representations by the Agent or the Arranger but have undertaken their own financial due diligence and will continue to do so. This is designed to protect the Agent and Arranger from liability for misrepresentation and from the argument by syndicate members that they were led to join the syndicate in reliance on the superior expertise of the Arranger and/or the Agent in relation to the proposed transaction.

10.017

Impaired Agent provisions

There are also optional provisions which are part of the Defaulting Lender 'kit' discussed in the Introduction at 0.155 and which

10.018

- require the Agent to disclose the identity of Defaulting Lenders on request either by the borrower or by the Majority Lenders
- allow the Majority Lenders to replace an Impaired Agent
- allow payments to be made through a different party – not the Agent (if it is an Impaired Agent), and
- require the Agent to provide the borrower with a list of the lenders, either monthly or on request.

CLAUSE 27: CONDUCT OF BUSINESS BY THE FINANCE PARTIES

Clause 27 provides that the lenders can organize their affairs (particularly their tax affairs) as they think fit, and that they are not required to claim any particular tax credit or tax relief which might be available to them. This clause is discussed in the context of clause 13.4 at 6.028.

10.019

CLAUSE 28: SHARING AMONG FINANCE PARTIES

Clause 28.1 Payments to Finance Parties and
Clause 28.2 Redistribution of payments

Clause 28 is the pro rata sharing clause. Its function is to ensure that each lender recovers the same proportion of its debt as each of the other lenders. The clause provides that if any lender recovers a greater proportion than any other, then it will share the excess with the others, reflecting the basic concept of a syndicated loan that, if there is a loss, the lenders should suffer equally.

10.020

This clause does not however oblige any lender to exercise its set off rights against the syndicated loan (see Box 10.4 on page 278).

> **Box 10.4**
>
> For example, assume lender A,
>
> (a) has a bilateral facility of $10 million to borrower B; and
> (b) is a member of a syndicate of ten lenders which have provided a loan of $100 million to B with each lender lending $10 million.
>
> Assume that B fails to repay either loan but has a bank account with A with $5 million in it and that the law in the country where the bank account is held allows set off rights as against either of the facilities. Lender A has two choices (absent any special relationship as discussed below):
>
> - It may use the $5 million deposit to set off against its $10 million bilateral facility. In this case, after the set off, it will be owed $10 million on the syndicated loan and $5 million on its bilateral facility;
> - Alternatively, it may use the $5 million deposit to set off against its interest in the syndicated loan. It would then need to share the $5 million with all other nine members of the syndicate – leaving A retaining a benefit of only $0.5 million from the set off. The result would be a continued debt to B of $10 million on its bilateral facility and of $9.5 million in respect of the syndicated loan.
>
> Clearly A would prefer to use the set off for the purpose of the bilateral facility. This is not prohibited by the clause.

It may be, however, that exercising a set off for the benefit of a different debt could be challenged if the lender in question had some special relationship[9] with lenders who would have benefited from the sharing clause had the set off been applied to this loan; those other lenders may be able to claim that the lender's action was in breach of a fiduciary duty (if they can show that such a duty exists).

Clause 28.3   Recovering party's rights

10.021   If a lender makes a payment of a surplus under this clause then clause 28.3 provides that the borrower still owes them the amount they have paid over. This clause is necessary since the exercise of the right of set off will have extinguished the debt owed to the recovering lender (see Box 10.5).

> **Box 10.5**
>
> In the example in Box 10.4, if the set off were exercised against the syndicated loan, after the set off the borrower would only owe A $5 million, as the other $5 million has been extinguished by the set off. However, after the sharing, A has a shortfall of $9.5 million. This clause provides that B now owes A the amount (i.e. $4.5 million) which A has paid over to the other lenders.

---

[9] For example, if it were the Agent or a lender of record with responsibilities to sub-participants.

Nevertheless, it is possible that this provision may not be effective in the insolvency of the borrower since it may contravene the pari passu principle which is applicable in insolvency (because the debt, having been paid to the lender, is then treated as not having been paid).[10]

The intention of course is that the lenders who have received payment under this clause should have their claim against the borrower reduced by the amount received, so that the total amount due by the borrower is unaffected by the clause.

Comment Borrowers might want an adjustment to the clause to state this expressly. 10.022

It is also worth noting that, as a matter of English law, the recovering lender is unlikely to be able to exercise set off rights in insolvency in relation to the amounts newly due to it as a result of the operation of the clause.[11] 10.023

Clause 28.4 Reversal of redistribution

Clause 28.4 provides for the payments to be reversed if, after the sharing has occurred, the lender that had recovered more than the others is required to refund that excess recovery to the borrower or other Obligor. 10.024

Given that some countries require rights of set off which have been exercised shortly before an insolvency to be reversed this is an important provision for the lender which originally had the extra recovery.

Clause 28.5 Exceptions

Clause 28.5 provides that the obligation to share additional recoveries does not apply if the result would be that the lender which had the additional recovery would not have a valid claim against the borrower (e.g. pursuant to clause 28.3) after the sharing. It also does not apply if a lender recovered a greater percentage of its loan than other lenders as a result of taking legal action (including amounts paid in settlement of that action) which others could have joined in but declined to do so. This exception is important if the right of individual action referred to at clause 2.2(b) (discussed at 2.006) is to have any real value. 10.025

---

[10] This is one reason for the exception in clause 28.5, relieving the lender of the obligation to share if as a result they would no longer have a valid claim against the borrower.
[11] See *International Loans, Bonds, Guarantees, Legal Opinions*, 2nd edn by Philip Wood at 7.030–1.

11 Administration

CLAUSE 29: PAYMENT MECHANICS

Clause 29.1   Payments to the Agent

11.001   Clause 29 sets out the payment mechanics. Payments are to be made to the Agent in the principal financial centre for the currency concerned (or in the case of Euro, in one of the principal financial centres or in London '*as specified by the Agent*'[1]). This effectively passes exchange control risk and risk of insolvency of intermediaries[2] to the borrower.

The Clause requires payment to be made in '*such funds specified by the Agent as being customary ... for settlement of transactions in the relevant currency in the place of payment*'. This refers to the practices in different markets from time to time, for example, payments may required to be made in **CHIPS**[3] in some markets.

Clause 29.2   Distributions by the Agent

11.002   This clause provides for the Agent to distribute moneys received to the bank accounts specified by the various parties, with at least five Business Days' notice of the bank account details being required.

Clause 29.3   Distribution to an Obligor

11.003   This clause allows the Agent to use moneys which are owed to an Obligor under the agreement in settlement of any moneys due from that Obligor.

---

[1] The ability of the Agent to specify the place of payment is intended to assist in the event of a Euro breakup, as it would allow the Agent to require payment outside the Eurozone.
[2] Other than the Agent's correspondent bank in the relevant country.
[3] See Goode *Commercial Law*, 4th edn, chapter 17 for a discussion of payment systems.

Clause 29.4 Clawback and pre-funding

Clause 29.4 provides protection for the Agent if it disburses sums (e.g. to the borrower) on the assumption that all others will contribute when due and any party (e.g. a lender) fails to do so. In these circumstances the party which received the payment must repay it to the Agent up to the amount of the missing contribution plus interest. This clause operates in both directions, that is, both for payments to the borrower which are to be funded by the syndicate, and for payments to the syndicate which are to be funded by the borrower. In relation to payments to the borrower, the clause provides that if the lender which failed to make its contribution also fails to compensate the Agent for its funding costs, then the borrower must do so.

11.004

The clause clarifies that the Agent is not obliged to make payments before they have received the corresponding sum.

Clause 29.5 Partial payments

Clause 29.5 deals with partial payments. It provides that where the borrower pays less than the full amount due, that payment will first pay the Agent's fees, costs, and expenses; then interest, other fees, and commission; then principal; then any other sums (e.g. broken funding). This clause prevents the borrower specifying how such a payment is to be allocated (see Box 11.1).

11.005

> **Box 11.1**
> For example, lenders would not want a partial payment to be applied against principal (and therefore reduce the amount on which interest was chargeable) when interest remained outstanding, particularly in countries where there are restrictions on the ability to charge interest on interest.

Comment Other lenders (e.g. a security trustee) who receive fees may wish to have their fees and expenses in the first level, pro rata with the Agent.

11.006

The clause provides that the order of application (excluding paragraph (i) providing for the Agent's fees and expenses to be paid first) may be amended by the Majority Lenders.

11.007

Comment The Majority Lender override may require adjustment in a combined facility where the lenders may be different for the different facilities, so as to ensure the order cannot be changed to the detriment of the lenders of one of the facilities.[4]

11.008

---

[4] See discussion of 'Majority Lenders' at 1.048 and see also 11.025

Clause 29.6 No set off by Obligors

11.009 Clause 29.6 provides for payment to be made by the borrowers, free of set off or counterclaim. If the borrowers have a claim or debt due from any lender, they must pursue their other remedies for that and not simply withhold payment under the loan agreement (which would cause the lender to incur additional costs in funding the amount withheld).

11.010 *Comment* Borrowers sometimes request amendment allowing them to exercise set off rights in relation to Defaulting Lenders. Lenders are likely to resist this as the lenders' ability to use the loan as collateral may depend on absence of set off rights.

See Box 11.2

> **Box 11.2**
> Clauses excluding rights of set off are potentially open to challenge under the Unfair Contract Terms Act 1977.[5] It has been held[6] that these clauses are reasonable in a loan agreement and therefore not unenforceable.

Clause 29.8 Currency of account

11.011 Clause 29.8 requires all payments to be made in the currency of the loan. As a result of concerns over the potential for a Euro break up, sometimes (such as in the Leveraged LMA) the clause is amended to require payment in the currency in which the loan is denominated 'pursuant to this Agreement' with the aim of reducing the risk of a redenomination in the event of a Euro exit.

Clause 29.10 Disruption to payment systems, etc.

11.012 Clause 29.10 provides an optional mechanism to deal with disruption to payment systems (defined to mean disruption to the payment system or financial markets or unavoidable systems error) and allows the Agent to bind the syndicate in relation to any payment arrangements which it agrees with the borrower to deal with such an eventuality.

CLAUSE 30: SET OFF

11.013 Clause 30 gives the lenders a contractual right of set off. This is more extensive than the right of set off they would have in the absence of express

---

[5] See discussion on exclusion clauses at A1.027.
[6] In Deutsche Bank v Khan (2013) EWHC 482 (comm)

provision if the bank account were in England. For example, it allows amounts due in different currencies to be converted into the same currency to allow a set off.

Comment Borrowers need to ensure that giving this right of set off does not breach any negative pledges they have signed. 11.014

Comment Borrowers also sometimes request that the right can only be exercised while an Event of Default is continuing. 11.015

CLAUSE 31: NOTICES

Clause 31 deals with notices. Any two parties to the agreement may agree between themselves that e-mail is an acceptable form of communication. Particular care should be taken with any notices of default or acceleration to ensure they are delivered in accordance with this clause. 11.016

It is also sensible to ensure that if other documents are involved in the transaction (e.g. security documents) the notices clauses in those documents conform to this.

CLAUSE 32: CALCULATIONS AND CERTIFICATES
Clause 32.1 Accounts

This clause provides that the lenders' accounts will be prima facie evidence of the existence of the debt. As far as English law is concerned, there is no need to have a promissory note to evidence the debt and market practice is not to require notes (see Box 11.3). 11.017

Box 11.3
Promissory notes are often found in loans with US lenders. There are two main reasons for requiring notes:

- Loans supported by notes could be used as collateral for loans from the Federal Reserve Banks.[7]
- Notes may give a procedural advantage in terms of enforcement since they are contracts quite distinct from the underlying arrangement and courts are reluctant to allow the debtor to raise a defence based on the underlying arrangement.[8]

---

[7] However, Lee Buchheit, *How to Negotiate Eurocurrency Loan Agreements*, 2nd edn, p. 150, indicates that loans without notes can also be accepted.

[8] Questions may arise under English law as to whether a promissory note which relates to a floating rate of interest would benefit from this advantage because of the requirement that a promissory note should contain a certain and unconditional payment obligation. Nevertheless, it is thought that, even if the promissory note relates to a floating rate of interest, it will benefit from the advantages of negotiable instruments as a result of commercial usage – see Goode *Commercial Law*, p. 518.

Clause 32.2 Certificates and determinations

11.018 This clause states that the lenders' certificates as to amounts due under the documents are conclusive except in the case of manifest error. Nevertheless, evidence which is conclusive under the agreement may not be accepted as such in court.

Clause 32.3 Day count convention

11.019 Clause 32.3 provides that calculations of fees, interest etc. will be based on a 360-day year except for currencies where that is not the market practice. The 360-day year convention matches the currency markets for most currencies (see Box 11.4). Some currencies (e.g. Sterling) work on a 365-day year. Regulations in some countries require the annual (i.e. on the basis of a 365-day year) interest rate to be specified. In this case the interest would still be calculated in accordance with the convention in the relevant currency market but there would need to be further description in the agreement converting the interest rate to a 365-day basis.

> **Box 11.4**
> The effect of the convention is to marginally change the interest calculation by assuming that there are only 360 days in a year. So, to calculate 30 days' interest on $3 million, the calculation is $3 million X 30/360 X interest rate (not $3 million X 30/365 X interest rate as one might expect).

CLAUSE 33: PARTIAL INVALIDITY[9]

11.020 This clause states that if any part of the agreement is illegal or unenforceable, that will have no effect on the rest of the document.

CLAUSE 34: REMEDIES AND WAIVERS

11.021 Clause 34 addresses the issues of waiver and **estoppel**.[10] In the principal case[11] Lord Cairns said that if one party leads another 'to suppose that the strict rights arising under the contract will not be enforced, or will be kept in suspense or held in abeyance, the person who otherwise might have

---

[9] A provision may only be severed under English law if it passes the 'blue pencil test' set out in <u>Goldsoll v Goldman (1915) 1 Ch 292</u>, which requires that the rest of the contract must be able to stand if the offending part is simply deleted.

[10] For further detail see Treitel, *The Law of Contract*, 13th edn at 3–077 onwards.

[11] <u>Hughes v Metropolitan Ry (1877) 2 App Cas 439.</u>

enforced those rights will not be allowed to enforce them where it would be inequitable having regard to the dealings which have thus taken place between the parties'.

The main concern in relation to a loan is that, following a default, the lenders may lead the borrower to believe that they do not intend to exercise their rights and, ultimately, they may be held to have waived the rights or be estopped from exercising them. This clause provides that that will not happen.

11.022

There is also a concern that if lenders continue to perform the loan agreement following an Event of Default, they will be held to have affirmed the contract and will therefore lose their right to terminate it.[12] The clause therefore also provides that no election by a lender to affirm the agreement will be effective unless in writing.

Nevertheless, the clause will be read **contra proferentem** and should not be relied on to be effective in the circumstances of any given case. If the borrower defaults and the lenders do not plan to exercise their rights immediately, they should write to the borrower advising that they are reserving their rights to be exercised as they see fit in the future.

CLAUSE 35: AMENDMENTS AND WAIVERS

Clause 35 regulates the level of consent between lenders required for amendment or waiver of provisions of the documents. The general provision is that Majority Lender[13] consent is required to amend or waive. However, consent of all lenders is needed for certain issues – generally the key issues which will have been subject to credit committee approval. These are set out in clause 35.2. They include the margin, interest, fees, commission, and so on; the loan amount; the drawdown period; the due dates for payment; the definition of Majority Lenders; the pro rata sharing clause, the change of control clause, the governing law and jurisdiction clause (particularly important in the context of issues such as a potential Euro break up, as well as for the general assessment of the credit risk involved in the transaction); and clause 35.2 itself, as well as certain changes to the structure of the facilities (see Box 11.5 on page 286). Clause 35.3 also provides that changes relating to the rights or obligations of the Agent or Arranger can only be made with their consent.

11.023

---

[12] See Tele2 International Card Co SA v Post Office (2009) EWCA Civ 9.
[13] See discussion of 'Majority Lenders' at 1.048.

> **Box 11.5**
> One of the changes which is stated to require unanimous approval is *'any requirement that a cancellation of Commitments reduces the Commitments of the lenders rateably under the relevant Facility'*. This was added following the emergence of a trend in secured financings, to arrange 'amend and extend' and similar facilities. These essentially involve restructuring existing debt by extending the maturity. In some cases (where unanimous agreement to change the repayment dates could not be obtained), a new tranche was added to the existing loan, with a new maturity. Lenders who wanted to participate in the new tranche would swap their commitments in the existing loan for commitments in the new tranche. In that way, borrowers could arrange a refinancing, with the benefit of existing guarantees and the like, even if all lenders were unwilling to agree a rescheduling. Those who did not participate in the new tranche simply kept their existing participation in the loan with the original repayment dates. Such a restructuring would not be possible if the loan agreement had contained this new provision relating to consent for cancellation of commitments on a non-pro rata basis.
>
> It is noteworthy that the Leveraged LMA (which is the market in which this type of restructuring emerged) has added a provision which allows 'structural adjustments' to be made without majority lender consent, but only requiring consent of the affected lenders.

11.024 It is important that alterations to the due dates for payment cannot be made without the consent of all lenders as otherwise the rights of individual lenders discussed at clause 2.2 (see 2.006) would be illusory. Similarly, a clause saying that due dates can only be changed with the consent of all lenders will be of little comfort if individual lenders can only take action to recover their debt with the approval of Majority Lenders.

11.025 *Comment* Lenders need to consider whether any other issues should require unanimous approval to change. This may include:

- release of security;
- any particular conditions precedent which are key such as any relating to security;
- any provisions which one lender requires as a matter of policy, but which other lenders may not be concerned about (such as environmental and social policies); and
- any provisions designed to protect one group of lenders in a facility which has different lenders participating in different parts of the facility.

11.026 *Comment* The borrower may also consider requesting that a provision be included to deal with lenders not responding to requests for consent. A non-response has the same effect as a no vote, since generally, where consent is sought, the requirement is to obtain consent from whatever constitutes 'Majority Lenders'. See Box 11.6.

> **Box 11.6**
> There are two common alternatives for dealing with this. In one version ('delay and it's OK') a lender is treated as giving consent if it does not respond to the request within a specified time. In the second (preferable) version, a lender who fails to respond is ignored for the purpose of calculating the level of consent obtained – this is referred to as a 'snooze you lose' clause.

This is also where you might see a 'yank the bank' clause discussed at 4.026. 11.027

There is also an optional provision here which is part of the Defaulting Lender 'kit' referred to in the Introduction at 0.155. This provides that

- the voting rights of any Defaulting Lender will be calculated on the basis of moneys actually advanced – ignoring the undrawn Commitment of the Defaulting Lender 11.028
- the Defaulting Lender will not be taken into account for the purpose of consents if it fails to respond to a request within a specified period; and 11.029
- the borrower may require a Defaulting Lender to transfer its entire participation in the loan to a company nominated by the borrower. 11.030

CLAUSE 36: CONFIDENTIALITY

Clause 36 is an express confidentiality undertaking by the lenders. It was inserted as a result of increased participation of non-bank lenders in syndicates (see 0.189). 11.031

The Clause imposes duties of confidentiality on the lenders. It allows disclosure of confidential information in specified circumstances which are 11.032

- to Affiliates of lenders and their professional advisers (note, borrowers may request that recipients be asked to sign a confidentiality undertaking, so as to commit only to use the information received for a permitted purpose);
- to actual or potential secondary market purchasers and investors including sub-participants and parties to credit derivatives (and anyone financing such purchasers and investors), provided they have signed an agreed form of confidentiality undertaking;
- to a representative for a lender (this is designed to avoid difficulties with any lenders who do not want to receive non-public price sensitive information as discussed at 0.191) provided they have signed an agreed form of confidentiality undertaking;

- to anyone to whom disclosure is required by law, regulation, or the rules of a relevant authority or stock exchange;
- to anyone who provides services to the lenders in connection with the administration of the loan (provided they have signed a confidentiality undertaking);
- to anyone to whom a lender has given security over this loan if that person has been advised that the information is confidential;
- as required in litigation or similar proceedings;
- to a rating agency; and
- to a numbering service provider[14] – of very limited information which is not (and which the borrower represents is not) price sensitive information.

11.033 *Comment* A lender's duties of confidentiality are expressed to expire 12 months after it has ceased to be a lender. Borrowers may want to consider whether 12 months is a sufficiently long period. They may also want to consider whether there should be overriding prohibitions on giving confidential information to certain categories of persons such as competitors.

11.034 *Comment* Sometimes borrowers ask to be kept informed of the people to whom confidential information has been passed, but in many cases this will be impractical for lenders.

11.035 Finally, it is worth noting that these confidentiality undertakings can be hard for the borrower to police. If confidential information is leaked, the borrower may not discover the fact; if it does it will be hard to identify the source of the leak; and it is hard to identify the loss caused by the leak.

CLAUSE 37: COUNTERPARTS

11.036 Clause 37 allows the agreement to be executed in counterparts. In this case, the Agent's lawyer will produce a **conformed copy** which indicates the signatories.

---

[14] Securities which are traded such as bonds and debt instruments, are given a Securities Identification Number, which is unique to that instrument, to allow them to be readily identified and traded efficiently. The agency responsible for issuing this number needs details of the security – hence the need to allow certain information to be provided for this purpose.

12 Governing Law and Enforcement

CLAUSE 38: GOVERNING LAW

Clause 38 provides that the Agreement will be governed by English[1] law. Choosing English or New York law for loan agreements makes syndication of very large loans easier than many other **governing laws** because the market customarily deals in agreements under English or New York law. Another factor is the predictability of these laws. They respect freedom of contract to a large extent and are reluctant to interfere in negotiated agreements, making for a fair degree of certainty in relation to the effect of the agreement. Nevertheless laws of many other countries are increasingly acceptable and, in recognition of this, the LMA has produced template documents for French, German and Spanish law transactions.

12.001

The ability of a party to choose the law which applies to a contract may be limited and this is an issue for due diligence. Many countries disallow a choice of law if it is made in order to avoid a mandatory provision of the law which would otherwise apply. Others require there to be some connection between the transaction and the law chosen.[2]

The LMA Term Loan also contains optional wording choosing English law to apply to non-contractual obligations (such as claims in negligence or other torts or delicts[3]) arising in relation to the agreement. This wording stems from Rome II[4] which allows parties who are pursuing a commercial activity to agree in advance on the law which will apply to non-contractual obligations. Where the loan is unsecured and the loan agreement is the only document governing the relationship, choosing English law for non-contractual obligations may be sensible so as to have all issues dealt with in a single forum. However where there are security documents which will be governed by different laws, choosing English law for non-contractual obligations arising out of those documents would probably be inappropriate since issues may arise in relation to the assets over which security is taken, which would be best dealt with under the law of the location of the asset.

12.002

---

[1] Incidentally there is no such thing as UK or British law. Technically it is the law of England and Wales.
[2] See discussions on Schedule 13 at 13.062.
[3] See A1.012.
[4] *Regulation 864/2007*).

CLAUSE 39: ENFORCEMENT
Clause 39.1 Jurisdiction

12.003 Clause 39 gives the English courts 'exclusive' jurisdiction (subject to the points discussed at 12.004) to deal with disputes relating to the Agreement. Lenders commonly require borrowers to submit to the jurisdiction of the courts of the country of the chosen governing law. Clearly it makes sense, if English law has been chosen as the governing law, to choose the English courts to settle disputes so that they will be applying a law they are familiar with. English and New York courts are also popular because of their expertise in dealing with this nature of transaction and because of the predictability of the results.

Note that it is usual to submit to the jurisdiction of courts rather than submitting disputes to arbitration because, for claims in debt (as opposed to claims in damages) courts are usually faster and cheaper than arbitration. See also Box 12.1.

Box 12.1

Would arbitration be better?

Arbitration is unusual for loan agreements. It may be considered in cases where the alternative is to use courts which are known to be slow, expensive, and/or unpredictable. It may also be considered if the due diligence unearths the fact that the country where the borrower's assets are located will not necessarily enforce a judgement given by the chosen court. In this event, it may be that an arbitration award would be more effective than a court judgement, at least in relation to an unsecured loan.[5] Whenever arbitration is considered as an alternative to the courts however, it will be necessary to consider whether it will be necessary to have recourse to the courts in any event in order to enforce any security. In many jurisdictions, security can only be enforced with the assistance of the courts and/or the assistance of the courts may be necessary to enable the lenders to give good title to the property which is the subject of the security.

One option which is increasingly popular is to include 'optional' arbitration provisions – that is, to submit to the jurisdiction of the courts but also to give the lenders the option of arbitration. This may be helpful if the borrower is expected to have some assets in countries which will enforce judgements of the chosen courts and some in countries which may not do so. Such clauses are permissible in England but may not be so in other countries.[6]

---

[5] This may be the case if the relevant country is party to international treaties as to reciprocal enforcement of arbitration awards (the 1958 United Nations Convention on the Recognition and Enforcement of Foreign Arbitral Awards – the 'New York Convention').

[6] In 2012 a Russian case Telefonnaya Kompaniya (RTK) v Sony Ericsson Mobile Communication Rus held that a clause submitting to arbitration but giving the lenders the sole right to litigate contravened the rights of equal access to courts.

The submission to the jurisdiction of the English courts is expressed (in clause 39.1(c)) to be for the benefit of the lenders. The intention behind this wording (and its effect under English law) is that the lenders should be entitled to take action in other countries, while the borrower should not. Lenders generally want the right to take action in other countries as well as the courts specified as they may find, in practice, that it is simpler to start proceedings directly in the country of the borrower or guarantor rather than obtaining an English judgement which they will then need to enforce locally. This is often referred to as a 'one way' jurisdiction clause.

12.004

However, if the lenders seek to take action in a country other than England, that country will apply its own law in interpreting the effect of clause 39.1(c) and in deciding whether to accept jurisdiction.

One way jurisdiction clauses came under scrutiny in 2012 and 2013, when a French case[7] found that they were invalid and that the effect was as though no jurisdiction had been agreed upon. The LMA issued a note in January 2013, with some alternative clauses for consideration. The alternatives suggested were:

12.005

- Simple exclusive jurisdiction of chosen court;
- One way jurisdiction with a fall back provision that if that was ineffective, the parties agree a simple exclusive jurisdiction; and
- A clause giving exclusive jurisdiction to the courts of more than one specified country.

Subsequently, the English court[8] held that as a matter of English law, one way jurisdiction clauses were effective. Nevertheless, until the matter is settled by the Court of Justice of the European Union, the prospect remains that courts in some EU countries may follow the French approach.

Which type of jurisdiction clause to use will therefore need consideration based on the location of the borrower and its assets. Provided that the borrower's assets are in (and are likely to remain in) countries which will enforce a judgement from the courts chosen to have jurisdiction then the lenders may be best served by using a simple exclusive jurisdiction clause (i.e. option 1 of the three LMA options). The principal advantage of this approach is certainty and reduced opportunities for the borrower to cause delay and expense by disputing the jurisdiction of the English courts.[9]

12.006

It should be noted that disputing the jurisdiction of the specified courts can be a litigation tactic for borrowers wishing to frustrate their lenders'

12.007

---

[7] The decision of the Cour de cassation in Mme X v Rothschild Civil Division 1, 26 September 2012, 11–26022.
[8] In Mauritius Commercial Bank Ltd v Hestia Holdings [2013] EWHC 1328 (Comm).
[9] Additionally the one-sided jurisdiction clause does permit lenders to take action against each other in any jurisdiction – in an increasingly litigious environment this is another factor in favour of a simple exclusive jurisdiction clause.

enforcement action. Pre-2015 this could be achieved by a so-called 'Italian Torpedo'. See Box 12.2. This will no longer be possible post-2015, where an exclusive jurisdiction clause has been agreed. However, if the lenders include a one-sided jurisdiction clause then, as a result of the French case referred to at 12.005, this will reopen the door to the borrowers to dispute the jurisdiction of the chosen courts. See Box 12.2.

> **Box 12.2**
>
> Italian torpedoes
>
> In an 'Italian torpedo' borrowers would start proceedings in one European country (even if that country clearly did not have jurisdiction) simply to delay the ability of lenders to take action in the jurisdiction which had been agreed on under the documents. This was possible because the Brussels I Regulation[10] said that if one European country was dealing with a dispute then no other European jurisdiction could hear it until the first had come to a decision even if it was clear that the court which was dealing with the dispute did not have jurisdiction. In some countries, the court decides on whether it has jurisdiction at the same time as it decides on the substance of the dispute. This could give the borrower ample ability to delay the start of substantive proceedings in the 'correct' court.
>
> This practice has now been addressed by changes in the regulation, which will become effective in 2015.[11] Article 31(2) of the recast regulation provides that where the parties have given exclusive jurisdiction to one EU court, that court may proceed to hear the case even if another EU court is dealing with the dispute. The question remains as to whether a one way jurisdiction clause amounts to an exclusive jurisdiction clause for this purpose.

Clause 39.2: Service of process

12.008   The lenders will require non-English borrowers irrevocably[12] to appoint someone in England to accept service of any proceedings on their behalf under clause 39.2. This will be a condition precedent to advance of the loan. This avoids the need to serve proceedings abroad, which can be a time-consuming process.

Some lenders do not like borrowers to appoint group members because of the risk of sale or dissolution, and prefer that the borrower use a third party which specializes in providing agents for service of proceedings as a commercial service. Using embassies or consulates is not a good idea as they are immune from legal proceedings.

---

[10] Council Regulation (EC) No 44/2001.
[11] Regulation 2015/2012/EU.
[12] Even though the clause states that the appointment is irrevocable, it is clear that (except in the special case of an appointment of an agent coupled with an interest) an agent's appointment nay be revoked by the principal.

13 Schedules

SCHEDULE 1: PARTIES

Schedule 1 specifies the parties. **13.001**

SCHEDULE 2: CONDITIONS PRECEDENT

Part I Conditions precedent to initial utilization

For the original borrowers, the conditions precedent set out in the LMA Term Loan consist of **13.002**

- corporate documents;
- legal opinions; and
- other.

Corporate documents

Conditions (a) and (b) require constitutional documents and board resolutions

It is normal to require copies of the constitutional documents and of board resolutions of the Obligors despite the provisions of section 40(1) Companies Act 2006,[1] as lenders do not want to be involved in unauthorized transactions. The resolutions will, of course, need to have been made in accordance with the company's constitution, including such matters as quorum, notice of meeting and declaration of directors' interests. **13.003**

Condition (c) requires specimen signatures of the people who are authorized to sign the documents. **13.004**

Condition (d) optionally requires a shareholders' resolution from the shareholders in the guarantors. This will be required if there are concerns as to breach of directors' duties; see Box A1.23 on page 344. Such a resolution will not assist if the company was insolvent at the time of, or as a result of, the guarantee (not **13.005**

---

[1] Which reads 'In favour of a person dealing with a company in good faith, the power of the board of directors to bind the company or to authorize others to do so shall be deemed to be free of any limitation under the company's constitution.'

13.006 least because the question of **transaction at an undervalue** will be relevant in those circumstances).

Condition (e) requires a certificate confirming that the borrowing will not exceed any applicable borrowing limits. This is because it is not unusual for the powers of the directors to authorize borrowings or guarantees to be limited by the company's constitution, sometimes with reference to matters which are not a matter of public record. This condition precedent addresses this issue.

Legal opinions

13.007 Condition 2 requires two legal opinions, both to be issued by the Agent's lawyers:

- An opinion in the country of incorporation of any Obligor – this opinion will cover capacity, tax, choice of law and enforceability of judgements and possibly enforceability; and
- An opinion in the country whose law was chosen to govern the agreement – this will cover enforceability.

Lenders will also need to consider asking for opinions in other jurisdictions – principally, in a secured transaction – in the location of the asset over which security is taken.

In some cases lenders should also consider taking advice in relation to insolvency and enforcement of judgements in any places where the Obligors have any significant presence if that is not the same as the place of incorporation. See further 13.037 onwards.

Other conditions precedent

13.008 The other conditions precedent required by the LMA Term Loan are

- an acceptance by the person appointed to accept service of legal proceedings in the English courts (see clause 39.2 at 12.008);
- delivery of the Original Financial Statements; and
- payment of fees and expenses.

In most cases additional conditions precedent will be required reflecting the credit decision, as discussed in the comments on clause 22 at 8.190.

Part II Conditions precedent to additional obligors

13.009 The key conditions precedent to future Obligors are

- the delivery of an accession letter;[2] and
- the corporate authorities, legal opinions,[3] financial statements, and process agent letter relating to the new Obligor.

---

[2] See Schedule 7 at 13.023.
[3] See comments on clause 25.2 at 9.060.

Conditions precedent in other commercial circumstances

Conditions precedent in asset finance

In an asset finance transaction, because some conditions, such as those relating to security over the asset being acquired, cannot be satisfied before the loan is advanced there will be two sets of conditions precedent –

- those which are to be satisfied on or before the time of the drawdown notice (as with a corporate transaction); and
- those (e.g. the mortgage) which are to be satisfied on drawdown.

13.010

The first set will generally include approval of insurances and delivery of a copy of the purchase contract in addition to the conditions precedent normally required for a corporate loan. For the sake of practicalities, the legal opinions will often be delayed and will form part of the second set of conditions (to enable the opinions to cover the mortgage issues). However, the lender's lawyer will usually agree the form of legal opinion with the relevant lawyers before the loan agreement is signed.

The additional conditions precedent applicable on drawdown will include

13.011

- experts' reports (e.g. environmental and/or safety issues and reports on the insurances);
- evidence of ownership and registration of the asset;
- delivery (and registration as needed) of the security documents;
- evidence of the state of repair of the asset; and
- evidence of all consents, etc. needed for operation of the asset.

The moneys will be advanced direct to the seller and/or the seller's mortgagee. The agreement should provide for the conditions precedent to be satisfied by a specific time of day on the drawdown date, to ensure that they are satisfied in sufficient time to enable the lenders to authorize payment. See also Box 13.1 on page 297.

13.012

Conditions precedent in project finance

In a project finance transaction there will be at least two different circumstances in which conditions precedent will be required: the first drawdown, and subsequent drawdowns. There may be an additional requirement for conditions precedent (e.g. to the release of certain guarantees or security which apply during the construction period only) to be satisfied once construction is complete and the project moves into the operational phase.

13.013

13.014
Conditions precedent to first drawing
These will include similar documents and facts to those required in a corporate transaction (corporate authorities, process agent's letter, legal opinions, specimen signatures plus a requirement that there is no Default and that Repeating Representations are true).

In addition there will be other conditions precedent, such as:

- All contracts necessary for the project (such as a construction agreement, offtake agreement, concession agreement, shareholders' agreement, and any supply contract) must have been signed and become effective.
- All financing documents (such as funding commitments from other lenders and shareholders, intercreditor arrangements and security sharing arrangements) must have become effective.
- All security must have been constituted and perfected.
- All necessary consents and licences must have been obtained.
- The insurance must be in place and have been approved by the lenders.
- Auditors must have been authorized to communicate directly with the lenders.
- The financial model (containing budgets and assumptions of income) must have been agreed.

13.015
Conditions precedent to subsequent drawings
These may include (as well as a requirement that there is no Default) such issues as

- confirmation of completion of a particular stage of construction of the project;
- updating of the assumptions in the financing plan and compliance with financial ratios (possibly more strict than those which justify acceleration);
- injection by other lenders and shareholders of a specified amount of funds; and
- evidence that the relevant funds are required for the project.

The funds will be paid to a Disbursement Account and only available for drawing from that account on production of invoices or other evidence of their utilization.

13.016
Conditions precedent to release of security on completion of construction
This will include confirmation from an expert that the project is in all respects ready for operation, and, in many cases, confirmation that it has been operating in accordance with the plans for a given period of time.

> **Box 13.1**
> In asset finance, given that some conditions precedent to drawdown (e.g. the mortgage) cannot be satisfied until after the moneys have been drawn, and the lenders will not want to advance until the conditions are satisfied, the parties will need to agree how this issue is to be resolved.
>   One solution is to use a 'payment letter'. The lender tables a letter irrevocably undertaking to pay the relevant amount, for value on that day to the seller's account. The seller will exchange the title document for this payment letter. Of course the lender will not proffer the payment letter for exchange until it is satisfied that:
>
> - all conditions precedent to the loan (other than the title document and the mortgage) are in order; and
> - the original title document and mortgage are acceptable (and, if applicable, are acceptable for registration in any relevant registry).
>
> This solution relies on the seller (and its banker) accepting the credit risk of the lending bank.

SCHEDULE 3: REQUESTS

Schedule 3   **13.017**
Schedule 3 sets out the form of various notices to be given by the borrower.

1 Part 1 – Utilization request

This specifies the date, currency, amount, and interest period for the drawing as well as the account to be credited. It also confirms the factual conditions precedent set out in clause 4.2 (no Default and all Repeating Representations are true). The main purpose of this is to ensure that the borrower considers these issues at the time of drawing so that it does not issue a drawdown request if these statements are untrue.   **13.018**

2 Part 2 – Selection notice

This selects the interest period for a loan (after its initial advance) and specifies any required change of currency. As with the utilization request, if there is to be a change of currency, the form requires the borrower to confirm the factual conditions precedent (no Default and Repeating Representations true). This is because a change of currency can result in the lender advancing additional funds to the borrower.[4]   **13.019**

---

[4] See clause 6 at 3.019 onwards.

SCHEDULE 4: MANDATORY COSTS FORMULA

13.020 Schedule 4 is for the insertion of a formula for the calculation of Mandatory Costs if these costs are to be charged in addition to LIBOR. Mandatory Costs are the costs to the lenders of contributing to the running costs of banking regulators to the extent that cost is attributable to the loan in question. Because the cost is different for different lenders (depending, among other things, on whether they are lending through a branch or a subsidiary) Agents found that the administrative expense involved in collecting and distributing the moneys was excessive. The LMA therefore withdrew the formula for calculating these costs in 2013, leaving it up to the lenders to decide whether to charge Mandatory Costs in addition to the Margin (and, if so, how to calculate them), or to include them in the Margin.

SCHEDULE 5: FORM OF TRANSFER CERTIFICATE

13.021 Schedule 5 sets out the form of transfer certificate.

This document is used to transfer interests in the loan to new lenders. It confirms

- relevant contact details;
- tax status for the purpose of withholding tax (if applicable);
- the limitation on the seller's responsibility to the purchaser in respect of the loan interest purchased; and
- details of the amount transferred and the effective date of the transfer.

It is signed by the seller, buyer and Agent and, under the LMA Term Loan, takes effect as a novation. There will be an additional document between the parties detailing issues such as apportionment of interest (if interest is not to be apportioned by the Agent under the optional Clause 24.9).

SCHEDULE 6: FORM OF ASSIGNMENT AGREEMENT

13.022 This sets out the form of document to be used if a new lender chooses to purchase a participation by assignment rather than by a transfer using the transfer certificate mechanism in Schedule 5.[5]

SCHEDULE 7: ACCESSION LETTER

13.023 Schedule 7 sets out the form to be signed to add a borrower or guarantor. The letter simply has the new party:

- agree to be bound by the agreement;
- confirm its country of incorporation; and
- provide contact details.

---

[5] See 9.001 onwards for a discussion of assignments and transfers.

There is an option to effect the document by a deed, which may be useful, for example, in the case of the addition of a guarantor, to avoid **consideration** issues.[6]

SCHEDULE 8: FORM OF RESIGNATION LETTER

Schedule 8 sets out the form to be signed by a borrower or guarantor which is ceasing to be an Obligor under the agreement. As well as requesting release from the agreement, the Obligor confirms that no Default exists.

13.024

SCHEDULE 9: FORM OF COMPLIANCE CERTIFICATE

Schedule 9 sets out the form of certificate to be signed to confirm compliance with specified undertakings in the agreement (such as the financial covenants in clause 21, and confirmation that no Default has occurred).

13.025

SCHEDULE 10: EXISTING SECURITY

Schedule 10 is to list existing security for the purpose of the negative pledge.

13.026

SCHEDULE 11: FORM OF CONFIDENTIALITY UNDERTAKING

Schedule 11 is the form of confidentiality undertaking required under the confidentiality clause, for example, if confidential information is to be given to proposed sub-participants.

13.027

The LMA form of this letter contains the undertaking to keep 'Confidential Information' confidential. These provisions largely mirror the terms of clause 36 of the Agreement, discussed at 11.031.

Additionally, in relation to information provided before the issuer of the undertaking decides whether or not to make the proposed investment in the loan, there is an undertaking

- only to use the Confidential Information for the purpose of deciding whether to invest or not; and
- to return the Confidential Information and destroy all records of it on request.

'Confidential Information' is information which is not publicly available and which the signatory of the letter did not already have. The 'Permitted Purpose' is the consideration of buying an interest in the loan.

13.028

For the letter to be enforceable there needs to be consideration for its issue. The consideration is usually the provision of the information. It is

---

[6] See A1.025 for an explanation of deeds and consideration.

important that the letter is signed before the information is delivered, both for practical reasons and because otherwise, the consideration would be past, and therefore ineffective. See A1.024.

SCHEDULE 12: TIMETABLES

13.029 Schedule 12 sets out timings for notifications for requests for different currencies and in different markets.

SCHEDULE 13: LEGAL OPINIONS

For the sake of convenience, the form of a legal opinion is discussed here as though it was attached to the LMA Term Loan as Schedule 13.

13.030 This commentary on legal opinions is not intended to be a comprehensive review of the subject,[7] but rather an overview of the process and of the expectations of the parties involved. In particular, suggestions as to qualifications which may be necessary for certain opinions, and issues which need to be considered before an opinion can be given, are intended as examples only.

SECTION 1   INTRODUCTION

Types of opinion

13.031 In financial transactions, legal opinions usually address some or all of the following:

- capacity and authority (the power of the company to enter into the transaction and the fact that it has been properly authorized). This opinion is sought in the jurisdiction of incorporation of the relevant borrower or guarantor;
- enforceability. This opinion is sought in the jurisdiction of the governing law of the documents (and sometimes, to a limited extent, in the jurisdiction of incorporation – see 13.052);
- tax consequences; and/or
- choice of law and enforceability of judgements. This opinion is sought in the jurisdiction of incorporation of the borrower.

Limits on scope of opinion

13.032 The legal opinion does not cover insolvency issues, questions of fact, or priority and enforcement of security.

---

[7] For which, see Michael Gruson, Stephan Hutter, and Michael Kutchera, *Legal Opinions in International Transactions*, 4th edn, 2003.

Insolvency issues

The types of insolvency law issues on which the lenders may need advice but which are not covered by the opinion include   13.033

- the circumstances in which a liquidator will be able to avoid certain aspects of the transaction;
- priority of the lenders' claims in an insolvency;
- the circumstances in which lenders may find that they have to agree to a rescheduling of their debt, or might find themselves unable to enforce any security, as a result of some compulsory rehabilitation of the company under insolvency procedures; or
- directors' duties in insolvency such as the point at which they must stop trading – these may have a significant impact on the ability to organize a rescheduling of the debt if difficulties arise.

These issues are not covered because they are too complex to be summarized usefully and they often involve a lot of discretion for the liquidator.

Factual issues

The opinion also does not usually cover issues of fact such as the location of a company's 'centre of main interests' (see 8.198) or whether performing obligations under the documents breaches any other contract signed by the borrower. The lawyer issuing the opinion is unlikely to have personal knowledge of such factual issues.   13.034

Often the legal conclusion (such as the conclusion that the documents are binding) depends on factual issues (such as the fact that certain specified persons attended the board meeting which approved the transaction). In this case the lawyer will state those factual assumptions which they have made in order to come to the legal conclusion stated in the opinion. This is the role of the 'assumptions' in the opinion discussed at 13.045. It may be sensible to request the borrower/ guarantor to give representations in the loan documents to the effect that those factual assumptions are correct.   13.035

Priority and enforcement of security

The opinion does not generally deal with issues such as   13.036

- priority of the security;
- how long enforcement might take;
- what it might cost;
- whether self help is available;
- the predictability of the courts;
- any restrictions which may be imposed on the sale of the asset concerned in the event of enforcement (e.g. restrictions on the identity of any

purchaser or any requirement for consent, such as an export licence, before such sale can proceed); or
- duties of the security holder such as duties to give the security provider an opportunity to pay before enforcing, duties to other mortgagees, or other duties such as interference with contracts.

Locations of opinions

13.037 In an international transaction, the laws of many countries may impact the legal effect of the transaction, as discussed in the analysis of the opinion which follows at 13.042 onwards. The usual practice is to require legal opinions only from the place of incorporation of the relevant borrowers/guarantors; the country of the law chosen to govern the agreement; and the location of any asset taken as security. Sometimes advice (which may or may not include a requirement for a legal opinion) is also sought in other jurisdictions (e.g. perhaps if a borrower has significant assets in a given location or the place where its centre of main interests may be – see 8.198).

Which lawyers?

13.038 A legal opinion is only an opinion. Its value depends on the expertise of the lawyer giving it. The choice of lawyer is of course very important. It is also important that the lawyer is adequately insured.

Advice from the borrower's in-house counsel is helpful in relation to factual issues which external lawyers would be unable to confirm (e.g. as to no breach of other contracts). However, generally, lenders will require an opinion of external lawyers, rather than in-house counsel.

Practice differs in different countries as to which lawyers should be asked to issue opinions. In the US, borrowers' external lawyers are asked to issue enforceability opinions to the lenders. In England, the normal practice is to require the enforceability opinion from the Agent's lawyer and not from the borrower's lawyer. Sometimes the borrower's lawyer may be asked for a capacity opinion, particularly if the lenders do not have lawyers in the borrower's place of incorporation. For more detail on precisely what an English lawyer will cover see the Guide issued by the City of London Law Society.[8] That guide also highlights the professional conduct and other issues which an English lawyer needs to consider before issuing an opinion in favour of a person who is not their client (referred to as a 'third party opinion').

---

[8] Practice of English lawyers in giving opinions on financial transactions is explained in some detail in 'A guide to the questions to be addressed when providing opinion letters on English law in financial transactions', issued by the City of London Law Society and available at www.citysolicitors.org.uk under the financial law committee section.

The lawyers' roles

The purpose of a legal opinion in a loan transaction is to ensure that the lenders are aware of the legal risks involved in that transaction and that those risks are kept to a minimum. It is the responsibility of the Agent's lawyer to arrange the issue of appropriate legal opinions. **13.039**

The legal opinion is not an insurance policy, but rather it is an expression of a professional opinion as at the date of the opinion. Ultimately, precisely what the opinion says is up to the issuer. There is no obligation on the lawyer to advise recipients if the law changes after the opinion is issued.

The Agent's lawyer's role is not simply to request the correspondent lawyers to issue an opinion, but also to try to ensure that those lawyers address the issues and advise of all potential problems. This can be a difficult task if the relevant country has laws which are completely different to those in the country of the Agent's lawyer. For example, the concept of overcollateralization[9] (relevant, e.g. under German law) is unknown to lawyers in many other countries. As a result, unless the coordinating lawyer happens to be aware of the overcollateralization concept, they are unlikely to ask for advice on that topic. **13.040**

To minimize the risk that the Agent's lawyers will only raise queries on legal issues with which they are already familiar under their own law, the usual opinion obtained in the context of a loan financing addresses very broad principles which should, together, cover all potential issues.[10] **13.041**

The risk remains that the coordinating lawyer and local lawyer may have different understandings of the meaning of the opinions requested (e.g. did they both appreciate that the opinion on power – referred to at 13.048 – required confirmation that the transaction was within the company's express power rather than a confirmation given in reliance on protections given by law?), or that the breadth of the opinions requested will result in the local lawyer failing to give specific advice.[11] If those involved in agreeing legal opinions are aware of these hazards, they are more easily avoided.

SECTION 2 FORM OF OPINION

The advice obtained will often be encapsulated in a legal opinion. The usual form of opinion is divided into **13.042**

- the introduction
- the assumptions

---

[9] The idea that security may be open to challenge if the value of the asset taken as security is substantially greater than the amount secured.

[10] These general principles are: due incorporation and continued existence, power, authority, due execution, no contravention of law or constitution, valid and enforceable obligations, effectiveness of security, no consents or filings needed, no unexpected tax consequences, choice of law and jurisdiction, and enforcement of judgements. Each of these topics is discussed in more detail at 13.043 onwards.

[11] See, for example, the comments at 13.055.

- the opinions
- the qualifications.

Introduction

13.043 The introduction sets out the lawyer's role in the transaction and specifies the documents reviewed.

> *We have acted as solicitors to the Agent in connection with a credit agreement dated [] (the Credit Agreement) made between [] (the 'Borrower'), the lenders party to the Credit Agreement and [] (the 'Agent'). Terms defined in the Credit Agreement have the same meaning in this letter.*
>
> *We have examined the following documents.* [This section will list the documents reviewed which will usually be the Credit Agreement itself plus the appropriate corporate authorities and any consents reviewed and searches of public records which have been conducted.]
>
> *and such other documents as we have deemed necessary as a basis for the opinions set out in this letter.*

13.044 This section may also identify who is entitled to rely on the opinion. In a syndicated loan, the opinion must be able to be relied on not only by the lawyer's client (that is the Agent), but also by all other syndicate members. It would be unusual for the opinion to allow reliance by any party which is not a direct lender at the stage of primary syndication.

Assumptions

> *We have made the following assumptions*

13.045 The assumptions will cover issues which are outside the opinion of the lawyers such as:

- that copies of documents supplied are complete and accurate;
- that signatures are genuine;
- that information provided by searches is up to date;
- that certain statements of corporate officers (e.g. as to the persons attending board meetings and the issue of notice of meeting and the like) are true.

The assumptions will also include relevant assumptions as to the effect of laws of other countries.

Opinions

The opinions give the legal confirmations required. The opinions themselves mirror, to a large extent, the representations in the loan agreement. Adjustments to one often need also to be made to the other. **13.046**

The legal opinions will cover some or all of the points discussed here, and those points will be addressed by the lawyer in the relevant jurisdiction, as identified by the conflict of law analysis conducted by the Agent's lawyer. For example, the due incorporation opinion may be required from a different lawyer than the lawyer who issues the opinion on the effectiveness of the security.

For each opinion discussed in the following paragraphs, it is discussed in relation to the principal jurisdiction(s) from which that opinion is usually required.

Due incorporation and continued existence

We are of the opinion that the Borrower is a limited liability company, duly incorporated and validly existing [in goodstanding] under [English] law. **13.047**

Giving this opinion involves not only ensuring that the company is indeed a limited liability company, but also ensuring that no resolution for winding up (or similar in the relevant jurisdiction) has been passed nor has an administrator or similar officer been appointed. This opinion will be required in the place of incorporation.[12] In countries such as the US, which have a concept of goodstanding (where, for example, failure to pay an annual registration tax may result in the company being struck off or its licence to conduct business removed) the opinion will include confirmation of goodstanding.

Power

The execution, delivery and performance by the Borrower of the Credit Agreement are within the Borrower's corporate powers. **13.048**

This opinion will be required in the place of incorporation.[13] Lenders want to be sure that the transaction is specifically within the company's power. They do not generally want to rely on protections (such as those in s40 (1) Companies Act 2006 in England) for those dealing with companies where there is a problem with the company's capacity (power) to enter into

---

[12] A company may also be the subject of an insolvency process (such as an English administration) in its place of business. For example, a company may be made the subject of a winding up procedure in the EC in the country where it has its 'centre of main interests', regardless of the place of incorporation of the company. Advice on insolvency may therefore sometimes also be sought in those places although this is unusual due to the difficulty in identifying the location of the centre of main interests – see Box 8.32 on page 216.

[13] In some cases the 'seat' of the company is the place which determines these issues.

particular transactions. Hence, this opinion requires the lawyer to confirm that the transaction is within the company's power.

Authority

13.049 *The execution, delivery and performance by the Borrower of the Credit Agreement have been duly authorized by all necessary corporate action (if any).*

This opinion will be sought in the place of incorporation.[14] The requirement is for the lawyer to confirm that the company has complied with whatever procedures (such as holding a board meeting and associated issues, e.g. notice of meeting, quorum, voting at the meeting, and disclosure of interests, and, if a power of attorney has been used, due authorization of issue of the power of attorney) as are necessary to authorize the signing of the agreement and that the directors are not exceeding their powers in authorizing the transaction. In some cases there may be internal, non-public limits on the directors' authority which do not affect third parties. Nevertheless, lenders will not wish to become involved in a transaction which was not properly authorized, so will usually require specific confirmation that the directors were authorized.[15]

Due execution

13.050 *The documents have been duly executed by the Borrower.*

This opinion will be required in the place of incorporation at the minimum and is often also required in the place of the law chosen to govern the agreement.[16] The opinion requires the lawyer to confirm that all necessary signatures were obtained, all necessary formalities observed (e.g. any requirement for witnesses or for initialling each page) and that those who signed the documents had authority to do so.

This opinion is a mix of fact and law and often involves considering legal issues in a number of places, including the place of execution as well as the place of incorporation (or seat) and the place of the law chosen.[17] Assumptions will therefore be needed in relation to the impact of those other laws and also as to relevant factual issues, such as that the person who signed the document is the person he claimed to be.[18]

---

[14] Also relevant may be the place of the seat.
[15] This opinion usually involves a mix of fact and law and the opining lawyer may have to rely on certificates from directors (such as a certificate confirming who attended at a board meeting or a certificate as to compliance with any non-public restrictions on the directors' authority) and include an assumption that those certificates are accurate.
[16] The law chosen to govern the agreement may impose requirements as to formalities, such as the English law requirement that a document which confers a power of attorney must be executed as a deed, with the formalities which that necessitates.
[17] See *Legal Opinions in International Transactions*, pp. 137, 221.
[18] The lenders may obtain comfort on this by requiring notarization of the documents.

No contravention of law or constitution

> *The execution, delivery and performance by the Borrower of the Credit Agreement do not contravene any provision of [the Borrower's constitutional documents] or any law rule or regulation applicable to the Borrower in [England].* **13.051**

This opinion is usually required in all places from which an opinion is sought. This opinion is required because some breaches of law may result in fines or other sanctions but not unenforceability of the documents. This opinion therefore supplements the enforceability opinion. It will be necessary for the lawyer giving this opinion to ascertain what regulatory authorities (e.g. authorities regulating the banking and insurance businesses, or the offering of investments, etc.) the borrower's business, and the transactions contemplated by the loan agreement are subject to.[19] Given that sanctions may be imposed in any country with which the loan, or the borrower, is connected, this opinion should be sought (but excluding the reference to constitutional documents, which will only be needed in the place of incorporation or seat), in all countries in which an opinion is sought.

Valid and enforceable obligations

> *The agreement constitutes the legal, valid, binding and enforceable obligations of the Borrower under [English] law.* **13.052**

This is the essence of the enforceability opinion. The opinion will usually be required in the place of the law chosen to govern the agreement and, in the unlikely event that it is different, the law of the country chosen to have jurisdiction. The lenders often also require confirmation from lawyers in the place of incorporation and/or business that the agreement will be enforceable against the borrower in those places.[20]

It is expected that the lawyer providing the opinion will consider all circumstances in which the agreement or any clause of the agreement may not be enforceable as expected. So if, for example, there is a risk of recharacterization[21] or there may be a problem enforcing the grossing-up clause, this should be stated (usually in the qualifications). **13.053**

---

[19] For example, might any aspect of the transaction, such as a swap, be regarded as insurance, or gambling, in the relevant jurisdiction, and therefore be subject to regulatory approval?

[20] This opinion from any place other than that of the law chosen to govern the agreement requires careful consideration of the conflict of law issues – see paragraphs 55–56 of the commentary on legal opinions at the City of London Law Society website quoted at 13.038. See also *Legal Opinions in International Transactions*, pp. 145–151, pp. 207–211 and pp. 222–228. It is also worth noting that the City of London Law Society publishes a precedent for an enforceability opinion from the place of incorporation in the context of transactions involving real estate in England – available from the precedent section of their website at www.citysolicitors.org.uk.

[21] See Appendix 2.

The opinion is only that the local court will give a remedy.[22] Further advice as to costs, procedures, priorities and the likely time involved in any enforcement may also be needed. These issues are normally addressed in advice but not included in the legal opinion itself.

13.054   A number of qualifications need to be made in relation to this opinion, for example,[23]

- the insolvency qualification;[24]
- the equitable principles qualification;[25]
- qualifications and/or assumptions as to all defences which may be available to the borrower, such as mistake, commercial benefit, financial assistance, duress, fraud, or lapse of time;
- assumptions as to corporate existence, capacity, authority, and due execution (unless these are governed by the law of the country from which the opinion is sought);
- qualifications in relation to any individual clause which may be unenforceable for any reason not already covered by the other qualifications. So, for example, an English opinion will probably include qualifications as to the enforceability of the default interest clause,[26] the severability clause,[27] any clauses requiring the borrower to pay the lenders' costs of enforcement,[28] any clause stating that certificates are conclusive,[29] and the effectiveness of exclusion clauses.[30]

Effectiveness of security[31]

13.055   *The security documents constitute legal, valid and enforceable security interests over the property expressed to be the subject of the security documents and constitute valid security for the Outstanding Indebtedness.*

---

[22] This is why an English lawyer would not state that the agreement 'is enforceable in accordance with its terms' because an English court will not necessarily actually require the borrower to do what they have promised, by ordering specific performance. The court may order specific performance, but that is at the discretion of the court. A simple statement that the agreement is 'enforceable' rather than 'enforceable in accordance with its terms' is generally accepted to mean that it is actionable in court.

[23] This is not a complete list. For example, some lawyers may wish to include a qualification that specific performance is not available, or assumptions as to acceptance of jurisdiction – see further *Legal Opinions in International Transactions*.

[24] See 13.066.

[25] See 13.067.

[26] Is it a penalty? See Treitel 13th edn, 20.130 onwards for a discussion on the law on penalties.

[27] For example, clause 33 of the LMA Term Loan – on the basis that such a clause may not affect the basis (outlined in Goldsoll v Goldman (1915) 1 Ch 292) on which a court will disregard (or 'sever') provisions of a contract.

[28] Since, in any legal proceedings, the court will make its own award on payment of costs.

[29] Such a clause will not necessarily make such certificates admissible in evidence.

[30] For example, liability for fraud cannot be excluded, and exclusion clauses will be read contra proferentem – see further Goode *Commercial Law*, p. 107 onwards.

[31] An opinion may be required as to the priority of the security as well as its effectiveness. Given the different regimes affecting priority of security, the formulation of the opinion and appropriate

This opinion will be sought in the place of the proper law[32] of the security (not necessarily the same as the law chosen to govern the loan agreement) from the lawyers responsible for drafting and if applicable, registering the security.

The ability to give this opinion will depend on many factors including: 13.056

- Whether it is possible under the proper law to create security over the assets in question (e.g. property which does not yet exist, intangible property, movable property, or property which has been mixed with, and cannot be separated from, other property such as oil in a pipeline).
- Whether it is possible under the proper law to create security for the type of liability in question (e.g. as security for a future debt, such as might be constituted if the loan is transferred by novation, or is repaid and redrawn, as in a revolving credit or a multicurrency loan, or for a debt which is uncertain or fluctuates in amount).
- Whether the security can be created in favour of that security holder (e.g. are there restrictions on the identity of the security holder or are there problems with a charge back?[33]).
- Whether the security over the asset in question has been correctly established in accordance with the requirements for creating security over that asset (e.g. are there notification requirements, registration requirements, or formal requirements, for example, as to delivery or as to the form in which such security must be created?) (see Box 13.2).

Box 13.2
Where the security needs to be registered, that will be referred to here. There may be a timing issue if the security is to be registered after the opinion is to be given. In that case the Agent will usually rely on the lawyer (acting for the Agent, not the borrower) who is responsible for the registration to confirm that that will be done and that lawyer will need to ensure they are in possession of everything which is necessary to ensure that the registration will be effected.

- Whether the security has been correctly constituted so as to create security for the debt in question (e.g. can the security be given to an Agent on behalf of the lenders or must it be given to the person to whom the debt is owed? If the secured debt is repaid and redrawn, as in a revolving credit or, often, a multicurrency agreement, or if it is novated, as in a loan trans-

---

assumptions will be made on a case-by-case basis.
[32] Other laws may be relevant depending on the type of asset over which security is being taken as discussed below.
[33] Creating security in favour of A over a debt owed by A.

ferred by novation, will the security be discharged by the intermediate repayment or by the novation?).
- Whether there are any restrictions on the enforceability of the security, such as overcollateralization issues.

13.057 The opining lawyer will need to include all the assumptions and qualifications which are necessary for the enforceability opinion as well as any other assumptions as necessary under the proper law, such as, in England, assumptions that the transactions do not involve unlawful financial assistance and that the lenders do not have notice of any facts which could taint the security (such as knowledge that it is created in breach of the provisions of a negative pledge).

As with the enforceability opinion, the opining lawyer is expected to state if any specific provision of the security documents may not be enforceable as stated.

13.058 Lenders need to be aware that

- the opinion is only that a remedy will be available in the country of the proper law of the security; for example, it does not address the issues referred to at 13.036;
- it gives no comfort as to enforceability of the security anywhere other than in the country of the proper law (e.g. with security over moveable property or over a **chose in action** which may need to be enforced in other jurisdictions); and
- the opinion is subject to the insolvency qualification; lenders and their coordinating lawyers need to consider the circumstances in which an insolvency of any person could have an impact. For example,
  - If the borrower becomes insolvent, in what circumstances might the security be set aside (e.g. transactions at an undervalue if the borrower is English)?
  - If security is taken over rights under a contract, will that security be recognized in an insolvency of the parties to the contract?

No consents or filings needed

13.059 *No authorization or approval (including exchange control approval) or other action by, and no notice to or filing with, any government, administrative authority or court is required for the due execution, delivery and performance by the Borrower of its obligations under the Credit Agreement except for [] [which has been effected].*

This opinion is usually required in all places from which an opinion is sought. This opinion is required because some absences of approval may result in fines or other sanctions but not unenforceability of the documents. This opinion therefore supplements the enforceability opinion. It will be necessary for the lawyer giving this opinion to determine whether any aspects of the transaction may require approvals or filings and also to ascertain what regulatory authorities the borrower's business is subject to that may result in a need for approvals. The lawyer will also be expected to consider the effect on any necessary consents etc. of any intermediate payment of the loan, as in a revolving credit or multicurrency loan, or any transfer of the loan by novation. Will the relevant consent apply to all future advances and all novated loans or will it fall away as a result of the intermediate payment or novation?

Given that sanctions may be imposed in any country with which the loan, or the borrower, is connected, this opinion is usually sought in all countries in which an opinion is sought. 13.060

No unexpected tax consequences

> *There is no tax imposed by [the Borrower's country] or any taxing authority thereof either (i) on or by virtue of the execution of the documents or (ii) on any payments to be made by the Borrower pursuant to the documents and neither the Agent nor any of the Lenders is or will be resident or subject to taxation in [the Borrower's country] by reason only of the execution, delivery performance or enforcement of the documents.* 13.061

There may be tax consequences (in addition to the normal corporation tax issues of the lender and the borrower) in the place of execution (e.g. stamp tax), any place from which payment is to be made (e.g. withholding tax), or from which payment *may* be made, for example, under a guarantee (e.g. deemed tax residence of lender), as well as in any other country with which the loan, or the borrower, is connected. This opinion is therefore usually required in all places from which an opinion is sought.

Choice of law and jurisdiction

> *The choice of [English] law to govern the documents and the submission to the jurisdiction of the [English] courts are valid under the law of [the country chosen to have jurisdiction] [the borrower's country].* 13.062

This opinion is usually sought in the place of the courts chosen to have jurisdiction (probably the same as the law chosen to govern the agreement) as well as in the country of incorporation. The lenders will wish to be satisfied that (all else being equal[34]) the country chosen to have jurisdiction will accept jurisdiction and will apply the chosen law.

The lenders may also want lawyers in the country of incorporation to confirm that the choice of law and jurisdiction is valid from their perspec-

---

[34] The opinion does not require confirmation that the courts will actually accept jurisdiction and apply the chosen law, since that depends on the facts at the time – for example, whether proceedings have started elsewhere. The opinion, instead, requires confirmation that the submission, and choice of law are 'valid'.

tive. For example, they want to be sure that there is no prohibition on citizens of that country submitting to the jurisdiction of other courts.

Enforcement of judgements

13.063 *Final and conclusive judgements issued by the courts of [England] are recognized and enforceable in [the borrower's country of incorporation/ business].*

This opinion is usually required in the place of incorporation.[35] This opinion will, of course, need to be qualified by whatever matters as are relevant to the enforceability in the relevant country of foreign judgements. For example, these might include qualifications that the original proceedings did not contravene natural justice and that enforcement will not contravene public policy.

Pari passu

13.064 *The obligations of the Borrower under the Credit Agreement rank at least pari passu with all other obligations of the Borrower which are not secured and which are not mandatorily preferred by law applying to companies generally.*

This opinion (if sought at all – see 13.033) will usually be sought in the place of incorporation and/or potential insolvency. The lawyer giving the opinion will need to consider whether there are, or may be, any obligations of the borrower which may be preferred over other obligations, or whether this particular debt may be subordinated to other debts, other than as a result of security, or as a result of law affecting companies generally. Examples are the subordination that affects loans to English borrowers[36] where the lenders' return varies with the profitability of the borrower,[37] and the priority that may be obtained in certain jurisdictions[38] by executing a loan agreement as an escrita publica.

Qualifications

13.065 Finally come the *qualifications*. These list the legal issues that may result in difficulties for the lenders. Given that the purpose of the opinion is to ensure the lenders are aware of the risks inherent in the transaction before they advance funds, it is important for lenders (with assistance from the co-coordinating lawyers) to ensure that they understand the implications of the qualifications for the transaction in hand.

---

[35] Other places which may be relevant include any place of business or location of the borrower's assets.
[36] And borrowers in other jurisdictions whose law is based on English law.
[37] See s3 Partnership Act 1890 discussed at 1.050.
[38] Whose law is based on Spanish law, for example, the Philippines.

Insolvency qualification

> *The enforceability of the rights and remedies provided for in the documents may be limited by insolvency, bankruptcy, reorganization, moratorium or other similar laws affecting generally the enforceability of creditors' rights from time to time in effect.*

13.066

This qualification is necessary in relation to the opinions as to enforceability and effectiveness of security discussed at 13.052 onwards. However, acceptance of the qualification without further investigation may result in the lenders failing to be made aware of issues which are important in the assessment of the transaction. It is therefore often necessary for the co-coordinating lawyer to investigate the details behind this opinion to determine how insolvency of an obligor might affect the lenders. In particular they will be concerned to investigate

- in what circumstances[39] might the lenders need court approval to enforce their rights against the borrower or the assets which are the subject of the security? and
- are any transactions vulnerable to be set aside if the company is insolvent or wound up?[40]

Equitable principles qualification

> *The enforceability of the rights and remedies provided for in the documents is subject to general principles of equity including application by a court of competent jurisdiction of principles of good faith, fair dealing, commercial reasonableness, materiality, unconscionability and conflict with public policy and other similar principles.*

13.067

This qualification is necessary in relation to the opinion as to enforceability discussed at 13.052 (see Box 13.3 on page 314).

13.068

Other qualifications

The opinion will then list the other qualifications necessary for the opinions, as discussed in relation to each opinion above, plus any other qualifications which the lawyer giving the opinion considers necessary.

13.069

The lenders and the co-coordinating lawyer need to examine each qualification (and assumption) and decide:

- if the risk it discloses is acceptable (e.g. in relation to the issue on the risk that default interest may be unenforceable as a penalty, are the lenders happy to proceed nevertheless);

---

[39] See 'Administration' in Appendix 2.
[40] For example, transactions at an undervalue or preferences under English law. Set off under some laws.

- if the risk is likely to be a real risk in the circumstances of the case (e.g. if the lawyer has included an assumption or qualification as to mistake, is there a possibility of mistake being an issue in this transaction); and
- if anything can be done to reduce the risk (e.g. if the opinion shows that judgements may not be enforced, would submission to arbitration be a better arrangement).

> **Box 13.3**
> Some countries have general principles requiring lenders to act reasonably in exercising their rights. This may (e.g.) prevent them from relying on an Event of Default if the event is minor in nature but the lenders' remedy (acceleration) is disastrous for the borrower. In England, outside of consumer areas, there is no general principle of fair dealing but there are a number of principles which apply in specific instances, such as estoppel, the contra proferentem rule, relief against forfeiture, restitution for unjust enrichment, the law on exclusion clauses, and equitable principles which apply to equitable remedies. There is also a rule of interpretation that the more unreasonable an item in an agreement seems to be, the more unlikely it is that that is the true intention of the parties.[41] Courts may also interfere with the exercise of discretions if they are exercised perversely or capriciously or in a manner which no reasonable person could have believed was reasonable[42] Because of these various principles and rules, this qualification is included in an English legal opinion.

---

[41] See Lancashire County Council v Municipal Mutual Insurance Limited (1997) QB 897.

[42] There is an implied term (known as the Socimer implied term) that discretions will not be exercised capriciously. See the note at 10.003. See for example Ludgate Insurance Co Ltd v Citibank (1998) Lloyds Rep 221, Abu Dhabi National Tanker Co v Product Star Shipping (No 2) (1993) 1 Lloyds Rep 397, and Concord Trust v The Law Debenture Corp plc (2005) 1 WLR 1591.

APPENDIX 1: Some English Law Concepts

This Appendix seeks to give those readers who do not have an English legal background a very basic road map to some of the areas of English law which are important for the purpose of international lending and which are not covered in other parts of this book. It is intended to be a brief introduction to the topics covered and where to look for further information on those subjects. It is not intended to be a comprehensive list of the relevant topics nor a comprehensive treatment of any of those subjects.

SECTION 1 SOME BASIC CONCEPTS

1 English law

English law is more strictly known as the law of England and Wales. England is part of the United Kingdom, which comprises three different legal jurisdictions.

Scotland has its own laws. Northern Ireland has similar but not the same law as England and Wales.

English law comprises statutes and common law[1] as well as European law.[2]

2 Sources of law[3]

Common versus civil law

To a certain extent, the distinction between common and **civil law** is historical (see Box A1.1 on page 316).

---

[1] See A1.002.
[2] By which we do not mean the laws of different countries within Europe, but rather the laws promulgated by European bodies such as the Council of the European Union or the European Parliament. Some types of European law are directly enforceable in English courts without a requirement for further steps to be taken by the national legislature to transpose this law into the English national law. Others must be transposed into the domestic law of England before they become effective in England.
[3] See Goode, *Commercial Law*, 4th edn, pp. 11–25.

> **Box A1.1**
> Civil law systems developed from Roman law, which was the earliest significant example of a legal system. It influenced most of the legal systems of the world. In the fifth century BC, the Twelve Tables of Rome were engraved on bronze tablets. They were largely a declaration of existing customs concerning such matters as property, payment of debts, and appropriate compensation or other remedies for damage to persons. These Tables and their Roman successors, including the Justinian Code, led to civil law codes that provide the main source of law in much of modern Europe, South America and elsewhere.
>
> The common law system of England developed in a different manner. Before the Norman Conquest (1066), England was a loose confederation of societies, the laws of which were largely tribal and local. The Anglo-Norman rulers created a system of centralized courts that operated under a single set of laws that superseded the rules laid down by earlier societies. This legal system, known as the common law of England, began with common customs, but over time it involved the courts in lawmaking that was responsive to changes in society.

A1.003 The most significant distinction between civil law systems and common law systems is that civil law systems are based on a codified set of rules, while common law systems develop through cases which come to court, and with decisions in those cases binding in (or creating 'precedents' for) future cases unless they can be distinguished from the earlier cases.[4] Judges in a common law system help to create the law.

To an increasing extent this distinction is becoming blurred as, in common law jurisdictions, the case law is supplemented by an ever-increasing volume of formal rules and regulations (statutes or legislation) created by modern governments. Similarly, in civil law countries, the subtleties of judicial interpretation and the weight of judicial precedents are recognized as involving the courts in significant aspects of lawmaking.

Case law versus statute

A1.004 Case law is another expression for common law – that is, the law which emerges from cases which come before the courts. Statute (or legislation) is the expression used for the formal rules and regulations issued by the government of the relevant jurisdiction.

Common law versus equity[5]

A1.005 The distinction here is based on the origin of the law (or the right or remedy) in question. Equity was the system of rules which were applied in one system of courts (the Courts of Chancery), while the common law was applied in other courts (Box A1.2 on page 317).

---

[4] That is, if a difference can be identified which justifies a different decision being reached.
[5] See Hanbury and Martin, *Modern Equity*, 19th edn, 2012, chapter 1.

> **Box A1.2**
> Until 1854 there were two sets of courts in England which gave two different types of remedy and recognized different rights and obligations. One court applied the common law and the other (the Chancery Court) applied 'equity'. The historical reason for this was that, before the establishment of the courts of equity in the fourteenth century, the remedies available in courts were limited to damages and delivery of property and there was no relief available for breach of faith. Claims for other relief were to the King, who delegated these issues to the Lord Chancellor who decided these issues in the Courts of Chancery. So the Courts of Chancery arose in order to mitigate the harshness of the common law courts. The Courts of Chancery applied 'equitable' principles and remedies.

Now all English courts apply all law, whether it derives from common law, equity or statute. However the concept of equity is still important, for example, because certain principles (some of which are discussed in the following paragraphs by way of example) apply to equitable remedies and equitable interests which do not apply in other circumstances.

A1.006

Equitable remedies which are available include (among an array of other equitable remedies):[6]

A1.007

- Specific performance (requiring a party to perform their obligations, as opposed to requiring them to pay damages instead). Specific performance will not be granted where damages is an adequate remedy (e.g. in the case of a breach of a contract for sale of generic goods) or for breach of a contract for personal services.
- Injunctions (usually requiring a party not to do something).
- Restitution (requiring a party to refund assets if he has been unjustly enriched at another's expense).

Equitable concepts developed by the courts include (again, by way of example, and among an array of other equitable concepts):

A1.008

- the distinction between legal and beneficial ownership,[7] giving rise to the development of trusts;[8] and
- mistake and misrepresentation.

Some equitable principles are that

A1.009

- Equity treats as done that which should have been done. So, for example, an agreement to create a mortgage of an asset will, subject to certain conditions, be given effect to in equity as if the mortgage has been

---

[6] See I.C.F. Spry, *Equitable Remedies*, 9th edn, 2013.
[7] See A1.019.
[8] See Appendix 2.

effected and so will create an immediate equitable interest[9] in the asset for the transferee.[10]
- Parties must come to equity with clean hands. So an equitable remedy will not be available to a party which has not acted in good faith.
- An equitable interest can be defeated by a bona fide purchaser for value without notice.[11]

3 Types of claims and rights

Action in rem versus action in personam[12]

A1.010 This is the distinction between the method of enforcement of a 'real' right (or right in property, otherwise known as a 'proprietary interest') and the method of enforcement of 'personal' rights (which is simply a right to sue a legal entity). 'Real' rights are rights in property, for example, ownership is a real right. Security is also a real right – someone with security has a right, in certain circumstances, to take the property over which he has security and use proceeds of that property to pay the secured debt. That is a right in property as opposed to the personal right to require the borrower to pay the debt.[13]

Chose in action

A1.011 This is the name given to an asset which is not a physical asset but which is simply a right which must be enforced by taking legal action. For example, money in a bank account is not a physical asset. It is a claim against the bank with whom the account is held. If the bank does not pay the moneys over on request, the only right which the person who deposited the money has is to take legal action against the bank. Hence the name chose (French for thing) 'in action', that is, enforceable only by taking legal action.[14]

Contract versus tort

A1.012 Contracts are agreements or promises which are enforced by the courts. Tort is the word given to the law relating to the circumstances in which a person will be liable for the consequences of their actions in circumstances where there is no contract. (It is similar to the continental concept of 'delict').

Damages for breach of contract are broadly based on the loss which arises as a result of the breaking of the arrangement, and so will generally cover lost profit.

---

[9] See A1.019.
[10] See Goode, *Commercial Law*, p. 668.
[11] See A1.022.
[12] See further, Goode, *Commercial Law*, p. 28.
[13] Or, more accurately, it is a right enforceable against all the world (a right in rem) as opposed to a right which is enforceable only against specific person(s) – (a right in personam).
[14] See further, Goode, *Commercial Law*, p. 32.

Tort is based on liability for the foreseeable consequences of your actions for others (e.g. negligence). Damages in tort are therefore based on the extent to which the harm caused by the tort was foreseeable.

Damages versus debt[15]

A claim for a debt is a claim to be paid a sum of money which is outstanding (e.g. the purchase price of goods delivered, or a claim under a guarantee). A claim in damages is a claim for monetary compensation for some action or inaction by another party, which has resulted in loss. So, for example, if one party does not perform its obligations under a contract, the other will have a claim in damages. See Box A1.3.

A1.013

> **Box A1.3**
> This distinction is particularly important in those structures (such as are common in structured, project and asset finance and also in secured corporate-based lending) where loans are made to a company, relying in part on the security of contracts (such as an offtake agreement in project finance, or a **residual value guarantee** in asset finance) which that company has with a third party. The lender is taking security over a particular payment, or series of payments, which will be used to service the debt in certain circumstances. In the event that there is a default by the third party under the contract, however, the claim on which the lender is relying is usually a claim for damages for breach of the contract.

The main disadvantages of a claim in damages, as opposed to a claim for a debt which is due, are

A1.014

- the claimant will have to prove that the loss he suffered was caused by the other's action or inaction;
- the amount which will be recovered will be calculated on the basis of the loss which would have been suffered had the claimant taken reasonable steps to mitigate its loss;[16] and
- the amount which will be recovered under a claim in damages is uncertain.[17]

A provision in a contract for payment of liquidated damages avoids these difficulties, although the issue may arise as to whether such a provision is a penalty.[18]

A1.015

---

[15] See Goode, *Commercial Law*, pp. 126 at para (v) onwards.

[16] Often (misleadingly) referred to as the 'duty to mitigate', as this is a rule of the measure of damages – there is no 'duty' involved.

[17] Of course, there is also the commercial disadvantage that, if the contract is onerous on the counterparty, they may seek to renegotiate for lower payments, and, in practice, acceptance of that lower rate may be better for the borrower than the alternative, of insisting on maintaining the original terms and, in the event that the counterparty is unable to pay, claiming in damages against the counterparty, potentially making it insolvent, and receiving only a small proportion of the damages awarded.

[18] See Appendix 2.

Joint versus several

A1.016 A joint obligation is one which a number of parties owe jointly, as in the situation where two parties borrow a sum of $10 million and undertake to repay it jointly. The lender must join both borrowers in any claim on the debt. The borrowers must, together, pay the full debt and if either one is unable to pay, the other is liable to pay the full amount.

A1.017 A **several obligation** is an independent obligation of one party which is not affected by the obligations of other parties. So if two parties each had a several liability to pay $10 million, the total due would be $20 million. Each debt is entirely independent of the other. The lender may pursue each party on its debt without involving the other party, and non-payment by one party of its debt does not give the lender a claim on the other party.

A1.018 A joint and several obligation is a combination of the above. So if two parties borrow $10 million and undertake, jointly and severally, to repay it, the lender may sue both parties together on their joint undertaking or it may sue either individual borrower on its several undertaking (which, under English law at least, is to repay the whole loan of $10 million).

Obligations of borrowers and guarantors are usually made joint and several so as to allow lenders the option of choosing which parties to pursue and not involving parties where there may be procedural or cross border difficulties or where it would be uneconomic to do so. Obligations of lenders are usually several since lenders are not prepared to take responsibility for the actions of other lenders.

Legal versus beneficial interest[19]

A1.019 The legal owner of an asset is the person who has title to it. The beneficial owner may be different – it is the person who is *entitled in fairness* to the benefit of having that asset. He is also described as having an 'equitable interest' in the asset (see Box A1.4).

Where legal ownership is with someone who is not also the beneficial owner, the legal owner holds as trustee[20] for the beneficial owner (or **beneficiary**). A trust may be created by a document, or it may arise simply as a result of the circumstances, as in the example referred to in the Box A1.4.

Box A1.4
For example, if two people (A and B) pay for something, but one only (A) gets title, that one may be both the legal and the beneficial owner if it is clear that the other (B) intended to make a gift. If B did not intend to make a gift, then A will be the legal owner and both A and B will be beneficial owners (those entitled to the benefits of ownership) with beneficial interests (also known as 'equitable interests') proportionate to their contribution to the price.

---

[19] See further Goode, *Commercial Law*, pp. 34–49.
[20] See A1.039.

Ownership versus possession[21]

Ownership involves having title. This gives the person having it the right to deal freely with the thing, for example, to sell it. A1.020

Possession is a much more limited concept. The person with possession may or may not have the consent of the owner. They do not have the right to dispose of the thing, and their continued right to possession depends on the terms agreed with the owner (e.g. a lease or licence) or on the law (e.g. a lien created by operation of law).

The difference can be illustrated by the situation in which a company sells its warehouse to a purchaser (the purchaser has ownership), and where it temporarily lets the warehouse to another company (the lessee has possession). A1.021

4   Miscellaneous legal concepts

Bona fide purchaser for value without notice

Otherwise sometimes called 'equity's darling', because an equitable interest can be defeated by such a purchaser (see Box A1.5). A1.022

> **Box A1.5**
> This concept is relevant where two entities have conflicting interests, for example where one party has security over an asset but another person has bought the asset without knowing of the security. The buyer will take free of the security if the security was an equitable interest only (such as a **charge**,[22] but not a legal mortgage) and the buyer is a **bona fide purchaser for value** without notice.

The expression means a party A1.023
- acting in good faith ('bona fide');
- which acquired a legal interest, either a security interest, such as a mortgage, or an ownership interest (a 'purchaser');
- which gave value for that interest ('for value'); and
- which had no notice of the prior equitable interest.[23]

Consideration[24]

Some benefit given in exchange for a promise (but see Box A1.6 on page 322 Gratuitous promises (e.g. gifts) may be enforceable if the agreement to make them is made by a **deed**.[25] Otherwise, English contract law requires A1.024

---

[21] See Goode, *Commercial Law*, pp. 34–49.
[22] See A1.045.
[23] See Richard Calnan, *Taking Security*, 3rd edn at 7,65 onwards.
[24] See Treitel, *The Law of Contract*, chapter 3.
[25] See A1.025.

some form of exchange, or benefit, or 'something of value in the eye of the law'[26] in order for a promise to be enforceable. There are numerous rules relating to consideration (such as the rule that past consideration is no consideration) that are outside the scope of this book.[27]

> **Box A1.6**
> One aspect of consideration which many non-English lawyers find strange is that the courts will not enquire into the value of the consideration, and that, for example, a contract under which a company disposes of an asset for a price which is only a very small percentage of the value of the asset, will nevertheless not be open to challenge on the basis of absence of consideration.
> Nevertheless, shareholders and creditors of companies which enter into uncommercial bargains are not without redress. In relation to shareholders, the directors have a duty to promote the success of the company – see Box A1.23 on page 344. Creditors are protected by the provisions relating to transactions at an undervalue – see A1.082.

Deed

A1.025 An agreement will only be enforced by a court if either

- there is consideration for it; or
- the agreement is executed as a deed.

So, executing a document as a deed will have the effect of making the agreement enforceable by a court even though there is no consideration for it, and the agreement is gratuitous (e.g. an agreement to give a gift).

A1.026 Originally deeds were formal documents which the person signing had to seal with their personal wax seal. This formality helped to ensure that those agreeing to make gifts were prompted to consider their action before proceeding. With the disappearance of personal wax seals (and their substitution by red stickers) much of the extra formality involved in executing a deed fell away. In 1989, legislation was introduced in England[28] which abolished the need for a seal at all[29] and stated that a document would be a deed if it made clear on its face that it was intended to be a deed;[30] and if it was executed as a deed (and, in relation to execution as a deed, set out

---

[26] Thomas v Thomas (1842) 2 QB 851 at p. 859.
[27] And for which see Treitel, *The Law of Contract*, chapter 3.
[28] s1(2) Law of Property (Miscellaneous Provisions) Act 1989.
[29] At least, in relation to execution of deeds by individuals and by companies incorporated under the Companies Acts.
[30] Of course, countries with laws based on those of England and Wales may still require deeds to be sealed and sealing is still required in England for bodies in relation to which the common law requirements have not been modified by statute.

requirements for witnessing without the need for sealing); and if it had been delivered.[31]

Deeds are required for certain types of transactions, such as powers of attorney.[32]

Exclusion clauses[33]

Exclusion clauses are included in a wide variety of transactions. This explanation focuses on exclusion clauses in the types of documents which are common in international finance – therefore, it does not look at exclusion clauses contained in transactions with consumers.

A1.027

An exclusion clause is a clause which seeks to reduce the circumstances in which one party will have liability to another, or to reduce the amount of that liability (see Box A1.7).

> **Box A1.7**
> Clauses will be subject to the same restrictions as exclusion clauses if they have the effect of restricting liability even if that is done indirectly (e.g. by an 'entire agreement' clause,[34] which seeks to exclude the possibility of reliance on representations made outside the written agreement) or only partially (e.g. by restricting the counterpart's remedies in respect of any breach – such as restrictions on rights of set off).[35]

Exclusion clauses may be challenged under the common law on a variety of grounds.[36] In particular, they are read contra proferentem.[37] They are also subject to a statutory test of reasonableness if they attempt to exclude liability for statutory misrepresentation[38] or negligence, or if they are included in a transaction which is conducted on one party's standard terms.[39] Exclusion clauses in standard form documents and any attempt to exclude liability for statutory **misrepresentation** or negligence will only be effective in circumstances where the court considers it reasonable for this to be effective on the facts in question (but see Box A1.8 on page 324).

A1.028

---

[31] See Treitel, *Law of Contract* at 3–172 for further discussion of the requirement for delivery.
[32] s1 Powers of Attorney Act 1971.
[33] See Goode, *Commercial Law*, p. 107.
[34] A clause which states that the written document constitutes the entire agreement between the parties – the intention of which is to prevent parties from asserting that representations made prior to the agreement being signed had any contractual force and therefore, indirectly, of limiting liability in relation to any such representations.
[35] See Elizabeth Macdonald, *Exemption Clauses and Unfair Terms*, 2nd edn, 2006, pp. 70–79.
[36] See Goode, *Commercial Law*, at p. 107 onwards.
[37] See Appendix 2.
[38] s3 Misrepresentation Act 1967.
[39] s2(2) Unfair Contract Terms Act 1977. The reasonableness test will also apply to clauses excluding liability for breach of contract (i.e. not only to clauses excluding liability for negligence) in certain cases involving consumers and standard form documents – s3 Unfair Contract Terms Act 1977.

> **Box A1.8**
> This reasonableness requirement is subject to a rather unusual qualification.[40] That is, in most cases,[41] the reasonableness test will only apply to exclusion clauses in contracts which are governed by English law and would have been governed by English law had there been no express choice of law. Many international loan agreements are only governed by English law by choice and therefore the exclusion clause will not be subject to the reasonableness test.[42]

Misrepresentation[43]

A1.029   There are numerous types of misrepresentation under English law, each of which has different consequences. This explanation relates only to liability for negligent misrepresentation, which is (hopefully) the most likely category in the context of international finance.

A1.030   Liability for negligent misrepresentation may arise either at common law[44] or under the Misrepresentation Act 1967 (statutory misrepresentation). In each case, liability arises if a person is induced to enter into a contract by a statement which was misleading. Broadly speaking liability will only arise if

- a person gives information negligently;
- the other person relied on it;
- the person giving the information entered into a contract with the other (in the case of establishing liability under the statute) or owed a duty of care to the other (in the case of establishing liability under the common law); and
- the other suffered loss as a result and that loss was foreseeable at the time the misrepresentation was made.

An exclusion clause in relation to liability for misrepresentation[45] will be effective only if the courts hold that it is fair and reasonable for it to be effective (which will depend, among other things, on how much opportunity there was for the recipient to verify the information).

Statements of opinions and forecasts are capable of being representations, particularly if those relying on the statements reasonably perceive that the person making the statement (e.g. an Arranger in an information

---

[40] Contained in s27 Unfair Contract Terms Act 1977.
[41] Excluding, that is, exclusion clauses relating to statutory misrepresentation and certain other issues such as personal injury which are not relevant for our purposes.
[42] Except to the extent it attempts to exclude liability for statutory misrepresentation.
[43] See Treitel, *The Law of Contract*, chapter 9.
[44] See Hedley Byrne & Co Ltd v Heller & B Partners Ltd (1964) AC 465.
[45] Including clauses which will have a similar effect, such as an 'entire agreement' clause – see Box A1.7 on page 323.

memorandum) is in a position, for example, because of its special expertise, such that its opinions carry weight.[46]

Under English law (apart from any specific legislation which may apply in particular circumstances, such as prospectus legislation) there is no duty to disclose information but information disclosed must not be misleading. There is a duty to disclose if subsequent facts make a statement untrue before it has been acted on.[47]

A1.031

Pari passu

Pari passu means having an equal level of priority. If two pari passu debts owed to A and B respectively are due on the same day and there are not enough funds to pay both – neither of them has priority over the other.[48]

A1.032

Debts are pari passu even if due on different dates. Therefore it is quite feasible for A to recover in full while B faces a shortfall simply because A's debt falls due first. Moreover, the general view is that voluntarily paying one debt while leaving another unpaid is perfectly permissible even for pari passu debts,[49] unless such payment constitutes a preference (see 'preferences' in Appendix 2).

Subordination[50]

Giving one debt a lower ranking in terms of its priority of payment than another debt. The expression encompasses a wide variety of arrangements.

A1.033

Subordinate security
This does not necessarily involve subordinated debt (see Box A1.9).

A1.034

> **Box A1.9**
> For example, assume Company A borrows $10 million from B and gives B a mortgage on land as security. It then borrows $10 million from C and gives a second (subordinate) mortgage to C. Assume A is wound up and the land sold at a price of $5 million. A has other assets worth $3 million and no other creditors. B will recover $5 million from the security. A's remaining assets ($3 million) will be shared pro rata between B and C, with B recovering $1 million and C recovering $2 million.[51]
>
> If the loan to C had been subordinate to B's loan (as well as the security being subordinate) then B would have recovered all of the surplus $3 million and C would have recovered nothing.

---

[46] See further Treitel, *The Law of Contract*, at 9-008.
[47] See further Treitel, *The Law of Contract*, at 9-132.
[48] See Appendix 2.
[49] See commentary on clause 19.12 of the LMA Term Loan at 8.052.
[50] See Philip Wood, *Project Finance, Subordinated Debt and State Loans*, 2nd edn, chapters 6–11.
[51] The assets of $3 million are shared in the ratio of the outstanding claims which, after B has taken the security, are $5 million to B and $10 million to C, which is 1:2.

Different levels of subordination of the debt

A1.035 The 'subordinate' debt may be subordinate

- as to principal only – that is, interest may be paid on the subordinated debt but not principal;
- as to both principal and interest – that is, no payments, whether of principal or interest, may be made on the subordinated debt;[52]
- in a winding up (or on the occurrence of some other condition such as an Event of Default) only – that is, unless the condition occurs, payments may be made on the subordinated debt; or
- at all times – that is, the prohibition on payments under the subordinated debt commences immediately.

Structural subordination

A1.036 It is not necessary to have a contractual subordination agreement in order for a debt to be subordinate. This can also be achieved through the corporate structure by lending to a shareholder without taking any rights against its subsidiary through which income is generated. By doing this, the lender is structurally subordinate to all creditors of the subsidiary, since it has no claim against the subsidiary and can only access the subsidiary's assets via any dividend which the subsidiary pays to its parent. That dividend can only be made after retention of sums to pay the subsidiary's creditors – (see Box A1.10).

> **Box A1.10**
> Assume a lender lends $10 million to a holding company (Company A), whose only assets are its shares in its subsidiary, Company B. The lender takes security, in the form of a mortgage on the shares in Company B. Company A has no business of its own, and is simply a holding company.
>
> Assume both Companies A and B become insolvent and are wound up at a time when Company B has assets worth $20 million and debts of $20 million. Company A's only debt is the loan.
>
> The assets of Company B will be used to pay its debts. There will be no surplus and the shares in Company B (and therefore the mortgage on those shares) will be worthless. The lender to Company A will therefore recover nothing as Company A has no assets. If, on the other hand, the lender had a guarantee from Company B, it would have been entitled to make a claim in the insolvency of Company B. Without such a claim, it is structurally subordinate to the creditors of Company B.

A1.037 For this reason, many lenders will normally only lend to operating companies and not their shareholders. Alternatively they will require guarantees

---

[52] This might be expected for a shareholder's loan, but not for a loan made by a commercial lender.

from the operating companies of loans to their shareholders (subject to any legal difficulties involved in giving upstream guarantees[53]) or will take assignments of intercompany loans made by the shareholder to its subsidiary.[54] This is also one reason why lenders may want to impose restrictions on borrowings by subsidiaries of their borrowers, as suggested as part of Moody's covenant matrix discussed at Box 8.22 on page 196.

Miscellaneous categories of subordination

There are miscellaneous other circumstances in which a loan may be subordinated to other debts including

A1.038

- Automatic subordination of shareholder loans in insolvency in Germany
- Equitable subordination in the US – which applies if a US court considers that a creditor has engaged in inequitable conduct to the detriment of other creditors in an insolvency; and
- Subordination resulting from the provisions of the Partnership Act in the UK or from the form of execution of the document in some other countries as discussed at 8.057.

Trustees versus agents

A trustee is the legal owner of property (the trust property) which it holds on behalf of others – who have beneficial ownership of that property as discussed at A1.019. The trust property, although belonging to the trustee, will not form part of its estate, so that in a liquidation of the trustee the trust property will not be available to the trustee's liquidator. Agency, on the other hand, also involves one person representing another, but, in the case of agency, the agent does not own property on behalf of another, they simply owe contractual duties to the persons they represent. Those persons have rights in personam, not the rights in rem which beneficiaries of a trust have.

A1.039

SECTION 2   SECURITY[55]

1   Introduction

Under English common law there are a number of ways to create security, each of which has a technical description (mortgage, charge, lien, **pledge**). These words are often not used in their technical sense. Moreover, statutes have added to the common law and created statutory mortgages and liens which have different characteristics to their common law equivalents. These

A1.040

---

[53] See A1.082.
[54] However, in some countries, for example Germany, shareholder loans are automatically subordinated to creditors so that an assignment of such a loan would not have the desired effect.
[55] See Ross Cranston, *Principles of Banking Law*, 2nd edn, 2012, chapter 15.

A1.041

factors make a focus on the common law meanings of the words used to describe different concepts of security of limited value. Nevertheless, we summarize those meanings in this section in the interests of clarity.

'*Security*' means a proprietary right (i.e. an interest in property) to secure a liability. In other words, security requires the secured party to have an ownership interest in an asset which it can use to secure a liability. See Box A1.11.

> **Box A1.11**
> Security is the right to take an asset and use its proceeds to pay the secured debt. It follows that when reviewing the security document there are two key clauses – the clause creating the security on the asset and the clause which identifies when and how the proceeds of the security will be applied to the debt.[56]
> A quick review of the clause which creates the security will establish
>
> - the identity of the asset on which the security is given,
> - the debt it secures, and
> - the identity of the holder of the security.
>
> The second key clause to review is the application of funds clause (sometimes referred to as a 'waterfall') which establishes what is to happen to the income and sale proceeds from the secured asset. It is particularly important in relation to the proceeds of the security prior to an Event of Default.

Guarantees do not fall within the definition of security given at A1.041 – they do not give an ownership interest.[57] Rights of set off also do not fall within the definition as they are procedural rights which do not amount to an ownership interest.

2 Types of security[58]

The types of security which can be created at common law[59] in England are:

Mortgages

A1.042

These[60] involve the borrower giving legal title (i.e. ownership) of the asset to the lender. The lender will own the asset subject to the borrower's '**equity of redemption**' – its right to redeem, or pay off, the debt and have title

---

[56] Of course there will also be undertakings relating to the secured asset as discussed at 8.238, as well as contractual powers in favour of the mortgagee supplementing the powers which they have as a matter of general law.

[57] They are referred to as personal security as opposed to real security.

[58] See Goode, *Commercial Law*, pp. 627–630.

[59] Excluding those which arise by operation of law, which are discussed at Goode, *Commercial Law*, pp. 660–664.

[60] Other than in relation to land, where the common law position has been supplemented by statute.

passed back to it. The most common example is a statutory assignment of a chose in action – see A1.053.

Pledges

These involve the borrower physically handing an asset (or something, such as a key or a document of title, which gives control of an asset) over to the lender (or other party), in order to persuade the lender to advance funds. Pledges can only be used with physical assets or documents of title representing assets, such as bearer shares or bills of lading.[61] The lender can retain the asset till the debt has been repaid or, in default of payment, the lender can sell the asset and apply the proceeds to the secured debt.

A1.043

Liens

A common law **lien**[62] is a right to retain goods to secure payment of a contract debt. As with a pledge, a lien involves one party having possession of an asset owned by another but, in the case of the lien, possession was given for some other contractual purpose and not for the purpose of raising funds. A common example in international finance is the repairer's lien – an item of machinery may be delivered to a third party for repair. The repairer can keep the equipment, and has a security interest in it, until he is paid for his services. The distinction between this and the pledge is the fact that, in the case of the lien, the security is not deliberately created for the purpose of raising money. Another difference is that the lien holder (unlike a pledgee), has no implied right of sale.

A1.044

Charges

Charges do not depend on title, or on possession. A charge gives its holder the right to take the charged asset in certain circumstances and apply its proceeds against the debt. A charge may be a **floating charge** or a **fixed charge**.

A1.045

Floating charge[63]

A floating charge is a security which gives the chargor the freedom to deal with the subject matter of the security until the charge '**crystallizes**'. A floating charge is generally expressed to crystallize on the occurrence of an Event of Default in accordance with the terms of the loan agreement (usually, whether or not the lender has delivered a notice accelerating the loan). The charge is usually (but not necessarily[64]) created over a category

A1.046

---

[61] Which can even be released to the borrower without discharging the security, by using the trust receipt device discussed at pp. 1122–1124 of Goode, *Commercial Law*.
[62] Note there are numerous other types of liens, such as maritime liens and statutory liens – see Richard Calnan, *Taking Security*, 3rd edn, chapter 10 (where common law liens are divided into legal and equitable liens).
[63] The expression 'floating charge' is a bit of a misnomer – 'floating security' would be a better name since the security interest in question does not need to be a charge, but could, for example, take the form of an assignment. Any security interest which gives the chargor the freedom to deal with the property may take effect as a floating charge.
[64] Re Cosslett (Contractors) Ltd (1998) Ch 495.

of assets (such as the chargor's stock in trade) and automatically catches new assets which the chargor acquires from time to time which fall within the relevant category.

The existence of this form of security allows a company to use, as security, those assets which the company buys and sells as part of its ordinary business. Without the concept of a floating charge this would not be possible because the security would need to be discharged to allow sale.

A1.047 However, a floating charge has three significant disadvantages over a fixed charge.

- First, if a company gets into financial difficulties it is quite likely to find itself unable to replenish stock. So, when a chargee enforces the security, there may be very few assets there.
- Second, unlike all other forms of security, the chargee cannot keep all proceeds of the security but must (except in some circumstances where the security constitutes 'financial collateral'[65]) use part of the proceeds to pay certain other creditors.[66]
- Third, it may lose priority to a subsequent holder of a fixed charge over the assets of the chargor (see Box A1.12).

For these reasons, a floating charge should only be used for assets in respect of which no other form of security is realistically available.

Box A1.12
A floating charge may lose priority to a later charge[67] because, by its nature, a floating charge does not prohibit dealings with the assets concerned, and so a subsequent fixed charge may be created and this charge will rank in priority to the previously created floating charge. The floating charge therefore usually includes a negative pledge. The registration of the floating charge with the Registrar of Companies will include a description of the charge as well as a copy of it, so that anyone searching the register will become aware of the existence of the negative pledge. The intention is to try to ensure that a subsequent fixed charge holder, who would probably be expected to inspect the register before taking a charge, knew of the existence of the negative pledge and that any charge taken by such a person would not have priority over the floating charge.[68]

---

[65] See Box A1.14 on page 335 and see also Richard Calnan, *Taking Security*, 3rd edn at 3.288 onwards.
[66] Under the Enterprise Act 2002 payments to tax authorities no longer have preferential status. However, under s252 of the Act a 'prescribed part' of a company's assets must be allocated to unsecured creditors, ahead of the holder of a floating charge. The amount of the prescribed part was fixed by SI 2003/2097 at 50% of the first £10,000 of a company's assets, plus 20% of any surplus over £10,000, up to a maximum of £600,000.
[67] Unless the floating charge has crystallized at the time the fixed charge is created and the fixed charge holder has actual or constructive notice of the crystallization.
[68] For more on this topic see Richard Calnan, *Taking Security*, 3rd edn at 7.286 onwards.

Difficulties often arise in determining whether a given security document creates a fixed or a floating charge. The answer depends on the degree of control which the giver of the security has to deal with the asset – can they dispose of it in the ordinary course of business? Care therefore needs to be taken to ensure that any exceptions to a no disposals clause do not have the effect of changing what was intended to be a fixed security into a floating one by allowing disposals of charged assets in the ordinary course of business.[69]

A1.048

There are particular problems when security is taken over the borrower's income, either by taking an assignment of a stream of payments under a particular contract or by taking security over all of a borrower's present and future book debts without being more specific as to the source of those debts. This issue was considered by the House of Lords in 2005,[70] and it was held that the determining factor in deciding whether a security interest was fixed or floating was the degree of control which the borrower retained over the assets which were the subject of the security. The case held that, in the context of security over debts, if the proceeds of the debts are required to be paid to a specified account, but the borrower is able to draw on that account in the ordinary way, the security over the debts is floating security. The case did not decide how much control the lender would need to have over the bank account in order to ensure that the security was fixed security.

A1.049

As a result there is uncertainty about the effect of those arrangements which are integral to, for example, project finance, where security is taken over specific income streams and use of the income is highly regulated but, nevertheless, the borrower, in normal circumstances, has access to the income for payment of operating expenses. Pending further cases being decided, it is unclear whether such security is fixed or floating security over the income stream although there is a body of opinion to the effect that the security is fixed.[71]

Fixed charge
A fixed charge (like a floating charge) is equitable. As such it may be defeated by a subsequent mortgage or by sale of the charged asset. This is because any equitable interest may be defeated by a bona fide purchaser for value without notice.[72] In practice, for many assets, this potential defect of a charge is not relevant since the existence of the charge is registered

A1.050

---

[69] See <u>Ashborder BV v Green Gas Power Ltd (2004) EWHC 1517</u>. See also commentary on clause 22.4(b) of the LMA Term Loan at 8.214.
[70] <u>National Westminster Bank Plc v Spectrum Plus Limited (2005) 3 W.L.R. 58</u>. In that case a borrower had given security over all its book debts, and agreed to pay those book debts to a specified bank account to which the borrower had free access. The court held that the security over the book debts was a floating charge.
[71] See Richard Calnan, *Taking Security*, 3rd edn at 4.120 onwards.
[72] See A1.022.

with the Companies Registry[73] and therefore subsequent purchasers and mortgagees will be put on notice of the existence of the charge when they search the register. If the subsequent purchaser or mortgagee did not search the register then they will be treated as having notice of the prior charge if they could reasonably be expected to have searched the register.[74] A charge may therefore be vulnerable if the assets over which the lender is taking security are assets of the type which purchasers may ordinarily be expected to buy without first doing a search of the Companies Registry (which would generally be the types of assets over which a floating charge would be taken).

Assignment[75]

A1.051 In addition, security may be created over rights (such as rights under contracts) by way of assignment or by way of a charge.[76]

A1.052 Assignment may be used either to sell a debt or to give security over it. The difference is that where the assignment is being given as security, the lender's interest in the debt will last only until the secured claim has been paid.

There are three main categories of assignment in England,[77] each of which may be used as a method of sale or as a method of creating security.

A statutory assignment under s136 Law of Property Act 1925

A1.053 This form of assignment must be of the whole debt; notice must be given to the debtor and it must be absolute (see Box A1.13).

> **Box A1.13**
> The expression 'absolute' is used to mean a complete transfer, in which the assignor does not retain any interest in the property assigned. It is commonly compared with an assignment by way of charge. Nevertheless, this is not to suggest that just because an assignment is being used as a method of security, the result is that that assignment cannot be absolute.[78]

---

[73] See A1.056.
[74] See Richard Calnan, *Taking Security*, 3rd edn at 7.293.
[75] See Goode *Legal Problems of Credit and Security*, 5th edn 3–13 to 3–21
[76] A chose in action, like any other asset, may have security created over it either by passing title to the asset (as in a mortgage) until the secured debt is repaid, or by agreeing (as in a charge), that the asset may be taken and its proceeds used to pay the secured debt if there is a default in payment. If the route of passing title is to be used, the chose in action will be transferred by assignment, since that is the only way to pass title to a chose in action. If assignment is not used, the security can be created by a charge, that is, an agreement which creates security but does not amount to a transfer of title.
[77] Ignoring assignments of proceeds of the debt and the different mechanisms by which equitable assignments can be created as discussed in Goode, *Legal Problems of Credit and Security*, 5th edn, 3–17 to 3–20.
[78] See Treitel, *The Law of Contract*, at 15-011 on absolute assignments.

This form of assignment results in the debtor having to make payment direct to the assignee. It has a minor procedural advantage over an equitable assignment of which notice has been given to the debtor (described at A1.054), in that, in order to take legal action against the debtor, the assignor does not need to be joined in the proceedings.

If any of the three requirements of a statutory assignment are missing then the assignment will still take effect in equity and its effect will depend on which of the three requirements are missing.

An equitable assignment with notice given to the debtor[79]
This form of assignment effectively[80] results in the debtor having to make payment direct to the assignee. It has a minor procedural disadvantage to a statutory assignment in that the assignor needs to be joined in to any proceedings against the debtor.

A1.054

An equitable assignment without notice given to the debtor
This form of assignment results in the debtor having to make payment to the assignor, which will then be obliged to account for the moneys to the assignee.

A1.055

There are three main disadvantages of this form of assignment –

- payment will be made to the assignor so that it will be necessary to make a claim against the assignor in order to be paid;
- priorities of competing assignments of the same debt depend on who gave notice to the debtor first.[81] Hence this assignment can be defeated by a subsequent assignment of the same debt which has been notified to the debtor;
- once notice is given the debtor cannot gain any new rights such as set off against the assignor. Not giving notice means that these types of rights may increase and so reduce the value of the assigned debt.

3 Registration requirements

There are two potential registration requirements for security created by companies[82] under English law. One is registration against the asset and the second is registration against the company which created the security.

A1.056

---

[79] In this case, the assignment will either be of a part of the debt or it will not be an absolute assignment.
[80] In fact if the assignor objected then the debtor would need to pay the money into court and not to the assignee but any such objection would normally be a breach of the terms of the assignment.
[81] The rule in <u>Dearle v Hall (1828) 3 Russ 1</u>.
[82] The <u>Bills of Sale Acts 1878 and 1882</u> impose registration requirements on security created by individuals. Security created by individuals is beyond the scope of this book. There are also registration requirements for limited partnerships which are substantially similar to the requirements for companies.

Registration against the asset

A1.057　In England there are asset registers for certain types of property including land, ships, aircraft and intellectual property. Security over any of these types of property needs to be registered in the asset register. Generally,[83] registration against the asset creates priority so that priority will be governed by the date of registration.

Registration against the company

A1.058　In addition to any applicable registration against the asset, most security created by an English company (except financial collateral, security created by physical possession such as pledges and liens and certain other limited exceptions such as security in favour of a central bank) must be registered on the company's public records at the Companies Registry. That is the case wherever the asset which is the subject of the security happens to be.

Failure to register against the company in accordance with these requirements within 21 days of creation of the security has the effect of making the security void against an English liquidator, but, outside liquidation, as long as all security is registered within the required 21 day period, this registration has no effect on priorities.

Overseas companies do not need to register security at the Companies Register but they need to keep a register, available for inspection, of any security they give over land, ships, aircraft or intellectual property, and of any floating charge which covers assets in England.[84]

4　What types of asset can security be created over?

A1.059　Under English law, security can be created over most types of assets. Some of these are discussed in the following paragraphs.

Future property

A1.060　This may be made the subject of floating security through a floating charge. It may also be made the subject of fixed security through an agreement now to create security when the property is owned. This is because of the equitable principle that 'equity treats as done that which ought to have been done'. So an agreement to create security is an effective (equitable) security.

Intangible assets

A1.061　Security can be created over intangible assets such as intellectual property by using an assignment as discussed at A1.051 onwards.

---

[83] Although there are special procedures for land.
[84] Overseas Companies *(Execution* of *Documents* and Registration of Charges*) (Amendments) Regulations 2011 (SI 2011/2194)*.

Shares or other investments

Security can be created over shares or other investments in a company. How this is achieved and what effect it has depends on whether the security has been 'delivered' to the security holder (how much control does he have?) such that the security constitutes a 'financial collateral arrangement' (see Box A1.14) and on the nature of the investment, including, in particular, whether the investments are traded on a public market, and on whether the investments are held directly or through an intermediary.[85]

A1.062

> **Box A1.14**
> If the security constitutes a 'financial collateral arrangement' it will be governed by the <u>Financial Collateral Arrangements (No 2) Regulations 2003</u>. In that event it will benefit from a number of simplifications to the general law, including abolition of the need to register the security, continued ability to enforce the security despite the appointment of an administrator, and, broadly speaking, if the security is a floating charge, abolition of the requirement to allocate a 'prescribed part' of the proceeds of realization of the security to other creditors. Additionally financial collateral can be enforced by simply 'appropriating' the security – that is, taking ownership. This method of enforcement is, under English law, unique to financial collateral arrangements although relief from forfeiture may still be available to the security provider – see <u>Cukurova Finance International Ltd v Alfa Telecom Turkey Ltd 2009 WL 908215.</u>

Moveable property

Security can be created over moveable property without the need for the lender to keep possession – this is achieved by way of creation of a fixed or floating charge over the property. But see Box A1.15 on page 336.

A1.063

An entire business

This is achieved by a document (known as a **debenture**, or, more accurately, a mortgage debenture[86]) which contains a combination of mortgages, charges (fixed and floating), and assignments over all items of the company's property.

A1.064

A bank account

Security can be created over a bank account held by the borrower with the lender. There are four possible routes for a lender to take an interest in a

A1.065

---
[85] See Lingard on *Bank Security Documents*, 5th edn, 2011, at 15.18–15.22.
[86] See 'debenture' in Appendix 2.

bank account.[87] In practice, security documents usually provide for all the options to be available, so as to give greatest flexibility to lenders at the time of enforcement. The lender may:

- rely on general rights of set off;
- extend rights of set off by contract (note this is only effective outside insolvency);
- use a netting or conditional payment route (see Box A1.16 on page 337) – note, this is particularly useful in countries which have limited rights of set off in insolvency;
- take a charge.[88]

Box A1.15

The main problem with security over moveable property is the question of recognition of the security if the property moves into a different jurisdiction.[89] Many jurisdictions have a conflict of law rule which recognizes interests in moveable property if those interests were validly created in accordance with the law of the jurisdiction where the property was at the time the interest was created. Other jurisdictions will not recognize interests in property if they cannot be 'translated' into an interest which is equivalent to some legal interest which could have been created under the local law. Even if the interest is recognized, it may be defeated for lack of registration.[90]

For certain major assets however, the issue of recognition (if not of registration) is addressed by international treaties[91] under which countries which are signatories to such conventions[92] agree to recognize 'foreign' security in those assets.

---

[87] See Richard Calnan, *Taking Security*, 3rd edn at 12.171 onwards.
[88] Rather than an assignment. Note Re Charge Card Services (1987) Ch 150 held that neither an assignment nor a charge over a bank account in favour of the bank which held the deposit could be effective. This was effectively overruled in relation to charges (but no mention was made of assignments) in Morris v Agrichemicals Ltd (1998) AC 214.
[89] See generally, Philip Wood, *Comparative Law of Security Interests and Title Finance*, 2nd edn at 39-030 onwards.
[90] For example, the Australian case of Luckins v Highway Motel (Caernarvon) Pty Ltd (1975) 133 CLR 164, discussed at 14-049 of Philip Wood's *Conflict of Law and International Finance* 2nd edn, where security over a bus failed for lack of registration in the jurisdiction where the bus was seized by creditors, although the security was recognized as valid security and would have been effective had it been registered.
[91] For example, Brussels Convention of 1926 relating to Maritime Liens and Mortgages, the Geneva Convention of 1948 on the International Recognition of Rights in Aircraft, and the Cape Town Convention on International Interests in Mobile Equipment 2001.
[92] It should not be assumed that these conventions are worldwide in their operation, or anything like it. For example, the 1926 Brussels Convention was acceded to by only 19 countries.

> **Box A1.16**
> In a conditional payment arrangement, the documents provide that the obligations of the bank to pay the borrower the amount in the bank account is conditional on the borrower repaying the secured loan. In a netting arrangement, the documents provide that the only liability of the parties is to pay a net figure calculated with reference to the value provided by each of them to the other from time to time.[93]

There are a number of detailed differences between the effects of these arrangements, with some of the most significant being as follows:

A1.066

- Security can be better than set off if the debt 'secured' is a contingent debt or is in a different currency than the bank account (each of which therefore requires valuation on an insolvency before a set off can be applied, and that valuation may not be accurate).
- Set off can be used without the consent of an administrator in the event of administration, while security cannot unless the security constitutes a 'financial collateral arrangement' as discussed at Box A1.14 on page 335.
- If any security on the bank account is construed as a floating charge (see A1.046) then unless the security constitutes a 'financial collateral arrangement' the lenders will retain less funds through a security interest than they would through set off.
- Under English law, use of set off is not open to challenge, for example, as a transaction at an undervalue, while security may be.

For these reasons security on a bank account in England will usually include all the arrangements described here so as to give the lenders the option of choosing which rights to pursue at the time of enforcement.

Comingled property

It is not however possible to give security over assets which have merged (or comingled) with assets belonging to a third party – such as gas in a pipeline. In this case the lender will need to take a pledge on a document of title or security over some other asset representing the merged property, such as the right to take delivery.

A1.067

5 What can the security secure?

Security can be given under English law for debts in any currency, for future loans,[94] for actual or contingent debts,[95] and without the need to specify a maximum secured amount.

A1.068

---

[93] See Richard Calnan, *Taking Security*, 3rd edn at 12.10 onwards.
[94] Such as the new loans which are made on rollover under a revolving credit facility, or under a multi-currency loan which operates by re-payment and re-drawing.
[95] Such as the contingent liability in respect of the exposure which would arise if a swap were to terminate early.

A1.069   A priority issue arises[96] if a lender has a security in an asset but another security interest is granted in the same asset to a different entity. The issue is that the first lender may find that even though their security purportedly secures future advances (e.g. as in an overdraft facility), nevertheless any advances made after the first lender becomes aware of the existence of the second security may rank behind the second security.[97] For this purpose, registration of a subsequent mortgage does not give notice.[98] In the case of land, there is protection for the first lender if he was obliged to make the further advances, although in practice, this will rarely be the case – see Box A1.17.

> **Box A1.17**
> Invariably, security documents include a prohibition on the granting of additional security on the asset. So, if the borrower creates second security on the asset that will be an Event of Default. That Event of Default will release the lender from its obligation to advance funds. Any further advances may therefore lose priority to the second security.

An example may help – see Box A1.18.

> **Box A1.18**
> For example, assume
>   A lends $10 million to B taking security over assets which secure the $10 million plus any future advances.
>   C then lends $5 million to B taking second security over the same assets.
>   A then lends a further $2 million to C.
>   If the advance of the additional $2 million was pursuant to an obligation binding on A then A's $2 million will have priority over C's $5 million.
>   If A was not obliged to lend the additional $2 million, A will have priority if he was unaware of C's advance at the time he lent the additional $2 million. Otherwise, the additional $2 million will rank behind C's debt.

A1.070   Lenders should not advance further moneys against the security if they are aware of the existence of second priority security (unless, of course, they are obliged to do so or there are inter-creditor agreements[99] documenting the position).

---

[96] The issue is referred to as 'tacking' of further advances' although, as Richard Calnan points out in *Taking Security*, this is misleading as it would actually be better described as 'restrictions on tacking further advances'
[97] See Richard Calnan, *Taking Security*, 3rd edn at 7.207 onwards.
[98] Law of Property Act 1925 s94 (2).
[99] See Appendix 2.

SECTION 3 GUARANTEES[100]
1 The nature of a guarantee

The expression 'guarantee' may be used to describe a variety of instruments including suretyship guarantees, bank guarantees, demand guarantees and performance bonds. Moreover the names given to different instruments are not particularly helpful, particularly because they may be used differently in different jurisdictions. The clearest example of this is the expression 'demand guarantee' as discussed at A1.075.   A1.071

This lack of clarity can easily lead parties to enter into documents which have quite a different effect from that which they intended, so it is important to focus on the various different characteristics of the different instruments rather than their names. The expression 'guarantee' when used here, is used to mean a suretyship guarantee. The following paragraphs highlight the key differences between the different instruments.

Guarantee versus indemnity

A suretyship guarantee is an agreement to be answerable for the debt of another if that other does not pay.   A1.072

An indemnity, on the other hand, is an agreement to make payment in certain circumstances (see Box A1.19).

> **Box A1.19**
> This can be illustrated by the difference between the following two situations
> - A buys goods from B and C states 'If A does not pay you, I will'. That is a guarantee.
> - A buys goods from B and C states 'I will make sure you are paid for those'. That is an indemnity.
>
> In the first case, C is only liable to pay if A does not. In the second case, C must pay whether or not A is liable to pay.

The indemnity is an independent debt; no underlying claim is necessary. In legal terms, it is a primary obligation, while a guarantee is a secondary obligation; it depends on the existence of an underlying debt.   A1.073

Primary versus secondary obligation

An indemnity is simply an example of a primary obligation. A primary obligation is any obligation which is not dependent on the existence of an underlying debt. Any undertaking to pay is usually a primary obligation (e.g. the undertaking to pay the price of goods ordered) (see Box A1.20 on page 340).   A1.074

---
[100] See Goode, *Commercial Law*, chapter 30.

> **Box A1.20**
> As discussed in the context of clause 18.1(b) at 7.002, English law guarantees commonly include indemnities as well as guarantees. Some English law guarantees do not do this but instead state that the guarantor guarantees 'as primary obligor.' This shorthand approach is not recommended as it may have a number of different interpretations.[101] The clearest solution is to insert a primary undertaking to pay the debt on its due date as well as a guarantee.

Indemnity versus demand guarantee[102]

A1.075 A **demand guarantee** (as opposed to a first demand guarantee discussed at A1.077) is not a suretyship guarantee. Instead it is an instrument under which the guarantor must pay, regardless of whether there is an underlying debt, and, if applicable, regardless of whether the underlying debt is legally due and unpaid. Payment must be made by the guarantor on demand by the beneficiary of the demand guarantee and without looking into the merits of the claim against the debtor. A demand guarantee is similar to, but not the same as, an indemnity. One key difference is that under an indemnity the beneficiary needs to show that they have suffered a loss but even that is unnecessary under a demand guarantee. See Box A1.21. They are usually issued by banks and may, for example, take the form of a standby letter of credit.

> **Box A1.21**
> It may help to illustrate the nature of a demand guarantee to look at the example of a performance bond, which is an example of a demand guarantee. This is an instrument issued by a bank which states that if the bank's customer does not perform the relevant obligations to which the performance bond relates, then the bank will pay a specified sum of money to the holder of the performance bond. The bank must pay whenever the holder of the bond states that the relevant circumstances have arisen to trigger a payment. There is no defence to payment except fraud. The amount due does not need to reflect any loss suffered by the holder of the bond.

A1.076 It is simply a question of construction as to whether any document takes effect as a suretyship guarantee (under which default must be demonstrated before demand may be made), a demand guarantee (under which there is no defence to payment except fraud and there is no need to prove a loss), or an indemnity (under which the amount of loss needs to be

---

[101] See Philip Wood, *International Loans, Bonds, Guarantees and Legal Opinions*, 2nd edn, 19-015. See also Heald v O'Connor (1971) 2 AER 1105, and General Produce Co v United Bank Ltd (1979) 2 Lloyds Reps 255.
[102] See Goode, *Commercial Law*, p. 1124 onwards, for further detail on demand guarantees.

established in order to make a claim). However it is often very unclear as to whether a document is intended to be a suretyship guarantee or a demand guarantee, and this has resulted in a number of cases on the issue.[103] Moreover, the simple fact that an English law guarantee is expressed to be payable 'on demand' does not make it into a 'demand guarantee', see Box A1.22.

> **Box A1.22**
> English law guarantees are expressed to be payable on demand so that the limitation period during which claim must be made only starts on the making of a demand. If these words were not there then the limitation period would start on the date of the borrower's default.

Courts will be reluctant to find that an instrument is a demand guarantee and, if that is the intention, the best way to achieve that is to incorporate the uniform rules for demand guarantees issued by the International Chamber of Commerce.[104]

Need to claim against borrower

A1.077 Another distinction which is sometimes made is as to whether the lender can claim under the guarantee without first having taken enforcement action against the borrower. Unfortunately, the expression 'first demand guarantee' is sometimes used to describe a guarantee under which a claim can be made on the guarantor without first enforcing rights against the borrower. Unsurprisingly this leads to confusion between this concept and 'demand guarantees' described at A1.075. Under English law, as soon as the debt is due from the borrower, it can be claimed under the guarantee without the need for the lender to take further action against the borrower. Of course, the full debt will only be due from the borrower once it has been accelerated, so in practice demand needs to be made on the borrower before it is made on the guarantor.

Continuing guarantees

A1.078 Just as loans may be revolving in nature, with the amount outstanding both decreasing and increasing in accordance with the borrower's needs,[105] so also guarantees may be continuing in nature and may secure, not simply a fixed loan, but instead a loan, such as a revolving credit, which may be

---

[103] See Vossloh v Alpha Trains [2010] EWHC 2443 (Ch). See also 'Guarantees and Performance Bonds – Problems of Drafting and Interpretation' *Butterworths Journal of International Banking and Financial Law*, November 2013.
[104] Meritz Fire & Marine v Jan de Nul [2011] 2 Lloyds Rep 379.
[105] As opposed to loans of a fixed sum, which, once advanced, must be repaid but are not available for re-drawing.

repaid and re-advanced from time to time. The guarantee relates to a fluctuating balance of the facility.

A1.079 A continuing guarantee may also be given on an 'all moneys' basis – to secure any money which is outstanding from the borrower when the guarantee is called on – whether under an agreement in place at the time the guarantee was entered into or under any subsequent arrangements. The guarantee relates to the amount outstanding when the demand is made under the guarantee. The question of what debts are covered by a guarantee is simply a question of interpretation of the wording of the guarantee.

Where the guarantee relates to advances which the lender is not committed to make at the time the guarantee is given (e.g. under an all moneys guarantee) the guarantor will be able to give notice terminating its liability in respect of advances not yet made at the time the notice of termination is given.[106]

Guarantee versus third party charge

A1.080 A guarantee is a right in personam.[107] A third party charge is a security interest (a right in rem) granted by a party which is not the borrower. The third party charge may be given as **security** for the third party's obligations under a guarantee or may be given directly for the borrower's obligations under the loan. Whichever route is chosen, the effect is that the third party is making its asset which is the subject of the charge available to meet the debts of the borrower. Since the third party is standing surety for the borrower to the extent of the value of the asset, it has the rights of a surety, and the various issues discussed in relation to guarantees (e.g. effect of discharge of security) apply equally to third party charges.

Guarantee versus letter of comfort

A1.081 A letter of comfort is sometimes intended to create a legally binding commitment which is something short of a guarantee. Alternatively, it may not be intended to create a legal commitment of any kind. Commonly a comfort letter will contain assurances as to the shareholder's policy towards supporting its subsidiaries. The precise effect of the document will of course depend on its wording. If, as is common, the shareholder does not intend to enter into any commitments as to the future then words of promise such as 'agree' and 'undertake' should be avoided. Similarly any statements as to policies should clarify that they are only statements of 'current' policies or 'current' intentions so that they cannot be construed as implied representations as to the future.

---

[106] See Goode, *Commercial Law*, p. 898.
[107] See A1.010.

If the intention is only to give a moral assurance then the document should clearly state that it is not intended to be legally binding. Simply calling it a letter of comfort does not result in it not being a legal commitment.[108]

2 Hazards with guarantees

Transactions at an undervalue[109]/commercial benefit

Under English law, guarantees may be vulnerable to be set aside as transactions at an undervalue[110] if

A1.082

- given at a time when the company was insolvent[111] or if it became insolvent as a result of the guarantee;
- the company subsequently goes into liquidation or administration under a process which commenced during the hardening period;[112] and
- the company cannot take advantage of the defence which is available. It is a defence if the guarantee was entered into in good faith and for the purpose of carrying on its business and there were reasonable grounds to believe it would benefit the company. In the case of a downstream guarantee[113] this benefit to the guarantor is often not hard to show – improving the financial position of a subsidiary generally improves the prospects of receiving dividends. In the case of an upstream or sister guarantee,[114] there may be more difficulty establishing this requirement.

In addition to the hazards of transactions at an undervalue, payment under a guarantee may be challenged on the basis of a breach of the directors' duties under s172 Companies Act 2006. That section states that directors must act in the way that he or she considers, in good faith, will be most likely to promote the success of the company (see Box A1.23 on page 344).

A1.083

---

[108] See Chemco Leasing SpA v Rediffusion plc (1987) 1 FTLR 201, and Kleinwort Benson Ltd v Malaysian Mining Corp (1989) 1 AER 785.
[109] s238 Insolvency Act 1986. See further, Goode, *Commercial Law*, pp. 916–917.
[110] A transaction under which a company gives substantially more than it receives. In a guarantee, an assurance is given and, in exchange the company receives the right to be indemnified by the original debtor if payment is made under the guarantee.
[111] That is, unable to pay its debts as they fall due or its liabilities exceed its assets, s123 Insolvency Act 1986. See also 8.253 onwards
[112] That is, the period during which the transaction is open to challenge. The longest hardening period under English law is two years.
[113] That is, a guarantee given by a parent for the benefit of a subsidiary.
[114] That is, a guarantee given by a subsidiary for the benefit of its parent or of a fellow subsidiary.

> **Box A1.23**
>
> The Companies Act duty was intended to be a codification and extension of existing common law rules and it expressly provides[115] that it is to be interpreted with regard to existing case law in relation to the equivalent common law provisions. The statutory duty to promote the success of the company is an extension of the pre-existing common law fiduciary duty of directors to act in the interests of the company. The principal case on the common law fiduciary duty is Rolled Steel Products (Holdings) Ltd v British Steel Corp and others (1986) Ch 246 where a guarantee was set aside due to a lack of corporate benefit to the company itself. The case held that where a third party knowingly (including someone with **constructive notice**) received a payment which was made in breach of that duty, it would be obliged to refund that payment to the company. Lenders taking guarantees therefore remain concerned to ensure that directors do not act in breach of their duty outlined in Rolled Steel and therefore to ensure that they (the lenders) do not have constructive knowledge of a misuse of the company's assets. In the case of a solvent company it is thought that this duty may be waived by all the shareholders.[116]

A1.084   Lenders will therefore be concerned to ensure that the guaranteeing company obtains a benefit from the guarantee, or alternatively, in the case of a guarantor which will be solvent after the giving of the guarantee, to ensure that shareholder approval of the guarantee is obtained (see comments on Schedule 2 at 13.005).

Subrogation/reimbursement

A1.085   A guarantor which pays another's debt is generally entitled to be reimbursed by the debtor. The scope of this right depends on whether the debtor requested the issue of the guarantee. If the guarantee is entered into voluntarily by the guarantor (e.g. in a risk sub-participation) the right of the guarantor to be reimbursed is more limited than it otherwise would be.[117]

Guarantees usually require guarantors to agree that any claim for reimbursement which they have will be subordinate to the guaranteed debt.[118]

A1.086   A party which pays under a guarantee is also entitled to take over (or be subrogated to) the creditor's rights against the debtor, including any security held by the creditor. This right of subrogation (unlike the right of reimbursement discussed at A1.085) appears to be available to a guarantor whether or not the borrower requested the issue of the guarantee.[119]

---

[115] At s170(4) Companies Act 2006.
[116] For more information on directors' fiduciary duties see Richard Calnan, *Taking Security*, 3rd edn at 5.32.
[117] See *The Modern Contract of Guarantee*, Dr John Phillips, 2nd English edn, 2010 at para 12.02.
[118] See comments on clause 18.7 at 7.014.
[119] For further detail on the guarantor's rights see Richard Calnan Taking Security 3rd edn at 11.146 onwards

Guarantees usually require guarantors to waive their right of subrogation until the lender is paid in full.[120]

Discharge by amendment and other defences

As discussed in relation to clause 18.4, care must be taken not to amend or waive the loan agreement or otherwise deal with it or any security for it, without obtaining the guarantor's confirmation that their guarantee will remain effective after the proposed action (or inaction) has been taken. See the discussion on clause 18.4 of the LMA Term Loan at 7.007.[121]

A1.087

---

[120] See comments on clause 18.7 at 7.014.
[121] See also Richard Calnan Taking Security 3rd edn at 11.88 for a discussion of the factors which can discharge the guarantee and how the lender can protect itself.

APPENDIX 2: Glossary of Terms Used in International Lending

This glossary is intended to assist practitioners by giving brief explanations of certain words commonly encountered in international finance. It includes technical legal and banking expressions as well as colloquial terms.

APPENDIX 2   GLOSSARY OF TERMS

Acceleration   The giving of notice to the borrower, following the occurrence of an Event of Default, requiring the loan to be repaid immediately.

Acceptance credit facility   A facility under which the 'borrower' may issue bills of exchange or letters of credit which require 'acceptance' (or agreement to pay the amount specified in the relevant instrument) by the 'lender.' Amounts which the 'lender' has paid under the instrument are treated as loans made to the 'borrower.'

Accrued interest   The interest which, on any given day, has been earned (but is not yet due and payable) on a loan, bond or similar instrument.

Acquisition finance   Finance provided for the purpose of funding a company acquisition.

Administration   An English legal expression describing the legal situation which results from the issue of an administration order under the Insolvency Act 1986 as amended. Such an order may be issued in relation to a company which is in financial difficulties and allows the reorganisation of the company's affairs or the realization of its assets for the benefit of creditors. While the order is in force, creditors cannot take action against the company, or enforce security against its assets, unless they obtain the consent of the court. Similar to 'Chapter 11' in the United States.

Administrator   The official who will take control of the business of a company while it is in administration.

Advance   A drawing of money under a loan facility.

Agent   In the context of a syndicated credit facility, the Agent is the party which administers the facility, acting as a channel between the borrower and the syndicate for the purpose of communications and payments.

In other contexts, an agent is anyone who represents another (his 'principal') in a negotiation or other transaction.

Agency fee An annual fee payable by the borrower to compensate the agent for the mechanical and operational work performed by it under the loan agreement.

Amend and extend An amendment to a syndicated facility agreement where certain of the existing lenders agree in advance to extend the maturity of some or all of their loans.

Amortization The repayment of debt in stages.

Annuity A basis for repaying a loan which results in the total amount paid by the borrower on each payment date being the same. In the early years, this amount will be made up largely of interest, while in the later years it will constitute mostly principal.

Arbitrage Profiting from the difference in prices between markets, for example, between Tokyo and London.

Arbitration A process for settling disputes without having recourse to courts of law. The dispute is decided either by a person appointed by the parties to the dispute or chosen by a third party they have nominated to make the appointment. See further Box 12.1 on page 290.

Arranger The lender which is originally mandated by the borrower to arrange a syndicated loan.

Asset Any thing which has value. It may be physical, such as a ship, intellectual, such as a patent, or otherwise intangible, such as a debt.

Asset backed securities Securities (such as those issued in a securitization) which are supported by assets such as credit card receivables (as opposed to normal debt securities issued by a company, which are often unsecured and pari passu with that company's general creditors).

Asset finance Finance which is provided for the purpose of funding the acquisition of a major asset.

Asset stripping Sale of assets for cash instead of keeping them to generate income.

Assignment A method of transfer of 'choses in action'. An English law assignment may be used in an outright transfer, such as a sale, (as to which see 9.010 onwards), or as a method of security, (as to which see A1.051 onwards). An English law assignment may only be used to transfer rights, not obligations. In the United States, the expression may also refer to a transfer (by assumption) of obligations.

Availability period The time during which a borrower may draw down advances under a loan.

Backstop facility   A facility to be used in the event of a problem with alternative financing arrangements.

Back to back transactions   A colloquial expression for two linked transactions on identical (or practically identical) terms – for example, a loan from X to Y and a corresponding loan from Y to Z.

Balance sheet lending   Lending on the strength of the borrower's balance sheet (as opposed to lending on the value of a particular asset or income stream).

Balloon repayment   A final repayment of principal on a loan transaction which is substantially larger than earlier repayment instalments.

Bankruptcy   The situation which arises if a person has been declared by a court not to be able to pay his debts and whose affairs have been put into the hands of a receiver. In England, this term is applied only to persons. Companies go into liquidation as opposed to bankruptcy.

Base rate   A fluctuating interest rate, peculiar to individual banks and used by them as a reference point for lending rates when lending on an inclusive (as opposed to a 'cost plus') basis. See 0.084.

Basel I   Framework agreed in 1988 by the Basel Committee on Banking Supervision relating to supervisory regulations governing the capital adequacy of international banks.

Basel II   The agreement updating the capital adequacy requirements which were originally set down in 1988. See 6.037.

Basel III   The various documents issued by the Basel Committee on Banking Supervision following the 2007–2008 financial crisis and which, in the EU, was implemented via the 4th Capital Requirements Directive (commonly referred to as 'CRD IV') in 2013. See 6.038.

Basis point   1/100 of one per cent (0.01%). It is the unit of measurement used to describe fees or spreads in most loan transactions.

BBA   British Bankers Association

Bells and whistles   Unusual features of a transaction.

Beneficiary   Any person for whose benefit assets are held in trust. See A1.019.

Bible   Complete set of copy or conformed copy documents relating to a particular transaction.

Bid bond   A bond provided by a bank which is payable if a bidder, on winning the bid, does not enter into a binding contract in accordance with the bid.

Bilateral facility   A loan facility between one lender and one borrower.

Bill of exchange   A form of short-term promise to pay, widely used to finance trade and provide credit. It is an instruction by the drawer to the person accepting the bill of exchange to make a payment to a third party. It differs from a promissory note in that a promissory note is a promise by one party to make a payment. It differs from a letter of credit in that a letter of credit is payable only against presentation of documents (and is usually issued by a bank at the request of a customer).

Bona fide   A Latin expression meaning in good faith.

Bona fide purchaser for value   An English legal expression meaning a person who, acting in good faith and acquiring, for a price, a legal interest in property, may defeat an equitable interest in the same property.[1]

Bond   In the context of capital markets, means a medium- to long-term promise to pay a certain amount at a certain date in the future, traded in the capital markets. It may or may not be interest-bearing, (if it is, it is referred to as having a 'coupon').

In other contexts (as in bid bond or performance bond) some form of assurance given (in the form of a promise to pay a fixed sum in certain circumstances) that a person will perform as promised.

Book debts   The items in a company's balance sheet which represent amounts owing to the company.

Book runner   The bank(s) appointed to run the books during the primary syndication of the loan. Responsible for issuing invitations, passing information to interested banks and informing both the borrower and the management group of underwriters of daily progress.

Book value   The value of a company's assets as shown in its balance sheet. It differs from the actual value because it simply shows the price paid less 'depreciation' which is a notional annual loss of value of an asset, based on its estimated valuable life.

Bridge financing   Interim financing used as a short-term stop gap until the intended long-term financing facility is available.

Broken funding costs   The cost to a lender of breaking its underlying funding if the lender is paid earlier than agreed.[2]

Bullet repayment   Repayment of a debt obligation in a single instalment at the date of maturity of the debt (i.e. with no amortization).

Business day   A day on which banks are open for business in the relevant country.

Call option   An agreement which gives the recipient the right, but not the obligation, to require the donor to transfer a specified asset to the recipient, normally at a specified price, on a specified date (or within a range of dates). The recipient of this right can be expected to exercise it if the value of the asset, on the date on which the option may be exercised, is higher than the

---

[1] See A1.022.
[2] See commentary on 'Break Costs' at 1.009.

price at which the option can be exercised. It therefore gives the recipient an option to participate in any increase in price of the relevant asset.

Cap A limit or ceiling, for example, setting the maximum interest rate on a loan.

Capital markets The markets for sale and purchase of tradeable financial instruments such as bonds and commercial paper.

Capitalized interest Interest which has accrued but which has been added to the principal amount of the loan and is itself bearing interest. Often interest is capitalized during the construction phase of a project finance transaction before there is any income to fund it.

Certain funds An English expression meaning funds with minimal conditions precedent to availability as necessary for meeting the requirements of the Takeover Code for financing the acquisition of a UK quoted company.

Chapter 11 US rules allowing a company a period of protection from its creditors while it seeks to reorganize its affairs and avoid winding up. Similar to English 'administration'.

Charge An English legal expression meaning a security interest under which the chargee does not get either title or possession but simply the right, in a default, to take the asset and apply its proceeds against the secured debt. See A1.045.

Chinese wall An artificial barrier restricting communication between different areas within an organization, allowing them to act for parties who may have conflicting interests. The concept originated in securities houses. It is also commonly used within large firms of solicitors and accountants.

CHIPS A clearing system used in the United States for settlement of large value payments.[3]

Chose in action An English legal expression meaning rights (such as rights under contracts) which can only be enforced by taking legal action.[4]

Civil law Codified systems of law which have developed from Roman law – see A1.002.

Clawback clause A clause enabling one party to retrieve money already paid out. An example is the clause (Clause 29.4 of the LMA Term Loan) found in syndicated loan agreements enabling an agent to recover money already paid out by it to a party, wrongly believing that the agent had received the corresponding payment from another party. This allows an agent to distribute money (e.g. a repayment instalment) to the bank syndicate without confirming receipt of the payment from the borrower, knowing if it does not receive the monies from the borrower it may 'clawback' the monies

---

[3] See Ross Cranston, *Principles of Banking Law*, 2nd edn, p. 279.
[4] See Martin Hughes, *Selected Legal Issues for Finance Lawyers*, at pp. 70–71.

paid out to the syndicate. Another example is clause 13.4 of the LMA Term Loan, relating to withholding tax and allowing the borrower to 'clawback' some of the moneys paid under the grossing-up clause (clause 13.2(c) of the LMA Term Loan) in the event that the relevant lender receives a tax credit which it attributes to those payments by the borrower.

Clean down period A requirement sometimes included in a revolving credit facility requiring the facility not to be used for a specified period in each year so as to demonstrate that it is not being used as part of the borrower's permanent capital. See 8.011.

Clean up period used in leveraged finance – this is a period after the acquisition of the Target company during which some of the provisions of the loan agreement are relaxed to give the borrower an opportunity to make the necessary arrangements to ensure compliance.

Clear market clause Clause in a term sheet by which a borrower undertakes, while its loan is being syndicated, not to put other offerings on sale which could compete with the syndication.

Club A small group of banks which finance a loan without the need for a full syndication process.

Co-financing A financing where a number of different lenders or syndicates are involved, each providing a different facility to the borrower, under a different facility agreement, often with common undertakings and events of default as set out in a 'Common Terms Agreement'. Generally, the lenders will share any security in accordance with pre-agreed rules which are not simply based on one lender being senior in all circumstances to another. Distinct from a syndicated loan in that there are different facilities, to be used for different purposes, and with different pricing.

Collar A combination of a cap and a floor limiting movement (e.g. of interest rates) to stay within a defined range.

Collateral Assets used to secure a loan or other financing transaction.

Collateralized debt obligation (or 'CDO') A bond or other tradeable financial instrument issued by an SPV which is secured by a portfolio of debts purchased by that SPV. A CDO is a type of securitization.

Collateralized loan obligation A CDO where the debt obligations are loans.

Comfort letter a letter of support which is intended to give rise to a moral rather than a legal commitment, or, if intended to give rise to a legal commitment, to stop short of a guarantee – see A1.081.

Commercial paper Short-term promise to pay a specified amount at a future date, traded in the capital markets.

Commitment The specified amount of money agreed to be lent by a lender in a committed facility.

Commitment fee An annual percentage fee payable to a bank on the undrawn portion of its commitment under a committed facility. The commitment fee is usually paid periodically in arrears.

Committed facility A facility which the lenders are committed to make (or keep) available, subject only to the satisfaction of conditions precedent and non-occurrence of an Event of Default.

Common law Law as laid down by decisions of courts, rather than by statute. See A1.002.

Compound interest Interest charged on interest.

Conditions A word with many meanings. It may refer to
- the provisions of an agreement generally;
- things which need to be done in order for particular parts of an agreement to become, or to remain, operative (as in 'conditions precedent' or 'conditions subsequent'); or
- those provisions of an agreement which are sufficiently important to warrant the termination of the agreement if there is a breach of the provision (as opposed to a warranty, breach of which gives rise only to damages).

Conformed copy A copy of a final executed document in which all signatures and any other handwritten words (e.g. dates or alterations) are printed in typed form. Conformed copies are often used to make up the transaction bible.

Consideration An English law expression meaning some benefit given in exchange for a promise in order for the promise to be legally enforceable.[5]

Constructive notice In many situations English law provides that a party's rights depend on whether or not it had notice of certain facts. In order to prevent parties from deciding not to enquire about things they might rather not know about, English law includes a concept of 'constructive notice'. Precisely what constitutes constructive notice in any given situation will depend on the facts of the case, but the concept is that a party will be treated as having notice (and will have constructive notice) if that party would have had notice if it had acted in a manner which the court decides that it should have acted, bearing in mind all the circumstances of the case.

Contingent debt A debt which may or may not mature. The obligation to pay it is dependent on the occurrence of some intervening event. An example is a guarantee, payment under which will only become due if the borrower defaults.

Contingent liability A liability which is dependent on the occurrence of an uncertain event (such as the liability under a guarantee).

---

[5] See A1.024.

Contra proferentem   A rule of interpretation. The rule states that, where there is ambiguity in the wording of any provision of a contract, that provision is to be read against the party at whose instigation it was included in the contract and who is now seeking the benefit of the relevant provision.

Counterparty   The other party to a contract.

Coupon   The interest which is paid on a bond.

Covenant   A promise to do or not do specified acts. Same meaning as 'undertaking'.

Covenant lite   Loans that have bond-like financial incurrence covenants rather than traditional maintenance covenants – see 8.073.

CRD IV   EU Capital Requirements Directive implementing Basel III in the EU.

Credit Default Swap (or 'CDS')   A financial instrument whereby, for valuable consideration, one party transfers credit risk to another party. Many CDSs have a pool of 'reference obligations' (i.e. the debts whose risk is transferred), which is often not static but may be changed over time. A CDS is a type of credit derivative.

Credit derivative   A derivative relating to a particular credit risk, such as a credit linked note, total return swap, or credit default swap. See 9.020.

Credit enhancement   A guarantee or other form of support which will enable the rating of a particular issue of securities to be improved.

Cross default   An event of default in a loan to a borrower which is triggered by a default in the payment, or the potential acceleration of repayment, of other indebtedness of the same borrower.

Cross security   Security given for one loan also being given as security for another loan and vice versa.

Crystallization   The termination of the freedom which a chargor has, under a floating charge, to deal with the assets which are the subject of the charge. See A1.046.

Current asset   Any asset which is not intended to be retained in a company and which is available to be turned into cash within one year.

Current liability   A liability of a company which falls due within one year.

Debenture   This can be a document, such as a bond or promissory note, which evidences a debt. Often these securities are freely transferable and listed. They may be secured on the company's property ('mortgage debentures'). A debenture can also be a document which creates security over all of a company's business. The document contains, in the charging clause, mortgages, fixed and floating charges, and assignments which together create the necessary security.

Debt service Payment of principal and interest in respect of the loan.

Deductible The amount which an insurer will deduct before making payment of a claim.

The expression is also used in relation to tax, meaning the ability to deduct a particular payment from profits for the purpose of calculating tax liability.

Deed An English law expression meaning a document which will be enforced by the courts without the need for consideration.[6]

Default In its ordinary sense, this means a breach or a failure to perform as promised under a contract. It is usually also a defined term in the loan agreement, meaning something which may, or may not, result in an Event of Default. See commentary on 'Default' at 1.018.

Defeasance A structure which creates certainty that a payment obligation will be met from a specific source other than by the original debtor.

Demand guarantee an instrument such as a standby letter of credit or a performance bond under which the 'guarantor' must pay, regardless of whether there is an underlying debt – see A1.075.

Dematerialize To transfer to a system which is based on book entries.

De minimis Too small to be concerned with.

Derivatives Assets (such as futures) which derive their value from underlying assets. See, for example, the discussion of credit derivatives at 9.020 onwards.

Disbursement account The account to which the proceeds of a loan provided in a project finance transaction are paid. Money will be drawn from that account against approved invoices.

Distressed debt Debt which is, or which the lender believes will be, non-performing (i.e. repaid late, partially, or not at all) and which is usually sold for substantially less than the value of principal outstanding.

Distributable reserves The amount which a company is allowed to pay to its shareholders at any given time by way of dividend.

Dividend A payment by a company to its shareholders out of profits.

Double dipping Structuring a transaction in such a way that it becomes possible to utilize the tax benefits on capital investments in more than one jurisdiction.

Double taxation treaty An agreement between two countries intended to limit the double taxation of income and gains, under the terms of which an investor which is tax resident in one country but invests in another may be able to apply for an exemption or reduction in the taxes imposed on his income or gains by the country of his investment, on the basis that such

---

[6] See A1.025.

income or gains will have tax levied on them in the country in which he is tax resident. This type of treaty encourages trade and financial transactions between countries. See 6.002.

Drawdown   The borrowing of money under a loan facility.

Drop dead fee   A fee payable to a lender in the event the proposed transaction does not proceed.

Due diligence   The process of checking all relevant facts before entering into a transaction. Involves both financial and legal due diligence.

EBITDA   Earnings before interest, tax, depreciation and amortization – see Box 8.17 on page 185.

Encumbrance   A general description of any restriction on rights of ownership. It includes all forms of security as well as other restrictions such as rights of way.

Engrossment   The final version of a contract, ready for signature.

Equity   Has a number of meanings –
- Moneys invested into a company by its shareholders (including, perhaps, accumulated profits not yet distributed)
- The principles of law which are embodied in equitable principles (see A1.009)
- Fairness

Equity cure   These provisions allow issuers to fix a breach of a financial covenant without having to request a waiver or amendment. Some agreements do not limit the number of equity cures, while others cap the number to, maybe, one per year or two over the life of the loan, with the exact details negotiated for each deal. See 8.119.

Equity kicker   An option, often included in certain loan transactions, particularly in mezzanine finance and venture capital, to take a share in the profits arising from the transaction financed by the loan.

Equity of redemption   A mortgagee's right to pay off the secured debt and obtain title back from the mortgagor.

ERISA   Employee Retirement Income Security Act of 1974 in the United States. Failure to comply with the requirements of the Act can result in penalties and security interests arising. US borrowers are therefore often asked to give representations and covenants as to compliance with ERISA.

Escrow arrangement   Documents held in escrow are executed documents given by one executing party to a third party (usually a solicitor) to hold to its order until a certain condition is satisfied, or event occurs. The third party will usually be instructed that, on the satisfaction of such condition or occurrence of such event, the documents must be released out of escrow, usually to the other executing party. Money may also be held in escrow – that is, held by a third party with irrevocable instructions as to how to dispose of it in different circumstances.

Estoppel   An English law principle that, in certain circumstances, it would be unfair to allow a person to do something (such as enforcing their legal rights) and that he will therefore be 'estopped' from doing it. See 11.021. In the classic case[7] a landlord, having promised not to charge the full rent he was entitled to, was subsequently estopped from suing for the full rent.

Eurobond   A bond denominated in a Euro currency and traded on the capital markets.

Eurocurrency   Traditionally, any currency held by a non-resident of the country of that currency.[8]

Event of Default   The circumstances listed in the loan agreement which entitle the lender to demand immediate repayment of the loan.

Evergreen   A colloquial expression which means that the relevant thing is always there. For example, an evergreen repetition of the representations is one which requires them to be repeated daily and an evergreen facility is one which is renewable annually.

Exclusion clause   A clause under which a person seeks to exclude the liability, which he would otherwise have had, to another.[9]

Execute   Sign.

Export credit   Support provided by a country's government or an agency on behalf of the government, for the purpose of encouraging exports from that country. The support may take the form of guarantees, loans at subsidized interest rates, or other. The terms of export credit are regulated by the OECD Guidelines for Officially Supported Export Credit.

Export credit agency   A government body created for the purpose of providing export   credit.

Facility   A generic description for any form of financial support, whether by way of loan, guarantee, acceptance credit, or other.

Factoring   The sale and purchase of receivables, either on a recourse or non-recourse basis. In other words, the seller may or may not remain subject to the risk of default in relation to the receivables sold.

FATCA   Foreign Account Tax Compliance Act – see 6.030.

Fiduciary duty   This is the duty of the trustee or agent (including directors of companies, who are agents of the company by virtue of their position as directors) to act in the interests of those he represents. The existence

---

[7] Central London Property Trust Ltd v High Trees House Ltd (1947) KB 130.
[8] But see *How to Read the Financial Pages*, Michael Brett, 5th edn, p. 276.
[9] See A1.027.

and exact scope of any fiduciary duty depends on the situation. In general, fiduciary duties include a duty
- not to make a secret profit,
- not to put oneself in a position where a conflict of interest may arise,
- not to sub-delegate, and
- to act in good faith.[10]

Finance lease   A means of financing involving a lease of an asset, the commercial effect of which is that the owner of the asset is in a similar position to a lender and the lessee is in a similar position to owner and borrower. Lease payments during the life of the lease are sufficient to enable the owner to recover the cost of the asset from the lessee, plus a return on its investment, regardless of any fluctuation in the value of the asset. For accounting purposes, the lessee under a finance lease is treated in the same way as if it were the owner of the relevant asset. Any lease which is not a finance lease is an operating lease.

Fixed charge   Security over a specific asset which prevents the owner from dealing with the asset. See A1.045.

Floating charge   Floating charges are security interests which allow the person giving the security to sell the items over which the security exists, free of the security until the security 'crystallizes'. They are often used to give security over categories of assets such as a trader's stock in trade from time to time. They have a number of disadvantages as against other forms of security; one of which is that the security holder cannot retain all the proceeds of the security. See A1.046.

Floor   An agreed limit below which a particular figure, such as an interest rate, is not allowed to drop.

Force majeure   A continental law concept meaning occurrences of a type (e.g. acts of God) which are outside the control of the parties and which justify the non-performance of obligations under a contract (without the contract itself having to set this out). Under English law, non-performance of a contract for reasons which are not specified in the contract but which are outside the control of the parties, is justified if the contract is 'frustrated'. This is a much narrower concept than the continental concept of force majeure. For this reason, many English law contracts contain force majeure clauses, specifically allowing non-performance in circumstances which would not amount to frustration.

Forward Start Facility   A committed facility used to refinance (repay) an existing syndicated loan on maturity. It is signed some time in advance (several months to a year) of maturity of the existing loan and is provided by some of the existing lenders.

---

[10] See further Goode, *Commercial Law*, 4th edn, p. 187.

Frustration The circumstances in which English law will release parties from further performance of a contract as a result of unanticipated occurrences. A contract is frustrated if it is incapable of being performed in a manner which will give the parties the same nature of benefit as they originally contracted for. Further performance is then excused.[11]

Full recourse In relation to an obligation, 'full recourse' means that the person who is owed the obligation has all the rights which the law gives in relation to enforcement of that obligation, for example, to sue the counterparty for all sums due and enforce any judgement against any of the assets of the counterparty.

Fungible assets Assets where the precise identity of the asset is irrelevant – each asset of that type is interchangeable. For example, in relation to cash, a deposit of £10 with a bank may be reimbursed by the bank returning £10 – even though the precise notes are not the same as those originally deposited.

Futures Contracts to buy or sell specific assets for agreed prices on an agreed future date.

GAAP **Generally Accepted Accounting Principles** – the common set of accounting principles, standards, and procedures that companies use in any given country to compile their financial statements and reports.

Gearing The ratio of a company's debt to its equity.

Gilts Securities such as commercial paper issued by the British government.

Goodstanding A concept which is relevant in some (e.g. some US) jurisdictions where failure to pay taxes may jeopardize the company's existence or ability to do business.

Goodwill The value attributed in a company's balance sheet to certain of the company's non-physical assets such as its name, reputation and customer base.

Governing law See 'proper law'.

Grace period The period of time given to a borrower, in relation to the events of default in a loan agreement, in which it is allowed to remedy any given situation, and to avoid that situation becoming an Event of Default.

Gross-up A borrower may be required to gross-up payments it has to make to the lenders, meaning it must make additional payments to compensate for withholding taxes, or similar deductions, which would otherwise reduce the amounts actually received by the lenders. See commentary on clause 13.2(c) of the LMA Term Loan at 6.004.

Guarantee A promise to pay a debt which has been made to another if that other defaults in payment. See A1.071 onwards.

---

[11] See chapter 19 of Treitel, *The Law of Contract*, 13th edn.

Haircut   A situation where a borrower has fallen into financial difficulties and lenders have agreed to accept a reduction in interest and or fees, or, principal. Also a situation where a borrower has fallen into financial difficulty and a lender has decided to sell its exposure in the secondary market at a significant discount to its par value.

Hardening period   The period of time before the commencement of an insolvency process (e.g. winding up) in respect of which a liquidator can challenge certain transactions entered into by the insolvent company. See 'Transactions at an undervalue' and 'Preference'. The longest hardening period in English law is two years (except in the case of fraud).

Hedge funds   An investment vehicle that is privately organized and not widely available to the public. Hedge funds are generally not constrained by legal limitations on their investment discretion and can adopt a variety of trading strategies.

Hedging   Arrangements made to protect against loss due to market or currency fluctuation.

Hell or high water clause   A clause which requires payment regardless of any eventualities (e.g. to continue paying hire for an asset, regardless of its destruction, as will be contained in a finance lease).

Hire purchase   A form of finance lease under which the lessee has the right to purchase the asset for a nominal sum at the end of the financing period.

ICE LIBOR   The ICE Benchmark Administration Limited's (ICE) fixing of the London Interbank Offered Rate (*LIBOR*). ICE LIBOR is often used as a benchmark or reference rate for short-term interest rates. It is compiled by ICE and released to the market at about 11am each day. It replaced *BBA LIBOR* on 1 February 2014.

IFRS   International Financial Reporting Standards created by the International Accounting Standards Board.

Indemnity   An agreement to hold another harmless against loss. See A1.072.

Information memorandum   A document prepared in connection with a proposed syndicated loan or issue of securities, providing information in relation to the proposed transaction for review by potential participants. See 'Prospectus'.

Insolvency   A company is insolvent if either
- it cannot pay its debts as they fall due (the cash flow test) or
- its liabilities exceed its assets (the balance sheet test).[12]

---

[12] s123 Insolvency Act 1986.

Failure to meet either of these tests does not necessarily result in the company being wound up but it does give rise to additional duties for directors (see 'wrongful trading') and to the potential for certain transactions entered into (see 'transactions at an undervalue' and 'preference') being subsequently set aside if an insolvency process (such as a winding up or administration) starts during the hardening period.

The expression is sometimes (inaccurately) used to mean the same as winding up. See also 8.253 onwards.

Institutional investor   An organization whose function is to invest its assets, such as pension funds and investment funds.

Intangible assets   Any asset which does not have a physical form. Examples are debts and patents.

Intercreditor deed   Any deed made between different creditors (or groups of creditors, such as different syndicates) of a company. Such a document may deal with any issues which those creditors seek to regulate among themselves, but commonly covers such issues as priorities of debts, (perhaps prior to insolvency as well as in the event of insolvency of the debtor), priorities of security, agreement on the application of proceeds of sale of assets belonging to the debtor, rights (or restrictions on rights) to take action against the debtor or its assets, commitments relating to provision of further funding and/or provision of information, and rights (or restrictions on rights) to adjust the existing contractual arrangements with the debtor. Such a document may also go by other names such as 'priorities deed', or 'subordination deed'.

Interest period   The period(s) with reference to which interest is calculated for the purpose of a loan agreement. See commentary on clause 10 of the LMA Term Loan at 5.012 onwards.

Initial public offering   A flotation of a company on a stock exchange.

Investment grade   Securities which are rated by the rating agencies at a specified rate high enough to be eligible for investment by certain organizations, such as pension funds.

ISDA   International Swap and Derivatives Association. An association responsible for publishing standard terms for swaps and other derivatives.

Joint venture   A business which is run by two or more companies in co-operation. The joint venture may take the form of a partnership between the companies, a separate legal entity, or other contractual arrangements.

Judgement currency indemnity   An indemnity sometimes included in credit facilities (e.g. clause 15.1 of the LMA Term Loan) to protect the lenders against losses they may suffer if judgement is obtained against the borrower in a currency different to that in which the facility is denominated. Such an indemnity may not be enforceable in all circumstances and this is an issue for due diligence.

Jurisdiction The concept that any given court is only able to deal with certain issues, being those which fall within its 'jurisdiction'. The jurisdiction of any court may be limited with reference to the type of issue concerned (e.g. the family courts), the amount in dispute or the country or countries with which the dispute or the parties to it have a connection. Parties to a loan agreement will expressly submit to the jurisdiction of the courts of a specified jurisdiction. These need not be (but usually are) the courts of the country whose law has been chosen as the proper law of the agreement.

KYC Various checks and investigations required of your customers as part of the procedures to prevent money laundering.

Lender of record A member of the syndicate, with direct claims against the borrower.

Lending office The branch or office of a lender through which the funds for a facility are provided.

Letter of credit A document commonly used in connection with the sale and purchase of goods. It is a written undertaking by a bank (the issuing bank) given at the request of, and in accordance with the instructions of, the applicant (the buyer of the goods) to the beneficiary (the seller of the goods), to effect a payment of a stated amount of money, within a prescribed time limit, against the production of stipulated documents (such as evidence of shipment of the goods).

Leverage Ratio of debt to equity. Also known as gearing.

Liability A legal responsibility (may either be a responsibility to do a specified thing or to make a specified payment).

LIBOR London Interbank Offered Rate. The rate of interest quoted by banks in the London Interbank Market at which they are able to borrow money, that is, obtain deposits in a particular currency for a particular period of time. See 0.081 onwards.

Lien A right to retain possession of an asset until paid where this right arises as a result of some commercial activity (such as repair of the asset) and was not created for the purpose of raising funds. In the United States the expression may be used to mean all forms of security interest. See A1.044.

Limited recourse A limited recourse loan is one with limited comeback (or recourse) to the borrower. The comeback is usually limited to certain specified assets – usually the assets involved in, and income derived from, the project being financed.

The expression may also be used in circumstances where there is full recourse to the borrower, but the borrower is an SPV, which only owns assets relating to the project being financed. In this case, the transaction is limited recourse to (or sometimes non-recourse to) the shareholders of the SPV. This is a structural limitation on recourse.

Liquidated damages A sum specified in a contract as being the amount to be paid by one party to the other in the event of a breach of (or of a specified provision of) the contract. Care needs to be taken in fixing the amount to ensure that it is not a penalty. See 'Penalty'.

Liquidation The winding up of a company and distribution of its assets.

Liquidator The official who will be responsible for collection and distribution of a company's assets in a liquidation.

Liquidity The ability of a company to pay its debts as they fall due. Often assessed by the liquidity ratio – the ratio of current assets to current liabilities. If a company is unable to pay its debts as they fall due, it is insolvent. See 'Insolvency'.

Liquidity coverage ratio the ratio between high quality liquid assets and expected outflows from a bank during periods of stress – see 6.040.

Liquidity premium the price charged by banks for taking a liquidity risk.

Liquidity risk the risk involved in the fact that banks borrow money on a short-term basis and onlend it on a long-term basis – see 0.098.

Listed A bond, note, company share or other instrument which is quoted on a recognized stock exchange.

Loss Given Default A measure of how much lenders lose when a borrower defaults. The loss will vary depending on the type of borrower and its value when it defaults. Secured creditors will of course lose less than unsecured creditors and senior creditors will loss less than subordinated creditors. Some calculations express loss as a nominal percentage of principal or a percentage of principal plus accrued interest. Others use a present value calculation using an estimated discount rate of an amount demanded by distressed investors.

Loss payee A person named on an insurance policy as the person to be paid in the event of a claim.

Mandate The authorization from one person to another to conduct the relevant transaction on the agreed terms. Usually given in the form of a letter signed by both parties.

Mandated Lead Arranger mandated bank at the highest level. The MLA, or at least one MLA in cases when there is more than one MLA, will act as the bookrunner.

Margin In relation to floating interest rates, the rate of interest charged by the lender over and above the relevant cost of funding, such as LIBOR.

Mark to market Valuing an asset against its current market value (particularly used for swaps and other derivatives).

Market disruption clause The clause in a loan agreement (clause 11.2 in the LMA Term Loan, discussed at 5.026), which deals with what happens if funds are unavailable in the specified market.

Market flex clause The clause in a term sheet which allows the Arranger to alter the terms if there are changes in market conditions.

Matched funding The process of matching a loan (asset) with a deposit (liability) of the same maturity.

Maturity The date upon which a debt is finally repayable.

Mezzanine finance or debt Usually high-interest-bearing debt, which ranks behind (i.e. is subordinate to) the 'senior debtors' so far as repayment and security is concerned. In terms of risk and reward it ranks between debt and equity. The debt may be structured as a subordinated loan or as preference shares, depending on the legal, regulatory and tax regime. See 'Subordinated debt'.

Misrepresentation An untrue statement inducing a contract. See A1.029.

Monoline insurer Insurer whose business is the provision of financial insurance.

Moratorium A period in which creditors agree to allow a borrower to delay payment of a debt, usually to allow negotiation of a rescue.

Mortgage A type of security interest. Under a common law mortgage, title passes to the mortgagee, subject to the mortgagor's equity of redemption. See A1.042.

Mulligan clause A clause that allows the borrower a second chance on the financial covenants. If, for example, a borrower does not comply with its financial covenants for one quarter but is back in line the following quarter, the previous quarter is disregarded as if it never happened.

Mutatis mutandis A Latin expression meaning 'with such changes as are necessary'. This is a shorthand expression, occasionally used in drafting. For example, the following statement may be used to avoid repetition. '*Clause [] (Agency) shall apply to the Security Trustee mutatis mutandis*'.

This avoids the need to repeat the clause replacing all references to 'the Agent' with references to 'the Security Trustee'.

Negative pledge Undertaking by a borrower not to allow indebtedness to be maintained on a secured basis.

Net present value The current value of a given future payment or payments, discounted at a given rate (see BoxA2.1 on page 364).

> **Box A2.1**
> For example, if the current interest rate is 5% per annum, the net present value of a payment of $105 due to be made in 12 months' time is $100, since that is the amount which, if deposited in an account today and bearing interest at 5% for the year, would yield a payment of $105 in 12 months' time.

Net stable funding ratio   The ratio between 'stable funding' of a bank and its mix of assets – see 6.039.

Novation   A method of transferring rights and obligations from one party to a contract to a third party.[13] This method involves the discharge of one contract and its replacement by a new, identical contract, with different parties.

Offtaker   A party which commits to purchase a quantity of the product produced in a project finance transaction.

Operating lease   A lease which is not a finance lease.

Originator   A party who sells its receivables in a securitization transaction.

Pari passu   Equally and without preference in terms of entitlement to payment (as opposed to pro rata, which relates to actual payment, and requires that all receive the same percentage of what is due to them.) Two debts which are pari passu will, when payment is made, be paid pro rata. See also 8.052 onwards.

Participation   A single lender's share of the overall loan facility.

Performance bond   A guarantee for a non-monetary obligation (such as due performance of a contract). The expression may be used in two entirely different ways. It may be used to describe a suretyship guarantee or, alternatively, to describe an instrument which is primary in nature.[14]

Penalty   An English law expression. Under English law, any provision of a contract which seeks to penalize a party to the contract if it fails to perform under the contract is a penalty and may be unenforceable. Such a provision will however be enforceable if, in summary, the provision is a genuine attempt to compensate the other party for loss it will suffer as a result of the failure to perform.[15] Common areas where this question arises are in relation to default interest and liquidated damages.

PIK notes   Payment in kind, typically, does not provide for any payments from the borrower to the lender between the drawdown date and the maturity or refinancing date. PIK interest accrues and capitalizes periodically

---

[13] See 9.004.
[14] See Goode, *Commercial Law*, 4th edn at p. 1124.
[15] See Dunlop Pneumatic Tyre Co Ltd v New Garage & Motor Co Ltd (1915) AC 79 at 87–88 for rules of construction as to whether a clause is penal or a pre-estimate of damages.

over the life of the debt, thus increasing the underlying principal (i.e. compound interest).

Plain vanilla   A colloquial term used to describe loan facilities with no additional features such as call options.

Pledge   The security created by the actual or constructive delivery of an asset to a lender where the possession of the asset was delivered for the purpose of raising funds (as opposed to a lien, where possession was delivered for some other purpose). See A1.043.

Pool   A combination of assets into a single unit, such as a single investment (e.g. commercial paper) which is based on a number of investment instruments.

Power of attorney   A legal document authorizing one person to act on behalf of another.

Preference   An English law expression for a transaction which puts a person in a better position in the insolvency of another than they otherwise would have been (see Box A2.2). Any such step is vulnerable to be set aside as a fraudulent preference.[16]

Box A2.2

For example, assume a company has two loans, one of which has been personally guaranteed by the company's directors. If the company starts having financial difficulties, it might decide to pay off the guaranteed debt in order to obtain the release of the personal guarantees. If it subsequently goes into liquidation during the hardening period, the bank which had been repaid might be required to refund that sum to the company on the basis that the original repayment of the loan was a fraudulent preference. The only reason the company chose to pay off that loan was because it would result in the release of the personal guarantee and put the directors who had given the guarantees in a better position on an insolvency of the company than they otherwise would have been.

Preference shares   Shares which receive their dividends before all other shares and are repaid first if the company goes into liquidation.

Preferential creditors   Those creditors (such as, in many countries, employees) whose debts must be paid in priority to other unsecured creditors in a winding up.

Prepayment   A payment made before it is scheduled to be made.

Pro forma accounts   Financial statements that include the 'side effects' of the current transaction. For example, in the case of an acquisition, pro forma EBITDA will reflect the combined EBITDA of the two companies

---

[16] s239 Insolvency Act 1986 (as amended).

plus synergies from their merger. It could, for example, include cost savings generated by headcount reductions.

Pricing grid (or margin ratchet)   A provision under which a borrower agrees to pay a margin which varies by reference to a specific financial ratio (e.g. leverage) or external credit rating,

Principal   This can be the amount which the lender advanced to the borrower and which the borrower must repay (as opposed to the interest due in respect of such amount), or, in relation to a person, the principal is the person for whom some other person acts as agent.

Privity   The common law doctrine that no person is entitled to enforce a contract unless they are a party to it. See Box 1.22 on page 77.

Process agent   The agent appointed by a non-English company to accept service of proceedings in the English courts on its behalf. See 12.008.

Project finance   The financing of a specific project, the revenue from which will provide the lenders with repayment of their investment.

Promissory note   A promise in writing to pay a fixed sum on demand or on a determinable future date.[17]

Proper law   The law which applies to a contract. Sometimes referred to as the 'governing law'. This is the law which the court in which a dispute is heard decides should apply. In general a court in the European Union will give effect to the law chosen by the parties.[18]

Pro rata   In the same proportion (see Box A2.3).

Box A2.3

If A owes $10 to B and $20 to C, and a sum of $6 is to be distributed pro rata between B and C, then A will recover $2 (20% of the amount due to it) and B will recover $4 (20% of the amount due to it).

Prospectus   A document relating to investments (such as an issue of securities, or, potentially, participation in a syndicated loan) which sets out the relevant information in relation to the investment and is circulated to potential investors. See 'Prospectus legislation'.

Prospectus legislation   The legislation which exists in many countries which regulates the contents of any prospectus distributed in that country and/or requires those issuing the prospectuses to be authorized to do so.

---

[17] See Goode, *Commercial Law*, 4th edn, p. 515.
[18] This is governed by the Rome Convention on the Law Applicable to Contractual Obligations 1980 as updated by regulation 593/2008. There are exceptions, for example, for real rights relating to immovable real property which must be governed by the law where the property is.

Put option   An agreement which gives the recipient the right, but not the obligation, to require the donor to take title to a specified asset (e.g. shares) from the recipient, normally at a specified price on a specified date (or within a range of dates). The recipient can be expected to use this right if the value of the asset is less than the specified price on the specified date. Hence, such an agreement may be used to cap one party's potential losses in relation to an asset.

Quasi security   A transaction, such as a finance lease, which has the same commercial effect as security. Otherwise referred to as 'title financing'. See 0.234.

Rating   Grading of a debt's quality as an investment.

Rating Agency   Agencies which provide independently derived credit assessments on borrowers or on specific debt instruments issued by a borrower.

RCF   Revolving Credit Facility.

Receivables   Money which is owed to a company.

Recharacterization   The decision by a court not to take a transaction at face value but instead to look at its commercial effect in order to determine its validity. For example, a court in certain jurisdictions may determine that the true character of a transaction which involves quasi security is one of security, not ownership, and, as a result, may require that the transaction be registered as security or may treat the transaction as ineffective. Similarly, in England, a document may be expressed to be a fixed charge but a court may determine its effect to be that of a floating charge.

Redemption   The repayment by a borrower of outstanding loans, in accordance with their terms, with the effect of extinguishing the outstanding debt.

Regulatory capital   The capital required to support a portfolio of assets as a result of the capital requirements set out in the Basel regulations – see 0.096.

Repo   The sale of securities with an obligation to buy back at a future date.

Representation   A statement. Statements made before another party enters into a contract (or as part of the contract as a condition to its effectiveness) may be 'mere representations' or they may be 'warranties'. Warranties go to the root of the contract and amount to promises that the statement is true, such that, if it is not, the other party is entitled to the contractual measure of damages. Representations do not go to the root of the contract. Generally speaking,[19] representations entitle the other party only to the tort level of damages[20] if untrue.

---

[19] There are four different categories of misrepresentation, each of which has different consequences.
[20] Which, unlike the contractual measure of damages, does not include loss of profit.

Repudiation   Evidencing an intention no longer to be bound by a contract to which the person repudiating the contract is a party.

Rescheduling   In relation to debt obligations, the renegotiation and agreement of revised terms of a loan facility (usually involving the spreading of interest and capital repayments over a longer period).

Rescission   Treating a contract as at an end as a result of a breach by the counterparty.

Residual Value Guarantee   A guarantee from one party that if the value of a given asset is less than a set figure at a particular date in the future (subject to specified conditions, such as the state of repair of the asset), that party will compensate the other for the shortfall in value.

Restitution   An equitable remedy[21] under which a party which has been unjustly enriched at the expense of another will be required to refund the amount of that unjust enrichment.

Retention   An ability by one person to keep moneys (or other assets) belonging to another, pending occurrence of a specified event.

Revolving credit   A loan which may be drawn, repaid, and redrawn as needed.

Ring fence   To separate valuable assets or businesses[22] from others and limit transfers and other cash flows, out of the area where the valuable assets or businesses are situated, into other areas. For example, funds may be ring fenced if they are separated and allocated for use only in payment of given debts, or companies may be ring fenced in a group and payments out of the ring fenced companies restricted.

Rollover   The renewal of a drawing under a loan facility, for example, at the end of an interest period, or the reissue of a short-term commercial paper on its maturity.

Rollover loan   In a revolving credit, any loan in respect of which the amount outstanding is equal to or less than the amount outstanding under the immediately preceding loan – see also Box 2.1 on page 79.

Same day funds   Funds which will be available to the recipient with good value on the same day as that on which the instruction to transfer the funds is made.

Screen rate   The rate of interest (e.g. for six-month LIBOR) specified on a computer screen such as Reuters screen – see 1.060.

SEC   The Securities and Exchange Commission. A US agency whose role is to oversee the US securities market.

---

[21] See A1.007.
[22] Or, indeed, assets which have the potential to give rise to extensive liabilities.

Second lien financing A European 2nd lien is a loan with a security on a borrower's assets ranking behind the 1st loan security but ahead of any mezzanine debt.

Secondary market the market where lenders trade loans among themselves as opposed to the primary market, where lenders make loans to borrowers directly.

Securities Tradeable financial assets such as bonds, notes, and commercial paper.

Securitization Packaging assets (usually receivables such as credit card receipts) in such a way as to allow them to be used to back up an issue of securities.

Security An interest in property to secure a liability. See A1.041. Thus it would not include a guarantee, which does not give an interest in property. A guarantee is personal (not real) security.

May also be used as in the singular version of 'Securities'.

Set off The right of a person who owes money to another but is also owed money by that other, to reduce the amount it pays by the amount it is owed. Set off is not a security, but a procedural right not to pay one debt to the extent that another is due from the payee to the payer.

Several liability Where there is more than one Obligor (such as in a guarantee, where there are a number of guarantors) if their liabilities are several, they are completely independent of each other. Payment by one Obligor has no effect on the liability of other Obligors.

Shadow director Anyone in accordance with whose instructions the directors of a company are accustomed to act.[23] Such persons will have the same liabilities as directors.

Snooze you lose A clause in the loan agreement which disenfranchises a lender's voting right in relation to a specific amendment or waiver request if that lender has not responded to the agent within a certain predefined period of time. See Box 11.6 on page 287.

Sovereign immunity In many countries, the assets of the sovereign government and organs of that government may not be seized by a court nor may the sovereign government or its organs be sued, but it may be possible for this immunity to be waived.

SPC/SPV/SPE Special purpose company/vehicle/entity. A legal entity (it may not be a company) set up for a specific purpose (e.g. the project company in a project finance or the issuer of securities in a securitization) whose assets are limited to those relating to the transaction for which it was set up.

---

[23] S251 Companies Act 2006.

Sponsors   In a project finance, the parties who join together to arrange the finance, being shareholders (usually) in the project company.

Spread   In relation to securities – the difference between the offer and bid prices, that is, the price at which a broker would buy those securities and the price at which he would sell them. The word may also be used as another word for profit – in relation to a loan, the margin may be referred to as the spread.

Standby letter of credit   A letter of credit issued by a bank but which is intended to be used as a fall-back if there is a payment default under a specified instrument such as a loan agreement. A beneficiary of this arrangement is able to make a drawing on the letter of credit merely by providing a certificate of non-payment of the underlying debt. It is an example of a 'demand guarantee' discussed at A1.075.

Statutes   Laws passed in Parliament. See A1.004.

Subordinated debt   A debt which, in the event of the borrower's liquidation, ranks behind senior debt holders. See A1.033.

Sub-participation   A method of transfer of the credit risk in the loan which does not result in the transferee having direct rights against the borrower, or becoming a lender of record. See 9.017.

Subrogation   The right to take over the rights and security of another. In relation to a guarantee it is the right to take over the rights and security of the creditor on making payment under the guarantee – see A1.085. In relation to insurance, it is the right of the insurer to take over the claims of the insured on making payment of the claim.

Supplier credit   Finance made available by a supplier by way of allowing delayed payments for the goods delivered or services provided. Supplier credit is often interest-bearing and with similar documentation to a loan.

Supranationals   Entities set up by several sovereign states, for example, World Bank.

Surety   A party (A) which agrees that, if a debt owed by another (B) is not paid, then A will pay B's debt or allow A's asset to be used towards payment of B's debt.

Swap   The exchange of one asset for another, usually currencies, interest streams, or securities.

Swingline facility   A facility which is available immediately and without notice, and which will be used to overcome short-term liquidity issues. For example, it may be used to pay commercial paper if it cannot be rolled over. Such a facility can only be provided by lenders with access to immediate funds in the currency concerned. So, if a Dollar facility is required, it cannot be funded in Eurodollars (which require a period of notice before they can be accessed) but must be provided by a lender with access to immediately available funds in sufficient quantities.

Syndicated loan   A loan made available by a group of lenders under a single loan agreement.

Synthetic   Manufactured. In the context of loans or derivatives, it is used to denote the fact that the synthetic instrument has been created out of more than one underlying instrument (such as a combination of a fixed rate bond and a swap to create a stream of floating rate payments which may be represented by a synthetic instrument).

Tacking   The right (or rather, the limits on the right) to advance further moneys against the security given for a debt in the event that there is a second security on the same asset. See A1.069.

Take or pay contract   A contract which commits the counterparty to purchase a given quantity of a particular product at an agreed price, even if it does not, in the end, need that quantity.

Tangible net worth   The book value of all the assets of a company minus its intangible assets such as goodwill.

TARGET Day   A day when the Trans European Automated Real time Gross Settlement Express Transfer System is operating for payments of Euros.

Tax lease   A finance lease under which the lessee benefits (by reduced rentals) from some part of the tax benefits available to the owner resulting from the owner's acquisition of the asset.

Term out   The conversion of a drawing (or part of a drawing) under a revolving credit into a term loan – see Box 4.1 on page 99.

Tenor   The period until maturity of a debt.

Thin capitalization   Thin capitalization is the situation which exists if the capital injected into a company by way of shares is low in relation to the capital injected by way of shareholder loans. It is often more tax efficient for a company to be financed by debt rather than equity, because payments of interest are deductible in calculating the company's taxable profits, while payments of dividends are not deductible. As a result, subsidiaries are often capitalized by a combination of shares and shareholder loans.

Title financing   Using title as an alternative to security. Otherwise known as quasi security. See 0.234.

Toggle   A feature in some credit agreements which, at the discretion of the borrower, allows the borrower to switch periodically back and forth the payment of interest due on certain tiers of its debt between cash payments and PIK.

Tombstone   An announcement, usually placed in the financial press, made by either the borrower or the lenders announcing provision of a loan facility. Tombstones are not intended as an advertisement to entice prospective lenders, they simply contain a brief description of the facility and a list of the participating banks.

Transaction at an undervalue   A transaction under which a company gives substantially more than it receives.[24]

Transfer fee   The fee charged by an agent bank for transferring a portion of a loan from one lender of record to another lender of record.

Trust   An English legal expression referring to the situation where the legal owner of property holds it on behalf of another (or others) – the beneficiary.[25] There are a number of different types of trust. Charities are an example where trusts are commonly used. The property of the charity belongs to the trustees who must use it for the benefit of those for whom the charity was established.

Where someone wishes to create a trust, that trust will be created provided there is certainty as to:
- the intention to create a trust;
- the property vested in the trust; and
- the beneficiaries of the trust.

A trust once created is irrevocable. See A1.019.

Trustee   A person who holds ownership of an asset on behalf of another (the beneficiary). In the insolvency of the trustee, the trust property will not be available to the trustee's creditors. This compares with agency which is a purely contractual relationship.

Undertaking
- the business of a company, or
- a promise (as in covenant) to do or not to do, specified things.

Underwriter   A lender which commits in advance of drawdown to take on a portion of the overall facility if it is not taken up in the initial syndication.

Venture capital   Equity finance made available to, usually, newly established businesses to enable them to expand.

Warranty   A word with many meanings. When used in connection with pre-contractual statements, a warranty is compared to a representation and means the more commercially important statement, which has contractual force and, if untrue, gives a right to the contractual level of damages.

When used in connection with provisions of the contract, a warranty is compared to a condition and means the less commercially important

---

[24] See A1.082.
[25] See A1.019.

provision, which gives rise only to damages if breached, as opposed to a breach of condition which gives the right to terminate the contract.

Withholding tax   A tax deducted at source on certain payments (e.g. interest or dividend payments). See 6.001.

Working capital   Money required by a company to run its day to day activities, for example, to finance payment to employees and suppliers pending receipt of income from the sale of the product which the company supplies.

Workout   Common term for the long-term rescue of a defaulting borrower by its lender(s) (and other creditors).

Wrongful trading   Carrying on trading after the point at which it should have been clear that insolvent liquidation was inevitable. Directors and shadow directors may[26] have to contribute to the company's assets on a winding up if the company has been guilty of wrongful trading.

Yank the bank   A provision sometimes included in a loan agreement which allows the borrower to remove a lender which has voted against a waiver or amendment request under the loan agreement, which, but for that lender, would have been approved. See 4.026.

Yield   The annual rate of return on an investment.

---

[26] Under s 214 Insolvency Act 1986 (as amended).

Bibliography

BOOKS

Michael Brett, *How to Read the Financial Pages*, 5th edn, 2000
Lee Buchheit, *How to Negotiate Eurocurrency Loan Agreements*, 2nd edn, 2000
Richard Calnan, *Taking Security*, 3rd edn, 2013
Ross Cranston, *Principles of Banking Law*, 2nd edn, 2012
Goode, *Commercial Law*, 4th edn, 2010
Goode, *Legal Problems of Credit and Security*, 5th edn, 2013
Michael Gruson, Stephan Hutter, and Michael Kutchera, *Legal Opinions in International Transactions*, 4th edn, 2003.
Hanbury and Martin, *Modern Equity*, 19th edn, 2012
Martin Hughes, *Selected Legal Issues for Finance Lawyers*, 2003
Lingard on *Bank Security Documents*, 5th edn, 2011
Elizabeth Macdonald, *Exemption Clauses and Unfair Terms*, 2nd edn, 2006
Dr John Phillips, *The Modern Contract of Guarantee*, 2nd English edn, 2010
Tony Rhodes, *Syndicated Lending – Practice and Documentation*, 5th edn, 2009
C. F. Spry, *Equitable Remedies*, 9th edn, 2013
Treitel, *The Law of Contract*, 13th edn, 2011
Philip Wood, *Project finance, Securitisations and Subordinated Debt*, 2nd edn, 2007
Philip Wood, *Comparative Law of Security Interests and Title Finance*, 2nd edn, 2007
Philip Wood, *International Loans, Bonds, Guarantees and Legal Opinions*, 2nd edn, 2007

ARTICLES AND PAPERS

Association of Corporate Treasurers' *Borrower's Guide to LMA Loan Documentation for Investment Grade Borrowers*, available from their website at www.treasurers.org
Lachlan Burn, 'Pari Passu Clauses – English Law After NML v Argentina', *Capital Markets Law Journal*, 2014, 9(1), pp. 2–9
City of London Law Society, *A Guide to the Questions to be Addressed When Providing Opinion Letters on English Law in Financial Transactions*, available at www.citysolicitors.org.uk under the Financial Law Committee section
Thomas Evans, 'Guarantees and Performance Bonds – Problems of Drafting and Interpretation', *Butterworths Journal of International Banking and Financial Law*, November 2013

Financial Market Law Committee, Report on pari passu clauses in sovereign debt obligations, issued in March 2005, available from their web site www.fmlc.org

Robin Henry, 'Defining the "Ordinary Course of Business"', *Journal of International Banking Law and Regulation*, 2004, 19(12), p. 513

Philip Hertz, Rick Antonoff, Mark Pesso, Tim Bennett and Leah Edelboim, 'Trading Places: Distressed Debt Trading in the US and UK Restructuring Markets', *Butterworths Journal of International Banking and Financial Law*, July/August 2013

Franck Julien and Jean-Marc Lamontagne-Defriez, 'Material Adverse Change and Syndicated Bank Financing', *Journal of International Banking Law and Regulation*, 2004, 19(6), pp. 193–198

Philip Rawlings, 'Restrictions on the Transfer of Rights in Loan Contracts', *Butterworths Journal of International Banking and Financial Law*, October 2013

Index

acceleration, 11, 152–5, 159
   from Default to, 222–3
   Events of Default and, 244–6
   incorrect serving of notice of, 239n133
acceptance credit facility, 7, 47
accession letter, 298–9
acquisition finance, 5
action in personam, 318
action in rem, 318
administration, 41,
administrative provisions, 10, 49–139
Agent
   agency clause, 10
   agency fee, 120
   appointment of, 272
   conduct of business by 277
   confidentiality, 276
   distributions by, 280
   duties of, 273–4
   exclusion of liability, 275
   fiduciary duties of, 274
   impaired, 34–5, 277
   instructions to, 272
   lenders' indemnity to, 275
   no duty to monitor, 275
   not responsible for credit appraisal 277
   payments to, 280
   relationship with lenders, 276
   resignation of, 276
   responsibility for documentation, 274–5
   rights and discretions of, 274
   role of, 271–2
   vs. trustee, 327

Agent, security to, 259–61
   as security for joint creditorship, 261
   as security for parallel debt, 260
   as security for underlying debts, 259–60
'agreed form', 57
'all moneys' guarantee, 143
all reasonable endeavours, 177
Alternative Reference Banks, 24n37
amendments and waivers, 285–6
anti-corruption laws, 100–1
arbitration, 290
arrangement fee, 119–20
Arranger, role of, 271–2, 274
asset finance, 4, 5, 40–1, 83
   conditions precedent in, 86, 295
   financial covenants in, 193–6
asset risk, 5
asset types as security
   bank accounts, 335–7
   businesses, 335
   comingled property, 337
   future property, 334
   intangible assets, 334
   moveable property, 335
   shares and investments, 335
asset stripping, 30, 208
assignments, 41
   assignment agreements, 268, 298
   assignment and assumption agreements, 235
   vs. delegation, 254
   effect on
      indemnities 253–4
      obligations, 254-255
      security, 254

assignments – *continued*
    LMA assignment provisions
        for Lenders, 265–7
        for Obligors, 268
    loan transfers via, 252–5
    notice of, 218
    types of assignment, 332–3
Association of Corporate Treasurers, 8, 9n6, 21, 193
Automatic Events of Default, 222
availability period, 34, 90

backstop facilities, 86, 92
balance sheet lending, 4
base currency, 54, 89, 194n59
Basel regulations, 18, 19
    Basel I, 18n26, 19, 133
    Basel II, 18n26, 19, 133–4, 136
    Basel III, 18n26, 19, 82–3, 134, 136–7
base rate, 16
beneficial owner, 320
beneficiary, 320
best endeavours, 177
bilateral facilities, 7
bill of exchange, 47
bona fide purchaser for value without notice, 321
bonds, 39, 47, 62
borrowers
    see also Obligors
    additional, 268–9
    key concerns of, 12–13
    resignation of, 269
break costs, 21, 54–5, 105, 118–19
bridge finance, 5–6
British Bankers Association, 72
broken funding costs, *see* break costs
business day, 56

calculations and certificates, 283–4
cancellation, *see* prepayment and cancellation
capital adequacy, *see* Basel regulations
capital expenditure restriction, 189
capital leases, 44
capital markets, 4
    convergence with, 39–40
caps, on expenses, 139

case law, 316
cashflow, 185–6, 233
cash pooling, 200–2
cash sweeps, 189
Centre of Main Interests (COMI), 216
certificates and determinations, 284
change of business, 211
change of control, 101–2
charges
    fixed, 331–2
    floating, 329–31
choice of law and jurisdiction, 311–12
chose in action, 318
circularity of definitions, 53
civil law, 315–16
clawback and pre-funding clause, 281
clawback clause, 130, 145
clean down period, 189
clean up period, 9n7
club loans, 7
collateral, 36
collateralised debt obligations (CDOs), 36n68
comingled property, 337
commercial paper, 6, 47
commitment fee, 34, 102–3, 119
committed facility, 3–4
commodification of debt, 36–40
common law
    vs. civil law, 315–16
    vs. equity, 316–17
company
    The "Company" in the LMA loan, 25, 27
    companies able to use the facility, 24-5
    insignificant companies, 29
    non-recourse companies, 29–30
Competition Commission, 215n103
compliance certificate, 57, 180, 299
compound interest, 108
compulsory prepayment events
    change of control, 101
    and the cross default clause, 229, 232
"conclusive" evidence clause, 284
conditional sale agreements, 45
conditions of utilization, 83–90
    documentary conditions precedent, 83–6, 294–5
    factual conditions precedent, 87–8

maximum number of loans, 89–90
relating to optional currencies, 89
relating to additional obligors, 294
relating to asset finance, 295
relating to project finance, 295–7
confidentiality, 131, 276, 287–8
confidentiality undertaking, 299–300
conflict of law, 40
conformed copy, 288
consideration, 321–2
contingent debt, 234, 235
'continuing', 74
continuing guarantees, 144, 341–2
contra proferentem, 285, 323
control, 12
    change of, 101–2
corporate reconstruction, 211
cost-plus lending, 16–17
costs and expenses clause, 138–9
counterparts, 288
covenant lite loans, 37, 39, 177–8
covenants, *see* undertakings
credit default swaps (CDSs), 38, 256–7, 262
credit derivatives, 2, 249, 250, 256–7, 262
credit support arrangements, 203–4
cross acceleration clause, 230–1
cross default clauses, 12, 170, 225–33
    compulsory prepayment events, 232
    consents, 232–3
    cross acceleration clauses, 230–1
    grace periods, 232
    reducing impact of, 231–2
currencies
    base, 89, 194n59
    change of, 96–7
    currency of account, 282
    Euro crisis 75, 282
    optional, 69, 89, 94–7
    selection of, 96
    symbols and definitions, 75–6
currency indemnity, 137–8

day count convention, 284
debentures, 40, 335
debt
    commodification of, 36–40

claims in, vs. damages, 319
security for
    parallel debt, 260
    parallel debt, alternative to, 261
    underlying debt, 259–60
subordination of, 326 (see also subordination)
types of
    contingent, 234, 235
    distressed, 38
    prospective, 234
    short-term, 220
    sovereign, 7, 171–2
deeds, 321, 322–3
Default, 27, 57–60
    see also Events of Default and Acceleration
    acceleration and, 222–3
    notification of, 182–3
    stages of, 227
defaulting lender provisions, 33–6, 60, 78–80, 104–5, 119
default interest, 107–9
deferral of guarantors' rights, 148–51
definitions and interpretations, 14–15, 51–77
    circularity, 53
    currency, 75–6
    in different contexts, 53
    in the LMA, 54–73
    operative provisions, 53
    out of context, 51–2
    rules of construction 73–5
    uncapitalized definitions 52
demand guarantees, 340–1
demand loans, 3
derivatives, 203–4, 226
    credit, 2, 249, 250, 256–7, 262
directors' duties, 246, 343
disruptions to payment systems, 282
distressed debt, 38
double taxation treaties, 121–2, 266
Double Tax Treaty Passport (DTTP) Scheme, 122, 124, 266
DTTP scheme, *see* Double Tax Treaty Passport (DTTP) Scheme
due diligence, 11, 45
duplication of provisions, 178–9

EBITDA (Earnings before Interest, Tax, Depreciation and Amortization), 185, 186
Employee Retirement Income Security Act (ERISA), 213
endeavours (degrees of) 177
enforceability opinions, 307–8
enforcement expenses, 138–9
enforcement representations, 166
English law
  basic concepts of, 315–27
  guarantees, 339–45
  legal concepts, 321–7
  security and, 327–38
  sources of, 315–18
  types of claims and rights, 318–21
'entire agreement' clause, 323
equitable principles qualification, 313
equity, 6, 316–18
equity kicker, 6
equity of redemption, 328–9
ERISA, see Employee Retirement Income Security Act (ERISA)
estoppel, 284
Euribor, 16, 60, 64–5, 106–7
Euro, 75–6
Eurocurrency, 16, 16n20
Euro Libor, 16
Events of Default, 3, 9, 12–13, 29, 58–60, 74, 220–46
  acceleration and, 222–3, 244–6
  automatic, 222
  control over relevant events, 221–2
  in the LMA Term Loan, 223–46
    breach of financial covenant, 223–4
    breach of other obligations, 224
    creditors' process, 236–7
    cross default, 225–33
    insolvency, 233–5
    insolvency proceedings, 235–6
    material adverse change, 238–44
    misrepresentation, 224–5
    non-payment, 223
    relationship with financial ratios, 190–1
  notification of Default and, 182–3
  objective vs. subjective, 220–1
  ownership of the Obligors, 237–8
  purpose of, 220
exclusion clauses, 267, 271, 275, 323–4
export credit, 7

facility, 3, 77–81
  backstop, 86, 92
  finance parties' rights and obligations, 79–81
  LMA (increase), 78–9
  revolving credit, 78
facility office, 60
FATCA, see Foreign Account Tax Compliance Act (FATCA)
fees, 119–20, 267
fiduciary duties, 156, 271, 274
Finance Document, 61
finance leases, 44
Finance Parties
  rights and obligations, 79–81
  sharing among, 277–8
Financial Accounting Standards Board, 44
Financial Conduct Authority, 19
financial collateral 335
financial due diligence, 277
financial indebtedness, 47–8, 61–3, 226, 228–31
financial ratios, 32, 180, 183–96, 243
  in asset finance transaction, 193–6
  breach of, 223–4
  common ratios
    cashflow, 185–6
    gearing, 187–8
    interest cover, 185, 186
    leverage, 186–7
    liquidity, 187
    security cover, 193–4, 195
    tangible net worth, 188
  consequence of breach of, 191–2
  definition of words used in, 192–3
  equity cure rights, 192
  group level to run, 189–90
  incurrence tests, 190
  maintenance, 190–1
  periods for, 190–1
  purpose of, 183–4
  material adverse effect and, 190–1
  summary of, 188–9

financial statements, 169–70, 179–80
  original, 70, 169–70
  requirements as to, 180–1
fixed charges, 331–2
floating charges, 329–31
force majeure, 43
Foreign Account Tax Compliance Act (FATCA), 131–3
  confidentiality and, 131
  Model 1 intergovernmental agreement, 132
  Model 2 intergovernmental agreement, 132
  passthru payments, 131–2
  payments affected by, 131–2
  provisions, 132–3
form of assignment agreement, 298
form of transfer certificate, 298
forms, LMA, 8–10
forward purchase, 46
forward sales, 46, 48
frozen GAAP, 181
funded sub-participation, 256
further assurance clause, 219
future property, 334

GAAP, 44, 62, 63–5, 74, 180–1
gearing ratio, 187–8
geographical limitations, 160
goodstanding, 162
governing law, 289
grace period, 11, 58, 232
gross up, 24, 25, 122–3, 125-9
  limitations, 126–9
group, 25, 26, 27, 29, 31–2
  business with, 274
  definition of, 228
group structure, 219
guarantees, 45, 143–51
  'all moneys', 143
  appropriations, 148
  continuing, 144, 341–2
  deferral of guarantors' rights, 148–51
  demand, 340–1
  discharge by amendment, 345
  in English law, 339–45
  hazards of, 343–5

  immediate recourse, 148
  vs. indemnity, 143–4, 339, 340–1
  interest and, 150–1
  vs. letter of comfort, 342–3
  nature of, 339
  need to claim against borrower, 341
  primary vs. secondary obligations, 339–40
  reinstatement, 144–5
  subrogation/reimbursement, 344–5
  vs. third party charge, 342
  waiver of defences, 146–7
guarantors, 25–6, 27, 28
  additional, 269
  resignation of, 270

Hague Convention, on trusts, 257
hardening period, 145, 252
hire purchase, 44

illegality, 99–101
impaired agent, 34–5
  provisions, 277
inconsistencies, repeating representations and, 156–8
increased costs, 133–7
  claims, 137
  exceptions, 137
  mitigation of, 138
Increase Lender, 34
incurrence tests, 190
indemnities, 10, 137–8, 154
  currency, 137–8
  effect of assignment on, 253–4
  vs. guarantees, 339, 340–1
  guarantees and, 143–4
  tax, 129–30, 131–3
information memorandum, 169
information undertakings, 179–83, 215–16
  compliance certificate, 180
  financial statements, 179–81
  'know your customer' checks, 183
  miscellaneous, 181–2
  notification of Default, 182–3
  provision via websites, 183
insignificant companies, 29

insolvency, 41, 233–5
　directors' duties on, 246
　legal opinions and, 301, 313
　limited recourse provisions, 234–5
　proceedings as an Event of Default, 235–6
instalment sale agreements, 45
insurance, 41, 214
intangible assets, 334
intellectual property rights, 219, 334
interbank markets, 15–16
interest
　absence of quotations from Reference Banks, 112
　calculation of, 106–9
　compound, 108
　default, 107–9
　guarantees and, 150–1
　interest periods, 22, 109–12
　　changes to, 112
　　selection of, 109–12
　interest provisions, LMA Term Loan, 22–4
　Interpolated Rate, 22
　LIBOR 64-65 (*see also* London Interbank Offered Rate)
　LIBOR based lending 15–24
　market disruption and, 113–17
　notification of rates of, 109
　payment of, 107
　pro rata interest settlement, 268
interest cover ratio, 186
interest rate swaps, 203
intergovernmental agreements
　Model 1 agreement, 132
　Model 2 agreement, 132
International Accounting Standards Board, 44
International Financial Reporting Standards (IFRS), 64
International Swaps and Derivatives Association (ISDA), 256
Interpolated Rate, 22
interpretation clause 52
Italian torpedoes, 292

joint creditorship, 261
joint (vs several) obligation, 320
judgement currency indemnity, 137–8

jurisdiction, 10, 160, 290–2, 311–12

knowledge limitations, 160
'know your customer' checks, 183, 267

legal concepts, 321–7
legal opinions, 294, 300–14
　assumptions in, 304
　the opinions
　　authority, 306
　　choice of law and jurisdiction, 311–12
　　due execution, 306
　　due incorporation and continued existence, 305
　　effectiveness of security, 308–10
　　enforcement of judgements, 312
　　no consents or filings needed, 310–11
　　no contravention of law or constitution, 307
　　no unexpected tax consequences, 311
　　pari passu, 312
　　power, 305–6
　　valid and enforceable obligations, 307–8
　form of, 303–14
　lawyers' role and, 302–3
　limits on scope of, 300–2
　locations of, 302
　qualifications, 312–14
　types of, 300
legal owner, 320
lender default, *see* defaulting lender provisions
lender of record, 38
lenders, 25, 26
　categories of, for tax purposes 123–4
　defaulting, 60
　key concerns of, 13
　majority, 66–7, 272, 281, 284
　non-bank, 36–7
　number of, 7
　of record, 250, 263–5
　rights and obligations of, 79–81
lenders, changes to, – *see* loan transfers
lending office, 25

letter of comfort, 342–3
letter of credit facilities, 35–6
letters of credit, 33, 35, 93
Leveraged LMA, 5, 9, 33, 266–7, 285
leverage ratio, 186–7
LIBOR, *see* London Interbank Offered Rate
LIBOR-based lending, 2, 15–24
   alternatives to, 21–2
   cost-plus lending, 16–17
   history of, 17
   interbank markets, 15–16
   personal LIBOR, 20
   regulatory environment and, 17–20
   Screen Rate of LIBOR, 17, 20–1, 22
liens, 40, 207, 329
limitations to scope of representations
   companies covered, 159
   geographical, 160
   with reference to knowledge, 160
   materiality 160
limited recourse financing, 5
limited recourse provisions, 234–5
liquidity, 19
liquidity coverage ratio, 82–3, 134, 135
liquidity ratio, 187
liquidity risk, 19
litigation proceedings as Event of Default, 173–4, 181–2, 207, 237
LMA, *see* Loan Market Association (LMA)
loan agreements, 2–3
   hazards in reviewing, 14–15
   key concerns for borrowers in, 12–13
   key concerns for lenders in, 13
   overview, 8–16
   scope of, 24–32
   structure, 10–11
Loan Market Association (LMA), 2, 5
   recommended forms, 8–10
loan markets, convergence with capital markets, 39–40
loan stock, 47
loan transfers, 249–68
   assignments, 252–5
   'behind the scenes', 262
   changes to lender of record, 263–5
   conditions of, 265–7

   consent to, 262–5
   credit derivatives, 249, 250, 256–7
   fees, 267
   by lenders, 265
   novation, 250–2, 265
   by Obligors, 268
   procedure for, 267
   restrictions on, 264
   secured loans, 257–61
   sub-participation, 255–6
London Interbank Market, 17, 113, 114, 116
   see also LIBOR-based lending
London Interbank Offered Rate (LIBOR), 20, 64–5, 106–7, 113, 116
   see also LIBOR-based lending

Majority Lenders, 66–7, 272, 281, 285
mandatory costs, 19–20, 106, 298
margin, 6, 67–8
margin ratchet, 67
market disruption clause, 10, 113–17
material adverse change clause, 238–44
   drafting points in 240–3
   objections to
      excessive power to lenders, 240
      fragility, 240
      lack of use, 239
      uncertainty, 238–9
   financial condition and, 242–3
material adverse effect, 68–9, 167, 173, 190–1, 240–3
materiality thresholds, 160
material subsidiaries, 159
mezzanine finance, 6
minimum tangible net worth, 231
mismatch facilities, 6
misrepresentation, 162, 323, 324–5
   as Event of Default, 224–5
   liability in, 154–5
mitigation, of increased costs, 138
money laundering, 100
month, 69
Moody's, covenant quality assessment matrix, 196
mortgages, 328–9
moveable property, 335
multicurrency loans, 93, 95–6, 194n59
multiple drawdown facilities, 86

negative pledge, 13, 170, 196, 197–208
  consequences of breach, 198
  content of, 199
  exceptions to, 202–8
    security arising by operation of law, 204–5
    prohibition on quasi security, 200–2
    prohibition on security, 199
    purpose of, 197–8
negligent mismanagement, 246
net present value, 54
net stable funding ratio, 134–5
netting arrangement, 202–3
no disposals clause, 196, 208–11
  exceptions to, 210–11
non-bank lenders, 36–7
non-competition clauses, 149
non-recourse companies, 29–30
non-recourse subsidiaries, 206
notification of Default, 182–3
novation, 249, 250–2, 265
  consents and, 252
  effects of, 250, 251–2
  hardening period and, 252
  mechanics of, 250–1
  security and, 252

obligations
  effect of assignment on, 254–5
  primary vs. secondary, 339–40
Obligors, 25, 28, 30, 31–2
  assignments and transfers by, 268
  changes to, 268–70
  conditions precedent to additional, 294
  distributions to, 280
  no set off by, 282
  ownership of the, 237–8
operative provisions, 53
optional currency, 69, 89, 94–7
optional provisions, 32–6
ordinary course of business, 205, 210
ordinary course of trading, 205, 210
Original Borrowers, 25
original financial statements, 70, 169–70
Original Guarantors, 25
overdraft facility, 3–4
Overnight Swaps Rate (OSR), 114–15

parallel debt
  alternative to, 261
  security for, 260
pari passu, 13, 170–3, 312, 325
partial invalidity, 284
partial payments, 281
payment letters, 296
payment mechanics, 280–2
penalty, 108
pensions, 219
PIK (payment in kind) financings, 8, 187
pledges, 327, 329
pre-funding, 281
prepayment and cancellation, 55, 99–105
  change of control, 101–2
  illegality, 99–101
  restrictions, 105
  right of repayment and cancellation in relation to single lender, 104–5
  voluntary cancellation, 102–3
  voluntary prepayment, 103
primary obligations, 339–40
privity, 77
project finance, 4–5, 41–3, 158
  conditions precedent in, 295–7
  disbursement accounts, 42
  distribution accounts, 43
  revenue accounts, 43
project risk, 5
promissory notes, 47, 283
pro rata, 7
pro rata interest settlement, 268
pro rata sharing clause, 277–8
prospective debt, 234
prospectus legislation, 250
Prudential Regulatory Authority, 19

qualifications in legal opinions
  equitable principles, 313
  insolvency, 313
qualifications to representations, 159–60
qualifications to undertakings, 176–7
quasi security, 43–7
  prohibition on, 200–2
quick ratio, 187
Quistclose trust, 82
quotation day, 70

rateable payment, 172
reasonable endeavours, 177
reasonableness requirement, 324
reborrowing, 98–9
receivables, 6
  selling, 45
recharacterization, 45
Reference Bank Rate, 22, 64, 70–1
Reference Banks, 70–1
refinancing, 6
registration requirements for security, 333–4
regulatory environment, 18
  capital adequacy, 18
  LIBOR-based lending and, 17–20
  liquidity, 19
  mandatory costs, 19–20
regulatory fees, 136
regulatory risk, 216–17
relevant jurisdictions, 160
remedies and waivers, 284–5
repeating representations, 15, 71, 88, 155–9, 161, 174–5, 270
  hazards of, 156–8
repos, 46
representations, 9, 152–75
  in different circumstances, 174
  disclosure and, 152
  drawstop/acceleration, 152–5
  liability in misrepresentation, 154–5
  limitations
    geographical limitations, 160
    knowledge limitations, 160
    materiality thresholds, 160
  in the LMA Term Loan, 161–75
    binding obligations, 162–3
    financial statements, 169–70
    governing law and enforcement, 166
    no Default, 167–8
    no filing or stamp taxes, 167
    no misleading information, 169
    non-conflict with other obligations, 163–4
    no proceedings pending or threatened, 173–4
    pari passu ranking, 170–3
    power and authority, 164–5
    status, 161–2
    tax deduction, 166–7
    validity and admissibility in evidence, 165
  purpose of, 152–5
  repetition of, 15, 71, 88, 155–9, 161, 174–5, 270
  summary of, 158–9
requests, 297
residual value guarantee, 319
resignation letter, 299
revolving credit, 4, 78, 94
  clean down period, 189
  conditions precedent and, 86–8
  repayment and, 98–9
  Rollover Loans, 88
  selection of interest periods and, 111–12
risk sub-participation, 255–6

sanctions, 100–1
scope of agreement, 13
Screen Rate, 17, 20–1, 22, 64–5, 71–2, 114, 115, 116
secondary market, 33, 287
secondary obligations, 339–40
secured loans, transfers of, 257–61
Securities and Exchange Commission (SEC), 44
securitization, 6, 45
security, 2
  for a syndicated loan
    to an agent, 259–61
    for joint creditorship, 261
    for parallel debt, 260
    to trustee for covenant to pay, 257–8
    for underlying debt, 259–60
  on different types of assets, 334–7
  effect of assignment on, 254
  in English law, 327–38
  novation and, 252
  tacking further advances, 338
  prohibition on, 199
  quasi, 43–7, 200–2
  registration requirements, 333–4
  subordinate, 325
  third party charge as, 342
  types of, 328–33

security cover ratio, 193–4, 196
    restrictions on acceptable assets, 195
    release of additional security, 195
    valuation of security, 195
    value of cash, 195
security over lenders' rights clause, 268
Security Trustee, 24, 25, 257–8
selection notice, 297
seller's credit, 47
separateness undertakings, 220
service of process, 292
set off, 46, 202–3, 282–3
several obligation, 320
shadow banking system, 36
shadow directors, 175–6
shareholder documents, 181
'snooze you lose' provision, 12
Socimer implied term, 273
sovereign debt, 7, 171–2
statute, 74, 316
Stockholm Interbank Offered Rate (STIBOR), 20, 22
structural subordination, 326–7
subordinated debt, 6
subordinate security, 325
subordination, 325–7
    categories of, 327
    of debt, 326
    structural, 326–7
    before winding up, 150
    on winding up, 150
sub-participation, 249, 250, 255–6, 257, 262
    funded, 256
    risk, 255–6
subrogation, 146, 344–5
subsidiaries, 72–3, 159–60, 206
subsidiary undertaking, 27, 28
substantive consolidation, 220
suspect period, 145
swingline facilities, 6–7

tangible net worth, 29, 188
TARGET Day, 70
tax
    lenders' tax status, 123–4, 129
    tax credits, 130

double taxation treaties, 121–2, 124, 266
FATCA, 131–3
gross-up, 122–3, 125–9, 131–3
indemnities, 129–30, 131–3
withholding, 121, 124–5, 266
term loans, 3, 94–5
third party charge, 342
third party opinions, 302
third party rights, 76–7, 216
timetables, 300
title financing, 40, 43–4, 45, 48
title retention, 45
toggle, 8
tort, 318–19
transaction costs, 138, 139, 266–7
transactions at undervalue, 343–4
transfer certificate, 267, 268, 298
transfers, *see* loan transfers
trust accounts, 35
trust arrangements, 47
trustees, 24, 25, 327
    security, 257–8
trusts, 257–8, 320

undertakings, 3, 9, 175–223
    covenant lite loans, 177–8
    duplication, 178–9
    in the LMA Term Loan, 196–220
        authorization, 197
        change of business, 211
        compliance with laws, 197, 212
        financial covenants, 183–96 *see also* financial ratios
        information, 179–83, 215–16
        mergers, 211
    negative pledge, 197–208
    no disposals clause, 208–11
    other common, 212–20
        relating to assets given as security, 217–18
        relating to legal risks, 216
        restrictions on business focus, 213
        restrictions on dealing with assets and security, 214
        restrictions on movement of cash, 214–15
        separateness, 220

    purpose of, 175
    qualifications, 176–7
    shadow directors and, 175–6
US Patriot Act, 101
utilization, 91–7
    completion of utilization request, 91
    conditions of, 83–90
    costs of, 106–20
    currency and amount, 91
    delivery of utilization request, 91
utilization request, 297

voluntary cancellation, 102–3
voluntary prepayment, 103

waiver of defences to guarantee, 146–7
withholding tax, 17n25, 121, 266
    see also gross up
    documentation, 124–5
wrongful trading, 246

'yank the bank' clause, 12, 287
yield protection clauses, 17–18, 135

Printed and bound by CPI Group (UK) Ltd, Croydon, CR0 4YY